STRANGE
WORDS

MARGARET JEWETT BURLAND

STRANGE WORDS

*Retelling and Reception
in the Medieval
Roland Textual Tradition*

UNIVERSITY OF NOTRE DAME PRESS   NOTRE DAME, INDIANA

Designed by Wendy McMillen
Set in 11.2/13 MrsEaves by EM Studio
Printed on 55# Nature's Recycle paper in the U.S.A. by Versa Press

Library of Congress Cataloging-in-Publication Data

Burland, Margaret.
Strange words : retelling and reception in the medieval
Roland textual tradition / Margaret Jewett Burland.
p.   cm.
Includes bibliographical references and index.
ISBN-13: 978-0-268-02203-7 (pbk. : alk. paper)
ISBN-10: 0-268-02203-8 (pbk. : alk. paper)
1. Chanson de Roland—Criticism, Textual. I. Title.
PQ1523.B87   2007
841'.1—dc22

                              2007019523

 This book printed on recycled paper.

This book is dedicated to

my parents, William and Julia Jewett,

who impressed upon me the importance of stories,

told with or without words;

my teachers, Grace Armstrong and Peter Dembowski,

who showed me how to read more closely than I had thought possible;

my husband, Daniel Burland,

que mervelles aim;

and our children, Grace and Karl Burland,

who, at ages five and one, already understand the value of frequent rereading.

[T]he Lord will go before you, and the God of Israel will be your rear guard.

—Isaiah 52:12

Contents

Acknowledgments

This book is the product of many years of research, writing, and rewriting and has been enriched by the contributions of many mentors, colleagues, and friends. I remain grateful for the guidance of Peter Dembowski, Robert Morrissey, and Françoise Meltzer during this project's first incarnation as a doctoral dissertation, completed with the support of a fellowship from the Whiting Foundation. I would also like to thank the Dickey Center for International Understanding at Dartmouth College for sponsoring a group review of the book manuscript. I was fortunate enough to receive extensive feedback on earlier drafts of the book from Joseph Duggan, Matilda Bruckner, and an anonymous reader for the Press, as well as a senior medievalist who may not wish to be identified in a book in which he saw so little potential. All of these professional assessments were of tremendous help to me, and I am mindful of the generous gifts of time and attention that they represent. This book gradually took shape while I was teaching in the Department of French and Italian at Dartmouth, and I could not have wished for a more nurturing atmosphere. On a regular basis, and even more during a series of personal challenges, nearly every member of that large department made a concerted effort to help, advise, and encourage me, especially those in the Chair: Lynn Higgins, John Rassias, and Kate Conley. During those years, Andrea Tarnowski and Monika Otter generously offered themselves as sources of expertise on medieval narrative, advice of all kinds, and loyal friendship. My other steadfast medievalist

friend has been Paul Creamer, whose frequent and often hilarious messages of support for this enterprise forced me to smile even on the dark-
est days. I am profoundly grateful for the gracious gifts of my friends,
Don and Dori Willeman, and of my family. During my research, my
husband and children taught me at least as much as did the books
I read.

Introduction

The *Song of Roland* and the Narrativity of Roncevaux

The *Song of Roland* has been unjustly neglected by generations of modern medievalists. This would be an absurd claim, of course, if I were using that title in the way that has become customary, referring to the single version of this medieval narrative that is contained in manuscript Digby 23 at Oxford University. That particular text, which specialists of the *chanson de geste* tend to call, instead, "the Oxford *Roland*," has probably received more attention over the past two hundred years than any other text in the medieval French canon. The single text most readers know as the *Chanson de Roland* or *Song of Roland* is widely considered to be required reading for students of French literature, world literature, and Western civilization. This text has also been the subject of an impressive number of published critical analyses, which have exerted upon it many different approaches yielding nearly innumerable individual interpretations. Indeed, offering one's own interpretation of this text has been described as an all but inevitable rite of passage for scholars of medieval French literature.[1] How does this consistent and widespread attention constitute neglect?

As scholars of the *chanson de geste* have long insisted, the text now known as the *Chanson de Roland* is really only one member of a larger narrative tradition that medieval authors and audiences understood to be a coherent entity transcending all of its individual manifestations. The story of the deaths of Roland and the twelve peers of France at the Battle of Roncevaux circulated in countless oral and written versions during the Middle Ages and has survived to the present day in dozens of manuscripts, each one differing considerably from the others in language, style, and content. Since the Oxford *Roland* cannot be claimed as the direct source for any of the other surviving manuscripts, this textual tradition does not represent the ongoing literary legacy of that individual text. Instead, the medieval Roncevaux textual tradition was the written stage of a literary legend that predated the Oxford manuscript in oral transmission and then continued independently for centuries afterward.[2] As Douglas Kelly has said of medieval texts in general, "For us the texts are artifacts; in the Middle Ages they illustrated stages in a dynamic process of social and moral reflection elaborated in textual commentary and correction."[3] The importance of this larger narrative of Roncevaux to medieval culture, particularly in France, is clear not only from its survival in multiple textual forms but also from references to the story in other medieval literary texts, from artistic representations of it in several pieces of monumental sculpture, and even from a documented trend toward naming pairs of sons Roland and Olivier well before the Oxford *Roland* was written down.[4] Since it is well known that the Roncevaux story occupied a position of great cultural prominence over a period of several centuries, why have so few scholars bothered to study any Roncevaux manuscript other than Oxford, and why has only one monograph, published over fifty years ago, offered readings of multiple versions of the story side by side?[5]

Modern critics' neglect of the larger Roncevaux textual tradition bespeaks an indifference toward the post-Oxford manuscripts in the present day that is a diluted remnant of the marked antipathy of nineteenth-century scholars. The positivist and nationalist sources and expressions of this antipathy have been amply documented by a number of scholars tracing the modern reception history of the Oxford *Roland*, so there is no need to restate them here.[6] Medievalists today are well aware of the prejudices of nineteenth-century medieval studies and consciously intend not to perpetuate them. When it comes to the Roncevaux textual tradition, however, it is worthwhile to recall that the enduring and misleading reputation of the post-Oxford *Roland* manuscripts as minor variants upon a singular, superior masterpiece is the result not of mere ignorance but rather of the fact that these texts were once relegated deliberately to critical oblivion and have never been entirely reclaimed.

Because a larger narrative tradition about Roland at the Battle of Roncevaux not only exists but actually generated the Oxford *Roland* rather than having been generated by it, applying the title *Chanson de*

Roland to that text alone is a distortion. It has become such a familiar distortion, however, that it sounds unnatural, and requires explicit commentary, to apply that title more appropriately to the entire Roncevaux textual tradition.[7] The issue of the title itself is relatively trivial, especially because the title *Chanson de Roland* is a modern invention that does not appear in any medieval manuscript of which I am aware. Moreover, the conventional usage of that title to refer to the Oxford manuscript is probably too entrenched to be changed at this late date. What is in need of transformation, however, is modern critics' perception of the Oxford *Roland* (whatever one chooses to call it) and of its place in the larger narrative tradition to which it belongs. That text was probably never intended to be read apart from its larger tradition: the ubiquitousness of the Roncevaux story in medieval culture would have made such isolated reception virtually unimaginable at the time when the text was written. One might even say that the Roncevaux narrative tradition is the textbook example of medieval literary *mouvance*: in his well-known *Essai de poétique médiévale*, Paul Zumthor used the manuscript tradition of the French Roncevaux texts as a visual aid to illustrate the notion of *mouvance*, specifically of the inherently multiform nature of literary works in the Middle Ages. Under the title "Oeuvre '*Chanson de Roland*,'" Zumthor lists as separate branches the names of several individual manuscripts and writes below that the subtitle "Textes: *Les Chansons de Roland*."[8] Zumthor's chart illustrates the idea that the individual manuscript texts are all examples of the larger work but that that work cannot be said to exist fully in any one text. This notion of the inherently multiform medieval work has been restated and elaborated many times since then, to the point where it has become an accepted commonplace of the field. Yet relatively few scholars of medieval literature put this notion into practice by granting equal attention and authority to all surviving versions of the texts they analyze, in spite of the ever-increasing availability of both manuscripts and critical editions of textual variants that were once considered too "minor" to merit the attention of modern researchers.[9]

This would be an opportune moment for any scholar of medieval French literature to give more thought to the implications of the Oxford *Roland*'s relationship to the larger Roncevaux textual tradition. These days, the Oxford version itself may be suffering as much as the more neglected *Roland* manuscripts from the inordinate amount of past attention devoted to it and from its resulting isolation from the rich intertextual field within which it was designed to signify.[10] Many scholars of medieval French literature now see the Oxford *Roland* as a unique and familiar entity whose form and meaning have been fully elucidated by past studies and about which there is little need to say more. At the same time, some university professors are giving the Oxford *Roland* a less prominent place in medieval studies curricula because of its reputation as propaganda for the Crusades, or for other repressive political agendas particular to its twelfth-century context; these aspects of its conventional reputation seem to place the Oxford *Roland* outside the category of what might be intriguing or even palatable to many of today's readers. This reputation not only oversimplifies the Oxford *Roland* itself but also stifles the Roncevaux story by shackling it to a single redaction and a single historical moment, a limitation that disregards the parameters of the literary field in which the Oxford version itself first circulated. The Oxford *Roland* shows ample evidence of its engagement with its immediate historical context, but as part of a larger cultural enterprise of enduring relevance, for the Roncevaux story in all of its forms is concerned with how people of different historical moments strive to understand themselves in relation to one another.

A central focus of the Roncevaux texts, and therefore of this book, is the formulation and reception of narratives about past and future events, narratives that serve to affirm and/or call into question the coherence of individual and collective identities across time. The Roncevaux texts all return repeatedly to episodes in which characters within the fiction compose, transform, and interpret such narratives. These episodes make the point (usually implicitly, though at times explicitly) that literary narratives perform for entire societies the same restorative or destructive functions that these texts ascribe to the narratives told and heard by individual characters. Thus the Roncevaux texts both dramatize and problematize the importance of narrative to lived experience, and in particular to identity formation and perpetuation.[11] By including in these dramatizations the reception of character narratives by other characters, these texts also implicate the audience prominently in their statements about the social functioning of narrative. Since the "audiences" within the Roncevaux texts frequently reject the narratives they hear, choose between competing narratives, or formulate alternative narratives of their own, a close examination of narration and reception within the fiction of the Roncevaux texts has much to tell us about how their authors perceived the reciprocal dynamics of narration and reception in which they were themselves engaged with their medieval audiences.

Of course, traditional readings of the Oxford *Roland* do see that text engaged, along with its contemporary audience, in a diachronic examination of collective identity, but in a way that tends to be too strictly circumscribed. Some of the best-known lines from that text owe their fame to the fact that they seem to announce prescriptive truths to medieval audience members about what their identity should be, on the basis of identities formulated by the narrator and characters of the text. For example, Charlemagne is called "our" emperor in the opening line, although the historical Charlemagne died three centuries earlier; Roland at one point pronounces the universal judgment that "[p]agans are wrong and Christians are right";[12] and as the audience prepares to witness the graphic violence of Ganelon's execution by drawing and quartering, the narrator intones, "Any man who betrays kills himself along with others" [Hom ki traïst, sei ocit e altroi] (v. 3959). Since these three lines occur at the beginning, middle, and end of the text, it is legitimate to view them as elements of a consistent thread running through the narrative as a whole, implying that this narrative about political events of the past should be taken as an encouragement or a warning to audience members about how to conduct themselves within the political context of the twelfth-century present. Such a reading is of limited utility, however, since there is much more to the issues of identity and diachronic exchange in the Oxford *Roland* than these three lines and others like them and, within the larger Roncevaux textual tradition, much more than the Oxford *Roland* in its entirety. The political and cultural viewpoints that have contributed so much to the modern reputation of the Oxford *Roland* as a single text actually cannot be fully understood apart from their signification within the larger complex of cultural issues that medieval authors associated consistently with the Roncevaux story in all its forms.

The project of this book is to access that larger set of issues, whose contours emerge more clearly from the narrative strategies characteristic of the surviving Roncevaux texts than from the particular events of the Roncevaux story. Although the Oxford *Roland* has been analyzed many times as a literary text whose primary purposes were political[13] because its plotline consists of a series of political and military conflicts, my interest is in reading it, alongside three other medieval Roncevaux texts, somewhat in the opposite direction. Within the dramatization of the multiple conflicts that animate the Roncevaux story from start to finish, my readings of that story in four different versions consistently identify instances of discourse by characters and narrators that provide insights about the role of narrative structures in articulating and eventually resolving psychological, social, political, and historical tensions.

These texts demonstrate in a fascinating variety of ways how the construction of narratives, and especially their subsequent reconstruction and reinterpretation, function as essential cognitive techniques for the Roncevaux characters. Each author reshapes this central preoccupation of the Roncevaux story with evident care because these portrayals of narrative retelling and reception in character discourse suggest the important contributions that these rewritten literary narratives themselves were making to their contemporary culture. Evidence of a deliberate metaliterary agenda underlying the character narratives emerges clearly from comparative analysis of multiple Roncevaux texts. The varying form, subject matter, narrative strategies, and dynamics of reception displayed by the discourse of characters in each text prove not only that narrative itself was a theme consistently associated with the Roncevaux story but also that authors frequently found ways to connect character narratives to contemporary trends in medieval literature.

My goal in bringing to the fore these instances of metaliterary discourse is not merely to make the point that the Roncevaux texts contain a reflexive or "self-conscious" component, and it is certainly not to claim that these texts saw themselves as expressions of an "art for art's sake" mentality. I believe that the Roncevaux authors made the functioning of literary narratives a consistent theme of their texts precisely because they understood the powerful influence of literature, and particularly of the "matiere de France,"[14] upon the "imagined community"[15] of Old French speakers that was being ever more forcefully converted into a nation throughout the period in which the Roncevaux texts of this study were composed (twelfth through fifteenth centuries). Yet the type of metaliterary commentary contained in the Roncevaux texts is quite distinct from some modern and postmodern brands of metafiction, in which the production and circulation of literature are the primary focus of the plot. As Robert Siegle has cautioned, it is severely limiting to make assumptions about the universal functioning of literary reflexivity only on the basis of recent forms of it, for, according to that perspective, "A reflexive narrative would . . . be about 'only' art and would tell us little else. It would not affect our view of reality, our essential values and philosophical assumptions—would be, in other words, a safe but frivolous project."[16] It will be easy for readers familiar with the Oxford *Roland* to understand that this is not an apt description of the Roncevaux story, whose very premise—a bloody battle (or battles) between the Christian Franks and the Muslim Saracens resulting from treachery at the highest levels—offers a troubling test to the "essential values" and "philosophical assumptions" of its audiences in all times and places. Rather than either ignoring or dictating their audiences' values and assumptions, the Roncevaux texts often seem to be testing or questioning them; reading the Roncevaux story in this spirit can transform some of our received ideas about the political and cultural stakes of the Roncevaux story and its implicit metaliterary commentary.

Although some readers of the Oxford *Roland* may think of the Roncevaux story as action driven, nearly every major articulation of the Roncevaux plot in every surviving version is also heralded by one or more instances of narration and interpretation by characters. This essential narrativity becomes increasingly complex as the story unfolds because the overall structure of the Roncevaux plot causes the majority of these narratives to be recapitulative, retellings that themselves constitute reinterpretations of past events and then also elicit alternative reinterpretations from the characters who hear them. The basic structure of the Oxford *Roland* can provide an initial example for readers familiar with that text. The narrative of Oxford begins with the council scenes in which Ganelon's plan for the attack at Roncevaux takes shape, while the Franks and Saracens debate among themselves the merits of making a peace agreement with the other side. The battle itself occupies the longest portion of the text, followed just after the structural center by the Franks' revenge battles against the enemy forces of Marsile and Baligant (whose responses to the Battle of Roncevaux are communicated to the audience along with those of the Franks). Charlemagne conducts funerary rituals for the warriors killed at Roncevaux, and further episodes show his return to France, burdened with the sad duty of informing surviving family members of what happened in the battle. The last major episode of the text, the trial and execution of Ganelon, brings a judicial resolution to the narrative; the specific crime of which Ganelon is accused is that of arranging to have twenty thousand of Charlemagne's men killed at Roncevaux.

The first observation to be made about this basic structure is that the Battle of Roncevaux provides the clear reference point for everything else that the text recounts, an observation that also holds true for the post-Oxford versions. For this reason most medieval authors of these texts described their subject matter in manuscript explicits as "Roncevaux" and seldom as "Roland" or, for that matter, as a "song."[17] Yet it is equally apparent that none of the surviving Roncevaux texts limit themselves to recounting the Battle of Roncevaux alone, so when their authors say that their narratives are about "Roncevaux," that label encompasses not only the battle itself but also the other episodes in which characters verbally anticipate, interpret, and retell it.[18] A basic structural comparison between the surviving versions reveals that the only three scenes to appear in every Roncevaux text are the Battle of Roncevaux, the mourning of Charlemagne and his warriors at the battlefield, and the episode in which Charlemagne brings the news of the battle to Aude (the fiancée of Roland and the sister of his companion Olivier). Therefore even the most abbreviated versions of the story include a triptych formed by the battle, an initial verbal grief response to it, and then a retelling of it to a new audience, one that constitutes a reinterpretation and meets with a newly disturbing reception when Aude dies of grief. Most surviving versions, but not all, add another layer of retelling and reception after Aude's death, in the form of Ganelon's trial, during which the characters engage in heated and explicit debate about how to interpret the initial causes and lasting consequences of the battle. Several versions also include the council scenes at the start of the text, which, along with Ganelon's trial, form a frame around the Roncevaux narrative as a whole within which its central tensions are verbally presented and contested in three stages: before, during, and after the battle. Lexical and structural echoes between these three stages of narrative articulation encourage audiences to perceive the interpretative development that these episodes elaborate through implicit comparison with one another. Thus the varying structures of the essential narrative of "Roncevaux" all reserve an important place for verbal retelling and reinterpretation of the battle among the characters, though they may offer more or less numerous and complex examples of it.

Audience reception is also a prominent component of the architecture of the Roncevaux narratives, although it, too, may manifest itself differently from one text to another. The most obvious way in which the structure of every Roncevaux narrative takes the audience into account is by systematically granting the audience privileged access to information about the future events of the plot before they occur, information of which the protagonists are (tragically) unaware at the same moment. It has been said that this audience awareness was inevitable because it was circumstantial: by the time the surviving manuscripts were written down, the Roncevaux story was so well known that narrators did not hesitate to discuss major events of the plot from the beginning of each text because they would not be spoiling its surprises for anyone (several such cases of "prolepses" by the primary narrator can be observed in the early scenes of the Oxford *Roland*, vv. 9, 95, 178–79, 710–16). Yet a more essential privileging of the audience is inscribed in the basic parameters of the Battle of Roncevaux as a narrative event. One of the defining features of this literary battle is that the audience observes it from start to finish in vivid detail, but Charlemagne and the rest of the Frankish army do not even realize the battle is underway until it is nearly over and thus never arrive in time to witness it for themselves. Different texts introduce variants to this model, but these only serve to emphasize further this traditional perceptual gap between the audience and the surviving characters within the fiction.[19]

These narrative parameters of the literary Battle of Roncevaux mean that it is as temporally inaccessible for the surviving characters within the fiction as was the real event that inspired it for medieval audiences.[20] Since Charlemagne reaches the battlefield very soon after the last of the warriors has died, his arrival at Roncevaux can be said to occupy a contiguous or even synchronic historical moment in relation to that of the battle. Yet the irrevocable nature of his warriors' deaths, and their incapacity to tell their own stories, place the direct experience of the battle in a past moment as inaccessible as if it had occurred centuries before. (This simultaneous contiguity and inaccessibility is portrayed vividly in the Oxford *Roland*, laisse 177.) Because of their privileged narrative perspective, the audience members themselves serve as the eyewitnesses to the battle that are conspicuously missing from the fictional universe. As such, they are capable of perceiving any discrepancies in the narratives about the battle that are told by Charlemagne and the other characters in the post-Roncevaux episodes. In a larger sense, then, this narrative strategy shared by all the surviving Roncevaux texts allows the audience to serve as infallible judges of the characters' own narrative strategies, some of which were also characteristic of storytelling in the medieval audiences' own literary culture.

One purpose of the closing episodes of the Roncevaux narratives seems to be precisely that of exploring the contours of the audience's complex relationship to the fictional characters and their competing discourses and, by implication, any audience's relationship to the multiple narratives that medieval literature told and retold about a number of legendary past events. On the one hand, the audience is encouraged to identify strongly with the fictional characters whom they watch fighting and dying at Roncevaux and therefore to judge harshly the fictional characters who later misrepresent the experiences of those beloved warriors in their recapitulative speeches. On the other hand, the audience also can identify readily with the dilemma of the surviving fictional characters, who are forced to perceive what happened at Roncevaux through the cloud of temporal estrangement and the imperfect illumination of speculative reinvention. Medieval audiences may or may not have cared about the historical accuracy of literary narratives, and perhaps there is more evidence to suggest that audiences did not value such accuracy than to suggest that they did. What is interesting about the Roncevaux narratives in relation to many other medieval literary texts, then, is that they all share a narrative mechanism that strongly encourages the audience to judge the accuracy and intentionality of narrative retellings. By making such retellings a consistent feature of their post-Roncevaux episodes, and indeed by making them a matter of life and death (Aude) and of basic justice (Ganelon's trial), the Roncevaux texts not only draw attention to the dynamics of narrative retelling and audience reception but also elevate these literary functions to the status of individual and societal duties of the utmost importance.

Indeed, as I will show with numerous examples in the following chapters, the Roncevaux retellings formulated and processed by these fictional characters have clear political, religious, and cultural implications for their audiences, in addition to serving as a source of psychological and ethical integrity for the characters themselves. The interplay of personal identification and objective judgment that I have just described as characteristic of the implied audience of these texts suggests that the narrative of Roncevaux was perceived consistently in the Middle Ages as a suitable forum for serious political, social, and literary commentary: the audiences were encouraged not only to sympathize with the characters but also to evaluate the profound effects of their discursive choices upon themselves and others. What I wish to emphasize most about the nature of this commentary, by analyzing four distinct forms of it in the four texts in this study, is that it did not always advocate the same political, social, or literary views. Instead, what all of these Roncevaux narratives have in common is that they seek to engage their audiences in interpreting actively the discourses they hear, rather than receiving such discourses passively, whether as sheer entertainment or as unexamined truth.

Both the importance and the complexity of the Roncevaux texts' shared focus on retelling and reception are encoded in the title of this book, *Strange Words,* a reference to Aude's famous rejection of the discourse about Roncevaux and its consequences that is told to her by Charlemagne in the Oxford version: "Cest mot mei est estrange" [This word is strange to me] (v. 3717). I emphasize from the outset the "strangeness" both of words themselves and of discursive dynamics between characters in the Roncevaux texts because my readings of specific instances of retelling and reception within the fiction often hinge upon the anomalies of characters' speech or upon its wary reception by other characters. Some readers may be surprised by this approach to discourse among the Roncevaux characters, having been predisposed by traditional *Roland* criticism to view the language of these texts, instead, as univocal and monologic.[21] Yet I am not alone in reading them differently: it has been a distinctive tendency of recent *Roland* criticism to focus on the indeterminacy of words and of representational and interpretative strategies in that text, a trait that certain scholars perceived in the Oxford *Roland* decades ago.[22]

Two books deserve special mention here because of their profound influence on my view of language, individual and social identity formation, and the function of competing narratives in the Roncevaux texts. Peter Haidu's *The Subject of Violence: The* Song of Roland *and the Birth of the State* (1993) uses a semiotic approach to reveal the profound instability and the active maneuvering lying just below the surface of the Oxford *Roland*'s veneer of stable, unified political and social identities.[23] The complexity and/or indeterminacy of particular words and symbolic gestures in the fictional universe of Roncevaux provide points of access for Haidu's readings of textual passages drawn from every section of the poem. Although my study does not share Haidu's political and historical focus, my approach to comparing successive, interrelated instances of character narration in the Roncevaux texts often makes use of a similar emphasis on particular words whose meaning becomes clear only through their recurring and at times shifting usage in the speeches of different characters. Sarah Kay's *The Chansons de Geste in the Age of Romance* (1995), on the other hand, deliberately sets the Oxford *Roland* aside in order to offer readings of other *chansons de geste*, in comparison to the contemporary romances with which they share many significant traits and outside the long shadow cast by the Oxford version in most previous considerations of the epic genre. Although Kay therefore does not devote much attention to the Roncevaux narratives or focus systematically on the functioning of character discourse, her observations about the narrative dynamics of many twelfth- and thirteenth-century *chansons de geste* do frequently emphasize their multivocality. For example, one recurring theme of Kay's study is the tendency of many *chansons de geste* to generate "alternative narratives" or "counternarratives" that emerge gradually through the unfolding of their plots, contesting the assumptions inherent in the more apparent narrative threads with which these *chansons* had begun and causing a "resulting ambivalence of epic textuality."[24] The introductory chapter of Kay's study of the *chansons de geste* as "political fictions" also posits the inherent indeterminacy of religious discourses in medieval literary/historical texts such as the *chansons de geste*, of a kind that reflects rather than belies their Christian perspective. Kay points out that medieval Augustinian notions of history as expressions of human sin presided over by a divine providence whose purposes are unknowable "acknowledge that power, although belonging in a totality, can only be perceived through partial, fragmentary, contradictory, and ultimately indeterminate representations."[25] Therefore, whether the events of the Roncevaux texts are perceived primarily as the products of human political maneuvering or of divine providence manifesting itself through the medium of imperfect human actors, it is to be expected that the verbal formulation and recapitulation of this series of events would be characterized by frequent conflict and indeterminacy.[26] Because the Roncevaux texts devote a great deal of attention to depicting this flawed process as it occurs among their fictional characters, both political and religious readings of this textual tradition can be enhanced by a closer examination of the way they are encoded in the characters' "strange words."

For example, if the Oxford *Roland* is regarded as a narrative structured around the articulation in three stages of the specific issues and high social stakes of character discourses and their reception, three famous and vehement verbal conflicts immediately leap to mind from the three major sections of the plot: the conflicting policy recommendations of Roland and Ganelon during the initial council scenes, the debate between Roland and Olivier during the battle about whether to sound the horn to summon Charlemagne, and the conflicting statements of Charlemagne and Ganelon on the issue of whether Ganelon should be prosecuted as a traitor. These scenes all dramatize the possibility that one person may reject entirely the discourse of another, and rightly so, for there are obvious flaws even in the speeches of those characters whose points of view are ultimately validated by the text. Indeed, one consistent approach of the Oxford *Roland* to the portrayal of these debates is to make the "wrong" point of view sound, initially, more logical and trustworthy than the "right" one. This is particularly true of Olivier's well-reasoned recommendations during the horn debates (with which nearly all modern critics are strongly sympathetic), but even the traitor Ganelon's public speeches are often logical and persuasive, an impression represented within the text by their initially positive reception by other characters. These three scenes, along with several others in the Oxford *Roland*, show not only that characters regularly refute the very basis of each other's discourse but also that the narrative strategies of the text as a whole encourage audiences to feel alienated on a regular basis, even from the discourse of heroic characters.

The verbal indeterminacy and contentious reception of character discourses in each individual Roncevaux text are compounded through the comparative analysis of multiple representatives of the textual tradition. What is fascinating about studying this verbal alienation in the larger Roncevaux textual tradition is that many surviving texts include it as a prominent and consistent feature but that each text does so in its own way. For example, the most significant difference between the Oxford *Roland* and the other surviving Roncevaux texts is in its treatment of the Aude episode, which lasts for thirty lines in Oxford and nearly a thousand lines in some other versions. The full-length version of this episode not only devotes more attention to Aude but also has Charlemagne lie to her, and sometimes to all of France, about what happened at Roncevaux and how many warriors died there. Since the audience knows the truth about Roncevaux, including how important it was to the dying warriors that their sacrifice be properly understood after the fact, the audience's natural sympathy lies with Aude, and the drama of this episode results from the suspense felt by the audience about whether and how Aude is going to learn the truth. In other words, the audience spends this entire portion of the narrative feeling alienated from Charlemagne's discourse and anticipating the moment when a character will express that alienation within the fictional universe by denouncing the emperor's lies. Thus Aude's characterization of Charlemagne's truthful but awkward discourse in the Oxford *Roland* as "strange" represents a greatly softened version of the more usual Aude episode from the larger tradition but nevertheless retains in that key term the verbal alienation whose source is abundantly clear in the longer redactions of this episode.

Furthermore, each Roncevaux text includes at least a few scenes that do not appear in any of the others, and quite often the focal point of these scenes is character discourse. The Châteauroux manuscript is the surviving version that most closely resembles the Oxford *Roland* in its early scenes, but even this reworking of modest scope interpolates into the familiar sequence of events at the Frankish councils some unusually hostile verbal exchanges between Charlemagne and Ganelon, including one in which Charlemagne calls Ganelon a proven criminal. These additional words from the Charlemagne of Châteauroux are enough to transform the audience's initial perception of the emperor, whose motivations for entrusting Ganelon with the mission to Marsile are difficult to fathom once he has voiced his mistrust so early and so explicitly. One distinguishing feature of the Occitan version, *Ronsasvals*, is that it includes frequent speeches by characters who are virtually silent or even absent from other Roncevaux texts. Moreover, a number of these speeches occur when these characters are alone, or when another character in their presence is unable to hear what they are saying. In other speeches, heroic characters deliberately say the opposite of what they really mean, and in some cases they are successfully understood nevertheless. Thus *Ronsasvals* not only features character discourse more prominently than some other Roncevaux texts but also ascribes to it particular variants of communicative "strangeness" not found elsewhere in the textual tradition. As for *Galïen restoré*, the final Roncevaux text in the medieval French textual tradition and in this study, its flagrant linguistic discrepancies make virtually every line of it sound "strange," as it combines Old French, Middle French, and improvised forms lying somewhere between the two. Furthermore, the content of its characters' speeches is at times surprising in light of the more common characterizations of these characters in other Roncevaux texts, such as when Roland disparages the power of prayer or when the mighty Charlemagne worries that his army will lose the battle against Baligant unless fresh reinforcements arrive from somewhere else.

The medieval Roncevaux authors' shared focus on discourse provides a key to medieval rewriting in general, indicating that authors may have chosen to rewrite a particular story as much for its stylistic possibilities as for their interest in its apparent subject matter.[27] As in the examples just described, the characters' discourse is designed to sound "strange" not only to other characters within each text but also to audiences who have the opportunity to hear the radically different ways in which the characters express themselves in different versions of the Roncevaux story. It is precisely the stability of the basic Roncevaux plot that makes the characters' varying discourses emerge with such startling force for readers of multiple Roncevaux texts. In spite of some plot variations between one Roncevaux text and another, as well as some discrepancies caused by apparently accidental textual lacunae in certain surviving manuscripts, the Roncevaux textual tradition as a whole is characterized by a strikingly consistent series of core episodes, by comparison with medieval French textual traditions that have received more attention from modern critics, such as those of the Grail quest or of Tristan and Yseut. What characterizes these other textual traditions is a common premise with certain predictable ramifications but also with built-in opportunities for individual authors to adapt the plotline to their own purposes. The Grail texts are inherently variable because there are always multiple knights simultaneously but independently searching for the Grail. As for Tristan and Yseut, the fact that they always experience periods of separation from each other, from King Mark's court, or both allowed medieval authors to devise many new contexts and combinations for these texts' common characters and themes. The Roncevaux textual tradition is far more cohesive than these subcategories of the Arthurian material because it is defined by a shared central event that, in turn, governs every other event recounted alongside it. Even the most radical examples of rewriting in the Roncevaux tradition are limited to omitting, reducing, or expanding existing episodes because the very parameters of the "Roncevaux" category inhibit the invention of entirely new episodes or the transformation of the context in which familiar episodes occur. Yet the Roncevaux tradition is also far more diverse than most manuscript traditions of a common text. Some Old French narratives, such as the *Floire et Blanchefleur* in verse or the *Perceval* in prose, survive in two distinct but clearly related textual forms that have come to be known in modern criticism by concise labels such as "redactions A and B," but no such convention has been devised for the Roncevaux narratives. Critics sometimes speak of the "rhymed *Roland*s," a group of six thirteenth-century Roncevaux texts, as if they were a single entity, but representations of the relationships between them in a chart as a conventional *stemma* tend to be wide and horizontal because there are as many differences as similarities between any one of these manuscripts and all the others.[28]

The cohesiveness of the Roncevaux plot and its consistent dramatization of retelling and reception work together to draw audiences' attention to the new elements introduced into the Roncevaux narrative by each of its individual manifestations and to heighten audiences' awareness of those changes as contributions to an ongoing conversation among the larger tradition's different versions.[29] In the Middle Ages, that conversation unfolded within the clearly delineated literary space called "Roncevaux," but its strategies of signification did not require that audiences be exposed to all of the narratives within that space or even to any particular subset from among them: the distinctive "Roncevaux" plot and narrative strategies facilitate their comparative interpretation even by audiences familiar with only two versions, any two versions. The lack of documentable relationships between most of the surviving manuscripts means that these texts probably were not direct commentaries upon one another. A comparative study of selected Roncevaux texts therefore simulates the conditions of medieval reception in that it allows for a kind of comparative consideration that is not contingent upon a proven relationship between specific texts. The flexibility of comparative reception made possible by the cohesive medieval literary entity "Roncevaux" also means that the possibility that these narratives circulated simultaneously or successively in oral and written forms may not pose as many interpretative problems as some commentators have imagined. It is clear that the story of Roncevaux was told in oral forms that predated the surviving written texts, but the combination of apparent autonomy and inherent relatedness that we can observe among the surviving texts is also the dynamic thought to prevail among orally composed versions of a common story.[30]

Each chapter of this book is devoted to an individual Roncevaux text, demonstrating the ways in which its approach to rewriting is both dramatized and problematized by the characters' spoken discourse. At the start of each chapter, readers will find an overview of the central arguments to follow as well as a short introduction to the material and editorial issues associated with the unique manuscript of the text to be analyzed in that chapter. The first chapter, on the Oxford *Roland*, considers the words and actions of several main characters as realizations or refutations of the characteristics associated with the term *geste*, which the closing line of the poem applies both to the Oxford *Roland* itself and to its sources. Since this text was probably one of the earliest written versions of the Roncevaux narrative, if not the earliest, its author would have had every reason to want to highlight both its novelty and its adherence to the preceding tradition that had formed the expectations of its contemporary audience. By comparing the narratives about the past formulated within the text by Roland, Charlemagne, Ganelon, and the primary narrator, I demonstrate that these narratives and their reception embody the Oxford author's own dilemma, implicitly portraying the writing of this text as a heroic enterprise undertaken for the collective good, in marked contrast to the potentially fraudulent and self-serving narratives contained in texts written by individual authors who do not hold themselves to the high standard of the *geste*.

The author of the Châteauroux manuscript, analyzed in chapter 2, rewrites the Roncevaux narrative in a way that privileges the process of reception in two major stages. First, the early episodes of this text include long passages drawn nearly unchanged from existing texts (including one source clearly related to the Oxford *Roland*), a mode of rewriting that displays prominently its own adherence to tradition. At the same time, carefully selected changes to these sources guide the audience systematically toward one particular interpretation of the motivations of Roland, Ganelon, and Charlemagne, whereas other contemporary texts (including the Oxford *Roland*) allowed for more ambiguity in the portrayal of these characters. Later in the text, transmission and reception are emphasized in a different way through the extended Aude episode, which dramatizes Aude's reception of the deliberate misrepresentation of Roncevaux by Charlemagne and a literate cleric, on the one hand, and of the inherently truthful Roncevaux narratives communicated to her by prophetic dreams and angelic messengers, on the other. The Châteauroux manuscript's focus on the reception of the Roncevaux story by the text itself, by the audience, and by characters within the story emphasizes the contribution of insightful reception to successful literary transmission, rather than privileging the contribution of skillful storytelling.

Chapter 3 examines the unusual multivocality and interiority featured in the Occitan version, *Ronsasvals*. By omitting the initial council scenes, the post-Roncevaux battles against Marsile and Baligant, and Ganelon's trial, this Roncevaux narrative finds sufficient space and time to linger over the characters' gradual cognitive and verbal processing of the battle itself (among the warriors) and then of the painful losses inflicted by it (among the surviving characters). The audience hears frequently what characters are saying and thinking during the battle and its aftermath; this interior view of the characters, as well as the absence of a number of traditional plot elements, represents Roncevaux more as a spiritual crisis caused by sinful attitudes than as a political crisis caused by characters' actions and reactions. Verbal discourse among the characters not only expresses these personal flaws but also may serve to overcome them, through rhetorical strategies such as saying the opposite of what one really means or communicating the essential meaning of a message through metaphors that may survive intact despite subsequent rewording by the messenger. These verbal exchanges among the characters exemplify the text's own rewriting strategy: a faithful transmission of essential content that operates, paradoxically, through deliberate and blatant transformations of form.

The late-fifteenth-century text *Galïen restoré*, to which chapter 4 is devoted, rewrites the Roncevaux narrative as a monument to the complex functioning of literary memory. The text begins with metatextual comments about the audience's responsibility for keeping alive the memory of past heroes and then places at the center of its version of the Roncevaux story a young hero, Galien, who operates according to a similar, though largely unconscious, intertextual memory of the heroic deeds of his ancestors. This harmony between the primary hero of the text and the narrator's charge to the implied audience is disrupted, however, by a certain antipathy toward Galien and his optimistic perspective on the part of Olivier, Roland, and the primary narrator during this text's account of the episodes at Roncevaux. Charlemagne and the other traditional Frankish survivors also have trouble at times negotiating between their grief over the warriors they have lost and their joy at finding in Galien the solution to many of their traditional post-Roncevaux problems. Thus *Galïen restoré*, like the other texts in this study but in its own unique way, represents within its fictional universe the tensions involved in its own composition and reception. This is a text that sought to strengthen the audience's memory of the preceding textual tradition, but its contemporary success ultimately caused it to overshadow its textual ancestors: *Galïen restoré* made an early transition into print and has continued to circulate ever since, while the other Roncevaux texts in this study probably stopped circulating by the fifteenth century and had to be rediscovered by scholars in the nineteenth century.

That modern process of rediscovery and reception of the Roncevaux texts has been nearly as fraught with political, social, and literary tensions as the Roncevaux fictional universe itself. The analyses in the following chapters make the point that the simultaneously autonomous and collaborative literary enterprise exemplified by the Roncevaux texts offers an approach to literary rewriting and reception that causes these tensions to enhance rather than to inhibit readers' understanding of the processes of representation and interpretation underlying them all. The goal of this book is not merely to defend the value of a group of neglected medieval texts but to document the ways medieval texts addressed themselves to sophisticated critical audiences for whom reception and comparative analysis could be simultaneous and multilayered.[31] At the same time, the high stakes of verbal representation and interpretation in the Roncevaux texts demonstrate with particular poignancy medieval authors and audiences' shared awareness of the limited capacities of human narratives to make sense of human experience. By subordinating the particular political and cultural viewpoints of each individual version to the metanarrative perspective shared by them all, I wish to magnify rather than to reduce the scope of these texts as collaborative dramatizations of human cognition, communication, and commemoration.

The Oxford *Roland*

I

La Geste and Reliable Rewriting

This chapter is devoted to the theory that the narrative strategies of the Oxford *Roland* (both those used by the primary narrator and those used by characters) can be read fruitfully as a consistent metaphor for the project of committing the Roncevaux story to vernacular written form for what may have been the first time. The many narratives elaborated within the fiction draw the audience's attention repeatedly to the issue of storytelling, and the structure and tone of the primary narration invite audience members to evaluate the relative worth of the various narratives they hear. This metaliterary strand of signification can be found in every Roncevaux narrative, but the particular form that it takes in the Oxford *Roland* is related to this poem's status as the oldest surviving Old French text containing the Roncevaux story and also to the status it explicitly claims for itself, that of a *geste*. The particular sense of *geste* in the Oxford *Roland* transcends the oral/written binary and can take the form of literature or of lived experience: as such, it provides an ideal narrative category within which to express ideas about the psychological and social significance of narrative retelling. After discussing the characteristics that define the category "*geste*" in this text, I examine the narrative style of Ganelon, which I see as the text's representation of anti-*geste* narration within the fiction. Next I analyze how the problematic reception of both *geste* and anti-*geste* styles of discourse at councils of the

Franks convened by Charlemagne dramatizes tensions fundamental to the fictional universe and to the author's textual project. Finally, I interpret the Oxford poet's unique ways (unique within the Roncevaux textual tradition) of narrating the deaths of Roland and of Ganelon as metaphorical representations of the culturally "life-and-death" stakes of the Oxford poet's literary undertaking of textualizing a formerly oral, collective epic. I draw parallels between the poem itself and Roland's heroic and ultimately self-effacing style of narration and material representation; I also observe the clear distinctions between the primary narration and Ganelon's duplicitous and self-aggrandizing style of narration (which is, itself, depicted in this text as a significant cause of Ganelon's execution). Whether or not the Oxford author had this aim in mind, these resemblances and distinctions between the primary narration and narration by fictional characters implicitly refute the possible contemporary allegation that the written transmission of the Oxford *Roland* might be an attempt to override the ultimate, collectively determined truth of the *geste* with the selfish and short-sighted goal of glorifying a single poet's knowledge and narrative artistry.

About the Text

The only surviving medieval manuscript containing this text is housed at the Bodleian Library, Oxford University, and bears the shelfmark Digby 23 because it was donated by Sir Kenelm Digby. A facsimile edition of the manuscript was published in 1933, and a digital facsimile has been made available on the Web site "Early Manuscripts at Oxford University."[1] The manuscript is generally thought to have been copied in the second quarter of the twelfth century, although some recent commentators have argued for a date closer to the end of the century;[2] in either case, this is the oldest surviving Roncevaux manuscript. The date of written composition for this text is often given as "circa 1100," although some scholars believe that the surviving manuscript may represent the earliest transcription of the text, in which case the date for the entire enterprise of its composition and transcription would be closer to 1150. If we accept the approximate date of 1100, then this text is also by far the longest Old French text from that time to have survived: earlier Old French texts measure in dozens or hundreds of lines, while the Oxford *Roland* contains approximately four thousand lines.[3] The manuscript contains one other text, Chalcidius's translation of Plato's *Timaeus*, which may have been bound with the *Roland* as early as the thirteenth century or as late as the seventeenth century.[4] Both the linguistic forms found in the Oxford *Roland* and its scribal hand are Anglo-Norman, suggesting that it was written down, as well as preserved, in England[5] and therefore that this particular version may not have been available to later Roncevaux authors writing in France. Numerous editions and translations of the text are available, most under the title *La Chanson de Roland (The Song of Roland)*.[6]

Like all of the surviving Roncevaux texts to be analyzed in this book, the Oxford *Roland* is written in verse and organized in epic *laisses*, stanzas of varying lengths. The lines of each Oxford laisse end with a common vowel sound (assonance), though the entire ending may not be consistent from one line to the next. In other surviving Roncevaux texts, the lines of each laisse rhyme with one another, meaning that not only the last vowel sound but the entire last syllable matches from one line to the next within the same laisse. Another distinguishing feature of this text, compared to other surviving medieval Roncevaux texts, is its stylistic similarity to epics of other times and places that were composed and performed orally. The clearest mark of this orality is the text's use of epic formulas, set expressions of four, six, or ten syllables that could therefore be used as convenient building blocks to generate ten-syllable lines (with a caesura after the fourth or sixth syllable). An example would be the often repeated "Ço dist li reis" (The king said this), which can also be changed to "Ço dist Rollant," "Ço dist li quens" (The count says this), or even "Ço dist la Geste" (The *Geste* says this). Similarly, characters' two-syllable first names are often expanded to more metrically pragmatic four-syllable epithets such as "li quens Rollant" or "Turpins de Reins." A different use of formulaic style can be observed in the following lines, whose repetitive basic structure is formulaic, especially since all of these are initial lines of laisses: "La bataille est merveilluse e pesant" [The battle is terrible and hard] (v. 1412); "La bataille est merveilluse e hastive" [The battle is terrible and intense] (v. 1610); "La bataille est e merveillose e grant" [The battle is terrible and widespread] (v. 1620). This consistent way of using a formula, as the start of a new laisse and with only one altered word in each instance, is an example of the rhetorical sophistication of this text's formulaic style. These three lines alone provide a good summary of this entire section of the text, in which the warriors of the rear guard summon all their strength to fight off the elite members of the attacking force ("hard battle"), only to see several of their own elite warriors killed, often prompting immediate and violent reprisals ("intense battle"), and then additional Saracen re-inforcements arrive ("widespread battle").

It can be neither proven nor disproven definitively that this text was composed orally, although the simpler use of formulas first mentioned makes that scenario a viable option, based on what is known about tech-niques of oral composition used in other times and places.[7] What can be said on the basis of the existing manuscript alone is that its formulaic style, characterized by repetition with small and significant variations, can be seen to operate at every level of the text, from epithets and indi-vidual lines, as above, to sequences of laisses (usually three) that nearly paraphrase one another with significant variations, to entire episodes that follow a similar structure.[8] Some degree of repetition is character-istic of many, if not most, medieval narratives, but the Oxford *Roland* is exceptional in the variety and pervasiveness of its stylistic and structural uses of repetition and formulaic expression. Indeed, one of the most puzzling things about this document is how firmly it appears to be rooted in both the oral and written realms of medieval literary culture. We are fortunate to have this surviving manuscript evidence of medieval French oral epic, such as it is, but in all likelihood this is not a faithful repre-sentation of contemporary oral literature. The fact that the oral narra-tive must have been changed through the process of its conversion into written form is not a trivial detail of interest only to specialists but rather a fundamental trait of this text's apparatus of signification, and one that has been described as a "glaring paradox."[9] Modern readers of the Oxford *Roland* have often assumed that this text's marks of orality resulted from a natural stylistic continuity between earlier oral perfor-mances of the Roncevaux *matiere* and this early written version, which some have imagined to be a transcription of an actual oral performance rather than an independent composition. Yet the very newness of the written format for vernacular literature in the early twelfth century, particularly for epic texts (written vernacular literature from the ninth to eleventh centuries seems to have included only relatively short hagio-graphic texts), suggests that the Oxford *Roland* represented a deliberate break with past literary tradition and perhaps even a calculated inaugu-ration of a new era of written vernacular transmission, which of neces-sity would be dominated by literate authors capable of gaining the sup-port of wealthy patrons.

Not only this major shift toward vernacular texts but in particular the writing down of epic material may well have been controversial at the time. Oral epic usually serves as the cultural locus for the expression of collective values, its credibility with audiences ensured by the very fact that it is thought to be the product not of a single author but rather of the collectivity. If the Oxford *Roland* was the product of a single author, as its final line may suggest, then that author could have been thought arrogant or even subversive for taking it upon himself[10] to compose a single textual version of the Roncevaux story. The Oxford *Roland*'s formulaic style is not definitive proof that this text was actually composed in oral performance, but it does show that the author wanted to evoke the style of oral epic. This desire seems to have been a function of the expectations of literary culture at that particular time rather than a permanent requirement for medieval epic, since authors of many epic texts written a century or more later include far fewer oral formulas. Perhaps the Oxford poet used this oral style and incorporated repetition into every level of the narrative as a way of implicitly denying the innovative or even subversive nature of creating a vernacular epic text. At the same time, traces of written literary culture permeate this text from beginning to end, most obviously in the text's periodic references to textual sources and authorities. The manuscript's bookhand may also reflect its provenance in an elite center of written literary culture; it has been suggested that the Oxford *Roland* was written down by a highly trained scribe who was used to copying large-format Latin texts and had some trouble writing down unfamiliar vernacular words in a smaller size.[11] Other manuscript evidence may indicate that, from the late thirteenth century onward, this text was the property of the Augustinian canons of Oxford, along with the heavily glossed *Timaeus* with which it was bound.[12] These links to oral literary culture and to learned written culture may reveal the text's attempt to bring the Roncevaux story to scholarly audiences, or they may represent an awareness of the estrangement between written and oral literary culture and perhaps a desire to find common ground that could be shared by all French-speaking audiences. In any case, what we can say with confidence is that this version of the Roncevaux story was thought worthy of preservation by medieval scholars and that its formulaic style also attested to an earlier oral provenance, whether this orality was the result of a genuine continuity or was deliberately fabricated by the author.

That this text could appeal to both popular and scholarly medieval audiences should be neither a surprise nor a disappointment to modern scholars who admire its poetic excellence, its political insights, and its psychological profundity. What might be a bit disturbing to some scholars, however, is the possibility that this text never circulated in France and that in that case it probably would not have been a direct source for the authors who wrote the surviving Roncevaux texts that did circulate in thirteenth- and fourteenth-century France. We can neither prove nor disprove that the Oxford version was known to authors or audiences in twelfth- and thirteenth-century France, but it certainly is not safe to assume that it was a direct source for all the later Old French texts that have survived, or indeed for any one of them in particular. What this means is that Oxford, even more than the thirteenth-century French and Franco-Italian rhymed versions, is to be understood as an isolated textual manifestation of the Roncevaux story rather than as an influential source for later manifestations of it. Thus the particular strategies of signification found in the Oxford *Roland* have about an equal chance of being the common heritage of all Roncevaux authors or of being variations unique to this version, invented for the particular purposes of its author. To identify the narrative strategies unique to this version, as well as the larger literary principles underlying those strategies, I will begin with an examination of the self-descriptive term for the poem that is used in its final line: *la geste*.

La Geste as the Heroic Standard for Words, Actions, and Interpretations

La geste is such an important entity in the Oxford *Roland* that its meaning has been subjected to scrutiny by generations of critics, who have generally agreed that it is a term without a single definition that would apply to all of its occurrences within the text. The term comes from the past participle of the Latin verb *gerere*, which has meanings ranging from "accomplish" to "carry on" to "wage war." Thus the most literal meaning of the term is simply "things that have been accomplished," with a clear implication that those "things" may have been wars. In its Old French usage, *geste* had the connotation of "lineage," meaning that a *chanson de geste* was not only a war narrative but a narrative about wars (and other things) carried out by a particular kin group with some connection or established significance to the song's implied audience. Certain historical texts also were known as *gestes* in medieval culture, as some references within the Oxford *Roland* acknowledge. Where a *geste* is cited as a source for the narrator's knowledge of the events (vv. 1443, 1685, 2095, 3262, 3742), it sounds like a textual chronicle such as the Latin *Gesta Francorum* (the resemblance is especially striking in the formulation *La Geste Francor*, vv. 1443 and 3262). Yet in two places (vv. 1685 and

2095) it occurs in the formula "Ço dist la Geste," which indicates that "la Geste" is a speaking entity analogous to the characters whose speech is introduced with the same expression, "ço dist." When it appears in a description of Charlemagne by the Saracen leader Baligant, it is in a plural form and has neither an oral nor a written character, though its function is still that of a reliable source of information, apparently available within the fiction: ". . . mult est proz. / En plusurs gestes de lui sunt granz honurs." [. . . he is very valiant. / In many *gestes* about him there are great honors.] (vv. 3180–81). In the closing line of the text, the Oxford *Roland* itself is called a *geste*, specifically the *geste* of Turoldus (a name that probably denotes either the author or the scribe of the poem). This usage implies that *geste* had no one fixed form: the *geste* was known to exist already, but it could also be regenerated by new authors and spoken of as their work.

The most ambiguous use of the term, however, is the first one in the text, which occurs when Roland explains why he will not agree to bring half of Charlemagne's army with him to serve as the rear guard: "Jo n'en ferai nïent; / Deus me cunfunde, se la geste en desment!" [I will do nothing of the kind; / May God confound me, if I dismantle [or give the lie to] the *geste*!] (v. 788). In this instance, Roland recognizes the *geste* as a supreme authority; his desire to respect that authority motivates him to make a decision with grave consequences for thousands of his fellow warriors, in opposition to a direct order from the emperor.[13] Many critics have combined the Latin and Old French meanings of the word *geste* in their interpretation of this line, concluding that what Roland means by *geste* is "all that has been done before," that is, the traditional behavior of members of his kin group and the noble reputation that resulted from that behavior, a reputation that Roland does not wish to jeopardize by taking an action that might appear cowardly. In spite of a certain amount of critical consensus on this point,[14] it is worth noting that a later use of the term by the Archbishop Turpin opens up the possibility that Roland is making a metatextual reference to the story in which he appears. As Turpin watches the rear guard fight off a far larger number of attacking Saracens, he comments with satisfaction (to no one but the audience, it would seem), "Il est escrit en la Geste Francor / Que bons vassals out nostre empereür" [It is written in the *Geste Francor* / That our emperor had good vassals] (vv. 1443–44). What is most jarring here is that Turpin speaks of Charlemagne and his vassals in the past tense, citing a historical account written after Charlemagne's death, and therefore after his own death as well. Similarly, Roland's vehement insistence upon upholding the truth of the *geste* could represent his foreknowledge of the role he and the rear guard are to play in the subsequent literary legend of Roncevaux, a heroic determination to play his part correctly in the text at hand. This reading of verse 788 is particularly appropriate in light of Roland's reference during the battle to the future songs that will be sung about his brave deeds (vv. 1013–16). Clearly Roland does already view himself as a future literary hero, so perhaps his concern about "dismantling the *geste*" in verse 788 disregards the chronology according to which the literary representation of his deeds would logically follow his deeds rather than anticipating them.

Karl Uitti's article on the meaning of *geste* explains this ambiguity between past and future, literature and life, by tracing the roots of the term in the Oxford *Roland* back to Einhard's *Vita Caroli* (c. 830), one of the earliest written accounts of the historical event that inspired the literary legend of Roncevaux.[15] By considering carefully both the spirit of this pre-Oxford source for the Roncevaux story and the literal meaning of the term *geste*, Uitti arrives at a consistent reading of the term, even in Roland's use of it, that is more complex and informative than either the "family tradition" reading or a strictly metatextual reading. Uitti begins by pointing out that the story of this battle had always functioned as an *exemplum*, even within Einhard's account, and that for that reason there are as many similarities as differences between the Oxford *Roland* and the account of Einhard, despite the obvious discrepancies between their two versions of the actual series of events. Because Einhard's text is presented not as a chronicle but rather as a biography of Charlemagne, the battle in question showed that Charlemagne was a great military leader not because he was always victorious over his enemies but because he maintained his resolve even in the face of discouraging setbacks. For that reason, Einhard inserts the account of this defeat among the accounts of Charlemagne's numerous victories during the same period and suggests that Charlemagne did exact revenge for this defeat through his military career as a whole, even though he was unable to do so immediately.[16] These aspects of Einhard's rhetoric lead directly to two aspects of the Oxford *Roland* that initially appear to be a contradiction of Einhard's account: Charlemagne's successful revenge battles, which merely realize within the space of a single *chanson de geste* the eventual revenge that Einhard had implied, and Roland's deliberate refusal to call for help from Charlemagne, which provides a concrete example of the way in which the fictional Roland mirrors Charlemagne's own heroic steadfastness.[17]

This mirroring of Einhard's Charlemagne by the Roland of Oxford does not merely multiply the models of heroism offered by the Oxford

Roland in comparison to Einhard's account; rather, the detailed exposition of Roland's heroism throughout the first half of the text helps to explain the very nature of the *geste*. This explanation is one of Oxford's central metaliterary enterprises, since the text, like Roland, claims *"la geste"* as a primary authority. For Uitti, the most revealing use of *geste* in the Oxford *Roland* may be that of Baligant (vv. 3180–81, cited above), who accepts Charlemagne's military might and personal bravery as factual because the stories told about him are *gestes*, inherently truthful accounts:

> [T]hey constitute a story within which Charles plays a role. He is a character in the book that tells his story, and as such he must live up, so to speak, in "real life" to the expectations this story raises. . . . This set of expectations is exactly what Einhard, in conjunction with the Frankish annalists and others, had created when, in the *Vita Caroli,* the facts of Charles's life were integrated into the patterns provided by Suetonius's very "literary" *Life of Caesar Augustus.* Consequently, when in v. 788 Roland proclaims, "Deus me cunfunde, se la geste en desment," *geste,* I believe, has less to do with his lineage . . . than with—to be precise—the story within which, he understands, he has been called upon to play a clearly defined role. . . . Just as Roland's part in the *geste* constitutes an element of Charles's *geste,* so Charles's story forms a chapter in a still longer continuity: the *geste* of what The Strasbourg Oaths call the *christian poblo* and its *salvament.*[18]

In this passage, Uitti allows for the harmonious integration of several different aspects of the notion of *geste* that can appear contradictory when isolated from one another. Perhaps the most surprising component of the *geste* as Uitti explains it is that it does not only convey past events, as one might reasonably assume on the basis of its derivation from a Latin past participle. Baligant's faith in the inevitable continuity between the *gestes* of Charles and the emperor's character in the fictional present and future informs us that *gestes* have an authority that transcends that of history or of storytelling because they also determine the course of seemingly spontaneous lived experience in the present. The fact that it is the Saracen king who expresses this concept of the *geste* confirms its universality. For the leaders on both sides of this conflict, the *geste* is irresistible and irrefutable: Baligant and Roland seem to share the same understanding of what the *geste* is, even though they do not agree on who God is. Of course, as Uitti suggests here, the ultimate function of the *geste* for the Christians of the Oxford *Roland* is that of manifesting God's will through human history. But its status as a manifestation in the form of lived experience confers upon it the advantage of tangible evidence: it can persuade people to agree upon certain facts in spite of their differing principles and beliefs. Similarly, *la geste* would have provided the perfect literary authority with which to persuade skeptical audiences to accept the new written vernacular epic.

In the context of the *geste*, the past events being recounted are perceived simultaneously as past instances of real lived experience, comparable to one's own life in the present moment, and as coherent narratives, comparable to any other narratives but most similar to biblical narratives and hagiography both in their truth value and in their exemplarity. Not only does the *geste* confer upon literary works a historical authority derived from "real-life" events, but it also performs the reciprocal function of endowing the lives of conscious historical actors with a literariness that guides their actions along coherent paths. As Uitti emphasized through his use of the terms *real life* and *literary* to describe different aspects of the *geste*, the unique power of this entity is that it forms a bridge between the reality of individual existence in the present moment and the collective, narrativized memory of past events. It is for this reason that, as Uitti points out, "past and present—'ongoingness'— are conjoined at the very start of the *Song of Roland*,"[19] that is, in the text's first laisse, whose verbs alternate between the present, preterite, and perfect tenses.[20] In similar fashion, I would add, "ongoingness" is the essence of Roland's most famous recommendation to Charlemagne at the Franks' council, the first scene in which Roland appears: "Faites la guerre cum vos l'avez entreprise" [Wage this war as you began it] (v. 210). Interestingly, Ganelon's later description of Roland to the Saracen Blancadrin also concludes with the notion of "ongoingness": "Li soens orgoilz le devreit ben cunfundre, / Kar chascun jur de mort sei abandonet. / Seit ki l'ocïet, tute pais puis avrumes." [His pride really should be his undoing, / For every day he exposes himself to death. / If someone kills him, then we will be entirely at peace.] (vv. 389–91). According to this statement, Roland's daring in battle is as profound and immutable an aspect of his character as is his pride: he continues to risk his life in battle every day, and he will continue to do so forever. Yet Ganelon does introduce a new element here that was denied or unacknowledged in the earlier statements by Roland and the primary narrator: he contemplates the question of how the inevitable chain of Roland's predictable behavior might be broken. The solution he devises only serves to confirm the "lived experience" aspect of the *geste*: Roland's *geste* can be terminated only through his death because for Roland fighting bravely is an inherent part of living. Ganelon's proposed solution thus reveals the chief vulnerability of the *geste*: because it is manifested through the lived experience of mortal individuals, its power can be extinguished through the death of such individuals.

Uitti recognized this vulnerability and therefore pointed out that the end of the poem raises and then refutes the notion that Roland's *geste* could be terminated simply through his death. This point is made most obviously through the example of Thierry, an apparently average member of Charlemagne's army who nevertheless becomes the champion of Charlemagne (and thus of Roland) in the judicial combat that proves Ganelon's guilt. Thierry's willingness to risk a battle against Ganelon's mighty champion is a reenactment of Roland's stand against Marsile's far greater attacking force, a revival of Roland's *geste*.[21] Furthermore, the Oxford *Roland* emphasizes that Thierry's act of courage changed forever the ending of the Roncevaux story as it would be told by future generations. Through the mechanism of judicial combat, a legal proceeding that initially appeared to be a matter of validating either Ganelon's or Charlemagne's verbal claims about the causes of the Battle of Roncevaux was transformed into a new mini-*geste*. Because Thierry's memorial to Roland took the form of a decisive public act as well as a speech, he ensured that his point of view would be preserved in subsequent stories about the Battle of Roncevaux and its aftermath. Thierry's victory in the judicial combat would not be open to reinterpretation because it was made manifest before so many witnesses, in the context of an established judicial procedure whose function and meaning were well known by everyone present. Thierry's victory thus serves both as a manifestation of the *geste* and as a dramatization of how it functions in storytelling and in public life. According to the Oxford *Roland*'s view of life and of literature, an essential function of the *geste* is to form a bridge between the customarily estranged realms of verbal expression, which is abstract and unreliable in the Christian culture of Oxford's Franks because it is tainted by human sin, and of lived experience, which constitutes a concrete and absolute truth because it is the work of God, who is without sin or error and who is sovereign over all world events. As Baligant's statement about Charlemagne suggests, and as the actions of Roland and Thierry exemplify, the *geste* is not limited to the verbal realm because it preserves real past events to inspire real future events. On the other hand, the *geste* must assume a verbal form to transcend the deaths of the individuals who make it manifest and to communicate its meaning effectively to future generations.

This notion of the *geste* converges with Eugene Vance's notion of "commemoration" as a primary force in Oxford's fictional culture, just as it was in medieval culture: "By 'commemoration' I mean any gesture, ritualized or not, whose end is to invoke, in the name of the social group, some remembered essence or event that is either anterior in time or ontologically prior to what is present, in order to animate, fecundate, mark, or celebrate some moment in the present. Commemoration revitalizes or redeems whatever in the world or in the self has become merely corporeal, deficient, and vacant of meaning."[22] Vance's description of such commemorative acts resembles Uitti's description of the functioning of the *geste* in its emphasis on the relationship that such commemoration creates between three entities: past history or eternity, lived experience in the present, and a collectivity for whom the commemorative gesture signifies this relationship successfully. While the verbal component of the literary *geste* seems initially to be excluded from this definition, Vance's examination of commemoration in the Oxford *Roland* gives a prominent place to the reciprocal relationship between Roland's actions and the subsequent performances of literary songs commemorating them: "For if it is the antique glory of the hero that animates here and now the voice and the gestures of the poet, reciprocally, it is the commemorative posterity of the future singer's voice that inspires the epic blows of the hero on the battlefield. . . . [B]y his own *essample* Roland constitutes himself as the 'author' of the future poem that will celebrate his memory."[23] Here Vance cites one of Roland's most famous formulations of his heroic, *geste*-oriented worldview: "Or guart chascuns que granz colps i empleit, / Male cançun de nus chantét ne seit! / Paien unt tort e chrestïens unt dreit. / Malvaise essample n'en serat ja de mei." [Now may each one ensure that he strikes great blows, / So that a bad song may never be sung about us! / The pagans are wrong and the Christians are right. / A bad example will never be made of me.] (vv. 1013–16).[24] Roland's statements here anticipate an absolute, unbroken continuity between his actions in the present, the content and tone of the songs to be sung about those actions in the future, and the interpretation of those songs by future generations of people from his culture. He does not entertain the possibilities that his actions might not be known or remembered at all, that future singers might misrepresent those actions, or that audiences might fail to grasp the intended meaning of his actions as a positive example to inspire their own values and conduct. Although the Oxford narrator does not explicitly point out these potential threats to the perpetuation of the *geste* through commemoration, each of them is dramatized later in the poem by other examples of character discourse and reception.

Elsewhere Vance stressed that it is the collective functioning of oral epic that most profoundly shapes the model of heroism provided by Roland, whom he describes as a "hero of orality, who lives (like a poet) at the center of a social group," as opposed to most heroes of chivalric romance, who usually encounter their adventures alone. Vance added that the isolated adventures of medieval romance heroes matched the solitude of authors who wrote down their texts rather than composing them orally. Thus Vance perceived in the case of both oral and written production a reciprocal relationship between the heroes and authors of medieval literary works.[25] The remainder of this chapter will be devoted to examining the possibility of such a reciprocal relationship between Roland and the Oxford poet, for I believe that the Oxford *Roland* serves not only as a written record of Roland's heroism but as a commemoration of it, in Vance's sense of the term. Just as Vance and others have argued that Roland functions as a poet in certain scenes from Oxford, I wish to emphasize the ways in which the poet functions as a hero like Roland, in that his poem follows scrupulously the same criteria expressed by Roland's discourse and actions in service to the *geste*. Similarly, the Oxford poet attributes undesirable narrative traits to the villain of the poem, Ganelon, implicitly disassociating himself from those contemporary vernacular authors who might have shared Ganelon's disregard for the literary and behavioral requirements of the *geste*. This reading of the poem perceives the interactions between the main characters of the Roncevaux story as a dramatic space in which to display the literary and social tensions inherent in the project of writing down in the vernacular a story whose purpose was to privilege collective values over individual innovation.

The Burden of Proof: Ganelon as an Author and the Author as a Ganelon

These literary and social tensions emerge clearly from Ganelon's own retelling of the Roncevaux story during his trial near the end of the Oxford *Roland* because this is one of the most blatant cases of metaliterary character discourse in the poem. Although this is Ganelon's formal statement of his plea in a judicial proceeding, its similarities to a narrative performance encourage the audience to compare it to a literary narrative. This comparison has implications for the poem within which it appears, in part because Ganelon's statement is essentially a Roncevaux narrative (albeit an abbreviated and idiosyncratic one) and also because Ganelon can be seen to mimic, or perhaps even to parody, the traits of a heroic *geste*.[26] This scene dramatizes simultaneously the potential for storytellers to offer deceptive retellings of a *geste* and the dire threat to the *geste* posed by faulty audience reception, since all of Charlemagne's men but one initially fail to privilege Roland's version of events over Ganelon's. As I will show, clear links between Ganelon's narrative and others in the text show that this scene plays an important role in the poem's overall exposition of the defining traits of reliable and unreliable narration and of successful and unsuccessful audience reception.

Devant le rei la s'estut Guenelun:
Cors ad gaillard, el vis gente color;
S'il fust leials, ben resemblast barun.
Veit cels de France e tuz les jugeürs,
De ses parenz trente ki od lui sunt.
Puis s'escrïat haltement, a grant voiz:
"Pur amor Deu, car m'entendez, seignors!
Jo fui en l'ost avoec l'empereür,
Serveie le par feid e par amur.
Rollant sis niés me coillit en haür,
Si me jugat a mort e a dulur.
Message fui al rei Marsilïun;
Par mun saveir vinc jo a guarisun.
Jo desfiai Rollant le pugnëor,
E Oliver e tuiz lur cumpaignun;
Carles l'oïd e si noble baron.
Vengét m'en sui, mais n'i ad traïsun."

(vv. 3762–3778)

[There before the king Ganelon stood up:
He had a strong body, his face was a noble color;
If he were loyal, he would truly resemble a baron.
He saw the men from France and all of his judges,
Of his kin there were thirty who were with him.
Then he cried aloud, in a great voice:

"For the love of God, now hear me, lords!
I was in the entourage of the emperor,
And I always served him in good faith and in love/loyalty.[27]
Roland, his nephew, treated me with hatred,
Indeed he sentenced me to a painful death.
I served as the messenger to King Marsile;
Through my cleverness I managed to save myself.
I challenged Roland the warrior,
And Olivier and all of their companions;
Charles heard it along with his noble barons.
I avenged myself on them, but there was no betrayal in it."]

Ganelon's statement fulfills the literal definition of a *geste*, since it consists primarily of a list of "things done" by Roland and Ganelon. It also begins in the same way as many medieval narratives (especially *chansons de geste*), with an appeal for the audience's attention (v. 3768). His story proper then begins in a past tense marked by "ongoingness," as Ganelon describes in the imperfect tense the stable state of affairs that preceded the events at Roncevaux: "I served him [Charlemagne] in good faith and in love/loyalty." The event that changed all that was the sudden emergence of Roland's hatred for Ganelon, expressed with a decisive preterite verb (v. 3771); similarly, the plots of many *chansons de geste* are set in motion by an initial wrong committed against an innocent protagonist. Ganelon asserts that his subsequent actions should not be termed *traïsun* (which can denote either a "sneak attack" or an act of disloyalty toward one's lord)[28] because he formally warned Charlemagne's entire council of his hostile intentions toward Roland (vv. 3775–78); thus Ganelon was simply taking his proper vengeance against his sworn enemies (v. 3779). With this conclusion, Ganelon claims that the story of his actions in the larger Roncevaux plot falls into the same category as those of Roland and Charlemagne: like Charlemagne's act of vengeance against the Saracens, Ganelon's betrayal was an act of vengeance not only justified but necessitated by Roland's initial wrong against him. This justification of vengeance does not represent Ganelon's personal opinion but rather reflects the collective ethos of his society as expressed earlier in the text by Roland (v. 213), by Turpin (v. 1744), by Naime (v. 2428), by Charlemagne (v. 3012), and even by an angelic messenger (v. 2456). Ganelon's statement bears several distinguishing marks of a narrative performance and of a heroic *geste*, but as such it also contains multiple deficiencies, which are summed up by the phrase "par mun saveir vinc jo a guarison" [through my cleverness I managed to save myself] (v. 3774). This phrase is suggestive of all that is excluded from the literary entity of the *geste*: the primacy of individual existence and identity as well as the vagaries of individual perception, opinion, invention, and interpretation.

This is true, first of all, because the collective ethos of Frankish society as described in the Oxford *Roland* does not consider it an act of heroism per se to save oneself from death by any means, perhaps least of all by one's "knowledge" or "cleverness." More importantly for my metaliterary reading of the text, a heroic *geste* as described elsewhere in the poem is not a first-person narrative. Roland comments on his own heroic conduct in several scenes from the poem, but within the fiction these are not performances: when Roland refers to the *geste* or to future songs about his conduct, he explicitly states that someone else will be the ultimate author of the *geste* or the performer of the heroic songs. Even when Roland inscribes upon his own dying body a message about how his conduct in the Battle of Roncevaux should be interpreted, he does so precisely to influence a collective future account that will be told by others: "Pur ço l'at fait que il voelt veirement / Que Carles diet e trestute sa gent, / Li gentilz cuens, qu'il fut mort conquerant" [He did this because he truly wants / Charles to say, and all of his people, / That the noble count died conquering] (vv. 2361–63). It is not the place of the *geste*'s protagonists to sing their own praises or even to justify themselves after the fact; a fundamental trait of the *geste* is that it expresses a society's consensus about events in its collective history.

This same spirit of impartial collective consensus also characterizes the primary narrator's own references to "real" *gestes* that exist outside the fictional universe of the poem. At no time does the primary narrator seek to explain to the audience what his citations from the *geste* mean (which has allowed for the proliferation of interpretations among modern critics concerning certain of these passages), nor does he admit to any distance between what the *geste* actually contains and what he is saying about it. The narrator thus denies the existence of any process of interpretation or invention on his part; the narrator speaks of the *geste* as if it were an infallible source of truth, and its reception by the Oxford *Roland* performs its own reluctance to add or change anything about it. This immutable integrity and self-evidence of the *geste* can be explained by its implicitly universal availability to the audience. In fact, the context within which the primary narrator consistently evokes the authority of the *geste* is that of ignorance, which the *geste* can remedy because it is a product of reliable collective knowledge. This is the true *saveir* of which

Ganelon's *mun saveir* is a mockery. For example, Turpin's evocation of the great worth of Charlemagne and his vassals in the *"Geste Francor"* (v. 1443) follows immediately the narrator's dismissal of the interpretation by the people of France that the natural disasters that are suddenly taking place all over their country must be a sign of the end of the world: "Icil ne l' sevent, ne dïent veir nïent: / C'est li granz doels por la mort de Rollant" [They do not know this, they are not telling the truth at all: / This was the great grief for the death of Roland] (vv. 1436–37). Similarly, in the last line of laisse 155, just after an extensive comment about the sources of authority for the *geste*, the narrator concludes by telling the audience that they cannot understand what the current text is talking about unless they have knowledge of these previous *gestes*: "Ki tant ne set ne l'ad prod entendut" [Whoever does not know all this has not understood it at all] (v. 2098). While discussing the impressive number of men killed by Roland, Olivier, and Turpin, the narrator praises the empoweringly precise knowledge contained in written documents and affirmed by *"la Geste"*: "Cels qu'il unt mort, ben les poet hom preiser: / Il est escrit en cartres e es brefs, / Ço dit la Geste, plus de quatre milliers" [Those whom they killed, one can count them well: / It is written in charters and registers, / So says the *Geste*, over four thousand] (vv. 1683–85). The narrator's praise for the capacity of *gestes* to convey knowledge to the ignorant is not a major theme of the poem, but it is connected to one of the poem's most pervasive narrative devices: allowing the audience access to crucial information that is denied to the characters themselves at the same moment. All of the pre-Roncevaux scenes operate according to this dynamic, since the audience witnesses the councils of the Saracens as well as those of the Franks. The narrator explicitly reminds the audience of this dynamic when the rear guard arrives at Roncevaux, unaware of the fact that they are surrounded by four thousand Saracens who are about to attack them: "Deus! quel dulur que li Franceis ne l' sevent!" [God! how sad that the French do not know it!] (v. 716). "Knowledge" about Roncevaux is what the poem offers to its audience in retrospect, and both this knowledge (among audience members) and its lack (among the Frankish characters within the fiction) are collective states from the point of view of the poem as a whole.

Of course, only a reliable source of collective knowledge could live up to the narrator's characterization of *gestes* as universal points of reference for people both inside and outside the fictional universe. Yet the audience's collective, privileged knowledge about the Roncevaux plot, as communicated by the *geste* that this poem claims to be, is shared by two other individuals, Ganelon and the primary narrator, each of whose reliability might be either confirmed or contradicted by that of the other. The narrator appears to know in advance everything that happens in the poem, and, like the audience, Ganelon witnesses both the Frankish council and his own exchanges with the Saracens when he travels to Marsile's court as Charlemagne's messenger and commits his act of betrayal. This connection between the audience, the narrator, and Ganelon during the episode at Marsile's court assumes an uncomfortably metaliterary dimension when Ganelon serves as the author/narrator of a fictional anecdote about Roland. The fact that this narrative remains forever unknown to Roland, Charlemagne, and all the other Franks suggests that its existence was meant to fulfill a function for the audience alone. That function may have been to put into doubt the credibility of Roland, Ganelon, the narrator, or all three. In verses 383 to 388, Ganelon gives the Saracen Blancandrin an example of Roland's excessive pride. Just the other day, Ganelon claims, after pillaging in the region of Carcassonne, Roland offered an apple to Charlemagne, saying, "De trestuz reis vos present les curunes" [I present to you the crowns of all the kings in the world] (v. 388). This allegation appears to be untrue, both because the incident in question was not recounted earlier in the text and because it clearly draws upon biblical images of diabolical temptation (an apple like that offered to Eve in Gen. 3 and the same promise that the devil made to Christ in Matt. 4:8–9).[29] In other words, what Ganelon presents as a straightforward anecdote drawn from his lived experience is really a carefully constructed narrative that is both overtly intertextual and implicitly metatextual. Ganelon's story is intertextual not only in that it draws upon biblical narratives but also in that it functions, through such biblical allusion, in a similar way to many medieval literary works, including the Oxford *Roland* itself. Furthermore, it resembles the Oxford *Roland* in its emphasis on direct discourse.[30] Ganelon initially allows his narrative's protagonist to speak for himself, only afterward attaching the descriptive label "pride" to his fictive Roland: having told his story, Ganelon concludes, "Li soens orgoilz le devreit ben cunfundre" [His pride really should be his undoing] (v. 389). Rupert Pickens has noted a parallel between Ganelon's past-tense narrative here and Roland's narrative during the Frankish council in which he recounts Marsile's past treachery (vv. 196–209): both seek to offer past events as evidence of the moral character of the narratives' protagonists, with the crucial difference that the past events recounted by Roland are true while Ganelon's story is false. Pickens suggests the reflexive function of these two parallel past-tense accounts, concluding: "Thus the *Roland* text early on establishes models of truthful and untruthful narrative discourse. Truthful discourse is possible only in Christian culture, and the truth of Roland's account is reflected in other histories to which *La Chanson de Roland* refers directly and indirectly, such texts as the Bible, the *Geste Francor*, other *gestes*, and so forth—and most particularly in *La Chanson de Roland* itself."[31] As Pickens himself points out, however, a potentially disturbing feature of Ganelon's false narrative about Roland and the apple is that it, also, is designed to signify within Christian culture. Pickens argues that the Christian imagery of Ganelon's narrative was self-defeating in that the Oxford *Roland* as a whole clearly shows Ganelon, not Roland, to be the diabolical figure; the text's contemporary Christian audience would have been able to make that judgment for themselves, on the basis of their knowledge both of the Bible and of the roles of Roland and Ganelon in the Roncevaux story.[32] Yet the parallel between Ganelon's past-tense narrative and Roland's also allows for a parallel between Ganelon's narrative and the narrator's in the opening laisse of the text.

These two earlier narratives by the narrator and by Roland are almost explicitly linked by the text itself, since they begin with virtually the same words: Roland: "Set anz ad pleins qu'en Espeigne venimes" [It has been seven full years since we came to Spain] (v. 197); narrator: "Set anz tuz pleins [Charlemagne] ad estét en Espeigne" [Seven full, entire years [Charlemagne] has been in Spain"] (v. 2). The overall content of these narratives strengthens this initial parallel. The narrator's story in this first laisse consists of a comparison between Charlemagne's progress toward the conquest of Spain (vv. 3–6) and the obstacle provided by the obstinate non-Christian faith of Marsile (vv. 7–8); similarly, Roland's narrative consists of a comparison between his own contributions to the conquest of Spain, in faithful service to Charlemagne (vv. 198–200), and the treacherous actions of Marsile (vv. 201–9). During the council scene, this parallel serves to strengthen Roland's credibility. The narrative that he told about Marsile at the council could have been a matter of personal opinion or even a lie, but its resemblance to the opening words of the omniscient primary narrator suggests from the first that Roland's perception of the events and characters was entirely accurate: what could be said about Marsile in retrospect, on the basis of fact, is essentially no different from what Roland had said about him all along. Ganelon's narrative about Roland and the apple, however, triangulates the comparison and thereby threatens to transform its implications. Does the resemblance between these three narratives mean that the primary narrator is a storyteller like Roland or like Ganelon? Is the primary narrator, like Roland, telling the unvarnished truth about past events so that they may serve as an edifying example to the audience, or is the primary narrator, like Ganelon, inventing an entirely fictive history supported by a convincing apparatus of intertextual and biblical signification in order to persuade the audience of a skewed point of view?[33]

By not commenting on Ganelon's story about Roland and the apple, the primary narrator allows for this ambiguity: it is easy to infer that Ganelon's story is false, but the narrator does not take this opportunity to condemn the practice of such false, self-serving storytelling. It becomes clear only later that the narrator does not approve of Ganelon's narrative approach, for in laisse 54 the narrator does offer an uncharacteristically vehement condemnation of Ganelon for telling another false narrative about the past. When Ganelon returns from his mission to Marsile, he does not bring with him the Caliph, Marsile's uncle, even though it was an explicit condition of Charlemagne's written terms that the Caliph be one of the prisoners used to guarantee Marsile's compliance with the peace agreement (v. 493). Ganelon must explain this discrepancy, which he does by claiming that the Caliph chose to sail away with four thousand of his men as a protest to converting to Christianity; no sooner had their ship left land, however, than it was broken up by a storm, killing everyone on board (vv. 680–90). Ganelon claims to have seen all this with his own eyes (v. 682), but the event was not narrated earlier and is proven definitively to be false when the Caliph reappears during the Battle of Roncevaux and strikes the killing blow to Olivier (laisses 146–47). There is no need to wait for this confirmation of the story's falsehood, however, because the narrator introduces Ganelon's story with a string of words denoting Ganelon's evil and deceitful character (vv. 674–75). It is rare for the Oxford narrator to make such explicit moral judgments about the Christian characters, even about Ganelon: we hear several characters make moral judgments about one another (both positive and negative), but as a general rule the narrator does not speak in these terms. Wolfgang van Emden assembled a list of such judgments by the Oxford narrator, and it is a short one. Van Emden also observed that the narrator is particularly reticent about offering such explicit evaluations in contexts "where crucial issues are being debated," a piece of evidence in support of the notion that this text encourages audiences to formulate their own judgments of the characters at such crucial moments.[34] What is interesting about the few examples that do exist is that they accompany direct discourse by the character in question and form echoes of one another through their consistent context and syntax. Consider the narrator's two identical prefaces to Naime's speeches before Charlemagne's council, which comment upon preceding speeches by Ganelon and Roland respectively:

laisse 16	laisse 62
Après iço i est Neimes venud—	Anprès iço i est Neimes venud—
Meillor vassal n'aveit en la curt nul—	Meillor vassal n'out en la curt de lui—
E dist al rei: "Ben l'avez entendud."	E dist al rei: "Ben l'avez entendut."
(vv. 230–32)	(vv. 774–76)

[After this Naime came forward—
There was no better vassal at the court than he—
And said to the king: "You have heard him well."]

In similar fashion, the narrator's prefaces to Ganelon's speeches echo one another in a more complex way. One is before the start of the first Frankish council:

Guenes i vint, ki la traïsun fist.
Dés or cumencet le cunseill qu'en mal prist.
(vv. 178–79)

[Ganelon came to it, who committed the betrayal.
And now he begins the council that he used for evil.] [35]

Another is before Ganelon's first address to Marsile:

Par grant saver cumencet a parler
Cume celui ki ben faire le set
(vv. 426–27)

[With great skill he begins to speak
As someone who knows well how to do it]

And still another is before Ganelon's false past narrative about the drowning of the Caliph:

Guenes i vint, li fels, li parjurez;
Par grant veisdie cumencet a parler
(vv. 674–75)

[Ganelon came forward, the traitor, the foresworn;
With great deceit he begins to speak]

The Oxford *Roland*

This last passage not only echoes the words and syntax used in the first two passages but also references the moment in which Ganelon swore his loyalty to Marsile and their plot upon holy relics, a scene that makes a substantial contribution to the text's ongoing meditation in the pre-Roncevaux section upon the reliability of discourse. After Ganelon proposes the betrayal plot to Marsile, the Saracen king demands concrete proof that he actually intends to carry it out:

> Ço dist Marsilies: "Qu'en parlereiens mais?
> Cunseill n'est proz dunt hum fïance n'ait.
> La traïsun me jurrez e le plait!"
> Ço respunt Guenes: "Issi seit cum vos plaist!"
> Sur les reliques de s'espee Murgleis
> La traïsum jurat, si s'est forsfait.
>
> (vv. 603–8)

> [This is what Marsile says: "Why should we talk any more about it?
> Talk is worthless when a man has no assurance of it.
> You will swear to me the betrayal and our agreement!"
> This is what Ganelon replied: "Thus may it be, as you please, here and now!"
> On the relics in his sword Murgleis
> He swore the betrayal, and thus condemned himself.]

Marsile's statement of wariness about trusting *cunseill* (talk or advice) is an ironic elaboration on the speeches of both Roland and Ganelon at the Franks' council, since Marsile responds to Ganelon's apparently sound advice in the spirit that Charlemagne and his men would have done well to adopt toward Ganelon's advice themselves. The solemnity of this moment is indicated not only by the fact that Ganelon swears upon relics but also by the narrator's closing statement that it was at this precise moment that Ganelon was transformed into a criminal, only from then on meriting the formulaic epithet "Guenes li fels." Up to this point, Ganelon still could have turned back from the betrayal plot and taken back his earlier advice and spiteful words; once he swears to the plot upon relics, however, that action gives his words an irrevocable solidity. In fact, Ganelon's solemn vow translates his discourse into a kind of *geste* by transforming his words into "things done."

Thus the narrator's unusually negative introduction to Ganelon's story about the drowned Caliph in laisse 54 has two important functions. First, it reminds the audience that Ganelon's discourse has been untrustworthy all along. When Ganelon tells his story about the Caliph, the narrator brings together several verbal markers of earlier prefaces to Ganelon's speeches, communicating to the audience that Ganelon's proven evil character poisoned each of these earlier speeches retrospectively, regardless of their rhetorical power. In light of the narrator's silence concerning the unreliability of the apple story, it is also important to note that the narrator did not confirm or deny the validity of Ganelon's many threats and harsh words at the council after his having been nominated as the messenger to Marsile and that the narrator let pass without comment the obvious irony of Ganelon's words in refusing to let his men accompany him on the mission: "Mielz est sul moerge que tant bon chevaler" [It is better that I die alone, than that so many good knights [die along with me]] (v. 359). For, indeed, this statement only becomes clearly ironic after the fact, when Ganelon has the entire rear guard killed to save himself and carry out his personal vendetta. Although the other characters are quick to criticize Ganelon for his threats at the council, the narrator does not criticize Ganelon on the basis of his words alone, reserving criticism for the moment when those words are translated into action. It can be said, then, that the narrator's evaluation of Ganelon's moral status and credibility remains ambiguous in the scenes preceding his sworn betrayal. To be sure, the narrator had announced to the audience from the first that Ganelon was the one "who committed the betrayal," but that description of Ganelon only serves to add more weight to the moment in which Ganelon actually makes his vow upon relics because it implies that Ganelon was a neutral moral actor up to that moment. Ganelon's story about Roland and the apple belongs to the portion of the text that occurs before Ganelon becomes a lying criminal, and thus that story signifies within the portion of the text during which audiences are free to judge the validity of Ganelon's discourse for themselves.

As Pickens noted, the Christian imagery of the Roland anecdote suggests that it was addressed more to the audience than to Ganelon's Saracen interlocutor, Blancandrin.[36] And herein lies the second function of the narrator's negative preface to Ganelon's story about the Caliph, a reflexive function: its implicit, retrospective judgment against all of Ganelon's stories, including the one about Roland and the apple, strengthens the impression that it would be unfair to compare the narrator's own brand of storytelling to that of Ganelon. One recurring accusation of Old French authors against one another, particularly in the twelfth and early thirteenth centuries, was that individual authors merely invented stories according to their own whimsy and then passed them off as authoritative artifacts of collective cultural memory. Given the early date of the Oxford *Roland* and its many references to collective historical and literary knowledge, this text would have been particularly vulnerable to such an accusation. The fact that the narrator ascribes two narratives to Ganelon, which occur "pre-treachery" and "post-treachery," suggests that the second narrative exists to resolve a doubt raised by the first, a doubt concerning the narrator's high standards for storytelling. The audience learns as much about the narrator as about Ganelon during this series of scenes: the narrator's voice proves itself to be one of moderation and fairness by reserving explicit judgment against Ganelon until after he has proven himself to be a traitor through his own actions. Even the negative epithets that the narrator applies to Ganelon while introducing his story about the drowned Caliph meet the standard of impartiality imposed by the category *geste* because they directly pertain to Ganelon's proven past actions rather than merely communicating the narrator's personal opinion. In fact, the narrator's use of the epithet "the foresworn" to condemn Ganelon and his brand of storytelling in laisse 54 not only reminds the audience that the narrator is condemning Ganelon for a specific criminal act but also suggests that proper storytelling (i.e., a narrative approach contrary to that of Ganelon) would require maintaining one's fidelity to an existing order. Within the Oxford *Roland*, that existing narrative and social order is represented by the term *geste*.

The Burden of Reception: The Franks' Two Councils and the Emperor's New Narrative

Nearly as rich in intratextual and metaliterary portent as Ganelon's speech at his trial is the immediate response he receives to it: "Respundent Franc: 'A conseill en irums'" [The Franks' reply: "We will go into a council about this"] (v. 3779). In the context, the word *conseill* is entirely appropriate and to be expected: now that Charlemagne's barons have heard statements from Charlemagne and Ganelon, they must discuss among themselves whose testimony to believe. Yet by this point in the poem, the word *conseill* also carries some negative associations, of which the audience has just been reminded by Ganelon's account of Roland's nomination of him to be the messenger to Marsile. This nomination took place at an earlier council, recounted near the beginning of the poem, which the narrator described as "the council that Ganelon used for evil" (v. 179). Furthermore, Ganelon's statement that "through my cleverness I saved myself" refers most precisely to the very moment when he committed himself to the betrayal by a formal oath, in response to Marsile's reluctance to trust him on the basis of words alone (*cunseill*, v. 604). Finally, the term *conseill* here suggests an inappropriate indeterminacy: since the audience for the poem knew without a doubt that Ganelon's narratives could not be trusted and that Ganelon would not, in the end, be acquitted, they might expect the judges' consultation to be a mere procedural formality preceding a unanimous verdict affirming the truth of Charlemagne's word over Ganelon's. What actually follows in the judges' council, however, is nearly the opposite result. After a short deliberation, the judges not only recommend clemency for Ganelon but also twice recycle Ganelon's own discourse when they suggest, among themselves and then to Charlemagne, "Let Ganelon be acquitted, and may he serve the king in good faith and in love" (vv. 3800–3801 and 3809–10).[37] In other words, Ganelon's judges wish to reestablish the state of affairs that prevailed before the episode of Roncevaux began— the state of affairs as Ganelon has just portrayed it, that is. They are not only accepting Ganelon's story as true but also attempting to implement it as official policy. The consequences of this act of narrative reception by the judges would be staggering: a dangerous criminal would be reinstated to a position of great power and influence among Charlemagne's barons, and the memory of Roland's heroic sacrifice at Roncevaux would be forever tarnished by Ganelon's unchallenged allegation that the battle had been Roland's own fault. The barons seek to minimize the damage they are doing to Roland by emphasizing his status as a dead man who cannot be brought back to life in any case: "Morz est Rollant, jamais ne l' revereiz; / N'ert recuvrét por or ne por aveir; / Mult sereit fols ki or s'en cumbatreit!" [Roland is dead, you will never see him again; he will not be recovered for gold or other possessions; he would be quite foolish, the man who would engage in judicial combat over that!] (vv. 3802–4). This reasoning improperly privileges Roland's physical person over the transcendent value of truth: as Uitti put it, Charlemagne's anger at this lenient response from his barons at Ganelon's trial shows that he "realizes that this will to forget signifies the end of the *geste*, of history."[38]

Appropriately, then, Charlemagne responds by calling his barons by a similar name to the one the narrator had reserved for Ganelon: "Ço dist li reis: 'Vos estes mi felun!'" [The king says this: "You are criminals to me!"] (v. 3814). Not only do Charlemagne's men resemble Ganelon here by recommending the wrong action (or inaction); they also bear a more literary relationship to Ganelon in that their failure to choose definitively the story of Roncevaux as "told" by Roland (through his actions and their subsequent interpretation) over the one told by Ganelon (in words at his trial) represents within the fiction a betrayal of their responsibility for proper reception of the *geste* of Roncevaux. The platitude that "life goes on" simply does not suffice as a response to a collective trauma such as the one that took place at the Battle of Roncevaux. As Uitti indicated in his study of the *geste*, the "ongoingness" that is one of the defining traits of literary *gestes* is a grammatical representation of the necessary continuity of collective identity from past to present to future. If the life of the collectivity is to go on, then a consensus must be reached concerning which path it will follow, and from which recognized turning points in the past. The judges at Ganelon's trial, however, seem to believe that their collective history can be manipulated retrospectively. As a summary of their collective judgment, they attempt to characterize themselves as conservative by saying, "Bien fait a remaneir!" [One would do well to leave things as they are!] (v. 3798). Yet, for them, "to leave things as they are" *(remaneir)* actually means to move backward in time to a point before Roland's death and then to proceed forward from that point in the past, converting Ganelon's betrayal and the Battle of Roncevaux into a kind of historical palimpsest to be written over by the "new and improved" Frankish society of the present and immediate future. The barons seem to consider it possible to accept the positive changes achieved by the recent battles—namely the now successful conquest of all of Spain—without acknowledging the unpleasant changes, namely that twenty thousand of their warriors have died and that they will now have to contend with the proven traitor in their midst. In other words, their reception and retelling to one another of the series of events just recounted by the poem as a whole are selective and manipulative, like those of an unreliable narrator of a fanciful literary account inspired by historical events. Furthermore, because they are serving in a judicial capacity, their false narrative about Roncevaux threatens to become the official story that will be preserved in the collective memory of their society. Similarly, early examples of written vernacular texts, such as the Oxford *Roland* itself, threatened to preserve certain authors' versions of what had once been the more inclusive common property of a variety of oral storytellers. This entire poem is haunted by the implicit question of whether the new authors of these vernacular texts, like Ganelon, might rewrite the past according to their own preferences and whether that individual perspective on the past (*mun saveir*) might, in turn, be perceived as collective truth (*geste*) by a naive or complicit audience.

The judges' failure to affirm Charlemagne's words and to condemn Ganelon's is, therefore, a major event in the text, though their verdict is immediately overturned by Thierry's victory in the judicial combat. For this *conseill* at the end of the text reminds the audience that the faulty reception of discourse by Charlemagne's barons has been a problem since the start of the poem and now threatens to become the most serious problem in the Roncevaux story, since it is likely to lead to more carnage and collective foolishness in the future, transcending the scope of this particular event. A closer look at the earlier Frankish council scene reveals that Roland perceived this as the principal threat all along, and that Roland's proposed remedy for it was already that of adhering to the standard of the *geste* in both word and deed. By contrast, Ganelon's betrayal of this discursive standard in his earlier council speech reveals that his betrayal of the Franks to Marsile was only the concrete realization of his more general subversion of his society's way of recollecting past history and of making history in the present. The competing speeches of Roland and Ganelon model the tension in early Old French texts between tradition and innovation, between collective wisdom and individual cleverness. The council scene as a whole also has implications for the primary narration because the characters' discourse here frequently assumes a narrative form. Nearly all the characters who speak at the council announce an explicit link between their perceptions, advice, and plans about the events taking place in the fictional present and their retellings of past events or their imagined scenarios for the future. These links are certainly logical—the context provided by the past and future does influence decisions people make in the present—but a *narrative* exposition of that context is not strictly necessary to the narrative exposition of events unfolding within the fictional present of the Oxford *Roland*. That is, characters could reference the most critical lessons learned from their past experience without retelling those events in a narrative sequence. Similarly, their representations of the future often emerge as unexplained statements of certainty, causing them to resemble fictional inventions more than hypothetical scenarios.

The characters' narration of past events in this fictional setting is particularly unnecessary in light of the fact that in many cases the events recounted by the characters have already been recounted by the narrator, and in a way that conveys the narrator's belief that most of the medieval audience was familiar with these events before the narrative even began. This redundancy puts nearly all of the characters' past narratives into the category of narrative retellings, giving them an enhanced reflexive dimension since they appear in a text that is also a narrative retelling of the preexisting Roncevaux story. That the characters' repetition of previous comments from the narrator is superfluous for the purpose of communicating basic information to the audience also suggests that it has some other purpose, which I believe to be that of creating a comparison between the primary narrator and the narrating characters. Although the narrator and the audience occupy the same temporal space, from which the events are recounted retrospectively, the narrator also performs the same function as many of the characters, both retelling past events and predicting future outcomes with confidence. As some specific examples of character narration will show, however, the primary narrator performs these narrative functions more effectively than the characters because of that temporal advantage of retrospection. When the narrator and characters agree about a particular past event within the fiction, the characters' status as historical figures enhances the narrator's authority; on the other hand, when they disagree about a future event within the fiction, the narrator is always right and the character proves to be not merely wrong but also threatening to political and social harmony.[39]

The reliability of discourse is itself the central issue of the first Frankish council, as is emphasized by the grammar Charlemagne uses in his opening summary of the terms of the peace agreement Marsile has proposed (vv. 180–91).[40] In the first half of his speech, he says that Marsile "wants to" give them a substantial payment in material goods, but in exchange he makes a demand in the subjunctive mood: "Mais il me mandet quë en France m'en alge" [But the terms he sends are that I go back to France] (v. 187). Following these two grammatical expressions of what Marsile desires, it is interesting to note the continuation of this same sentence, which shifts abruptly from the subjunctive mood into the future tense. Instead of continuing by saying, "and the terms are that Marsile then do X, Y, and Z in return," Charlemagne uses four future-tense verbs to describe what Marsile is offering to do in exchange for the Franks' withdrawal from Spain ("he will follow me to Aix," "he will receive baptism," "he will be a Christian," and "he will hold his lands as my vassal"). This grammatical choice on Charlemagne's part suggests the inevitability of these four actions, yet in reality those four verbs are out of Charlemagne's control, while the first two verbs are completely within his control. This meeting is all about the discrepancy between the actions that Charlemagne conveys in the subjunctive and future respectively: Charlemagne can refuse to leave for France until Marsile hands over the promised payment, but once he has withdrawn with his army it will become very difficult for him to enforce Marsile's promised subsequent actions.[41] Immediately after recounting Marsile's promised actions in the future tense, Charlemagne recognizes this very problem in his closing statement, "Mais jo ne sai quels en est sis curages" [But I do not know what his intentions are about this] (v. 191). And the Franks do not miss the point, responding in unison, "Il nus i cuvent guarde!" [We must be careful about this!] (v. 192).

Charlemagne's speech models an essential aspect of responsible audience reception at which most of the Franks do not excel: questioning a speaker's motives. Although the Franks announce their intention to consider Marsile's speech with care, they do not show as much care in their reception of the subsequent speeches by Roland and Ganelon. In addition, Charlemagne's implicit recognition here of the folly of making absolute statements about future outcomes might have heightened the audience's awareness of how frequently the Franks do precisely that as the council continues. To demonstrate that tendency, and Charlemagne's consistent censure of it, I have excerpted from the council scene a series of attempted nominations for the duty of carrying Charlemagne's message to Marsile (with future "narratives" in bold and judgments of or attempts to control characters' verbal expression in italics):

246 Respunt dux Neimes: "J'**irai** par vostre dun."
250 [Charlemagne]: "Vos n'**irez** pas . . .
251 Alez sedeir quant *nuls ne vos sumunt!*"
254 Respunt Rollant: "J'i puis aler mult ben!"
255 "Nu **ferez** certes!" dist li quens Oliver
258 "Se li reis voelt, jo i puis aler ben."
259 Respunt li reis: *"Ambdui vos en taisez!*
260 Ne vos në il n'i **porterez** les piez.
261 Par ceste barbe que vëez blancheier,
262 *Li duze per mar i **serunt** jugez!*"
263 *Franceis se taisent: as les vus aquisez!*
269 [Turpin]: "E jo **irai** al Sarazin espan
270 Si li **dirai** alques de mun semblant."
271 *Li empereres respunt par maltalant:*
273 *"N'en parlez mais se jo ne l' vos cumant!*"
277 Ço dist Rollant: "C'**ert** Guenes, mis parastre."
278 Dïent Franceis: "Car il le poet ben faire!
279 Se lui lessez, n'i **trametrez** plus saive."

289 [Ganelon to Roland]: "Se Deus ço dunet que jo de la repaire,
290 Jo t'en **muvrai** une si grant contraire
291 Ki **durerat** a trestut tun edage."
292 *Respunt Rollant: "Orgoill oi e folage.*
293 *Ço set hom ben, n'ai cure de manace.*
294 *Mais saives hom, il deit faire message:*
295 *Se li reis voelt, prez sui por vus le face."*

246 Duke Naimes responds, "**I will go** by your leave."
250 [Charlemagne]: "**You will not go** . . .
251 *Go and sit down, since no one called upon you to speak!"*
254 Roland responds: "I can very well go there!"
255 "**You will surely do no such thing!**" says Count Olivier
258 "If the king wishes, I can well go there."
259 The king responds: *"Both of you, keep quiet!*
260 **Neither you nor he will set foot there.**
261 By this beard which you see turning white,
262 *Woe to anyone **who will nominate** one of the twelve peers!"*
263 *The Franks fall silent: see how they are quieted!*
269 [Turpin]: "And **I will go** to the Spanish Saracens
270 And **I will tell them** something about what I think."
271 *The emperor responds in a bad temper: . . .*
273 *"Do not talk about it again if I do not tell you to!"*
277 This is what Roland says: "**It will be Ganelon**, my stepfather."
278 The Franks say: "For he can do it well!
279 If you leave it to him, **you will not send** a wiser man there."
289 [Ganelon to Roland]: "If God grants that I return from there,
290 **I will raise** against you such great opposition
291 That **it will last** all your days."
292 *Roland responds: "Pride is what I hear, and folly.*
293 *Everyone knows this well, that I am not troubled by threats.*
294 But it is a wise man who must carry the message:
295 If the king wishes, I am ready to do it for you."

Throughout this scene, when the characters state their intention to do
something in the form of a simple future-tense verb, other characters
are forced to contradict the initial speakers' future projections, and this
pattern of prediction and contradiction elicits ever-intensifying verbal
censure from Charlemagne, who is the only person with the power to
determine exactly how the diplomatic mission will be conducted and

thus the only person who can credibly discuss the mission in the future tense.[42] Finally, Roland insults Ganelon's threatening future discourse by describing it as if Ganelon were giving voice to the very essence of pride and folly. In keeping with the mutual distaste for inappropriate future discourse shared here by Charlemagne and Roland, it is worth noting that Roland and Olivier nominate themselves for the mission without using the future tense. Each of them says, "I can do it," not "I will do it," and Olivier even adds that he can do it only if Charlemagne wishes it so. In light of the relatively cautious terms in which Roland phrases his self-nomination, his use of the future tense to nominate Ganelon emerges with particular force. Even in his retort to Ganelon's threat, Roland avoids making future-tense statements by adopting the subjunctive mood and evoking the king's sovereign will in this matter, rather than contradicting Ganelon's menacing future scenario with a future scenario of his own.

Indeed, the grammar of Roland's nomination of Ganelon marks it as a moment of transgression against his usual speech patterns, for by this point in the meeting Roland has already established a marked preference for narration in the past. Just after Charlemagne's summary of Marsile's terms of peace in the future tense, cited above, the narrator prefaces Roland's response by saying, "si li vint cuntredire" [thus he came to contradict him [Charlemagne]] (v. 195). Yet Roland's remarks show that he is not so much contradicting the content of Charlemagne's summary, which reveals considerable doubt about Marsile's sincerity, as contradicting the future-tense scenario of Marsile's observance of the peace. Roland's first reaction is to burst out with "Ja mar crerez Marsilie!" [To your detriment will you ever believe Marsile!] (v. 196). Here he echoes Charlemagne's use of the future tense, but in a critical or even mocking way in that he introduces the future with the extremely negative phrase "Ja mar," making it clear that this future scenario is one that must never be allowed to develop. What he is contradicting, then, is Charlemagne's rhetoric, which allows for the possibility of trusting in Marsile's future actions even as Charlemagne voices explicit doubt about Marsile's motives. To explain his pessimism about Marsile's credibility, Roland then jumps immediately into a past-tense narrative. As has long been noted in scholarship devoted to this text, Roland takes care to situate his advice to Charlemagne in the context of past events whose truth is irrefutable and whose relevance is obvious.[43] He reminds Charlemagne of his own military feats, all of which Roland accomplished as his loyal vassal (v. 198), and then contrasts his own admirable and loyal behavior with the treachery of Marsile, who once offered a peace agreement and then violated the basic rules of war by murdering the messengers who were bringing Charlemagne's response (vv. 201–9). The purpose of comparing himself to Marsile is to convince Charlemagne to take Roland's advice rather than agreeing to a peace agreement formulated by Marsile. Thus the central issue of Roland's speech is one of trustworthy and untrustworthy behavior, which, he implies, will inevitably correspond to trustworthy or untrustworthy discourse (a theory with its roots in the worldview of the *geste*). Because Roland has always done the right thing, his words should be trusted; because Marsile has been known to do the wrong thing, his words should not be trusted. Beyond this clear contrast between himself and Marsile, however, Roland also suggests a contrast between his own good advice and the bad advice that others in Charlemagne's council gave him the last time Marsile offered a peace agreement. In the middle of Roland's description of Marsile's treachery, he refers to the council they had on that occasion, in which Marsile's messengers pronounced "cez paroles meïsmes" [these same words] (v. 204), and he reminds Charlemagne that in the council that followed, the Franks "Loërent vos alques de legerie" [Advised you with some imprudence] (v. 206), giving Marsile the opportunity to kill two of Charlemagne's men, the messengers Basan and Basile. The shocked silence that follows Roland's speech (vv. 214–17) suggests that Charlemagne and the Franks have not failed to grasp Roland's implication that it was the flaws of their discourse, as well as the treachery of Marsile's actions, that led to the deaths of the messengers. Roland's speech suggests that this council threatens to initiate a replay (or "commemoration") of the earlier incident of Basan and Basile, which can be averted only through collective remembrance of the Franks' shared knowledge of their own history (their *geste*). This resemblance between the past and present councils is to be thwarted: trusting in Marsile is an aspect of the *geste* that should not be commemorated but should instead be eliminated through conscious "reworking" in the present council. Thus an awareness of the knowledge contained in the *geste* can result in change for the better: commemoration in the present is not a mindless replication of the past but a mindful reworking through deliberate reference to the past.

In addition to its pointed critique of the discourse that he has heard in past councils, Roland's narrative offers an example of what kind of discourse he considers legitimate: words that are factual, consistent with the speaker's past behavior, and carefully considered. In his immediate response to Roland, Ganelon offers a different general criterion: for him, words should be believed if they are in the listener's self-interest. Ganelon states this view at the outset when he rephrases Roland's opening retort to Charlemagne in a way that appears to be both self-effacing and flattering to Charlemagne: "Ja mar crerez bricun, / Ne mei në altre, se de vostre prod nun!" [To your detriment will you ever believe a fool, / Either me or another, if it is not to your advantage!] (vv. 220–21). In the charged atmosphere that has just been created by Roland's speech, in which he questioned the judgment of Charlemagne and his advisors, Ganelon's remark sounds like an endorsement of Charlemagne's judgment: the emperor knows best, and he should decide for himself whose advice to believe. Furthermore, the reformulation "Ja mar crerez bricun" implicitly puts Roland in the position that Marsile occupied in Roland's remark "Ja mar crerez Marsile," suggesting that Roland's credibility and motives should be questioned. Ganelon's paraphrase of Roland's opening line has a relatively conciliatory tone in its immediate context, but, considered objectively, its implication is that Charlemagne should privilege the appeal of a speaker's content to him personally over all other criteria, even those of the facts at hand or the speaker's character. Ganelon then advises that this decision be made on the basis of general principles rather than on the basis of the personal credibility either of Marsile or of any of Charlemagne's advisors. As Naime's speech affirms in the following laisse, these are sound general principles (vv. 235–42). Nevertheless, they do not negate the crucial issue of personal credibility. Indeed, as Ganelon's betrayal later proves, it does no good to believe advice grounded on sound general principles if that advice is uttered by a person who cannot be trusted. The audience's likely previous knowledge of the Roncevaux story would probably be enough to ensure that they would not accept Ganelon's speech as trustworthy, but the narrator takes no chances, explaining to the audience just before the council begins that Ganelon is about to ruin it: "Guenes i vint, ki la traïsun fist. / Dés or cumencet le cunseill qu'en mal prist." [Ganelon came to it, who committed the betrayal. / And now he begins the council that he used for evil.] (vv. 178–79).

It is the combination of Roland's speech and of Ganelon's that gives the audience the complete picture of what constitutes legitimate and illegitimate discourse in this scene. Since the audience knows that Ganelon is a traitor, and has been specifically reminded that his participation in the council is what made it a critical turning point in history, the audience is also likely to reject Ganelon's entire rhetoric, as convincing as it proves to be for the majority of the Franks in the council.

Therefore the audience must also reject what may well have been considered conventional wisdom: that one should never refuse to grant mercy to a weaker enemy who humbles himself by asking for it and, similarly and more generally, that one should mistrust discourse that seems to be motivated by pride (v. 228). Yet Roland's speech itself offers the solution to that dilemma in that it sets up specific criteria for reliable discourse that are applicable not only to his speech before the council but also, reflexively, to the entire narrative in which he appears. We have already seen that Roland's speech is based on the idea that trustworthy past behavior is a predictor of consistently trustworthy discourse, and vice versa. Furthermore, Roland's narration of past events is entirely factual: even when he offers the opinion that Charlemagne was given bad advice in the earlier council, he offers factual evidence to support that assertion, and no one contradicts it because the events speak for themselves. Indeed, in spite of Ganelon's rhetoric of privileging abstract general principles over personal credibility, the only way in which he can attack Roland's speech is through personal insults, implicitly calling Roland a "fool" at the outset and describing Roland's speech as "the advice of pride" at the end; Ganelon leaves aside the factual content of Roland's speech because it is unassailable.

It is instructive to apply Roland's criteria for reliable discourse to the narrative of Oxford as a whole, and perhaps audiences were meant to do just that. The first general principle that emerges from this exercise is that the narration of past events must be entirely factual, with value judgments emerging directly from those facts. Yet the value judgments are as important as the facts themselves: as people make decisions and plans in the present, they are likely to repeat past mistakes unless they evaluate what those mistakes were and how they came about. What this means for the Oxford *Roland* is that the narrator has an obligation to tell the truth about what happened and that the audience has an obligation to learn the appropriate lessons from those events. The narrator may guide the audience toward those lessons, as Roland did in his speech, but the narrator may not omit the initial step of retelling the events, even if the audience (like Roland's audience in the council) is already knowledgeable about these events, for it is the accuracy of that retelling that attests to the validity of the lessons drawn from it. This consideration leads to the second reflexive principle of Roland's speech: someone who behaves appropriately will also speak reliably. Thus to the extent that the narrator retells the events of the story accurately, the audience may trust the value judgments that the narrator attaches to those events. If the narrator were to express an opinion that had no direct basis in the factual events, however, that opinion would not be trustworthy, no matter how persuasive its wording, and would cause the audience to develop a general suspicion of the narrator's motives. This is the lesson that can be drawn from Ganelon's council speech and also from the characters' use of the future tense: when anyone makes a judgment not based on verifiable past experience, that person should not be believed, and the listener should question the speaker's motives.

This last point about discourse and reception is explored further in another scene near the end of the text featuring character discourse with a narrative component: Charlemagne's speech to Aude informing her of Roland's death. What Charlemagne tells Aude is factual, but his motives are not entirely trustworthy, precisely because his own personal experience of the shock of Roland's death endows Charlemagne's speech to Aude with some of the traits of a narrative retelling whose goal is reinterpretation. For her part, as the audience for this innovative retelling, Aude therefore adopts an approach to reception that insists upon its own faithfulness to the spirit of the *geste*: in fact, her few, well-chosen words assert that she is a hero comparable to Roland. The first of these is her famously enigmatic statement "Cest mot mei est estrange" [This word is strange to me] (v. 3717). The primary sense of the word *estrange* in this text is "foreign" or "alien," and the word is used everywhere else in the text as a description of the enemy Saracens. Thus the connotation of Aude's statement is not merely bewilderment but hostility, as if Charlemagne's speech were an attack by a foreign enemy analogous to the Saracens' attack on the rear guard at Roncevaux. As Joseph Long has observed, this implicit parallel is strengthened by her use of the word *per* to describe what her relationship to Roland was to be following their planned marriage.[44] *Per* was used as a term for "spouse" in a number of Old French texts, but this usage was hardly universal. In the texts where it does appear, it seems consistently to denote a special relationship of mutual regard that did not always prevail among medieval literary couples. Within this text, of course, the most common usage of *per* is as a privileged term for the twelve elite barons of Charlemagne who died at Roncevaux, including Roland and Olivier. There is a consistent logic, therefore, behind Aude's opening description of herself as Roland's "peer" and her closing statement that it is her destiny not to outlive him: dying alongside Roland is what all of Roland's other "peers" had already done by this point in the poem. The conventional interpretation of this scene is that Aude displays here a heroic integrity and a spirit of loyalty and self-sacrifice comparable to Roland's own, and that impression is certainly strengthened by all three connotations of the word *per:* she was his equal, she was his loyal companion, and therefore she was perfectly suited to become his wife, and the wife of no one else. It may be in part the heroic connotations of Aude's discourse that explain the choice of Ian Short, in his modern French translation of the poem, to render Aude's response as "Ces paroles ne s'addressent pas à moi" [These words are not addressed to me]. This translation preserves Aude's sense of alienation from and resistance to Charlemagne's speech without suggesting any confusion on her part that might weaken the charge of her own speech: Charlemagne is speaking to her as if she were a different kind of person, as if her primary concern were not Roland himself but her desire to make an advantageous marriage. I think that Short has captured something else in this translation as well, however, and that is the more literal sense that Charlemagne is not really answering Aude's question, or even that his words are really intended for someone else.

Critics have long noted the parallel between Aude's question at the start of this scene, "Where is Roland?" and the question that expressed Charlemagne's grief earlier in the text when he first saw the battlefield, every square foot of which was covered with the corpses of his own men and of the enemy:

Morz est Rollant; Deus en ad l'anme es cels.
Li emperere en Rencesvals parvient;
Il nen i ad ne veie ne senter
Ne voide tere në alne ne plain piéd
Quë il n'i ait o Franceis o paien.
Carles escrïet: "U estes vos, bels niés?
U'st l'arcevesque e li quens Oliver?
U est Gerins e sis cumpainz Gerers?
U est Oton e li quens Berengers,
Ive et Ivorie, que j'aveie tant chers?
Qu'est devenuz li Guascuinz Engeler,
Sansun li dux e Anseïs li fers?
U est Gerard de Russillun li veilz,
Li duze per que j'aveie laisét?"
De ço qui chelt quant nul n'en respundiét?
"Deus!" dist li reis, "tant me pois enrager
Que jo ne fui a l'estur cumencer!"
Tiret sa barbe cum hom ki est irét.

(vv. 2397–2414)

[Roland is dead; God has his soul in heaven.
The emperor arrives at Roncevaux;
There is no path or trail there,
No bare ground, not a bit, not a foot,
Where there is not either a Frank or a pagan.
Charles cried out: "Where are you, dear nephew?
Where is the archbishop and Count Olivier?
Where is Gerin and his companion Gerer?
Where is Oton and Count Berenger,
Ive and Ivorie, whom I held so dear?
What has become of Angelier the Gascon,
Duke Samson and the proud Anseïs?
Where is old Gerard of Roussillon,
The twelve peers whom I left here?"
But who cares about that, since no one answered him?
"God!" the king said, "I can truly be enraged
That I was not here when the battle began!"
He pulls on his beard like a man who is distraught.]

In this earlier scene, Charlemagne enumerates the entire list of the twelve peers, asking for each one, "Where is he?" in adherence to a long rhetorical tradition associated with literary lamentation (usually referenced in criticism by the Latin question "Ubi sunt?"). The structure of the passage as a whole emphasizes the fact that Charlemagne's rhetorical questions resist acknowledging the obvious physical reality that the men he is asking about are lying dead on the ground in front of him. In case audiences fail to observe that contrast, the narrator asks a question of his own in line 2411 that emphasizes the futility of Charlemagne's speech: "Who cares about that, since no one answered him?"[45] This disparagement of character discourse by the primary narrator using the phrase "De ço qui calt?" is not unique to this passage, but its effect is always jarring because the narrator tends to use it at moments such as this, when the audience would naturally be moved to sympathize with the speaker.[46] Charlemagne's grief is quite understandable, and the terms in which he expresses it are precisely those that the audience would expect, but I believe that the narrator is deliberately disrupting the audience's natural sympathetic response at these moments in order to attract their attention to the characters' words and encourage them to consider other possible alternatives for discourse and reception. The explicit evaluation of Charlemagne's discourse by Aude in the later scene serves the same purpose: at a highly emotional moment in the narrative, the audience's natural sympathy with both Aude and Charlemagne is disrupted by Aude's rejection of Charlemagne's entire speech (not merely of its content, since it is his "words" that she calls "strange"). Once again, the audience is encouraged to consider both how Charlemagne speaks and how Aude responds. Audience expectations are called into question here: both Aude's youth and her gender would normally predispose her to accept Charlemagne's words and to comply with his plans for her future. In real life, she would have had no other choice. Within this text's ongoing examination of different forms of retelling and reception, however, the figure of Aude allowed the author to display a particular facet of the dynamic of retelling and its reception. For the parallel between Aude's "Ubi sunt?" question and Charlemagne's earlier in the text makes this scene a restaging of the earlier one, as Charlemagne himself seems to recognize when he pulls on his beard in response to Aude's question, just as he did at the end of the earlier scene and as he does in several other scenes from the text in which he has to confront a truth that he does not want to acknowledge. It is as if Aude's question transported Charlemagne involuntarily back to his own initial grief at the sight of the corpse-strewn battlefield, but this time he answers his own rhetorical "Ubi sunt" question literally: Roland is a dead man, one among thousands lying on that blood-soaked field. This literal and insensitive answer, as well as the pragmatic solution he offers to Aude's loss of her fiancé, are so uncharacteristic of Charlemagne's approach to discourse elsewhere in the text that they call for further examination.

As several critics have noted, Charlemagne uses the loaded term *escange* (exchange) to describe the proposed substitution of his own son, Louis, for Roland as Aude's future husband. This term creates the rhyme *escange/estrange* in the scene with Aude, which serves as an echo of Charlemagne's own emotional distress earlier in the text. When Roland and the rear guard first left for Roncevaux and Charlemagne expressed to a close advisor his suspicion of the traitor Ganelon and his anxiety about losing Roland on this mission, he said: "Jo l'ai lessét en une marche estrange; / Deus! se jo l' pert, ja n'en avrai escange!" [I have left him in a foreign land; / God! if I lose him, I will never have a replacement for him!] (vv. 839–40). Critics have pointed out this earlier use of the same rhymed pair, *estrange/escange,* and reproached Charlemagne for his hypocrisy in offering a solution to Aude that he himself considered unimaginable.[47] What I would like to emphasize about these parallel passages, instead, is that they suggest that Charlemagne's discourse to

Aude functions as an attempt to "rework" these familiar circumstances. He recognizes his own past attitudes in Aude, and he tries to spare her the grief he himself has suffered by offering her a new scenario where Roland's death could be a simple fact rather than a deep wound, and where the need to replace Roland could be an occasion for rebuilding social and familial ties in a way that would bring greater honor to him and to his fiancée. Aude's death proves that Charlemagne was right to sense a real threat in allowing her grief to be expressed naturally; on the other hand, Aude was also right in recognizing Charlemagne's evasive discourse as inappropriate to his audience.

The root cause of the impasse between Charlemagne and Aude, then, is that they see themselves within two different stories. Charlemagne wants his discourse to Aude to inaugurate a "happy ending" to the story of Roncevaux, while her discourse to him implies that she sees her death as a repeat performance (commemoration) of Roland's heroic self-sacrifice in the battle. What Charlemagne wants is to avoid reliving the pain of the past, which he does by orchestrating a marriage in the future whose purpose would be to compensate for Roland's loss but whose unintended side effect would be to obscure Roland's unique identity. This is also the quandary that faces every author of a literary reworking: like Charlemagne, these authors want to enrich familiar material by incorporating new insights into it, but in doing so they run the risk of changing the fundamental identity of this material and facing resistance from their audiences, whom they are asking to accept the replacement with open arms. The reteller's goal, then, especially when working with material as culturally significant as the Oxford *Roland* was for twelfth-century audiences, is to compose a reworking that preserves the conventional meaning of existing versions of the same material while also adding to it new meanings and a new relevance. While resemblance between past and present was the impetus for Charlemagne's approach to reworking, innovation, rather than preservation, was its distinguishing characteristic. On the other hand, Aude's "reworking," through the combination of her words and her death, meets the criteria of both conventional meaning and renewed relevance. Her utter faithfulness to the heroic model provided by Roland, and her verbal references to that model through the key terms *peer, strange,* and *may it not please God,* make her into a new kind of hero precisely because of the inherent differences between her situation and Roland's. Her gender and social status mean that her conscious restaging of Roland's heroism adds new dimensions to it: her death is a form of self-sacrifice normally shown by men rather than women, and her loyalty transcends that of the feudal bond between lord and vassal or even of the bond between husband and wife, since she and Roland were not yet married. Aude's death offers not only a refreshing twist on medieval heroism but also a creative embodiment of the enterprise of literary reworking. Her simultaneous resemblance to and difference from Roland is analogous to the ideal relationship between two medieval versions of the same story: in both kinds of reworking (in life for Aude and in literature for authors), a balance between resemblance and renewal at the level of meaning is achieved through a concerted effort to cross the distance already in place because of inherent differences at the level of context or content. The notion that Aude's death represents an approach to literary reworking helps to mitigate the otherwise puzzling notion that she is meant to serve only as a model of literary reception. There is no doubt that Aude does serve as an audience for Charlemagne's narrative, a function that receives considerable elaboration in later Roncevaux narratives, but real audiences would find it both impossible and undesirable to imitate her suicide as a protest against unsuitable literary reworkings. Her extreme response makes more sense, perhaps, as a dramatization of the notion that literary reception is a form of reworking, an act involving choices with real consequences rather than an entirely passive acceptance of a narrator's discourse on its own terms.

The self-serving narratives of Ganelon and Charlemagne, and their troubling reception by the Frankish barons and Aude, dramatize for the audience some of the potential problems inherent in the retelling and reception of weighty collective narratives such as that of Roncevaux. An awareness of the potential literary problems implicit in these other character narratives now allows for an assessment of the metaliterary implications of Roland's discourse at several key moments in the poem. The literariness of some scenes featuring Roland has long been recognized, such as when the hero imagines the future songs to be sung about him or when he arranges his body in a certain way to influence the Franks' interpretation of the battle and his role in it. In this last section, I will now consider more precisely what the poem's portrayal of Roland's heroic words and actions in accordance with the *geste* can tell us about the challenges of the Oxford poet's attempt to commemorate the oral *geste* of Roncevaux by putting it into written form. Just as Ganelon personifies the transgressions of authors whose narrative innovations sought to preserve and even glorify their own cleverness (a description that modern critics have applied frequently to "playful" Old French authors such as Jean Renart and Jean de Meung), Roland personifies the particular combination of pride and self-sacrifice that characterized new retellings of traditional narratives that sought to preserve and glorify the collective wisdom of the preceding oral tradition rather than the present author's personal knowledge or cleverness. Examining Roland's speeches in light of the *geste* shows that this organizing principle explains Roland's moments of both greatest apparent strength and greatest weakness. Thus the literary category *geste* enhances our understanding of Roland's heroism, while Roland's status as the hero makes him the character whose words and actions best express the spirit of the *geste* that the poem claims to be in its closing line.

The Burden of the Hero: Embodying the *Geste* and Passing It On

As we have seen, it is Roland who pronounces the word *geste* when it first appears in the text. It is also characteristic of the Oxford narrator that he makes no immediate attempt to explain or judge Roland's statement in verse 788, just as the narrator withheld judgment of Ganelon's words until Ganelon committed himself to the betrayal with an irrevocable act. The narrator's evaluation of Roland's discourse and character is, in fact, delayed until the end of Roland's first debate with Olivier about whether to sound the horn and summon the rest of Charlemagne's army to Roncevaux (vv. 1093–97), which suggests that it is through this debate that Roland (like Ganelon, but in a positive sense) makes his definitive commitment to his course of action (his *geste*). Viewing the horn debate through this lens gives more cohesion to some of Roland's controversial utterances in that famous exchange with Olivier.

Between the rear guard's departure for Roncevaux and the first horn debate, the audience hears a series of conversations between Marsile and his best warriors in which the Saracens also express their attitudes and intentions about the battle (laisses 69–78). The ordering of these pre-battle conversations among the Saracens and then among the rear guard repeats the ordering of the Saracen and Frankish council scenes earlier in the text: once again, we hear from the Saracens first and then from the Franks a number of similar ideas. Yet two aspects of the Saracens' discourse give their speeches an inherent irony in comparison with the speeches of Roland and Olivier that follow: the Saracen warriors all boast about their great exploits in the battle to come, but they do so in the future tense (a sure harbinger of doomed wishful thinking in this text), evoking with striking frequency the name of the battlefield, "Renc-esvals" (vv. 892, 901, 912, 923, 934, 944, 963, 985). This name is an ironic signifier in the mouths of the boasting Saracens because of what was perceived (falsely) among Old French speakers to be its etymology: this battlefield was thought to be called the "valley of thorns" because in many Roncevaux narratives, though not in the Oxford *Roland*, God mi-raculously distinguishes between the dead bodies of the Christians and Saracens lying all over the field by causing thorn bushes to grow out of the Saracen corpses.[48] Thus it is as if the Saracens are evoking their own future corpses every time they talk about what will happen at "Rences-vals": the construction of this irony seems to me to be the only reason for the insistent repetition of the name in all of these Saracen boasts. Similarly, the claim of every Saracen that he will be the one to kill Roland (vv. 867, 893, 902, 914, 923–24, 935, 963, 986–88) would strike the audience as nothing but empty words if the oral Roncevaux tradition already included Oxford's emphasis on the fact that Roland instead killed himself by the force of his exhalation through the horn. The overall role of these Saracen boasts, then, is to serve as a point of comparison and contrast for what Olivier and Roland claim about the battle to come in the horn debate that immediately fol-lows: if Olivier or Roland sounded too much like these vainly boasting Saracens, he would similarly prejudice the audience against his point of view.

There is, therefore, a certain comic effect to Olivier's tentative open-ing words in the horn debate, since they follow all of this Saracen boast-ing and comment directly upon the bold sounding of a thousand horns with which the Saracens have just announced their imminent attack: "Dist Oliver: 'Sire cumpainz, ce crei, / De Sarrazins purum bataille aveir'" [Olivier said: "Lord, my companion, I believe we may have a battle with the Saracens"] (vv. 1006–7). This mild and respectful state-ment seems a fulfillment of the narrator's positive evaluation of Olivier the first time he was mentioned in the text, "Oliver, li proz e li gentilz" [Olivier, the worthy and the noble] (v. 176): the unexpected blast of horns does not seem to frighten Olivier, nor does he immediately dis-play any anger or disrespect toward Roland. By contrast, Roland's re-sponse sounds bold to the point of recklessness: he immediately envi-sions with a certain relish the suffering this battle will cause among the rear guard, declares his intention to strike "great blows," and concludes by explicitly citing those blows as the guarantor of his future reputation in the lines I have already cited (vv. 1013–16), concluding with a vehe-mently negative future-tense verb: "Malvaise essample n'en serat ja de mei" [A bad example will never be made of me"] (v. 1016). To the ears of some audiences, Roland's discourse here would sound uncomfortably like that of the boasting Saracens: not only does he sound eager to shed blood in the coming battle, having given no thought to the feasibility of matching his force against Marsile's, but Roland even speaks of the future fame he will garner in this battle. In doing so, Roland uses the future tense to talk about his own future fame, while offering cautionary subjunctive verbs to describe what the rear guard should do collectively ("Now may each one ensure that he strikes great blows, / So that a bad song may never be sung about us!"). The issue of Roland's grammar within his rhetoric is particularly pertinent in that this opening to the horn debate can be seen as a replay of the earlier council scene, in which Roland's bold opening speech followed Charlemagne's respectful and understated presentation of Marsile's terms for peace.[49] The parallel between the two scenes continues as Olivier, like Ganelon at the council, offers specific and quite reasonable arguments against Roland's intention to proceed with the battle: anyone can see that the rear guard is outnumbered, and anyone can figure out that this attack represents Ganelon's promised vengeance against them, since he was the one who nominated them for the rear guard (vv. 1021–25).[50] Unlike Ganelon's council speech, however, which seems to have been motivated by cowardice, Olivier has nothing but good intentions in offering this analysis. As he proves repeatedly throughout the battle, he is not one to run from a fight, even one that he has no chance of winning or even surviving. The purpose of the parallel between the speeches of Olivier and Ganelon, then, is not primarily to suggest that Olivier is wrong or evil but rather to suggest that Roland is right once again, in spite of the troubling aspects of his bold discourse (which many modern critics have cited as evidence of Roland's "démesure" or "excess" in both scenes).

Leaving Ganelon aside, however, a different kind of comparison between the council speeches and the first horn debate does reveal a problem with Olivier's discourse: his focus on the concrete realities of the moment and on the unprecedented nature of the rear guard's situation violates the rules for discourse and reasoning that govern the poem as a whole, that is, the rules of the *geste*. As we have seen, the power of the *geste* resides in its ability to link lived experience in the past with lived experience in the present by means of its embodiment of a collective and infallible verbal memory. Without this link to the past, lived experience in the present constitutes, not a heroic revival of the *geste,* but merely a spontaneous reaction with no guarantee of success and no lasting significance. In laisses 80 to 85, Olivier makes four separate attempts to convince Roland of his point of view, but none of them are successful because they all offer present circumstances (and emphatically *not* past precedent; see laisse 82) as the basis for scenarios in the future tense (and not in a more tentative and deferential conditional or subjunctive form). In equally consistent fashion on the other side, Roland stakes his claims upon the authority of the *geste* in that he offers a combination of past precedent and of the very integrity of his existence as the basis for his own future scenarios. Perhaps it is for this reason that the heart of the horn debate takes the form of repeating laisses, in which Olivier advises Roland to sound the horn and Roland refuses each time: these laisses (83–85) might seem on the surface to freeze Roland and Olivier in two intractable positions, but their dynamism lies in Roland's gradual exposition of each link in the unbreakable chain between past, present, and future that is the *geste* itself. In laisse 83, Roland points out that sounding the horn would violate the collective perception of Roland within his society, and we can see immediately that this is true, since Roland offers a self-description that corresponds perfectly to Ganelon's earlier description of his relentless valor: "Sempres ferrai de Durendal granz colps" [Forever will I strike great blows with Durendal] (v. 1055), the Latinate word *sempres* implicitly emphasizing both the authority of this statement and the fact that Roland's future is founded upon a long-established history. The closing line of laisse 83 also evokes both the absolute authority of the *geste* and Roland's ability to revive the *geste* in the present, as Roland pledges the Saracens' immutable fate upon his own person: "Je vos plevis, tuz sunt jugez a mort" [I guarantee it to you, they are all condemned to death] (v. 1058). This statement means not only that Roland is predicting this outcome emphatically but also that he himself serves as the material pledge of this outcome; the subject of the verb *plever* could be either the person taking a pledge or the material sign representing the solemnity of the pledge, and Roland occupies both of those roles here. Furthermore, Roland expresses the death of the Saracens in the future through the grammatical conjunction of present and past: they *are condemned* to death, they exist already in a state of predestined imminent death, and this not primarily because of Roland's determination or his future actions but rather by virtue of the kind of impersonal, absolute, and ongoing agency characteristic of the *geste* and, ultimately, of God's will. Having explained in laisse 83 the inevitable continuity between past and present, Roland explains in laisse 84 the inevitable continuity between his future conduct in the battle and the future honor of his kin group and of France, the whole of it in accordance with God's will (v. 1062), which is also the ultimate authority standing behind the infallibility of the *geste*. On the basis of this enhanced authority, then, and with these expanded consequences related to the reception as well as the execution of his deeds, Roland repeats his pledge: "Je vos plevis, tuz sunt a mort livrez" [I guarantee it to you, they are all delivered up for death] (v. 1069). Again, the passive term *livrez* suggests that the Saracens will die because of their predetermined fate, not because of the military prowess of Roland or the rear guard.

This time, therefore, it is Olivier whose discourse seems excessive when, in laisse 85, he uses the same verbal pledge as Roland in an effort to strengthen his own future-tense scenario: once again advising Roland to sound the horn, Olivier adds, "Je vos plevis, ja returnerunt Franc" [I guarantee it to you, the Franks will then return] (v. 1072). Once Roland set the standard so high for the use of the phrase "je vos plevis," Olivier's use of it seems shallow and perhaps even deceptive. Olivier is claiming to "guarantee" nothing more than the logical and contingent human reaction to a previous human action: if you sound the horn, the Franks will return. Furthermore, he will in no way act as the material pledge for that guarantee: he never offers to sound the horn himself, and if the Franks were to return they would ask for an explanation of the horn call from Roland, not from Olivier. Most importantly, however, Olivier would not be "reviving" or "commemorating" anything, even if he were the one to blow the horn: as he stated himself, that horn call would communicate the unprecedented nature of the attack on the rear guard and thus in a more abstract sense the chaotic nature of human existence. Within the universe of the *geste*, what Olivier claims to "guarantee" here is not the unfolding of God's inexorable will but rather the material realization of his own sound reasoning, or even of his own innovation, since he believes that there is no past precedent to be commemorated here. From the standpoint of the *geste*, then, Olivier's pledge represents either ignorance or blasphemy, as Roland's response suggests: "'Ne placet Deu,' ço li respunt Rollant, / 'Que ço seit dit pur nul hume vivant / Ne pur paien que ja seie cornant!'" ["May it not please God," this is what Roland responds to him, "that that be said by any living man, nor [that it be said] by any pagan that I blow the horn!"] (vv. 1073–75). These lines are usually construed in translation as ". . . that it be said by any living man or by any pagan that I blow the horn," but the word *ço* could refer to Olivier's last statement rather than or in addition to serving as a grammatical placeholder for the later clause "that I blow the horn," making line 1074 a rebuke to Olivier for using the verb *plever* so casually. At the end of laisse 85, Roland reaffirms his consistent implication that in this battle the Christians will prevail, not purely through their own military prowess, but rather because the Saracens do not have any *guarant* ("guarantor" or "protector") outside themselves (v. 1081). The winner of this battle, then, will be the side with the stronger protector, not the side with the most numerous or even the most skilled group of warriors.

Thus it is possible to understand laisses 83 through 85 as the moment in which Roland both explains and definitively commits himself to his heroic role as the living person through whom God's will is going to be manifested in this battle and then eternally preserved and revived in the *geste*. Roland's conscious awareness of his assigned role in the ongoing *geste* was already evident in verse 788, and his definitive commitment to that role is affirmed in both word and deed when he "pledges himself" to the predestined purpose of this battle: the destruction of the Saracens and their strongholds in Spain (the rear guard's own destruction being merely the necessary means to that end). This interpretation makes of the famous horn debate between Roland and Olivier a conflict between their differing views of their own roles as historical actors, not as warriors or vassals. Perhaps this is what the narrator means by his evaluation of the two men and their speeches at the end of this scene: "Rollant est proz e Oliver est sage; / Ambedui unt merveillus vasselage: / Puis quë il sunt as chevals e as armes, / Ja pur murir n'eschiverunt bataille. / Bon sunt li cunte e lur paroles haltes." [Roland is worthy and Olivier is wise; / Both have an amazing sense of their roles as vassals: / Once they are on horseback and at arms, / Never for [fear of] death will they avoid battle. / The counts are good and their words are lofty.] (vv. 1093–97). The first line of this passage has been subjected to intense scrutiny by critics, for it is the only one in this evaluative passage that suggests any difference between Roland and Olivier, and the nature of this difference is difficult to pinpoint on the basis of the meaning of *proz* and *sage* alone because both words can convey a variety of meanings in Old French according to their immediate context.[51] Furthermore, as we have already seen, the narrator called Olivier *proz* from the moment he first appeared in the text (v. 176), while Roland implicitly described himself as a "wise man" when he said that such a man was needed for the mission to Marsile and that he would therefore be a promising candidate to take Ganelon's place (vv. 294–95). If anything, I think it is worthwhile to consider the theory that both of these adjectives are offered in a spirit of compensatory reassurance: in spite of Roland's apparent pride in the horn debates, he really is a worthy person rather than a braggart; in spite of the fact that Olivier's advice is based on sensory data and everyday logic, he really is a wise person. For similar reasons, the line that intrigues me most in this passage is the last one, in which the narrator asserts that neither man's words are superior to the other's because both speeches occupy the same lofty plane of signification. Considered purely in terms of the lexical fields within which each man operates in the first horn debate, this evaluation seems false: Roland consistently speaks in terms of moral character and values, not just his own but those of his entire society (except when he is describing the bloody carnage he plans to generate), and Olivier consistently favors terms of physical description, quantity, and sensory perception. What I believe the narrator means by both men's "goodness" and their equally "lofty words," therefore, is that each man makes his speech in earnest and that the two speeches can be considered faithful representations of their speakers' differing worldviews. It is easier to see Roland's discourse as a representation of his personal philosophy, but the narrator insists here that both forms of discourse are philosophical in that they represent each man's way of processing the most urgent matters in life. Olivier has failed to grasp the worldview of the *geste*, but that does not make him stupid, treacherous, or even mistaken about what would be the best solution to their immediate problem. Instead, the difference between Roland and Olivier is simply that Roland is the predestined hero of this episode of the *geste* and Olivier is not. If Roland is aware of this, and has been at least since verse 788 (if not since verse 277, when he uttered the uncharacteristic future prediction "It will be Ganelon"), it is because his role in the *geste* was as inevitable as that of the Saracens. His statements in the horn debates reflect his understanding of that fact, lending them an ironic underlying humility in spite of their apparently prideful sound. As the members of the rear guard soon recognize, Roland himself is their *guarant* (v. 1161), but only because he has pledged himself to the inexorable will of God as expressed through the *geste*. Roland cannot protect them from harm; what he ensures for the rear guard is that their deaths will be considered meaningful by future audiences.

Roland's "lofty words" in the first horn debate express his understanding of how the *geste* functions and how he must behave as its living manifestation in the fictional present. As critics have long noted, however, in their later debate (laisses 128–30) the earlier rhetorical positions of Roland and Olivier are reversed, as Roland looks at the dead bodies of the rear guard and proposes in simple and direct language that Charlemagne must be notified, while Olivier argues against sounding the horn at this point in the battle, at times citing Roland's earlier arguments as implicit reproaches that eventually develop into an angry tirade in laisse 131. Olivier's anger results from his belief that Roland's desire to sound the horn represents a belated change of heart, which is why he refers to Roland's earlier decision as "vostre legerie" [your imprudence] (v. 1726). At this point in the unfolding of the *geste*, however, Roland does not express regret about his previous decision not to summon Charlemagne, nor does he expect Charlemagne's return to result in victory or even in saved lives among the rear guard. In fact, what is striking about Roland's reasoning in the second horn "debate" is its simplicity: *all* that he says is that he wants Charlemagne to be informed about what happened in the battle and therefore that he will sound the horn so that Charlemagne will return. In truth, this is not a debate at all, for Roland does not respond to Olivier's criticisms or to his analyses of their situation. Instead, Roland's discourse is dominated by the singular obsession of informing Charlemagne about the battle, and this obsessive focus on communication represents the necessary second stage of his role in this episode of the *geste*. Beyond submission to what Roland sees as the will of God for him in this situation, his only other purpose for allowing the battle to proceed as it did was that of producing collective meaning for future members of his society; if there were no survivor to communicate Roland's heroic attitude to future generations, then the chain of the *geste* would be broken in spite of all that Roland and the rear guard had just sacrificed to perpetuate it. In other words, Roland's living manifestation (or performance) of the *geste* requires reception by an audience to produce its intended meaning. At this point in the poem, Roland does not attempt to compose a Roncevaux narrative himself: he does not send a messenger to Charlemagne to tell the story of the battle because the ideal reception of Roland's *geste* would be direct, unmediated by another narrator or by verbal representation of any kind. This desire for direct transmission of the *geste* to Charlemagne explains what otherwise appears to be one of the strangest utterances in the whole poem, Roland's address to the absent Charlemagne just before sounding the horn: "E! reis, amis, que vos ici nen estes!" [Oh! king, friend, [how terrible it is] that you are not here!] (v. 1697). Audience members not mindful of the way in which the *geste* functions would naturally respond with a certain incredulity to this line, given that it was Roland himself who made the decision not to summon Charlemagne, and audiences might respond with great sympathy to Olivier's line, "Se m' creïsez, venuz i fust mi sire" [If you had believed me [and sounded the horn], my lord would have come here [already]] (v. 1728). What Olivier fails to appreciate, however, is that Roland's purpose in summoning Charlemagne is not strategic but performative: Charlemagne's presence could no longer change the outcome of this particular battle, but it could result in successful subsequent interpretation of it by both sides. Turpin does understand this distinction: in his response to the conflict between Roland and Olivier in laisse 132, he points out two advantages of summoning Charlemagne. First, if Charlemagne avenges their deaths by defeating Marsile, a potential and undesirable audience response to Roncevaux will be prevented, for "Ja cil d'Espaigne n'en deivent turner liez" [The men from Spain must never return happy] (v. 1745). Second, the returning Franks will mourn them and give them a proper Christian burial rather than allowing their corpses to be eaten by scavenging animals (vv. 1746–51); in other words, memorial services will be conducted, which will provide a context for other lasting gestures of commemoration. Since Turpin conveys the importance of audience reception and of commemoration so succinctly in this short speech, Roland congratulates him for it: "Respunt Rollant: 'Sire, mult dites bien'" [Roland responds: "My lord, you are saying it very well"] (v. 1752).

Just as Roland guaranteed with his own person the successful revival of the *geste* through the battle itself, now by sounding the horn he again invests his whole person in an act of nonverbal communication whose meaning thus cannot be distorted through deceptive wordplay or faulty interpretation. Having completed these two stages of his heroic *geste* through two acts of combined communication and action, Roland immediately regains some vestiges of normal humanity, only now weeping over the dead members of the rear guard and viewing their deaths through an earthly lens rather than a purely heroic one. For example, in spite of Roland's own eloquent exposition earlier in the text of the past, present, and future functioning and heroic meaning of the *geste* as manifested by the deaths of the Saracens and of the rear guard, after the horn call in laisse 140 he describes his friends' deaths as a loss and perhaps even a waste (v. 1860) and grieves over the fact that he could be a "guarant" only for the will of the *geste*, not for the safety of his closest companions: "Jo ne vos pois tenser ne guarantir" [I can neither defend nor protect you] (v. 1864). In fact, Roland perceives this grief as the force that will destroy him: "De doel murrai, s'altre ne m'i ocit" [I will die of grief, if another man does not kill me here] (v. 1867). Roland's total commitment to a transcendent entity, the *geste*, brings about a fundamental disruption in his present existence: having committed this transcendent act, he cannot go on living, even if no one actually kills him. Later Roland reiterates this realization and lends further weight to the notion that he acted as a hero earlier in the text only because it was required by the *geste*, not because he is a truly superior being. When he looks at the mortally wounded Olivier, Roland's first reaction is to verbalize his own powerlessness and lack of further direction: "'Deus!' dist li quens, 'or ne sai jo que face'" ["God!" says the count, "now I do not know what to do"] (v. 1982).

Indeed, it appears that Roland chooses the wrong course of action when he tries to destroy his sword Durendal (laisses 171–73), since he is unsuccessful in doing so. Although he claims to do this because he does not want the sword to be used by the Saracens against the Christians (vv. 2336–37), his recital of the exploits that he has accomplished with Durendal suggest that he also has prideful motives for not wanting another warrior to use the sword. Yet in the third laisse in the series recounting this incident, Roland's contemplation of the holy relics inside the sword reminds him that Durendal is forever implicated in the larger Christian *geste*, rather than serving primarily as an accessory of Roland's individual identity.[52] This realization links Durendal not only to Christendom but to the *geste* specifically, since Roland's final words on this subject echo his earlier statements about the relationship between his own heroism, the Saracens' transgressions, and the ruling authority of God as expressed through the *geste*:

> Or guart chascuns que granz colps i empleit,
> Male cançun de nus chantét ne seit!
> *Paien unt tort e chrestïens unt dreit.*
> Malvaise essample n'en serat ja de mei.
> > (vv. 1013–16; emphasis added)

> [Now may each one ensure that he strikes great blows,
> So that a bad song may never be sung about us!
> *The pagans are wrong and the Christians are right.*
> A bad example will never be made of me.]

> *Felun paien mar* i vindrent as porz:
> Jo vos plevis, *tuz sunt jugez* a mort.
> > (vv. 1057–58)

> [*To their detriment will the evil pagans* come to these passes:
> I guarantee it to you, *they are all condemned* to death.]

> [to Durendal]:
> *Il nen est dreiz que paiens* te baillisent;
> De chrestïens *devez* estre servie.
> > (vv. 2349–50)

[to Durendal]:
It is not right that the pagans should possess you:
By Christians you *must* be wielded.]

In each of these cases, Roland's confidence ultimately derives from his faith that the right (Christendom) will prevail over the wrong (Saracen resistance to it). Roland pledges his entire being to be used as an instrument of God and the *geste* rather than believing that his individual identity or personal qualities are the source of his heroic deeds or of their subsequent commemoration. Even his sword is ultimately God's instrument rather than Roland's own, which is why Durendal "survives" Roland's death. Like a material avatar of the *geste* itself, Durendal will bolster the heroism of future generations because of the layers of past and ongoing signification embedded in it alongside its holy relics, meanings that can be cited through both physical and verbal performances by the sword's future owners. As Roland himself said before the battle: "Se jo i moerc, dire poet ki l'avrat / Que ceste epee fut a noble vassal" [If I die here, whoever will have it can say / that this sword belonged to a noble vassal] (vv. 1122–23). This statement expresses the essence of the *geste* through its characteristic blend of past, present, and future tenses and of uncompromising commitment to action leading inevitably to verbal commemoration by a potential future actor. Therefore Roland's subsequent expression of a desire to destroy Durendal could be compared to Ganelon's earlier statement of his desire to destroy Roland himself: either act of destruction has the potential to jeopardize the ongoing signification of the *geste*, and both acts of destruction are motivated by an excessive concern for the individual identity of a mortal person.

Just as Roland's sword Durendal can be seen as a material sign for the heroic functioning of the *geste* through lived experience, so can it also be seen to represent the literary functioning of the *geste*, and specifically of this text as a new material manifestation of it. Roland's initial error during the scene of his attempted destruction of Durendal was to believe that its power and meaning were invested in its physical being and thus that it could be used as the passive instrument of anyone who might happen upon it. If the sword were to fall into enemy hands, Roland feared, it could be made to signify and act against Christendom simultaneously, and in that sense Roland's anxiety about Durendal's future owner was an anxiety about the sword's meaning being converted so that it would work against (or *desmantir*) the *geste*. Yet this series of laisses is introduced by an immediate clue to Durendal's unique and inalterable status. Roland decides to destroy Durendal after a Saracen tries to steal the sword from him, mistakenly believing that the mortally wounded Roland is dead already; temporarily deprived of his sword, therefore, Roland strikes the Saracen dead by hitting him over the head with his horn. Afterward, Roland laments that as a result of this blow the horn is now dented and its crystal and gold decorations have fallen out (vv. 2295–96). The sword proves to be mightier than the horn, then, and this is because of the relics it contains, which are both more powerful and more valuable than the external material embellishments of gold and jewels on the horn. In similar fashion, it is the truthful and spiritually transcendent content of this text, not the particularities of its material form, that makes it a worthy verbal expression of the *geste*, and one that cannot be stolen and made to serve an agenda contrary to that of God. Even if an individual author (in similar fashion to the momentarily prideful Roland in laisses 171–73) attempted to claim a Roncevaux text as his own creation and to deny its identity as the common property of all Christians, the text's content, the lived experience and lasting meaning behind the Roncevaux story, would serve as its "guarant," resisting any profoundly transformative change and ensuring its own continued integrity because of its permanent and sanctified narrative status as a textual relic (or reliquary) preserving evidence of God's intervention in human history.

If Durendal functions as a reflexive symbol for the poem, then Roland's wish concerning the sword's future bearer may also reflect upon the Oxford poet: "Ne vos ait hume ki facet cuardie!" [May no man have you who would commit acts of cowardice!] (v. 2351). Putting the Roncevaux story into writing was not an enterprise for the faint of heart because of the immense cultural and spiritual charge of its content; for the same reason, however, anyone succeeding at this perilous cultural project would be richly rewarded by his association with a text endowed with so much inherent significance, just as wielding Durendal during his lifetime was Roland's reward for his proven worth from a grateful Charlemagne acting as a simultaneous representative of God and of the Franks (vv. 2318–21). As my analysis of Roland's relationship to the *geste* in several scenes has already indicated, the primary hero of the text models for the author what his own approach to the Roncevaux *matiere* should be; the combined discourse and action of the traitor Ganelon, conversely, sketch the dimensions of a potential literary transgression, serving as the specter of the threat of cultural betrayal inherent in this intended project of cultural commemoration.

Considering first the notion of Roland as a model for the Oxford poet, several previously cited characteristics link the missions of these two individuals. First and foremost is the explicit statement by both Roland and the primary narrator that their most urgent mission is to uphold the *geste*. Roland states this negatively in verse 788 by saying that he would be a man under a curse if he were to do anything to threaten the integrity of the *geste*; in the closing line, the poem as a whole is described as "la geste que Turoldus declinet," a line that can be interpreted in many ways but in which it is clear that "la geste" bears a direct relationship to the text at hand.[53] If Turoldus is understood as the author's name, which is a clear possibility, then the act attributed to him here is that of doing something to the *geste*, an activity described by the verb *decliner*. In the notes to his bilingual edition of the Oxford *Roland*, Ian Short cites several past translations of *decliner* as it is used here and then proposes a verb that would encompass all of them: *poétiser* (make into a poem).[54] According to that reading, then, what "Turoldus" is explicitly described as doing is making *la geste* into the poem at hand, a statement that acknowledges a difference between *la geste* and the text of Oxford but that also suggests that the text represents the presence of *la geste* itself within the new form produced by Turoldus (either as poet or as scribe). In addition, *decliner* can have the connotation of "leaning" or "bowing" because of its relationship to the verb *cliner,* meaning to bow before someone or submit oneself to someone. This connotation enhances the impression of a link between the Oxford poet's literary project and Roland's literary mission: the heroic status of both of these historical actors results from their submission of their individual identity to the transcendent authority of the *geste*. Thus if the poet names himself in the closing line, he does so as part of a larger statement that his project is to make the *geste* into this poem as a way of submitting himself to it, just as Roland claimed to guarantee with his own person the predetermined will of God in the battle (vv. 1058 and 1069). Either statement could sound like a prideful exaltation of self or like a humble sacrifice of self for the sake of a higher purpose. Thierry restates this heroic stance in a formulation particularly rich with intratextual echoes when he volunteers to champion Charlemagne's side in the judicial combat that resolves Ganelon's trial: "S'or ad parent m'en voeille desmentir, / A ceste espee, que jo ai ceinte ici, / Mun jugement voel sempres guarantir" [If he [Ganelon] now has any relative who wishes to contradict me, / With this sword, which I have girded on here, / My judgment I wish to guarantee immediately [forever]] (vv. 3835–36). For Thierry, as for the

Oxford poet, perhaps, it is the truth of his verbalized narrative perspective that is being "guaranteed" with a "sword" against those who would depict it as a lie *(desmentir)*. Thierry's *mun jugement* provides a contrasting term for Ganelon's *mun saveir:* Thierry is not inventing a new narrative or an innovative course of action but rather affirming the truth of the emperor's narrative through a course of action (judicial combat) that could hardly be more traditional within his society. Similarly, the Oxford poet's faithful transcription of the Roncevaux story privileges the kind of judgment that characterizes Thierry over the kind of cleverness that characterizes Ganelon.

Other parallels between the Oxford poet and Roland represent metaphorically the impossibility of the Oxford poet claiming the Roncevaux story as his own creation or even claiming that he has enhanced its meaning. I have already suggested the subordinate relationship of the text to the larger legend in the potentially reflexive symbolism of Roland's sword Durendal, rendered precious, impervious to theft, and indestructible by the holy relics encased within it. A more obvious place to look for parallels between Roland and the author, however, is in Roland's two acts of communication to Charlemagne about the battle. As I noted earlier, the horn call strikes me as a representation of the ideal of unmediated transmission of the *geste* because it is simultaneously a committed action and an act of communication (hallmarks of the *geste*) and because it avoids the trap of verbalization by using pure, nonverbal sound and by seeking to bring Charlemagne and his army to the battlefield to be direct witnesses to the end of the battle. The horn call succeeded in alerting Charlemagne to the existence of the Battle of Roncevaux, but because Charlemagne was unable to witness the battle a second act of communication was required to ensure that it would be interpreted correctly. Roland's deliberate arrangement of his dying body in the last moments of his life has an explicit purpose as an act of signification and a guide to subsequent interpretation and transmission. Roland turns his head toward the enemy: "Pur ço l'at faìt quë il voelt veirement / Que Carles dïet e trestute sa gent, / Li gentliz quens, qu'il fut mort cunquerant" [He did this for the reason that he truly wished / That Charles would say, along with all of his people, / That the noble count died victorious] (vv. 2361–63). The implications of this scene as a metaphor for literary transmission have been noted by several critics,[55] and Vance also observed that the parallels between Roland and a poetic performer were already in evidence over a hundred lines earlier, when Roland gathered around him the bodies of the twelve peers and pronounced formal laments over them with accompanying performative gestures.[56] What is perhaps most telling about this communicative act as a potential parallel for the poem's own transmission of the *geste*, however, is that its scope of signification was limited to its audience's capacity to recognize in it a meaning that had been previously transmitted orally. Roland composes this corporeal message to Charlemagne as the material realization of an oral boast he made long before: that he would never die in a foreign land without having first put himself at the very front of the battle lines, and therefore that he would die with his head turned toward the land of the enemy (vv. 2860–67). Interestingly, Charlemagne reminds his men of Roland's boast *before* he finds Roland's body, rather than being reminded of it himself by seeing it realized before his eyes. This act of "premeditated reception" on the part of Charlemagne corresponds well to the conditions of audience reception at the time when the Oxford *Roland* was written down. Because of the established context for Roland's act of corporeal signification, it would have been useless and perhaps counterproductive if he were to attempt to add any other symbolic components to it; similarly, the scope of the Oxford poet's innovation was limited by the dimensions of what audiences already considered at the time to be the essence of the Roncevaux story. Thus the incident of Roland's corporeal message for Charlemagne, through which he intended to influence the content of future heroic poems told about him (vv. 2361–63), might also serve as a representation of the Oxford poet's own process of composition of the text and its subsequent intended reception. If we read this incident as a metaphor for the composition of the Oxford *Roland* (a reading strengthened by the fact that this incident does not occur in any other Roncevaux text of which I am aware), the fact that Roland's medium of signification is his own body emphasizes the earnest solemnity of the Oxford poet's undertaking. The author probably did not have to die in the process of writing this poem, but equating the poem with Roland's dead body ascribes to it an analogous value as the long-awaited material realization of a recognizable entity from oral literary culture. This reading also implies that all future Roncevaux texts will have to take this text into account, just as Roland imagines his own act of signification as an episode within future heroic poems told by others.

The Oxford poet never explicitly states his intended faithfulness to the oral *geste* of Roncevaux in the form of a prologue or other metatextual commentary, and he might have sounded distastefully or even suspiciously boastful to some audiences if he had. In the final scenes of the text, however, the primary narrator of the text does express the opposite notion: that those who boast of their *un*faithfulness should be harshly punished. In one of the narrator's few judgmental asides to the audience, felonious narrators like Ganelon are condemned using Roland's *geste*-inflected phrase "it is not right." The narrator concludes the laisse describing vividly Ganelon's execution by saying: "Guenes est mort cume fel recrëant. / Hom ki traïst, nen est dreiz qu'il s'en vant." [Ganelon is killed like an evil traitor/unbeliever.[57] / A man who betrays, it is not right that he boast about it.] (vv. 3973–74). By saying that Ganelon was a criminal because of his boasting at the trial, as well as his act of betrayal, the narrator affirms explicitly what the events and narrative strategies of this poem have suggested several times already: that the consequences of the Roncevaux characters' "strange words" may be as serious or even more serious than the consequences of their actions. The narrator takes a certain relish in describing the violent punishment of Ganelon, whose narrative transgressions equate him with those medieval authors who attempted to draw attention to their own literary innovations at the expense of truth and with the effect of extinguishing the effective functioning of the *geste* among future generations of literary audiences. The poem dramatizes in several scenes, but nowhere more clearly than here, that this kind of literary innovation was not its enterprise. As the narrator says in the laisse preceding the description of Ganelon's execution, "Hom ki traïst, sei ocit e altroi" [A man who betrays, he destroys himself along with others] (v. 3959). This line suggests that, like Roland when he refused to increase the size of the rear guard, the Oxford poet would have been a doomed man, as well as a traitor to his culture, if he had undertaken the reworking of the Roncevaux story in a spirit contrary to that of the *geste*.

The Châteauroux Version

2   Retelling as Redemptive Reception

This chapter examines three sections of the Roncevaux narrative contained in the rhymed Châteauroux manuscript, each of which features a distinctive approach to rewriting. In the section devoted to the council scenes, I show in detail how the Châteauroux redactor offered a clear, consistent, and somewhat revisionist interpretation of the personalities of Roland, Ganelon, and Charlemagne by making only small and generally subtle changes to its source text. Indeed, the very modesty of the redactor's reworking is what makes it so persuasive and effective as a prescriptive reinterpretation of the Roncevaux material. This stealthy approach to reworking continues in the battle scenes but takes a new form: repetition of familiar elements, which reinforces certain interpretations at the expense of others. Of particular interest to my overall study of the Roncevaux tradition is the fact that these repetitions nearly always take the form of character discourse, rather than occurring in the primary narration. This strategy disguises these repeated ideas as the spontaneous reactions of the characters to their situation; if these ideas had been repeated by the primary narrator, they would have assumed a more didactic tone. Finally, my interpretation of the Aude episode (the longest redaction of it in the surviving Roncevaux tradition) emphasizes the process through which the audiences' sympathies are directed toward Aude and away from Charlemagne, who proves to be consistently self-absorbed, manipulative, and dishonest in this text. I argue that

Aude's reception of multiple Roncevaux narratives and interpretations throughout this episode corresponds to the dilemma of thirteenth-century literary audiences confronted with multiple verse and prose renderings of the same material, many of them arguing strenuously for their unique truth value. By granting transcendent authority to the oral narrative recounted by Olivier during a brief resurrection from the dead, Châteauroux expresses a desire to rise above the petty rivalry of individual authors and return to the inherently spiritual value that it ascribes to the Roncevaux story throughout its own retelling of it.

About the Text

The manuscript referred to in this study as "Châteauroux" is currently kept at the Bibliothèque Muncipale de Châteauroux, shelfmark MS 1. The Roncevaux narrative it contains is written in rhymed laisses that appear to have been adapted from the same Old French rhymed source text (now lost) as the Roncevaux text contained in the manuscript known as "Venice 7" (Venice, Biblioteca Nazionale Marciana Fr. Z. 7 (=251)).[1] Both surviving manuscripts also include some passages that appear to have been adapted from a different source text written in assonanced laisses. The language of both manuscripts has been characterized as a form of Franco-Italian resulting from the copying of an Old French source by Italian scribes. The Châteauroux manuscript is written in a French gothic bookhand, but with scribal conventions and decorations that attest to its Italian provenance and to a date of execution in the latter part of the thirteenth century. Both manuscripts are known to have been held in the private libraries of Italian owners until the early eighteenth century, at which point Venice 7 was given to the Republic of Venice and Châteauroux was acquired by Louis XVI for his library at Versailles. Châteauroux and Venice 7 are so closely related, in fact, that a recent edition by Joseph Duggan combines readings from both manuscripts in an effort to offer the best possible witness of the common rhymed source text from which both were copied.[2] The date of original composition for this Roncevaux narrative is thought to be earlier than the dates of the manuscripts but after 1190, based on references in the text to historical events of the late twelfth century and to other literary works composed between 1150 and 1200.

Because of its division into rhymed laisses, Châteauroux is often discussed by modern specialists of the *chanson de geste* as part of a cohesive group called "the rhymed *Roland*s," consisting of six versions of substantial length as well as some additional surviving fragments, most of which were probably composed in the thirteenth century. Significant variations do exist among the six surviving rhymed versions, particularly since three of them begin just before or during the Battle of Roncevaux, probably because of missing folios at the start of each of these surviving copies (these three versions are known as "Paris" (Bibliothèque Nationale ms. français 860), "Cambridge" (Trinity College, R, 3-32, thus siglum T), and "Lyon" (Bibliothèque municipale de Lyon ms. 743).[3] Yet the similarities in plot and structure among the surviving portions of the six rhymed versions are more consistent than is their collective resemblance to the Oxford version. Like Châteauroux and Venice 7, one other rhymed version, "Venice 4" (Venice, Biblioteca Nazionale Marciana, 225; thought to have been composed before all the other surviving rhymed versions), begins with material similar to that found in the opening laisses of the Oxford version. Indeed, the content of laisses 1 through 9 is remarkably similar for Oxford, Venice 4, Venice 7, and Châteauroux, and these four versions continue to present a generally similar series of events until the first debate between Olivier and Roland about sounding the olifant (Oxford laisse 81, Châteauroux laisse 89). Substantial agreement, with some notable exceptions, characterizes the group of all six rhymed versions plus Oxford for much of the Battle of Roncevaux and continues through the battle against Baligant (with the exception of the Lyon version, which omits the Baligant episode entirely). In the scenes following the battle against Baligant, however, all of the rhymed versions proceed in a different direction from that of Oxford, recounting at greater length the episodes of Aude's death and of Ganelon's trial and execution. Although both of these episodes do exist in the Oxford version, it is difficult to identify specific laisses in these portions of Oxford that correspond with any precision to specific laisses from the rhymed versions. Most of the content of the specific laisses from these latter portions of the six rhymed versions can be matched to one another, however, with significant variations between specific lines within certain of these generally matching laisses.[4]

In spite of the overall similarities in structure among the six rhymed versions, there are two reasons why I believe that it is important to restrict my focus to only one of them in this chapter. The first reason is that the status of the six rhymed Roncevaux texts within medieval literary culture tends to be diminished by the scholarly convention of talking about them as a single entity. There is a certain logic to combining Châteauroux and Venice 7, since their content and structure are so close to identical; the other four rhymed versions, however, clearly constitute independent "re-creations" of the Roncevaux *matiere*, including some unique episodes and many unique lines in each version.[5] These five separate articulations prove that the Roncevaux *matiere* was considered both important and open to new interpretations in thirteenth-century francophone literary culture. Nevertheless, an inattentive reader of existing Roland criticism might conclude that there were two medieval versions of the Roncevaux legend—the Oxford version and the rhymed version—because specialists of French epic tend to speak in those terms and to describe the rhymed versions as "late" contributions to the textual tradition. The fact that there were, instead, at least six versions (for it is impossible to know how many medieval versions did not survive to the present day) indicates that the Roncevaux tradition may have experienced its most intense period of development in the thirteenth century and thus, perhaps, that the Roncevaux *matiere* was perceived during that period as more relevant to contemporary concerns (of a literary kind, a political kind, or both kinds) than it had ever been before.

The second reason for taking this step of studying one rhymed Roncevaux text apart from the others is to gain a more profound understanding of the particular process of rewriting—or, to use Douglas Kelly's terms, of "commentary and correction"[6]—that resulted in the distinct but closely related structures of the six surviving rhymed Roncevaux texts. Both the similarities and the differences among the surviving rhymed Roncevaux texts provide crucial evidence about their anonymous authors' approach to rewriting: when these medieval authors worked with the Roncevaux *matiere*, their shared impression seems to have been that the task at hand was to effect significant changes in the audience's perception of the story as a whole but also to include most or all of a traditional set of characters and scenes. These shared elements are undeniable, but they can also be misleading for readers who do not examine the distinctive features of each of the texts apart from the others. My analysis of the Châteauroux version in this chapter, both alone and in comparison to the well-known Oxford version, will demonstrate the kind of rewriting techniques that were particularly appropriate to a medieval *matiere* that was defined by a central, predetermined series of events (those associated with the Battle of Roncevaux), rather than by central figures on a widely varying trajectory from a shared premise to a shared conclusion (as is the case for narratives of the Grail quest or of the couples Lancelot and Guenevere or Tristan and Yseut).[7] Because of the defining presence of the Battle of Roncevaux and the circumstances surrounding it, many of the observations that I make here about the implications of the sequence of events as presented in Châteauroux also hold true for the other rhymed versions, and some for the Oxford version. Yet my emphasis on the exact words used by the narrator and characters in this version sharpens the focus of this analysis to allow the unique perspective of Châteauroux to emerge. This perspective is a product of the interaction between the events and the characters' expressed attitudes toward those events, both of which would have coexisted, in the process of medieval reception, with the audience's memory of alternate perspectives provided by other contemporary Roncevaux narratives.

Of the six surviving rhymed versions, why choose Châteauroux for this kind of detailed examination? To some extent, the choice is arbitrary: a close reading of any of the six versions would provide interesting and valuable results. Yet Châteauroux is perhaps the best example among the rhymed versions of the way in which apparently conservative rewriting strategies can mask profound shifts of perspective. This is true, first of all, because this version provides the most complete witness of the overall structure common to the six rhymed *Rolands*. The surviving portion of Paris displays an attention to detail similar to that of Châteauroux, but its early laisses are missing; Cambridge is missing fewer laisses at the beginning of the text, but another important lacuna appears during the debate between Roland and Olivier about sounding Roland's horn. The account in Lyon is the shortest of the six, beginning just after the horn scene and also omitting the Baligant episode. Like Oxford, Venice 4 omits an important scene from the other rhymed versions, in which each of the twelve peers prepares himself for battle, and it also adds a unique account of the conquest of Narbonne (laisses 285–319), centered on the character Aimeri, which constitutes an obtrusive adjustment to the common structure of all the other surviving rhymed versions. Moreover, Venice 4 offers a noticeably more concise account of most sections of the Roncevaux *matiere* than do the other rhymed versions, a quality that has caused some modern critics to prefer it to the more long-winded Paris and Châteauroux versions but that also makes it an atypical representative of the rhymed group as a whole.

By comparison to these other versions, the structure of Châteauroux can be characterized as more thorough and consistent: no portion of the conventional structure is missing, and some episodes (particularly those of the horn debates and those involving Aude) are repeated or greatly expanded. This conservatism can also be observed in the passages from Châteauroux that appear to have been copied nearly verbatim from a Roncevaux text in assonance, with only the last word of each line modified to provide the superficial appearance of rhyme.[8] As I will show with specific examples in the following pages, however, Châteauroux's rendering of character discourse is often unique. As Duggan has pointed out, the attention devoted to Aude in both Châteauroux and Venice 7 is also unparalleled in the surviving Roncevaux tradition, as evidenced not only by their detailed rendering of the episode of her death but also by the recurring mentions of Aude earlier in the text by Roland, Charlemagne, and the primary narrator.[9] These distinctive features of Châteauroux are of particular value to this study, both because the analysis of character discourse contributes so much to my readings of Oxford, *Ronsasvals,* and *Galïen restoré* in other chapters and because the role of the Aude episode in the rhymed versions constitutes one of the most obviously metaliterary episodes in the Roncevaux *matiere*. Thus a number of aspects that all the rhymed *Roland*s share appear in particularly sharp relief in the Châteauroux version, making it a good representative of the rhymed group as a whole and also a good source of distinctive, rewarding evidence when examined line by line.

In spite of these reasons for my choice of Châteauroux as the single text used to represent the rhymed Roncevaux texts in this study, there is one great disadvantage to working with this text: its syntax is at times difficult to decipher because its Italian scribe seems not to have had a sophisticated grasp of the Old French lines he was copying.[10] The frequent, obvious scribal misreadings in Châteauroux imply, of course, that this text probably also contains other lines whose syntax appears logical but nevertheless is also the result of scribal innovation rather than what the author originally composed. Yet in spite of the likelihood that the scribe was responsible for introducing substantial variations between Châteauroux and the other surviving versions closely related to it (corruption), a significant number of variations remain that convey consistent shifts in narrative strategy and character development and that thus represent the author's deliberate reworking (commentary). These consistent and substantive variations point toward the particular interpretation of the Roncevaux story that the Châteauroux version was designed to communicate to its medieval audience: they indicate that this rhymed version was, indeed, intended to be different from others that were circulating at the same time, and they offer concrete evidence of the nature of that difference.

"Mas ne dist autre outrage": Discursive Correction and Commentary in the Council Scenes

Laisse 22 of the Châteauroux version, the first of its laisses that appear in no other surviving Roncevaux text, is almost entirely devoted to spoken discourse by Charlemagne and Ganelon. In retrospect, after a reading of the entire Châteauroux version, this verbal exchange and its reception by Olivier can be understood as an initial sketch of the consistent interpretative choices that distinguish the unique point of view of this version from those of other Roncevaux narratives. This laisse shows Charlemagne and Ganelon from the first as the primary enemies facing off against each other and portrays Roland as an innocent and largely passive bystander to this conflict between the emperor and the traitor. Furthermore, Roland's sacrifice in the Battle of Roncevaux is already foreshadowed here in an unmistakably favorable and heroic light. Olivier, on the other hand, behaves like a man of action and perhaps even of impulse, in contrast to the famous description of him in the Oxford *Roland* as the "wise" counterbalance to Roland's apparently rash bravery.

> Li enperere a la barbe florie
> voit Guenellon, fortment le contralie:
> "Cuvert, dist il, li cors te maudie!
> Ge t'ai prové de meinte felonie!
> Por cel Seignor qe tot a en bailie,
> se je te pren a ren de quiteritre,
> tot l'or del mont ne te gariroit mie.
> Gardez ben soit ma besoigne fornie."
> Guenes l'entent, de maltalant s'escrie:
> "Deus! dist li quens, dame seinte Marie!
> Tant ai alé qe li rois me castie!
> Mais par celui qi tot en bailie,
> jamais ne vesrai jor de la Pasqe fornie.
> Se truis Rollant en bataille fornie,
> tel li donrai de m'espee forbie,
> d'autrui daumage ne li prenra envige!"
> Olivers l'ot, tot li vis li rogie.
> Irez saut sus, jal ferist lez l'oïe
> quant François saillent qi font la departie.
> (vv. 357–75)[11]

[The emperor with the white beard
Sees Ganelon, and strongly contradicts him:
"Coward," he said, "may you be cursed!
I have proven you guilty of many crimes;
By that Lord who has all in his power,
If I catch you doing anything wrong,
All the gold in the world will not save you.
See to it that my mission is well served."
Ganelon hears this, and cries out resentfully:
"God!" said the count, "holy lady Mary,
I have gone so far that the king reproaches me;
But by the One who has all in his power,
I will never again see an Easter day;
If I find Roland in pitched battle,
I will give him such a blow with my sword,
That he will never wish to harm anyone else."
Olivier heard this, his whole face flushed,
Angry, he jumps up and strikes him on the ear,
And the French surge forward and separate them from each other.]

This laisse raises a number of questions. First, where is Roland in this scene? Why does he not respond to Ganelon's threats, and why is it Olivier who does? And second, why is Charlemagne entrusting this mission to Ganelon at all if he considers him to be a proven criminal and a coward? The immediate context surrounding this laisse is not as helpful as one might expect in answering these questions because this laisse announces clearly what many other surrounding laisses imply through more subtle means. Throughout the council scenes at the start of Châteauroux, in fact, Roland and Charlemagne seem to have exchanged the roles each of them played in the council scenes of the Oxford version: like the Charlemagne of Oxford, Roland remains largely silent during the council scenes while others exchange insults and threats that directly involve him; like the Roland of Oxford, Charlemagne takes advantage of every opportunity to fuel Ganelon's anger and self-pity.

As I will show in the rest of this chapter, this initial exchange of roles indicates not only a new starting point but also a new trajectory for both of the Roncevaux protagonists because neither Roland nor Charlemagne experiences much heroic development in this version: their roles in the council scene remain entrenched throughout the Châteauroux version. Charlemagne chooses both the wrong course of action and the wrong discursive mode in this scene, and we will see that the same is true of

Charlemagne in the scenes following the battles against Marsile and Baligant, in which both his words and his actions make a difficult situation far worse. Roland's discourse in the council scenes, on the other hand, is markedly more mild than in most other medieval Roncevaux narratives, and his choices and actions throughout this text prove that his words are a sincere reflection of his inner serenity about the prospect of sacrificing himself to make up for Charlemagne's mistaken policy decisions. Charlemagne's failings, rather than Roland's heroic powers or weaknesses, thus become the focal point of this Roncevaux narrative, causing Ganelon's betrayal and necessitating Roland's self-sacrifice. Of course, the Oxford *Roland*, or indeed almost any Roncevaux narrative, could be read in the same way: even in Oxford, Charlemagne does his part to provoke Ganelon at the council (especially when he refuses to guarantee his protection to Ganelon's wife and child, Oxford laisse 23), while it can be said that Roland does not immediately summon Charlemagne to the Battle of Roncevaux because Roland is willfully pursuing, against the emperor's wishes, his own earlier policy recommendation to continue the war against Marsile, which Marsile's treachery proves retrospectively to have been the right one (Oxford laisse 14). What is distinctive about the way Châteauroux conveys this possible anti-Charlemagne interpretation, in comparison to other Roncevaux narratives that also allow for it, is that the rewriting strategies and character discourse particular to Châteauroux do not leave room for a number of other possible interpretations made available to the audience in other contemporary Roncevaux narratives.

In particular, Châteauroux provides the audience with virtually no evidence of character flaws on Roland's part; on the contrary, the potential portrayal of Roland as a Christ figure, which emerges late in the battle in other Roncevaux narratives, can already be glimpsed in this unique laisse early in the Châteauroux version. When Ganelon proclaims his intention to kill Roland with his own sword, he is reacting directly to Charlemagne's words, not Roland's: he could not attack the emperor's person, but an attack on Roland would be the way to hurt Charlemagne the most (as Ganelon himself says later in his speech to the Saracen council). Interestingly, Roland does not respond in any way to this public threat from Ganelon, but Olivier jumps to his feet and strikes a blow to Ganelon's ear (vv. 373–74), in a visual echo of the apostle Peter's attempted defense of Christ when Judas came with soldiers to arrest him in the garden of Gethsemane and Peter cut off the ear of one of the high priest's servants (John 18:3–11). Christ rebuked Peter for attempting in this way to alter his chosen, inevitable course toward the crucifixion, and Roland's silent inaction in this scene fore-shadows a similarly determined resignation to his own predestined sacri-fice of himself at Roncevaux. Drawing a universal analogy between Ro-land and Christ would be exaggerated on the basis of this one detail of Olivier's blow to Ganelon's ear, but this implicit visual suggestion is confirmed repeatedly by Roland's later words and actions, particularly in passages found only in Châteauroux (and often Venice 7). Mean-while, as Roland's discourse and behavior become perceptibly more mild and sincere in this version, Charlemagne's words and actions con-tinue to be unusually bold, hostile, and even suspicious.

Because of the subtlety of some of Châteauroux's rewriting strategies, an appreciation of the consistency of this altered presentation of Ro-land, Charlemagne, and Ganelon requires readers to place the proper emphasis on Châteauroux's unique interpolations, such as the laisse just cited. An inattentive audience might fail to take the proper notice of these unique passages, however, because they are surrounded by so many other passages that were drawn more or less unchanged from other contemporary Roncevaux texts. Although Châteauroux's decidedly nega-tive portrayal of Charlemagne makes it an unlikely piece of promon-archy political propaganda, its approach to rewriting would be well suited to some kind of propagandistic function, in that Châteauroux seems to have been designed to persuade the audience of its point of view in a manner somewhat akin to subliminal advertising. Whether Châteauroux's variations consist of an altered line, a short new interpo-lation, or a systematic transformation of a character's portrayal, this version's approach to rewriting is usually unobtrusive and thus perhaps designed to bypass to some extent medieval audiences' habit of active, comparative listening and reading. This subtle approach to rewriting is particularly characteristic of the earliest passages of Châteauroux: as I mentioned in the above introduction to the text, the council scenes of Châteauroux follow the account found in Oxford very closely, with the general content of nearly every laisse matching. The actual source text for Châteauroux was probably an assonanced version other than Ox-ford, but since that source has not survived I compare Châteauroux to Oxford in the following pages to demonstrate the overall conservatism of the rewriting approach of Châteauroux in this section. Interestingly, when Châteauroux does make a change to its source, it consistently chooses character discourse as the appropriate site for transformation: these changes, sometimes explicitly marked as corrections to previous Roncevaux texts, actually function as commentary on the correct inter-pretation of the Roncevaux story as a whole.

The council scenes at the start of the Roncevaux story are always a place where the texts including these scenes devote considerable attention to the exact words spoken by each character, as has been demonstrated by my own reading of Oxford and by the analyses of many other scholars. A slight change made by Châteauroux to the narrator's introduction to the first council scene at the end of laisse 12 indicates a mindfulness of the importance of words here that was not present in the same passage of Oxford. The end of laisse 12 of Oxford also consists of the narrator's introduction to the first council scene, but this passage simply conveys a general sense of foreboding about Ganelon's role in the council: "Guenes i vint, ki la traïsun fist. / Dés or cumencet le cunseill qu'en mal prist." [Ganelon came there, who committed the betrayal. / Now [he][12] begins the council that he used for evil.] (vv. 178–79). At the end of laisse 12 in Châteauroux we find instead: "et s'i fu Guenes qi toz les a traïz. / Deus! or commence tes parole et teus diz / dont douce France torna en grant esliz." [And Ganelon was there who betrayed them all. / God! now he begins words and speeches that were such / that sweet France turned toward a great destruction.] (vv. 213–15). Line 214 of Châteauroux is typical of this version's rewriting strategy: it cites nearly verbatim the beginning of an assonanced line (179 of Oxford) but then changes the end of the line in a way that not only makes the stylistic shift from assonance to rhyme but also comments upon the function of this scene in the previous Roncevaux tradition.

By placing an enhanced emphasis on "words and speeches" in this introductory passage, Châteauroux shows its understanding of the importance of character discourse in previous Roncevaux texts and also prepares the audience to be particularly attentive to the characters' words in the following scenes. This explicit preparation is warranted, both because Châteauroux does make important changes to character discourse in the first council scene and because it simultaneously maintains many of the exact words also used in its assonanced source, so that even modern scholars with the capacity to compare Oxford and Châteauroux line by line (a luxury undoubtedly denied to medieval audiences) can be impressed by both its faithfulness to its source and its occasionally radical revisions of it. Laisse 13 of Châteauroux resembles Oxford quite closely, including Charlemagne's thorough presentation of the terms of Marsile's offer in the future tense,[13] but instead of ending with an expression of wariness on the part of the Franks as a group, laisse 13 of Châteauroux ends with Roland uttering his customary opening words of warning: "Respont Rollant: 'Certes, mar lo cresrez!'" [Roland responds: "For certain, it will be to your detriment if you believe him!"] (v. 232). As in laisse 12, the narrator's introduction to Roland's longer response at the start of laisse 14 maintains some exact words also present in Oxford's laisse 14 but eliminates the statement in Oxford that Roland was "contradicting" Charlemagne here, a single word that has attracted the attention of modern critics and that might well have been considered controversial by medieval audiences. Another significant change made to Roland's speech in Châteauroux laisse 14 appears in the similarly controversial line from Oxford, "Jo vos cunquis e Noples e Commibles" [I conquered both Noples and Commibles for you] (v. 198), which has been cited in modern criticism as evidence of Roland's excessive pride. In Châteauroux, this line instead includes as agents Charlemagne and all the members of his army: "pris avons Nobles et Merinde saisie" [We have taken Nobles and seized Merinde] (v. 240).

These slight adjustments to Roland's opening speech might pass unnoticed or be quickly forgotten when the scene continues with transcriptions of the speeches by Ganelon and Naime in laisses 15, 16, and 17 that are not identical to Oxford but nevertheless are faithful to its content in every detail. In laisse 18, however, Châteauroux actually suppresses Roland's self-nomination to be the messenger to Marsile, while still going to great lengths to maintain a familiar-sounding wording overall:

Oxford laisse 18	Châteauroux laisse 18
"Seignurs baruns, qui purruns enveier	Ce dist li rois: "Qi sera envoiez?"
Al Sarrazin ki Sarraguce tient?"	Dist Olivers: "Se vus mel commandez,
Respunt Rollant: "J'i puis aler mult ben!"	Sire dux Nemes, nes porterez les piez!
	Vostre talanz est mot pesmes et griez,
"Nu ferez certes!" dist li quens Oliver,	si doteroie qe vos ne meslïez;
"Vostre curages est mult pesmes e fiers:	Mais je irai s'entre vus l'otrïez.
Jo me creindreie que vos vos meslisez.	A Saragoze irai joios et liez.
Se li reis voelt, jo i puis aler ben."	Senpres sera vostre droiz derasniez!"
Respunt li reis: "Ambdui vos en taisez!	Li rois l'entent, aval est enbroncez.
Ne vos në il n'i porterez les piez.	Aprés lor dist: "Anbedui vos taissiez,
Par ceste barbe que vëez blancheier,	qe nus de vos n'i portera les piez!
Li duze per mar i serunt jugez!"	Por ceste barbe don li poil est meslez,
Franceis se taisent: as les vus aquisez!	des doze pers mar sera vus jugiez!"
	Franzois se taissent; es les vos acoisiez.

["Lord barons, whom can we send
To the Saracen who holds Saragossa?"
Roland responds: "I can very well go
  there!"
"You will surely do no such thing!"
  says Count Olivier,
"Your heart is very fierce and proud;
I would fear that you would start a fight.
If the king wishes, I can well go there."
The king responds, "Both of you,
  keep quiet!
Neither you nor he will set foot there.
By this beard which you see turning
  white,
Woe to anyone who will nominate one
  of the twelve peers!"
The Franks fall silent: see how they ar
  quieted!]

[The king says this: "Who will be sent?"
Olivier says: "If you command me,
Sir Duke Naime, you will not set foot
  there:
Your mood is very fierce and harmful,
And for this reason I would suspect that
  you would start a fight;
But I will go there if, between you, you
  grant it.
To Saragossa I will go, joyous and
  happy, and your cause will always be
  supported."
The king hears this, his head lowered.
Then he says to them: "Both of you,
  keep quiet,
For neither of you will set foot there.
By this beard, which has gray hair in it,
Woe to the twelve peers if they choose
  you."
The Franks fall silent, see how they are
  quieted.]

This reworking does maintain several of the most vehement, and therefore memorable, statements from its source, such as "you would start a
fight," "Both of you, keep quiet, neither of you will set foot there," and
the narrator's emphatic and somewhat conspiratorial closing aside to
the audience. Of these faithfully maintained utterances, "both of
you . . . neither of you" represents perhaps the most strenuous effort at
conservative reworking because the author took pains to incorporate
Naime into this passage to counterbalance Roland's absence. The traditional pairing of Olivier with Roland in nearly every scene from the
Roncevaux *matiere* featuring Olivier seems to have made it appear necessary to the author of Châteauroux that Olivier be refused by Charlemagne in the company of another warrior. By the same token, then,
the author's elimination of Roland's self-nomination was also a deliberate choice: it would have been easier to keep Roland in this scene,
since in any case someone would have to be paired with Olivier. Or perhaps we should conclude that the Châteauroux author wished to have
Roland's omission pass unnoticed, since he went to such lengths to

maintain the traditional wording in the laisse as a whole, including the idea of Olivier offering himself as a candidate in place of someone too hotheaded (though Naime's traditional role as a wise counselor made him a strange choice for that role). The least likely possibility, however, would be that the scribe accidentally substituted Naime's name in place of Roland's. Since the previous laisse is devoted to Naime, it is true that his name appeared on the same page and was available as an inadvertent substitute. Yet in comparison to the wording of the laisse as a whole, the first two lines in which Olivier disparages the possibility of sending Naime have been more altered than the rest. This alteration was necessary, of course, because it would have been illogical to have Naime utter Roland's line, "I can very well go there," immediately after Charlemagne had ordered Naime not to speak anymore at the end of laisse 17. Since Châteauroux rewords these lines to avoid that lapse in logic, the substitution of Naime for Roland seems to have been a deliberate decision and not a case of inadvertent textual corruption. The goal of this conservative rewriting seems to be that of silencing Roland unobtrusively here and denying Olivier the opportunity to characterize Roland as excessively fierce and proud, which follows logically upon the redactor's earlier suppression of Roland's proud boasting in his speech against accepting the peace agreement.

That Roland's portrayal is being systematically softened in this section of Châteauroux becomes abundantly clear when he does finally speak up to nominate Ganelon as the messenger to Marsile. Indeed, it may be that the narrator took care to announce to the audience explicitly that Roland's response to Charlemagne's renewed request for a nominee lacked any excess: "Rollant respont: 'Mas ne dist autre outrage! / Guenellon, sire, par son fier vasalage!'" [Roland responds, but he did not say any other insult:[14] / "Ganelon, sire, because of his proud service as your vassal"] (vv. 331–32). In spite of this mild and respectful wording on Roland's part, Ganelon's response is as furious as ever, which makes Ganelon seem completely unreasonable when he evokes Roland's excessive pride as the reason behind his immediate formal declaration of hostile intent against Roland and the twelve peers in the following laisse (21). This formal declaration appeared in the Oxford version (laisse 24), but not until after a series of hostile exchanges between Roland and Ganelon, as well as Charlemagne's dismissal of Ganelon's request that he take care of Ganelon's wife and son in the event of his death on the mission to Marsile. In Oxford, then, these indications that the twelve peers and Charlemagne did not respect or value Ganelon seem to have caused him to make his formal declaration against them.

Ganelon's comparatively unwarranted declaration of hostility in Châteauroux 21 represents the version's first deviation from following the order of laisses as it appears in Oxford, and this deviation was deliberate, since the content of Oxford 21 through 23 is not omitted from Châteauroux but rather included after the content of Oxford 24. In this way, Châteauroux polarizes its portrayals of Roland and of Ganelon: Roland is made to appear more respectful and reasonable than in Oxford, while Ganelon is made to appear gratuitously hostile, to the point of paranoia.

Roland does not even respond to Ganelon's initial outburst in laisse 21, which is immediately followed by laisse 22, unique to Châteauroux and Venice 7 (cited above), in which Charlemagne insults and threatens Ganelon while Roland remains silent. In laisse 23, Ganelon demands that Charlemagne protect his wife and son, as in Oxford laisse 23, but Ganelon's customary references to Roland's excessive pride in Châteauroux laisse 23 make his entire discourse seem somewhat deranged in the altered context provided by Roland's milder demeanor. This is a significant point, since Ganelon's request that his feudal lord care for his widow is otherwise a moment in which the audience might feel sympathy for Ganelon and surprise at Charlemagne's callous response (especially since Ganelon's wife is Charlemagne's own sister); Châteauroux 23 is transmitting faithfully the content of Oxford laisse 23, but the changed context provided by Châteauroux 21 and 22 lends a new "strangeness" to these familiar words. In Châteauroux 24, Roland does finally respond to Ganelon's threats, but apparently only because Ganelon addresses him directly, rather than talking about him in the third person before the entire council. Most of Ganelon's discourse to Roland here consists of lines unique to Châteauroux, interpolated into the same threatening speech Ganelon made in Oxford laisse 20. These new lines are interesting in that they summarize some of the faults that modern critics have ascribed to the Roland of Oxford. Ganelon claims that Roland, overconfident in his own military prowess, made excessive demands on the warriors fighting alongside him; moreover, Ganelon describes Roland's attitude (*corage*) as excessive (*desmesurez*), a specific accusation that has also been a recurring point of contention in modern Roland criticism.[15] These accusations, which some modern critics have believed to be well founded in the Oxford *Roland*, seem to appear in this passage from Châteauroux for the express purpose of being discredited. We have seen no evidence of these traits in Roland's character so far in Châteauroux, and Roland's calm response to these accusations only confirms the established impression in this scene that Ganelon's words have no validity whatsoever. As in Oxford 20, Roland announces in Châteauroux 24 that he is willing to take Ganelon's place on the mission to Marsile, but whereas Roland began that statement in Oxford with the scornful and provocative remark, "I hear pride and folly" (Oxford v. 292), in Châteauroux Roland expresses a more neutral, factual disagreement with the content of Ganelon's speech: "What you say is false" [Vos dites fausetez] (v. 411). The Roland of Châteauroux also emphasizes the value he places on self-control (or *mesure*) when he adds in another phrase unique to Châteauroux, "No wise man should lose control" [Nus sages hom ne doit estre esgarez] (v. 414). This remark, in turn, creates a logical immediate context for Roland's laugh in response to Ganelon's further threats in Châteauroux 25. Whereas Roland's laugh in Oxford 21 has struck many readers as scornful and provocative, in Châteauroux 25, following repeated suggestions that Ganelon has lost control of himself, the laugh seems more indicative of Roland's incredulity at Ganelon's deranged state.

The audience has no further evidence of Roland's attitude toward Ganelon, however, because in laisse 26 Ganelon resumes his direct dialogue with Charlemagne, and Châteauroux provides renewed evidence of the emperor's own discursive excesses. Laisse 27 is another passage unique to Châteauroux and Venice 7, in which Charlemagne dictates orally an extremely provocative message for Ganelon to bring to Marsile. After restating the terms of their agreement, Charlemagne adds that Marsile will govern half of Spain, with Roland ruling the other half. Then Charlemagne describes in the most offensive terms what he plans to do to Marsile if he does not live up to his side of the agreement: not only will he return with his army to conquer Saragossa, but he will also execute Marsile in a shameful way (in Châteauroux by burning him at the stake, in Venice 7 by bringing him back to Paris as a prisoner and beheading him there). This message conflicts with the kind of diplomacy represented by the proposed terms of the peace agreement, which is characterized by a combination of Christian mercy and mutual respect. Delivering this message in person would also be dangerous, since its recipient is an enemy king who has already killed messengers from Charlemagne in the past; Ganelon's fearful response shows that he immediately recognizes this danger to himself (vv. 456–59).

What is most interesting about this startling and dangerous speech from Charlemagne, for the purposes of this study, is that it represents another facet of Châteauroux's simultaneously conservative and radical approach to rewriting. This laisse could be seen as conservative in the sense that it existed in Oxford and Venice 4, but only as hearsay: in those versions, Ganelon tells Marsile that Charlemagne dictated this outrageous message to him, but in fact the earlier texts did not show the scene of dictation and implied that Ganelon invented the whole speech himself. Not only would the strong language of this message be uncharacteristic of Charlemagne as he is portrayed in the council scenes of Oxford and Venice 4, but the discrepancy between this oral message and Charlemagne's relatively respectful written letter to Marsile is what arouses the suspicion of Marsile's son against Ganelon in these other versions. As this scene unfolds in the Oxford version, Ganelon first delivers the oral message, which elicits a violent response from Marsile himself (laisses 33–34); it is only after Marsile reads aloud Charlemagne's far milder letter, however, that Marsile's son threatens to kill Ganelon, saying, "Guenes ad dit folie; / Tant ad errét nen est dreiz que plus vivet'" [Ganelon has said an outrageous thing; / He has gone so far that it is not right that he live any longer] (vv. 496–97). What so offends Marsile's son here is not so much the disrespectful oral message as the fact that Ganelon appears to have invented it himself, against Charlemagne's wishes. Furthermore, this case of Ganelon's invented false discourse is not unique in Oxford: as I discussed in the last chapter, he also tells an untrue story when he returns to Charlemagne, about the mass drowning of the Caliph and his followers who did not wish to convert to Christianity (Oxford laisse 54). Thus the theory that Ganelon's oral message from Charlemagne to Marsile in the Oxford version was supposed to be of his own invention would be more consistent with the overall approach to character discourse in Oxford (stressing Ganelon's penchant for deceitful narratives) than would be the theory that Charlemagne himself dictated the message to Ganelon in a scene not recounted by the Oxford narrator. It is possible, as has been suggested, that the Châteauroux author meant to fill in an obvious gap in the assonanced versions by adding this laisse in which Charlemagne does dictate the oral message that Ganelon later delivers to Marsile.[16] Again, however, the overall approach to character discourse in the council scenes of Châteauroux suggests otherwise: laisse 27 is only one of three passages unique to Châteauroux (and Venice 7) that feature within a short space of narrative time (laisses 22, 27, 28) a series of unusually harsh speeches by Charlemagne that all share the characteristic of condemning Ganelon for a crime he has not yet committed and of making his mission to Marsile all but impossible, even if Ganelon did have the intention of carrying it out faithfully. Thus the apparently innocent correction to the assonanced versions that laisse 27 could represent is more likely to have been a deliberate example of commentary on the part of the

Châteauroux author, a commentary implying that Charlemagne was guilty of the same crime as Ganelon: the nomination of a fellow countryman for a mission that he himself sabotaged from the start, motivated by a homicidal hatred and punctuated by outrageous discourse.

Laisses 28 and 29 of Châteauroux also do not appear in any form in Oxford or Venice 4, and they continue the trends already set in motion by both laisses 22 and 27. Here Ganelon first makes a bitter speech against Roland to which Roland does not respond; instead, it is Charlemagne who silences Ganelon (vv. 463–69). Charlemagne then gives Ganelon the bow signifying his official status as Charlemagne's messenger and addresses God, in a speech in which he explicitly states that he believes Ganelon will betray them to Marsile, with the most dire consequences imaginable: "car Guenelons est mult de mal pensé. / De felonie lo voi mot escaufé. / Li rois Marsille, se il lo sert a gré, / vers traïtor a tot son cors torné. / Toz nus vendra por sa grant cruauté; / terre de France hui chea en grant vilté." [For Ganelon is having very evil thoughts; / I see him very much warming to a crime. / King Marsile, if he serves him as he wishes, / Has turned his whole self toward treachery; / He will sell us all out of his great cruelty; / The land of France is now falling into great debasement.] (vv. 476–81). The fact that Charlemagne is simultaneously granting Ganelon formal responsibility for this mission and stating unequivocally that he believes Ganelon will use the mission for the purpose of betraying the entire nation once again makes Charlemagne himself appear to be guilty of great foolishness, if not some sort of complicity. It is interesting that he tells Ganelon to be quiet about his resentment against Roland and then addresses God himself: it is unclear whether this speech is audible to the other people present in this scene, who might therefore remain unaware of the degree of certainty Charlemagne is expressing here about his suspicion of Ganelon. In the following laisse (29), also unique to Châteauroux (and Venice 7), Ganelon addresses a speech to God asking for divine support for his revenge against Roland, and it is also unclear here whether his speech is meant to be audible to others. This series of scenes thereby emphasizes that Charlemagne and Ganelon are the deadly enemies pitted against one other here, and the prayers of the two enemies in these last two laisses suggest that the outcome of the battle will represent God's favor for Charlemagne rather than Ganelon.[17] Roland, having done very little to bring Ganelon's wrath upon himself in this version, merely becomes the scapegoat for Ganelon's resentment against Charlemagne and the instrument for God's redemption of France.

"Mes corage ne cange": Roland's Normative Discourse in the Battle Scenes

In the section of Châteauroux devoted to the Battle of Roncevaux, Roland fully realizes his function as the instrument of God's will, and this heroic role also reverses his passivity and silence in relation to the human characters around him. Roland's discourse during the council scenes of Châteauroux was relatively sparse and mild, but during the battle scenes Roland's frequent speeches set the tone for the discourse of all the other members of the rear guard, with the notable exception of Olivier. In the first section, Charlemagne and Ganelon serve as one another's primary discursive opponents: Ganelon insults and criticizes Roland in his council speeches, but it is Charlemagne who most often provides the direct response to the traitor's bitter vitriol. During the battle scenes, the primary verbal opponents become Roland and Olivier, with the rest of the rear guard not only supporting but also audibly echoing Roland's discourse. Thus Olivier's discourse, to which many modern readers of the Oxford *Roland* are quite sympathetic, is systematically weakened and marginalized by the altered context provided for it in Châteauroux. Olivier is not represented as a villain like Ganelon, but he does occupy a comparable discursive position in relation to the patterns set during the council scenes: his primary function is that of resisting Roland's stated viewpoints, in comparison to the strikingly univocal and compliant statements made by the other members of the rear guard. Since the battle scenes in Châteauroux continue the trend of the first section toward unambiguous validation of Roland, Olivier's role as the lone dissenter becomes particularly unattractive, so much so that Châteauroux eventually devotes a new episode in the final section of the text to the posthumous rehabilitation of Olivier's attitude.

Roland's discursive leadership in this section of the text begins with his public accusation against Ganelon in laisse 66, a bold speech in Châteauroux and Venice 7 that is lacking from every other contemporary Roncevaux text that has survived.[18] If Charlemagne's prediction of Ganelon's betrayal in laisse 28 was inaudible to others, then Roland is not only breaking with the rest of previous recorded Roncevaux literary tradition but also breaking a previous public silence within the Châteauroux version when he formally and publicly informs Charlemagne, before his own departure with the rear guard, that he believes that Ganelon plotted with Marsile to betray the twelve peers (vv. 1095–1103).

This explicit public accusation against Ganelon eliminates two potential criticisms of Roland that have been expressed by modern critics: first, that Roland was too foolish or prideful to believe that Ganelon betrayed him or that he could be defeated by such a plot, and second, that Roland did suspect the betrayal but kept silent about it because public knowledge of Ganelon's guilt would shame Roland's family. It should also be noted here that Roland expresses this belief in Ganelon's guilt without indulging in the harsh insults he directed at Ganelon in laisse 60 of the Oxford *Roland*. That laisse is one of only four out of the first one hundred laisses of Oxford whose content is omitted entirely from Châteauroux. Thus there is an essential continuity between Roland's unusual silence in the council scenes and the series of unusual speeches that he makes at the beginning of this section of the text devoted to the Battle of Roncevaux: Roland begins to express his views more vocally here, but he does so without indulging in excessive pride or malice.

Roland's public accusation against Ganelon makes for a more sympathetic portrayal of Roland, as has been the case for Roland's portrayal in all the scenes of Châteauroux thus far, and it also serves to intensify the audience's impression of Charlemagne's guilt for not doing anything to thwart the now officially alleged betrayal plot. Indeed, the change wrought in public opinion by Roland's accusation becomes evident immediately, when a traditional speech by Naime changes its opening focus from Roland's state of extreme anger (as in Oxford laisse 62) to Naime's belief in Ganelon's guilt: "Droiz emperere, entendez mon talant: / ne creez pas consel de soduiant! / Por cel apostre qi qerent peneant, / tot sunt traïz par lo men esciant. / Asez öez qe Guenes va disant: / il est mot fel, crüel et soduiant." [Just emperor, hear my feeling: / Do not believe the advice of a traitor. / By that apostle whom penitents seek, / They are all betrayed, by my way of thinking. / You hear what Ganelon has been saying: / He is very evil, cruel, and treacherous.] (vv. 1110–15). Not only does this speech provide proof that Roland's public accusation has convinced others of Ganelon's guilt; it is also an ironic echo of the speeches by Roland, Ganelon, and Naime at the beginning of the first council scene. When Naime says, "Droiz enperere . . . Ne creez pas consel de soduiant," this formulation brings to mind both Roland's "Ja mar cresrez qe Marsille vos die" (v. 237) and Ganelon's "Droiz enperere, jamay cresrez bricon" (v. 261). It is not for nothing that Naime mentions penitent pilgrims in his oath, for his reference to the earlier speeches by Roland and Ganelon represents an implicit acknowledgment that Naime chose the wrong position earlier when he supported Ganelon at the council and that now he wants to redeem himself by offering better advice. Furthermore, Naime's emphasis here on Ganelon's discourse as reliable evidence of his character and conduct shows that he is now convinced of Roland's view of the direct relationship between words, actions, and character. In Naime's earlier speech before the council, by contrast, he had stated that it would be "a great wrong" [granz torz] (v. 282) for Charlemagne not to accept Marsile's verbal promise of peace, in spite of Marsile's known character flaws.

Yet although Naime's explicit recognition of Ganelon's betrayal does represent a major change to his speech as it appears in Oxford, the actual advice that he offers remains unchanged: Roland should be given the command of the rear guard, but he should also be given a great deal of help. Why does Naime not advise Charlemagne to keep the entire army behind, or in some other way to prevent the rear guard from being defeated through treachery? The most likely reason is that such advice would violate the most basic requirement of the Roncevaux *matiere*: the Battle of Roncevaux must be fought in every Roncevaux text, and its basic nature could not be entirely transformed from a scene of great loss to a scene of unambiguous triumph. As I will show in my analysis of the scenes following the Battle of Roncevaux, the redactor of Châteauroux understood very well the importance of the grief of Charlemagne and Aude for the meaning of the Roncevaux story as a whole: that this was never a narrative about absolute defeat or victory may have been one of its very reasons for being. For the moment, however, we can derive from the immediate context another answer to the question of why the rear guard was still left behind even when Ganelon's betrayal was considered an established fact: Roland would not allow it to be otherwise.

In every surviving redaction of this scene, Charlemagne attempts to make the rear guard a stronger force than Roland would wish, and the fact that the emperor seeks to strengthen the rear guard in a different way every time further emphasizes Roland's consistent and absolute determination to select the rear guard according to his own criteria. In the Oxford version, Charlemagne offers Roland half of his army for the rear guard (v. 785); in Venice 4, Charlemagne offers his entire army ("Tuta mia host eo ve met in presant," v. 715). In Châteauroux, Charlemagne phrases it differently, offering "tot le meus alosé" [the very most praiseworthy] of his men (v. 1130). Roland's response also varies and becomes the most clear in its formulation in Châteauroux. In Oxford, Roland specifically mentions the figure of twenty thousand as the appropriate force to be included in the rear guard, and we see that men volunteer for the mission rather than being recruited in any active way. In Venice 4, Roland again asks for twenty thousand men, and then he arms himself and rides up on a hill on his great warhorse. Once Roland has struck this dramatic pose, the narrator explains, "Or vederà chi l'amarà o non. / Dist li François: 'E nu vos seguiron!'" [Now he will see who loves him and who does not. / The Franks say: "And we will follow you!"] (vv. 729–30). Twenty thousand men then offer themselves as volunteers for the rear guard. In Châteauroux and Venice 7, what was an explanatory note from the narrator in Venice 4 becomes Roland's explicitly stated intention. After riding up on the hill, fully armed: "A aute voiz li cons s'est escrïez: / 'Or verai je qi sera mes privez.' / Dïent Franzois, de cui il est amez, / qe par aus soit secoruz et gardez." [In a loud voice the count cried out: / "Now I will see who will be my friend." / The Franks by whom he is loved say / That he will be helped and preserved by them.] (vv. 1149–52). What might appear to have been a dramatic, prideful gesture in Venice 4 becomes an explicit plea for support in Châteauroux and Venice 7; whereas the whole French army appeared bedazzled by Roland's impressive appearance in Venice 4, only those men who have been faithful followers of Roland all along offer to join the rear guard in Châteauroux and Venice 7, and they do so because they know that Roland greatly needs their support, not because they expect him to lead them to victory.

In the scenes recounting the actual Battle of Roncevaux, Châteauroux's approach to rewriting remains conservative, in the sense that it operates by repeating familiar ideas far more often than by incorporating entirely new material. The most obvious example of this kind of repetition appears at the structural level, in that Châteauroux is the only surviving Roncevaux narrative in which the debate between Roland and Olivier about sounding the horn occurs twice, once in wording that follows the assonanced source (laisses 87–99) and once in wording close to what appears in other rhymed versions (laisses 117–24). In similar fashion, Châteauroux devotes "extra" laisses to its account of some scenes that were already present in Oxford in only one laisse, such as the scene in which Roland's death is presaged by ominous natural phenomena (Oxford 110, Châteauroux 151–52). As a general rule, Châteauroux tends to lengthen laisses from the battle scenes whose overall content is faithful to a specific laisse found in Oxford and/or Venice 4. The overall resemblance between these laisses from Châteauroux and from its predecessors might cause readers to overlook these interpolations in their closing lines, but my examination of these passages has revealed that they most often consist of new direct discourse by characters. Indeed, another general rule that holds true throughout the battle scenes is that Châteauroux devotes ample space to character discourse, which gives the impression that the audience is hearing characters recount their experiences in their own words. Yet the fact that the characters nearly all express the same thoughts in similar terms suggests that the motivation behind incorporating this direct discourse was not to enhance the complexity of the portrayal of individual characters but rather to use their discourse to reinforce certain ideas about how their circumstances should be interpreted. Having characters repeat multiple times something that the audience fully expects to hear in a Roncevaux text is a strategy that makes certain aspects of the Roncevaux story clearer and more memorable for the audience without attracting the audience's attention to that enhanced emphasis; the more frequent presence of an expected element of a familiar story would not attract the audience's attention in the same way that the presence of a new element would. In this way, Châteauroux assigns to character discourse the kind of explanatory, didactic function that other Old French texts of the thirteenth century more often assigned to the primary narrator. Because the discourse of other characters tends to repeat Roland's discourse, the ultimate source of the characters' collective wisdom in these scenes appears to be Roland himself.

The innovative structure of the horn debates in Châteauroux multiplies the opportunities for characters to verbalize their interpretation of their circumstances before the battle, not only because the debates themselves occupy twice as much space as in other versions but also because the textual space between the two horn debates is filled with other speeches by various members of the rear guard. The horn debate is first told in a way that follows closely the structure and even the specific wording found in the Oxford version (Châteauroux laisses 87–99; Oxford laisses 79–91), Olivier pointing out the presence of the Saracens to Roland and Roland refusing to sound the horn and summon Charlemagne to return. Then, after hearing mass in laisse 103, Roland goes up on a hilltop alone in laisse 104 and prays to God to support his revenge against Ganelon. In laisse 105, Roland addresses a speech to the rear guard predicting their deaths in the battle in accordance with God's will, but this is for all practical purposes a soliloquy, since it is only in laisse 106 that he actually returns to the rear guard and orders them more confidently to arm themselves. The fact that there are no witnesses within the fiction to Roland's speech on the hill is significant for at least two reasons. First, it suggests that this speech was meant for the ears of the audience, building a complicity between Roland and the audience from which the other members of the rear guard are excluded. Second, the lack of witnesses within the fiction was almost a necessity, since the content of this speech conflicts in certain ways with what Roland says to the rear guard in laisse 106 and what he says in both horn debates with Olivier.

In fact, Roland's soliloquy on the hill in laisse 105 includes some statements typical of Olivier's prebattle discourse, against which Roland has just protested in laisses 87 through 99: Roland predicts the most terrible battle in history and blames it on Ganelon's betrayal (vv. 1626–30). This speech is also marked by thoughts that Roland himself expresses in the Oxford version later in the battle, just before sounding the horn, those that critics have cited as evidence of his change of heart after seeing his closest friends killed: "Franc, dist Rollant, bone gent honoree, / sor totes autres cremue et redotee, / com vos voi de seignor esgaree! / Vendu i somes par male destinee! / La traïson ne puet estre celee." ["Franks," Roland said, "good and honored people, / Above all others feared and respected, / How I see you bereft of a lord! / We were sold here by an evil fate. / The betrayal cannot be concealed."] (vv. 1623–27). It is somewhat surprising to hear Roland express such pessimism about France as a whole before the battle even begins, and his mention of the nation's lack of a lord to lead them also has a different ring when removed from its former context. In the Oxford version, Roland expresses similar thoughts, but with significant differences, in the following lines that he utters just before deciding to sound the horn quite late in the battle: "Tanz bons vassals vëez gesir par terre! / Pleindre poüms France dulce, la bele, / De tels barons cum or remeint deserte! / E! reis, amis, que vos ici nen estes!" [You see so many good vassals lying on the ground! / We can pity beautiful, sweet France, / which will now remain bereft of such noble men! / Oh! king, friend, [how terrible it is] that you are not here!] (Oxford vv. 1694–97). The general sentiment is the same, but the passage in Châteauroux both anticipates the deaths of the rear guard before they occur and describes the problem of France as that of lacking the leadership of a singular "lord," which makes these lines an accusation against Charlemagne. The problem is not that Charlemagne is absent from the battlefield at this moment, which is what the Roland of the Oxford version seems to see as the problem, since he acts immediately to rectify it by sounding the horn; instead, the Roland of Châteauroux is suggesting a more systematic leadership vacuum that will somehow be remedied by proceeding with a battle between the rear guard and Marsile's larger force. In his subsequent public speeches, Roland never voices to others this reproach against Charlemagne, but the author of Châteauroux clearly believed that it was important for the audience to understand this as a significant component of Roland's own decision to proceed with the battle. The last line of this speech confirms that Roland intends to kill as many Saracens as he can, in spite of the likelihood that the rear guard will ultimately lose the battle, because by doing so he will restore the reputation of France that Charlemagne's peace agreement with Marsile has put at risk. Having prayed that God will allow him to bloody his sword thoroughly before he dies, Roland concludes: "Aprés ma mort en ert France doutee" [After my death, France will be feared because of this] (v. 1638).

Roland's attitude of self-sacrifice for the good of France during a time of poor leadership could be seen as a product of his own arrogance: since Charlemagne did not follow Roland's advice not to accept the peace agreement, Roland is taking matters into his own hands. The rest of the battle scenes do not support this reading, however, because they repeatedly emphasize that Roland made the right decision for the right reasons, though not the reasons he articulated in his debates with Olivier. The fact that the other twelve peers (except Olivier) immediately support Roland's position by echoing his earlier rhetoric takes on a certain poignancy in light of the more controversial aspects of Roland's private discourse in laisse 105. Roland does not contradict himself, but he certainly does mask his privately stated view that France is "lacking a lord" when he announces to the rear guard that they can expect to hear him shouting Charlemagne's battle cry throughout the coming battle. The narrator then adds, "Li cons Rollant ot le cuer mot loia; / desoz son eume a regar de vasal" [Count Roland had a very loyal heart; / beneath his helmet he had the look of a vassal] (vv. 1650–51). As always with this text's portrayal of Roland, then, he is being validated here at Charlemagne's expense: we come away from this pair of laisses with the conclusion that Roland is steadfastly loyal to a lord who does not deserve that loyalty. Roland is sacrificing himself and the rear guard in this battle because Charlemagne has made the wrong official policy for France; what is more, Roland is doing so in Charlemagne's name and for his glory.

Laisses 107 through 117 show each of the twelve peers arming himself, with several of them verbalizing their thoughts as they prepare for battle. Olivier remains mostly silent during this section (though his physical presence is frequently mentioned), perhaps because the author believed that the audience had already heard enough about Olivier's feelings and wanted to show that his was the minority opinion. Although the other warriors show signs of pessimism about the possible outcome of the battle, their words are characterized by three common themes: they encourage each other to prepare quickly for the battle and to fight without retreating; they pray for their souls to be received into heaven if they are killed, and they seem to believe that this will be the case; and they think and speak about their common conviction that this battle is the result of Ganelon's betrayal. These individual speeches by members of the rear guard could have provided an opportunity to show either dissent or ill-considered overconfidence among them, but instead their words prove that they all share Roland's attitude of determination and resignation and that, unlike Olivier, none of them believes that Roland is wrong to lead them into the battle without calling for reinforcements. Laisses 117 through 124 then offer another debate between Olivier and Roland about sounding the horn, this time with wording that is farther removed from the wording of Oxford. This section could be considered the "rhymed *Roland* horn debate," since it is the only account of the horn debate that appears in Venice 7; a similarly worded debate also appears in the Paris version.[19] The fact that this second horn debate does not re-peat the same wording as the first one from laisses 88 through 100 sug-gests that this structural doubling was deliberate, not a case of inadvertent textual corruption. As usual in Châteauroux, such a choice represents an approach to rewriting that reinforces certain ideas through the repe-tition of familiar character discourse already present in available source texts rather than composing new material that might attract undue at-tention to itself. It is probably for this reason that Châteauroux re-counted first the horn debate much as it had appeared in its source in assonance: this version contained the traditional wording that audi-ences expected to hear. Minor changes to this first version, however, already reveal the interpretation favored by the Châteauroux redactor throughout the battle scenes: that Roland did not act to prevent the battle because he understood it to be the manifestation of God's will, not because of rashness or any selfish motivation.

The first such change occurs in laisse 87, in which Châteauroux omits a single line from a series of thirty lines otherwise drawn directly from a source in assonance. Roland's first response to Olivier's announcement that the Saracens are about to attack reads as follows in Oxford: "Res-pont Rollant: 'E Deus la nus otreit! / Ben devuns ci estre pur nostre rei: / Pur sun seignor deit hom susfrir destreiz / E endurer granz chalz e granz freiz'" [Roland responds: "And may God grant it [battle] to us! / We must remain here for our king: / For his lord a man must suffer hardship / And endure great heat and great cold"] (vv. 1008–11). The same passage in Châteauroux omits the line saying that they are fighting for their king, giving the word *lord* a meaning that could be either reli-gious or feudal: "Respont Rollant: 'Deus nos en soit amis! / Por son seignor doit hon estre penis / et endurer grant calt et grant fris'" [Roland responds: "May God be our friend in this! / For his lord a man must suffer, / and endure great heat and great cold"] (vv. 1383–85). Similarly, Châteauroux adds another single line of religious discourse from Roland in the middle of a thirty-five-line passage that otherwise corresponds almost exactly to its assonanced source (as in Oxford, vv. 1023–58). Although in the passage as a whole Roland is offering his usual arguments about guarding the honor of his family and France, this interpolation stresses that he could not undertake the battle without God's help: "Ce dist Rollant: 'Deus li granz nus aiuz!'" [Roland says this: "May the mighty God help us!"] (v. 1421). In laisse 92, as well, Châteauroux makes only one change to the text as it appears in Oxford, and it is a change that replaces the idea of feudal service with the idea of God's sovereign will. In Oxford, the line reads, "Franceis sunt bon, si ferrunt vassalment" [The Franks are good, they will strike as vassals] (v. 1080); in Châteauroux, the line reads, "François feront, se Deu plait, ensemant" [The Franks will strike, if it please God, in the same way [as I]] (v. 1442). A final two-line change is worth noting in this first version of the horn debate, for it seems to announce, somewhat ironically, Châteauroux's approach to rewriting. In Oxford laisse 86, Olivier points out the small size of the rear guard in comparison to Marsile's force, and Roland immediately retorts, "Mis talenz en engraigne!" [My desire [for battle] increases because of that!] (v. 1088). In the same passage from Châteauroux, Olivier points out the small size of the rear guard and then reiterates that Roland should therefore sound the horn to summon Charlemagne. Now that Roland's retort addresses the issue of sounding the horn, rather than the issue of the smaller rear guard, he quite appropriately says in this changed context, "Mes corage ne cange" [My attitude is not changing] (v. 1460). Thus in one of the few places in the horn debate where Châteauroux does transform the content of the assonanced version, it uses character discourse to deny the very notion of change.

The second version of the horn debate, found in Châteauroux laisses 117 through 124, does contain obvious changes to its source (as reflected by the Venice 7 and Paris versions), several of which intensify Roland's trend toward religious discourse. At the start of this sequence of laisses, most notably, Roland is mindful not only of God's will but also of Christian doctrine. Whereas in the first horn debate Roland merely evoked the names "Deu lo pere" and "Marïen, la soë douce mere" (Châteauroux vv. 1446–47), in laisse 117 he gives a narrative description of who "Deu" is: "Rollant respont: 'De folie parlez! / Ja Deu ne place, qi en crois fu penez / et el sepoucre cochez et repoussez. / Fors ad enfern fu Nostre Sire alez / por ses amis traire de dolentez. / Felon paien seront a mort tornez / qe ja li cors soit de par moi sonez!'" [Roland responds: "You are talking nonsense! / May it never please God, who suffered on the cross, / And was laid and buried in the tomb, / Out of there and to hell our Lord went / To release his friends from torment, / The evil pagans will be put to death / Before the horn is ever sounded by me."] (vv. 1878–84). This summary of Christ's death, burial, and descent to hell might seem a mere stylistic flourish without any particular significance, except that it also ends with a new formulation of Roland's attitude that suggests a prescience analogous to that of Christ during his life on earth. Rather than saying (as in the first horn debate) that he will never sound the horn under any circumstances, Roland says that he intends to kill all the attacking Saracens first, as if it had been his plan all along to wait until a more advanced stage of the battle before sounding the horn. As was the case with Roland's public accusation against Ganelon before leaving for Roncevaux, his implication here that he fully intends to sound the horn at a future moment of his own choosing tends to belie a potential interpretation of the Roncevaux story that would be unflattering to Roland: namely that Roland was mistaken for not sounding the horn the first time and that his eventual decision to do so represented a repentant change of heart. His description of Olivier's discourse as "folie" also emphasizes that Roland's own discourse has an entirely different basis: it communicates not merely his own opinion but timeless Christian doctrine. Yet it is not clear in this particular passage what the relationship is between Roland's refusal to sound the horn and Christ's descent into hell: in fact, one might say that, by leading the rear guard into a hopeless battle, Roland is actually dragging his friends with him into torment at this moment rather than releasing them from it. In a later passage, however, the narrator returns to the same description of Jesus in a prayer for Roland, when the wounded Roland faints while praying over the dead bodies of the rear guard: "Jesu li soit aidis, / qe fors d'enfer a jeté ses amis!" [May Jesus help him, / who threw his friends out of hell!] (vv. 3995–96). In this later passage, as in laisse 117, Roland is associated with Jesus's descent into hell in order to save his friends, at the very moment in which he is praying for his own friends to be kept out of hell and instead sent to heaven. This second reference to the descent into hell therefore appears as the logical realization of the first reference: before the battle, it was not at all clear how Roland's behavior was beneficial to his friends fighting alongside him, but Roland's attention to their souls after their deaths (not only in this prayer but in his accompanying act of dragging their bodies over to Turpin to be blessed one last time) is a much more appropriate setting in which to evoke this parallel with Christ's descent to hell. The fact that it is the narrator who does so suggests a retrospective affirmation of Roland's course of action by the voice of the text itself: the horn debates are traditionally a place in which Roland's position is put to the test, but through later statements such as this one from the narrator the Châteauroux version ensures that the audience understands that Roland's position has been the right one all along.

The rewritten versions of the horn debates make Roland's discourse more religious and imply that Roland's refusal to sound the horn was part of a planned strategy, but at the same time neither version of the horn debate in Châteauroux changes the substance of the arguments offered by Olivier and Roland. Olivier still emphasizes the concrete reality that a larger force is about to attack them and the logical conclusion that this attack is part of a betrayal plot devised by Ganelon. Roland, more surprisingly in light of his less prideful characterization during the rewritten council scenes, still emphasizes that it would be shameful to him, to his family, and to France to sound the horn; this version even maintains the traditional lines in which Roland reproaches Olivier for accusing his stepfather of treachery (Oxford vv. 1026–27; Châteauroux vv. 1400–1401), even though Roland himself has already made the same accusation in a more public forum. Perhaps, then, the audience is supposed to be puzzled by the discrepancies between the less prideful Roland that Châteauroux revealed to us in the council scene, the self-centered discourse Roland utters in the customary horn debate, and the new religious references that have entered into the horn debates in their articulation here. One way to resolve these discrepancies in Roland's discourse would be to consider that in the horn debates he is offering a series of arguments that he believes will make sense to Olivier, rather than stating his real motivation for continuing with the battle, which is that he believes that the battle represents God's will for himself and for Christendom. According to this interpretation, the stakes of the conflict between Roland and Olivier would be, not the apparent issues of appropriate military strategy or honorable versus dishonorable conduct, but rather the issue of whether the rear guard as a whole will resist or accept God's will for them. That Roland's refusal to sound the horn represents his resignation to God's will (or to his fate, as some prefer to put it) is an interpretation that has been articulated for the Roland of the Oxford version by some commentators, but it has always met with resistance from others who quite rightly stress Roland's self-centered logic in the horn debate and elsewhere in the text. The interpretation of a Roland resigned to God's will makes more sense in the context of Roland's overall portrayal in Châteauroux: once the audience has come to know the humble Roland of the council scenes and the analytical Roland of the soliloquy on the hill, it becomes easy for them to believe that Roland's discourse about his honor in the horn debate is insincere, a smokescreen hiding his real motivation to martyr himself for God.

As I have shown, preparation for this interpretation of the Battle of Roncevaux as Roland's voluntary martyrdom began with Roland's behavior throughout the council scenes in Châteauroux, culminating in the moment when an anguished Charlemagne hands Roland an official symbolic token of his responsibility for the rear guard: "Li rois li done, irez et corozant; / li cons la prent, dou cuer liez et joiant." [The king gives it to him, upset and angry. The count takes it, with a happy and joyous heart.] (vv. 1122–23). Since Roland has just predicted Ganelon's deadly betrayal of the rear guard about thirty lines earlier, his happiness here is not a sign of his overconfidence but rather a sign that he believes that there will be a greater reward to this mission than success or victory as measured in worldly terms. Roland's beliefs and motives concerning the battle to come are further clarified in his soliloquy on the hill in laisse 105. Although the horn debates leave some room for doubt about Roland's position, subsequent scenes cast far greater suspicion on Olivier's views. This is true not only because the text as a whole consistently validates Roland, as does the discourse of the other members of the rear guard, but also because Olivier's discourse becomes increasingly negative and worldly as the battle progresses and the religious tone of all the other characters (including the primary narrator) intensifies. As was also the case in the Oxford version, Roland and Olivier have several conversations during the course of the Battle of Roncevaux in Châteauroux, most of them directly related to the action of combat and then one further debate about sounding the horn, once Roland decides to do so. But Châteauroux also adds two new conversations between Roland and Olivier whose only apparent purpose is to strengthen the impression that Roland's attitude is right, since it is motivated by spiritual concerns, and that Olivier's attitude is wrong because he has no spiritual sensibility and continues to see Charlemagne's return as the only possible solution to a physical, tactical problem.

In laisse 164, found only in Châteauroux, Venice 7, and Paris, Roland and Olivier see several members of the rear guard killed, and then Olivier exclaims that they are gaining nothing and losing everything in this battle, since they are all going to die that day: "Dist Oliver: "Ci a male gaaigne! / Encui ferons dolerouse bargaigne; / tuit i morons sanz nulle recovreigne.'" [Oliver said: "This is a bad harvest; / Today we are making a grievous deal; / We will all die with no chance of recovery."][20] In the following laisse, Roland's restatement of the same idea in more religious language elicits a scornful response from Olivier: "'Deus,' dist Rollant, 'qi sofris pasion, / mot m'a fait Guene doloros guiredon! / Vendu nos a par male traïson. / E Charlle, sire, com grant perdicion / recevras hui del meus de ta maison.' / Dist Olivers: 'Laissez vostre sermon, / car n'en donroie vaillant un esperon!'" ["God," said Roland, "who suffered the passion, / Ganelon has given me a grievous recompense! / He has sold us through evil treachery. / And Charles, my lord, what a great loss / you will receive today from the best of your house." / Olivier said: "Leave off from your sermon, / For I would not give as much as a spur for it."] (vv. 2684–90).

The fact that Olivier calls Roland's speech a "sermon" suggests that it has not escaped him that Roland's allusion to the crucifixion of Christ (which was set in motion by the betrayal of Judas) is immediately followed by its parallel within the fiction, Ganelon's betrayal of the rear guard and their resulting deaths. Perhaps what Olivier is rejecting here is the very notion of such a parallel in the context of a bloody battle that he saw as preventable. Roland's own response is predictably mild: rather than taking offense at Olivier's rebuke, Roland worries that he is losing his friend, in which case he would consider his life worthless (vv. 2694–95). In the conversation where Roland proposes sounding the horn to summon Charlemagne as it appears in Châteauroux, Roland therefore makes a more concerted attempt to convince Olivier to give his consent to the sounding of the horn, most notably when he substitutes "Ge cornerai, se vos bien le volez" [I will sound the horn, if you are truly willing] (v. 2989) for "Jo cornerai, si l'orrat li reis Karles" [I will sound the horn, so that King Charles will hear it] (Oxford v. 1714), and also when he flatters Olivier for his wisdom while asking for his opinion about what to do. Yet Roland also says in this scene that Olivier is wrong ("merveillos tort avez!" v. 2985), a forthright statement lacking from the account in Oxford.

These conversations create a shift in the audience's perception of the dispute between Roland and Olivier. The Oxford version is careful to say that Olivier is a great warrior and that his reasoning is sound, most famously in the lines "Rollant est proz e Oliver est sage; / Ambedui unt merveillus vasselage" [Roland is brave and Oliver is wise; / Both are marvelous vassals] (vv. 1093–94), which Châteauroux dutifully cites twice (vv. 1465 and 1939). Yet the two later conversations encourage the audience to see Roland as the more sympathetic and conciliatory of the two men, eventually incorporating the idea that Olivier is wrong into the otherwise faithful rendering of the traditional debate in which Roland decides to sound the horn. In a laisse not found in Oxford, it is the narrator who later says outright that Roland is teaching Olivier a valuable lesson, and that lesson turns out to be the very idea of their deaths being inevitable and for a good cause: "Li cons Rollant a Oliver mostree; / une raison li a dite et enseignee: / "Ensanble Frans devon morir, beau frere, / por lor amor, en estraige contree" [Count Roland taught Olivier, / A speech he said and taught to him: / "Together with the Franks we must die, my brother, / For love of them, in a foreign land"] (vv. 3235–38). One can readily imagine the Roland of the Oxford version saying the same thing, but what is interesting about this passage is the narrator's assertion that this is a lesson that Olivier needs to learn from Roland. At this point the relationship of equality between the two men that is present in most Roncevaux narratives has shifted, with Roland being the wiser of the two and Olivier still struggling to understand the transcendent meaning of the battle in which he is about to die. Again, as with the narrator's prayer for Roland, the fact that this explicit endorsement of Roland is uttered by the primary narrator gives it enhanced weight because of the narrator's retrospective omniscience and the narrator's role as the implicit voice of the text itself.

As we have seen, the section of Châteauroux devoted to the Battle of Roncevaux features more religious discourse than does the Oxford version, and it often connects that religious discourse to its changed portrayal of Roland. Yet it is as interesting to note what remains the same between the account in Châteauroux and in its assonanced source as it is to observe what changes. Critics who accept the account in the Oxford version as normative have not emphasized the conservatism of Châteauroux's approach to rewriting because they tend to view the unchanged elements as accurate and the changed elements as errors or at least imperfections introduced into that normative model. It is possible to consider Châteauroux's rewriting strategy quite differently, however, if one takes into account that Châteauroux deliberately set out to offer a new witness of the Roncevaux *matiere* by combining material from assonanced and rhymed source texts, rather than attempting without success to copy an assonanced source. Another important factor to consider is Châteauroux's rejection of the legitimate possibility of composing a new Roncevaux narrative from start to finish without using any specific source whatsoever, a possibility that we will see realized in both *Ronsasvals* and *Galïen restoré*, the subjects of the following chapters of this study. In light of these last two considerations, we can understand the religious emphasis of Châteauroux as more than a general "tone" and less than a complete overhaul of the previous textual tradition. The conservative rewriting strategy of Châteauroux implicitly but consistently emphasizes that the changes it makes to its assonanced source are not really changes at all but rather interpretative choices that were always available in assonanced versions such as Oxford. Thus there is both a subtlety and an ostentatious virtuosity in Châteauroux's approach to rewriting, in that it transforms the audience's perception of Roland's personality and motivation by making consistent changes to its assonanced source that are extremely limited in scope. This approach to rewriting is a form of literary reception because its primary aim is to choose a consistent interpretation of previous Roncevaux texts rather than to offer an entirely new interpretation or compositional strategy. The very fact that this author/reader's response to the preexisting Roncevaux textual tradition took this form provides further evidence of the indeterminacy of the Oxford *Roland*, and perhaps of earlier rhymed texts as well, since it seems to have been this redactor's primary goal to reduce the number of possible interpretations of Roland that were offered to the audience in other versions.

I believe that the author of Châteauroux also aimed his "reader response" at both assonanced and rhymed source texts because he had something to say about the Roncevaux *matiere* as a whole and about written vernacular literature in general. This metaliterary message emerges most clearly in the episodes of mourning at Roncevaux and of Aude's death, which, in contrast to Châteauroux's restrictive "re-production" of earlier episodes, actually expand the possible interpretations made available by these episodes in the Oxford *Roland*. Yet these new interpretative possibilities prove to be all the more convincing and troubling for the very reason that they are built upon a generally similar account of the council and battle scenes. Like the earlier sections of the text, these final episodes continue to be focused on character discourse, showing more clearly than ever that the words used to tell a story are a measure of the health and stability of both individuals and entire societies.

"Nostre chancons va toz tens amendans": Aude's Death and the Redemption of Narrative

As an introduction to the metaliterary implications of discourse in the final section of Châteauroux, it is worth noting that, toward the end of the battle, the narrator distinguishes repeatedly between this account of the Roncevaux story and the kind of text written by a *clerc* ("clerk," a term that generally refers in Old French literature to an author who received a religious education but then focused his attention on composing secular literary texts). These statements imply that the redactor of Châteauroux was not a clerk and regarded that category of author with suspicion or even contempt, a viewpoint that might help to clarify the particular character and goals of Châteauroux as a rewritten narrative. The most striking statement about clerks appears at the moment of Roland's death, when this narrator remarks that clerks would be incapable of putting into words Roland's ascent into heaven: "Il joint ses meins, l'arme s'en va cantant. / Angle enpené l'emporterent a tant; / en paradis le poserent riant / devant Jesu, ou a de joies tant. / Nel vos pot dire nus clerc, tant fust lisant." [He joins his hands, his soul goes away singing. / Winged angels carried him away then; / In paradise they set him down, laughing, / Before Jesus, where there are so many joys. / No clerk could tell it to you, no matter how much reading he did.] (vv. 4176–80). This portrayal of Roland singing and laughing as he arrives in heaven is a new interpolation in this version, and an uncharacteristic one for this generally modest reworking so far, in that it encourages the audience to see Roland differently rather than simply to hear different words emerge from his mouth. Perhaps this is one implication of the last line of the passage: that Roncevaux authors cannot find all their most important source material in other Roncevaux texts, or in any written source, and that the imagination of author and audience will always be a crucial element of telling this story of spiritual transcendence in a way that can do justice to it. Another implication may be that the Châteauroux redactor considered clerks to be generally lacking in imagination or in sensitivity to spiritual matters. A last possibility may also be worthy of consideration: this narrative voice may be disparaging private reading and/or written literary transmission, given the claim here that extensive reading does not equip one to tell a complete version of the Roncevaux story.

There is a noticeable increase in metatextual references to sources in the section of the text devoted to the end of the Battle of Roncevaux and the battle against Baligant, but they do not help very much to elucidate Châteauroux's relationship either to its sources or to the literary trends of its own time. These references suggest that Châteauroux draws upon a variety of sources: local folklore (vv. 4125–26), oral storytelling or singing (v. 4272, vv. 5032, 5042), written *gestes* (vv. 5029–30), and a storyteller or "estoire" that may or may not be "lying" (v. 5358, 5377). The Châteauroux narrator uses the term *song* several times to describe this narrative itself but does not systematically privilege oral over written transmission in commentaries about sources: the narrator's comments about "jongleurs" can be as dismissive as those about "clerks." The only thing that this narrator asserts unambiguously about this narrative in relation to others is that the audience has never heard a better or truer song than this one and that this song is getting better as it goes along: "Nostre chançons va toz tens amendans, / jamais joclere de meillor ne vos chant" [Our song continues to improve all the time, / A jongleur never sings a better one for you] (vv. 5031–32); "Humais amende por voir nostre chançons. / Puis qe Jesus suscita Lazarons— / ce trovent clerc e livre de sermons— / ne vos fu dite plus veraie chançons." [From now on, truly, our song improves. / Since Jesus raised Lazarus— / as the clerks and sermon books tell it—[21] / Never has a truer song been said before you.] (vv. 5038–41). The reference to Jesus raising Lazarus in this second quotation does provide one possible clue about the nature of the "improvement" being made in this narrative's final section: it suggests a connection between the unprecedented truth claimed for this Roncevaux narrative and the later episode in which Olivier is briefly resurrected from the dead to perform a narrative of his own for Aude. Thus the final section of this chapter will treat Olivier's speech as the conclusion toward which Châteauroux's ever-increasing metaliterary commentary is directing itself throughout the final section of the text. As is the case in the Roncevaux textual tradition as a whole, Châteauroux chooses to dramatize its most significant instances of metaliterary commentary through character discourse and action, rather than putting them into the form of explicit metatextual asides from the primary narrator.

Both modern editors of the Châteauroux version have documented that the section of the text that recounts the scenes following the battle against Baligant bears no direct (i.e., laisse-for-laisse) resemblance to the Oxford version and that there is no evidence that this section is based on any other source text in assonance. Moreover, in spite of a general resemblance among the surviving rhymed texts in the episodes following the Battle of Roncevaux,[22] Châteauroux and Venice 7 do make one unique structural adjustment to this section: they eliminate the return of Charlemagne and his army to Roncevaux after the rout of Marsile's force and before the battle against Baligant, so that there is no pause between the two battles. Most of the other versions place Charlemagne's return to Roncevaux after his defeat of Marsile to bury most of the rear guard, then the battle against Baligant, and then another return to Roncevaux for further mourning and burial rituals. One effect of the simplified structure of Châteauroux is that it emphasizes a distinction between the heroic portrayal of Charlemagne during the post-Roncevaux battles and a far more troubling portrayal of the emperor once he falls into a state of grief after his return to Roncevaux and then to France. Châteauroux (along with Venice 7) is thereby able to imply that Charlemagne is so transformed by the grief that overtakes him at Roncevaux that he becomes incapable ever afterward of the kind of valor he had to muster for his single combat against Baligant; in the versions featuring two mourning scenes at Roncevaux, on the other hand, there is an implication that Charlemagne is able to emerge from his state of grief when his duties require it.

The contrast in Châteauroux between the conquering Charlemagne of the immediate post-Roncevaux episodes and the grieving Charlemagne of the post-Baligant episodes serves to dramatize for the audience exactly what Charlemagne's problem is: it is not merely his grief but the abandonment of spiritual principles that that grief causes in him. During the battles against Marsile and Baligant, therefore, as if to underline this point deliberately, Châteauroux makes repeated references to the soundness of Charlemagne's spiritual orientation: his propensity for prayer before undertaking a battle, his gratitude to God for his victories, his knowledge of biblical narratives and of Christian doctrine, and of course his privileged communication with God by way of angelic messengers. Charlemagne's preparation for his pursuit of Marsile's retreating army (laisse 249) includes several of these elements, yet we can also note that the opening words from the angelic messenger indicating God's willingness to immobilize the sun in the sky to make that pursuit possible already include a warning about the danger of a paralyzing grief that was not present in the same scene from Oxford: "Rois, ne te dementer! / En grant duel faire ne puez ren conquister" [King, do not despair! / By grieving greatly you can conquer nothing] (vv. 4259–60).

This warning about grief is warranted because when Charlemagne returns to the battlefield at Roncevaux after defeating Baligant, the power of the grief hanging over that place overwhelms him. Laisse 329 begins with the line "Granz fu li deus, la nuit en Rencevaus" [Great was the grief, that night at Roncevaux] (v. 5888), and that line begins in both Châteauroux and Venice 7 with a large decorated initial, indicating the start of a major new section of the narrative.[23] This first line of the new section appropriately indicates its subject matter: from now on, this text becomes the story of grief and of the spiritual struggles that accompany it. As if to emphasize that point, in the space of that laisse and the next, the words *duel, dolor,* or *dolant* appear eleven times. The last usage in this run of two laisses occurs in the form of a rebuke from Otes after he sees one hundred Franks faint in sympathy with the grieving Charlemagne. Otes warns Charlemagne that the visual spectacle of the mutual grief demonstrated by the emperor and his men is evidence that Charlemagne is failing in his leadership role and that serious consequences could ensue: "Et Deus!" dist Otes, "or voi je duel d'enfant. / Pur coi t'ocis, bons rois, nos els voiant? / Ja voiz qel gent te traient a garant. / Se il te perdent, qe feront il, dolant?" ["Oh, God!" said Otes, "here I see a childish grief. / Why are you killing yourself, good king, in our sight? / You see what kind of people count on you as their protector. / If they lose you, what will they do in their grief?"] (vv. 6006–9). This reproach shows that the damaging effects of grief become evident right away to Charlemagne's advisors, and what is particularly interesting in this speech is Otes's use of the word *garant* to describe Charlemagne's ideal leadership role. This is the word that is used to describe Roland's function as leader of the rear guard at several important moments in the Battle of Roncevaux in both Châteauroux and Oxford; to find it here implies that Charlemagne's duty now is not only to carry on as emperor but also to replace Roland as the source of hope and inspiration for the men following him into a daunting situation, that of confronting the consequences of the Battle of Roncevaux. Already, then, Otes's speech suggests that the grief resulting from Roncevaux poses a threat to the well-being of French society as serious as the threat of the battle itself was.

At the same time, laisses 329 through 335 also provide evidence that God does not entirely disapprove of Charlemagne's mourning and burial rituals, because several miraculous revelations from God take place in this section of the text in direct response to Charlemagne's prayers. When Charlemagne utters a long prayer filled with biblical narratives and Christian doctrine asking that God allow him to find Roland's body (vv. 5965–85), he immediately sees the body the next time he turns his head. When Charlemagne and the Franks together utter several prayers asking that the Christian and Saracen bodies be distinguished from one another so that they can give the Christians a proper burial, God causes a hawthorn bush to grow over each Saracen body, bushes that the narrator claims are still visible to pilgrims on the road to Compostella (vv. 6079–83). This miracle (recorded in all the surviving rhymed texts, as well as the Norse version) is offered as the source of the name "Roncevaux" in the literary legend, meaning "valley of thorns."[24] Charlemagne responds to this miracle with two speeches, whose parallel function is emphasized by their presence in the same laisse, so that they are built around the same rhyme. His first reaction is to feel hope about the evidence this miracle provides that God takes care of the bodies (and souls) of Christians who have died: "'Baron,' dist Karles, 'ben devons Deu servir! / Nus ne se doit esmaier de morir'" ["Lords," said Charles, "it is right that we serve God! / No one should worry about dying"] (vv. 6091–92). But just a few lines later, he begins a new speech of despairing grief: "'A, Deus!' dist Karles, 'or devroie morir / quant teus barons voi en terre covrir'" ["Ah, God!" said Charles, "now I ought to die, / since I see such noble men buried in the ground"] (vv. 6097–98). Clearly, then, Charles is wavering between worldly and spiritual perspectives: at times he is inclined to trust in God and move forward, and at other times his grief at the very sight of the carnage paralyzes him. God's final miracle in this scene therefore appears to be meant as an encouragement to Charlemagne, one for which the emperor did not pray but one that God realizes that he needs. After Charlemagne orders Ganelon to be brought before him (threatening his men that anyone who lets Ganelon escape will eventually be executed with him), he has a sudden impulse to look toward the sky, where he sees the angels and the souls of the Christian dead rejoicing in heaven (vv. 6118–21).[25] Yet this vision of the joyful reward of the dead warriors does not succeed in changing Charlemagne's attitude. As he and his men carry the bodies of Roland and Olivier away from Roncevaux, the narrator comments that they are weeping so loudly in their grief that no one there would be able to hear a thunderclap sent from God (vv. 6134–35).

As this scene of mourning at Roncevaux ends, then, not only do we see that the grief of the Franks is continuing, but the narrator even states explicitly that because of their demonstrations of grief these men cannot hear God. In accordance with this statement, Charlemagne receives no further messages or revelations from God for the remainder of the narrative. This, then, is the turning point where Charlemagne opts for a pessimistic, worldly attitude toward the losses at Roncevaux, rather than accepting the perspective offered to him by God: that these apparent losses were really joyful self-sacrifices that the rear guard made for the benefit of France and of Christendom. As we have seen, this Christian perspective was also the one advocated consistently by Châteauroux's rewriting of the battle scenes, which prepares the audience to favor this more spiritual outlook themselves, rather than sympathizing with Charlemagne. Just as the audience usually is aware of Ganelon's betrayal long before Charlemagne or the rear guard, apparently because Charlemagne ignores warning signs of the betrayal until it is too late, here the audience is aware of the rear guard's willing sacrifice and joyful reward after the battle, but Charlemagne willfully rejects God's efforts to communicate the same interpretation of the battle to him. In other words, Charlemagne's stubborn grief after Roncevaux puts him in the position of an unenlightened audience member and rewriter of the Roncevaux story: he is not drawing the correct conclusions about the meaning of the battle of Roncevaux, and he communicates this misunderstanding to others through his public and personal discourse in the following scenes.

The Châteauroux author is quick to dramatize that Charlemagne's refusal to understand the dead at Roncevaux as martyrs who are now rejoicing in heaven immediately spreads to others. When the Frankish army stops at a monastery on their way back to France, the crowd gathered there shows a grief similar to that of Charlemagne and his men, and this is Charlemagne's fault, for "Li enperere ne puet nul conforter" [The emperor could not comfort anyone] (v. 6162). Charlemagne does soon take action to prevent the further spread of such grief, but he does so by lying and making his messengers swear to do the same. In this way, a false representation of the Battle of Roncevaux is communicated to others as the official story. In laisse 337, Charlemagne sends one hundred men to Vienne to bring back Olivier's uncle Girart and his sister Aude, with the message that Aude is to be married right away, although this is impossible now that Roland has been killed. Charlemagne has the messengers swear on holy relics that they will not tell Aude about the deaths at Roncevaux because "S'ensi nel faites, ja n'i porai parler, / ainz li vesrai le cuer el cors crever" [If you do not do it this way, I will never be able to speak to her, / Before I see her heart collapse in her body] (vv. 6194–95). This warning implies that Charlemagne already expects Aude to die of grief, even though her death in other versions seems to come as a complete surprise to him; thus we might say that Charlemagne is attempting here to "rework" a series of events that he has already witnessed somehow, as if he had access to the same knowledge as the Châteauroux redactor. Yet Charlemagne then also orders another group of messengers sent to bring back his sister (Ganelon's wife) to conceal the deaths from everyone they meet along the way (vv. 6215–17). This second group of lying messengers suggests that Charlemagne's effort to conceal the truth about Roncevaux is not limited to Aude as a special case and thus that it is not motivated merely by a desire to preserve Aude's life but also by a desire to preserve his own reputation, or even to use his unique power of public communication to transform the story of Roncevaux in the minds of the entire French populace.

No sooner has Charlemagne sent these lying messengers out than Ganelon escapes from custody, and as the narrator announces this escape he also changes the crime of which Ganelon is accused. Here the narrator does not emphasize that Ganelon betrayed the rear guard to Marsile: instead, the traitor is described as "Guenes li fel, qi mut la grant dolor / dont doce France torna en grant freor" [Ganelon the criminal, who set in motion the great grief / because of which sweet France turned to great turmoil] (vv. 6245–46). The narrator asserts here, from a privileged retrospective vantage point, that, in spite of Charlemagne's victories over Marsile and Baligant, the grief resulting from Roncevaux was still able to cause profound instability in France. The narrator blames Ganelon for this instability, but the incident of Ganelon's escape also suggests a parallel between Ganelon and Charlemagne in that Ganelon asks a group of merchants he meets on the road to lie on his behalf (laisse 343), just as Charlemagne has just asked his messengers to do (laisses 337–39). This conversation with the merchants includes a mininarrative of Roncevaux according to Ganelon's perspective, the same perspective he presents later in his trial: "Ci venent gentz qi tos me vont chaçant. / Ocis lor ai un lor ami vaillant: / je n'en poi mais, jel fis moi deffendant." [Some people are coming this way, who are all pursuing me; / I killed a valiant friend of theirs: / I could not do otherwise, I did it in self-defense.] (vv. 6280–82). This version of events is clearly wrong because it represents Ganelon's orchestration of the deaths of twenty thousand warriors from his own country as a personal dispute between two individuals. But what is the difference between this false narrative about Roncevaux and the one being circulated by Charlemagne? Both narratives skew the facts according to an individual's self-centered perspective, and both serve the purpose of avoiding the consequences that would otherwise follow if the real story of Roncevaux were known to each man's "audience" within the fiction. Since Ganelon is soon recaptured (laisse 350), it is difficult to see what purpose this incident serves other than that of bringing to mind this very parallel.

Even if we understand Charlemagne's decision to lie about what happened at Roncevaux to have been sincerely motivated by his concern for Aude and the other family members of the dead, and by his desire to take personal responsibility for delivering the bad news himself, it is uncomfortable to witness in the following scene the doomed initial joy of Girart and Aude upon hearing from Charlemagne's lying messengers the "good" news about the Spanish campaign and about Aude's upcoming marriage to Roland (laisses 355–60). In case the audience fails to respond with appropriate chagrin to this spectacle, the messengers model the proper reaction at the end of this scene. When Girart urges Aude to get ready to leave as soon as she can, the narrator tells us that "Lors ont grant duel tuit li cent chevalier" [Then all one hundred knights felt great sorrow] (v. 6587). As the party sets out to meet Charlemagne, the narrator describes Girart's upcoming meeting with Charlemagne as a meeting with pain itself (vv. 6624–27). The narrator clearly means to build anticipation for this meeting with Charlemagne, but already these preparatory scenes project a negative outcome, not allowing for the possibility that Charlemagne really might be capable of telling the news in a way that would reduce the shock of it or of offering anything in the way of lands or alliances that would compensate for the family's loss. As is the case before the Battle of Roncevaux, then, the audience is put in the position of watching a terrible event unfold, knowing what will happen when Aude hears the news of Roland's death and witnessing the characters' inevitable failure to prevent it.

What makes the version of Aude's death in Châteauroux and the other rhymed versions more enjoyable to witness than the carnage at Roncevaux, however, is the direct intervention of God, not to prevent her death but to transform her attitude before it occurs. It is interesting, in light of the metanarrative character of all the Roncevaux texts, that this divine intervention occurs in the form of two different narratives that recount the Battle of Roncevaux in ways that directly conflict with Charlemagne's false representation of events to himself and to others. God's first representation for Aude of the Battle of Roncevaux and of her own circumstances takes the form of a dream so disturbing that Aude seeks help in interpreting it from a clerk who is described as literate and also knowledgeable about astronomy and the occult ("nigromance," v. 6790). The detailed imagery of this dream is interesting in itself and has already attracted the attention of scholars.[26] For the purposes of this study, however, what matters most about this dream is that it correctly predicts future events and therefore must have been sent to Aude by God rather than simply expressing a vague foreboding on her part.

Before addressing the future, however, the dream tells the past. Aude sees the highlights of the Battle of Roncevaux with the two armies represented as groups of animals (in a clear parallel to Charlemagne's prophetic dreams in multiple Roncevaux texts), although Roland does appear as himself, using his sword Durendal to cut off the right paw of an attacking lion (vv. 6663–67). Aude correctly infers that the dream is about a real battle against Marsile that left no Frankish survivors and that was a direct result of Ganelon's betrayal (vv. 6668–75). Although the messengers from Charlemagne reported to Girart and Aude a battle in which Marsile attacked the Franks at Roncevaux, they said nothing about Ganelon's betrayal or, of course, about the heavy losses on the Frankish side (vv. 6507–14), so Aude's interpretation, as well as the dream itself, shows signs of divine inspiration. Aude herself implies as much after she recounts a second scene from her dream representing the devastation at Roncevaux and once again concludes that it must have been the result of Ganelon's betrayal: "la traïson ne poet estre celee! / Je l'ai songié, si est vertez provee." ["The betrayal cannot be concealed! / I dreamed it, and so it is proven truth."] (vv. 6718–19). The audience is equipped to understand this as a supernatural insight not only because they witnessed what actually happened at Roncevaux but also because they heard Roland utter the same statement in his soliloquy before the battle began: "The betrayal cannot be concealed" (v. 1627). This insight thus appears to pass directly from Roland to Aude across the normally prohibitive distances that time and death have placed between them, connecting not only the perspectives but also the narrative functions occupied by the two characters. Just as Roland consistently embodied and gave voice to the text's favored perspective throughout the battle scenes, so does Aude in the series of scenes leading up to her death. Furthermore, the implicit reproach against Charlemagne in Roland's earlier speech becomes explicit in Aude's echo of it: there was no individual agent of concealment when Roland said these words, but now, when Aude says them, that agent clearly is none other than Charlemagne himself. Thus the link between Roland and Aude represented by this repeated line also strengthens the link between Ganelon and Charlemagne that was suggested by the episode of Ganelon's temporary escape: Charlemagne may believe that his lies about Roncevaux are in Aude's best interest, but in fact they both serve Ganelon's interests and emulate Ganelon's traditional modus operandi, the deliberate twisting of discourse for selfish reasons.

After these two dream sequences representing the past accurately, and after their accurate interpretation by Aude, the audience has been prepared to put their trust in the dream sequences Aude recounts afterwards, which foretell the immediate future. In the first of these prophetic dream images (laisse 365), Aude is being attacked from every direction by a crowd of bears, when an old man carries her away to a church, where she seems to be safe but where she also sees the dead bodies of Roland and Olivier lying side by side. In a second dream image, Charlemagne leads Aude to a forest where Roland and Olivier are hunting and then abandons her there. She tries to call for help from Roland and Olivier as they pass, but they do not speak to her and she sees them buried in a landslide. She then appears to wake up from this dream to find herself in a church again ("Quant m'esveillai, si fui en un mostier," v. 6775), where she sees Roland and Olivier embracing one another, but they still do not speak to her ("mais onqes moi n'i volsent arasnier," v. 6779). She foresees the deaths of the two men (v. 6782), and then she wakes up. Since these images foretell the future, the audience is not equipped to interpret them in detail at this point, except that listeners already know that she is right about the deaths of Roland and Olivier. The audience occupies the unusual position of having some privileged knowledge about what Aude is telling here but not enough, and they would therefore listen with interest to the interpretation of the dream that is offered by the clerk.

The audience would also share Aude's frustration, then, when the clerk consults a book and then lies to Aude about what he reads there:

Il prist un livre, si i list sanz falance:
la mor des contes i vit et la pesance,
et comme Guenes les vendi en balance
au roi Marsire qi en Deu n'ot creance.
De vint mellers n'en ala pié en France.
Li clers ot duel, nel tint pas a enfance,
mais par belle Aude en fist gente contenance.
                                        (vv. 6791–97)

[He took a book, and he read there without missing a thing:
the death of the counts he saw and their pain,
and how Ganelon sold them in exchange
to King Marsile, who did not believe in God.

Of twenty thousand, not one returned to France.
The clerk felt grief, he did not take this lightly,
But for the sake of Belle Aude he put a pleasant face on it.]

Depending upon how one interprets the content of this clerk's book, this may be the most blatant example of combined reflexivity and reception in the surviving Roncevaux tradition. This man may simply be consulting a book on dream interpretation that leads him to interpret Aude's dream with perfect accuracy, or, as the wording of the passage suggests, he may actually have seen the Roncevaux plot laid out in the book. In either case, this scene dramatizes vividly the capacity of literate clerks to engage in deliberately faulty oral retransmission of the written material to which they had privileged access in medieval culture. If an illiterate audience did not hear the truth about Roncevaux from the person reading about it from a book, it was the fault not of the book's author but rather of the reader/performer. Yet some complicity between the Châteauroux narrator and this lying reader within the fiction is suggested by the fact that the narrator does not take this man to task for his false interpretation but instead praises him for his wisdom and kindness in hiding the truth from Aude (vv. 6802–5), in flagrant disregard of Aude's supernatural insight that "the betrayal cannot be concealed." The clerk tells Aude that the dream means that Roland will leave her for another woman but that she will have Roland's child and that the child will be greatly honored by Charlemagne. The audience knows, of course, that this interpretation is both false and dishonoring to Roland's love for Aude, which the audience has glimpsed in Roland's thoughts of Aude during the battle (laisse 229). Aude's reception of this interpretation might express a similar skepticism, and it definitely expresses a submission to God's will that is reminiscent of Roland's attitude while he was preparing for the battle: "Respont belle Aude: 'Si ert cum Deu plaira'" [Belle Aude responds: "It will certainly be as God wishes!"] (v. 6822). What happens in this scene, therefore, is that the audience is guided toward embracing Aude's perspective, becoming alienated from both Charlemagne and the narrator in the process.

As if to emphasize this alienation, the narrator concludes this laisse (367) by stating once again that Aude's destination in this scene is the place "o sa dolor trova" [where she encountered her grief] (v. 6827) and then begins the following laisse with "Savie est li clers qi le duel ot celé; / en altre sen a le songe atorné. / Gerart chevauche, et o lui si privé. / E, las! qel duel quant seront asanblé!" (Wise is the clerk who had hidden the grief; / he turned the dream toward another sense. / Girart rides, and with him his followers. / Alas! what grief [there will be] when they are all together!] (vv. 6828–31). It is somewhat surprising that the narrator indulges in a third passage praising the clerk's "wise" misinterpretation here, and the occurrence of three words for grief in the space of five lines tells us that the narrator believes that loss and sadness are the essence of the next scene, in which Aude and Girart finally learn the truth about the deaths at Roncevaux. What the audience actually learns in this next scene, however, is that the narrator is making the same mistake as Charlemagne and the "wise" clerk by adopting this perspective. Of course Girart and Aude feel grief when they hear about the deaths of Roland and Olivier, but Aude's prophetic dream has also equipped her to seek out a discourse of spiritual transcendence directly from her dead brother's mouth. Charlemagne's anticipation of his meeting with Aude just before this scene begins affirms that an alternative source of discourse is necessary because he is still looking for some kind of rhetorical trick that will transform the bad news into good news, asking Naime, "per quel engin serons nos porpensé / coment il soient de cest duel conforté?" [What trick will we be able to devise / by which they will be comforted from this grief?] (vv. 6853–54). Naime's solution, which Charlemagne adopts, is to have everyone put on a performance of joy as they enter Blaye, dancing and singing; then Charlemagne, on meeting Aude, explains that Roland and Olivier are not with him because they have run off with Saracen women (laisses 370–72). Aude's response shows that she believes neither this story nor the general demonstrations of joy going on around her because of her dream and because of her certainty of Roland's love for her alone (vv. 6938–43). She is so insistent upon hearing the truth that Charlemagne finally tells it to her, and her first reaction is just like his: when she sees the blood-soaked bodies of Roland and Olivier, she makes great demonstrations of grief such as scratching her own face with her fingernails until she makes blood fly through the air (vv. 7050–61).

At the start of laisse 383, however, Aude has a sudden change of heart ("le cuer prist a changer," v. 7096), apparently because of her memory of her dream image of the stubbornly silent Roland and Olivier: she asks to be left alone in the church with the bodies in order to talk to them one last time in private. It is not only Aude who does the talking, however, because she prays to God to allow Olivier to come back to life and speak to her (laisses 384–85). In this prayer, as in the most sincere battlefield prayers of Roland, Turpin, and Charlemagne earlier in the Châteauroux version, Aude mentions biblical events with a clear connection to her current situation: the way various biblical characters

(Longinus, Joseph of Arimathea, and the three Marys) treated the body of Christ during and after his death and cases in which God raised someone from the dead (Lazarus, Jesus).[27] What she asks, specifically, is that Olivier be allowed to say whatever he wants to say to her ("Qe Oliver me die son talent," v. 7160; "tant qe il m'ait sa volonté gehie," v. 7180). Her insistence that Olivier be allowed to speak freely adds additional weight to his joyful speech about the experience of heaven that she will soon share with him. An angel leans down beside Olivier's body and causes him to utter the following words, which constitute an entirely new kind of Roncevaux narrative:

> Bele suer Aude, ne vos esmaiez mie:
> ne remandrez ne soule ne mendie.
> O moi venrez en la Deu compeignie
> amont el ciel, o joie est esclarcie.
> Tote bauté nos est amoneïe.
> Poi aproiseriez la terïene vie;
> el ne valt pas la moité d'une alie,
> or ne argent une pome porine.
> Cil qi Deu sert conqiert grant manantie
> ensanble as angles, o ja n'avras bosdie.
> Levez vos en, si soiez esbaudie;
> je n'ai congié qe plus raison vos die.
>   (vv. 7186–97)

> [Beautiful sister Aude, do not be dismayed:
> you will not remain here alone or in need.
> With me you will come into God's presence,
> above in heaven where joy is made clear.
> All beauty is given to us.
> You would value very little your earthly life;
> it is not worth half a crab-apple,
> gold nor silver [is worth] a rotten apple.
> The one who serves God conquers a great domain,
> together with the angels where you will never be deceived.
> Arise from there, and be joyful;
> I am not at leisure to say any more to you.]

This speech from Olivier might surprise us at first because it seems so out of character for a man whose personality on earth was so oriented toward the reality he could see and touch, but of course this is precisely

Strange Words

the point: we see here that Olivier's glorification in heaven has transformed the aspects of his personality that steered him wrong during his life. The sincerity of his description of the worthlessness of life on earth is implicitly affirmed by his not saying a word about what happened at Roncevaux. The anguish he once felt about Ganelon's betrayal and the bloody battle that resulted from it is entirely gone, and he does not seek to set the record straight with an eyewitness account of the battle because that is not the information he considers to be of utmost urgency to the survivors trying to make sense of the losses at Roncevaux. His description of life in heaven is general, even banal, telling Aude nothing that she would not have heard from a priest on earth if she asked a priest to describe heaven to her. By the same token, however, here we find the ultimate confirmation that Roland was right and Olivier was wrong throughout all the battle scenes in which their perspectives had clashed, because Roland understood all along the transcendent value of dying in the battle as a way of serving God. The inherent truth value of Olivier's speech, in that it is uttered by someone who is in heaven and therefore cannot lie, confirms the same idea in a reflexive sense by demonstrating that, if the rear guard themselves could tell us the story of Roncevaux, they would tell us that what matters most about the battle is not how it happened, how many deaths it caused, or what Charlemagne did in response to it, but rather that it won for them a place in heaven and enabled Christianity to spread on earth. The fact that it is Olivier's voice that articulates this message makes the consensus of the rear guard absolute on this point, since he was the only dissenter during the battle scenes, and also fulfills the posthumous reconciliation of Roland and Olivier that was represented in Aude's dream by the image of the two men embracing in a church like the one in which Aude is now enclosed with their two corpses.

The one implicit reference Olivier does make to the events currently unfolding within the fiction is when he promises Aude that in heaven she will no longer be deceived, a reminder to Aude and the audience of Charlemagne's campaign of misinformation, which has necessitated this alternative representation of the ultimately joyful significance of Roncevaux. Aude's name suggests a parallel between her position and that of a literary audience, as does the fact that her primary function in every surviving text is simply that of being told one or more versions of the story of Roncevaux. In this text, Olivier's heaven-centered Roncevaux narrative, the misreading of the Roncevaux dream narrative and book by the clerk, and Charlemagne's false official story all represent different ways in which the Roncevaux story can be reinterpreted for audiences. This proliferation of Roncevaux stories within the fiction in Châteauroux, and Aude's quest to identify the most truthful and inspiring one among them, seems an appropriate representation of the state of affairs facing audiences of the multiple Roncevaux narratives that were circulating in the thirteenth century. Aude's reception of Olivier's narrative shows not only that she is capable of recognizing the right interpretation but that that interpretation inspires her to right action, in this case using spiritual truth to resist grief: "Aude est sus sallie. / 'A, Deus!' fait ele, 'com ore sui garie! / Jamais por duel ne serai esbaïe.'" [Aude jumped to her feet: / "Oh, God!" she says, "how I am protected now! / Never again will I be disturbed by grief."] (vv. 7198–7200). Yet Aude's correct interpretative choice in response to a spiritually oriented narrative of Roncevaux is thwarted by Charlemagne's wrong choices: as soon as she emerges from the church, she learns that Charlemagne plans to marry her off to a high-ranking noble, an idea that she refuses even to discuss (v. 7209, which resembles the Aude episode in the Oxford version). She then begins to talk about how her grief is going to kill her, and she continues to make comments in this vein for the next thirty lines until she falls dead (vv. 7210–43).

This traditional representation of Aude's death does not suggest that her joyful reception of Olivier's speech was insincere; rather, like Roland's insincere discourse in the horn debates, Aude's distraught public discourse before her death communicates to the people around her what they expect to hear from a person in her situation. Just as sounding the horn was not an option for a Roland preparing himself for a voluntary martyrdom at Roncevaux, marrying another man and continuing with a meaningless life on earth is no longer an option for Aude, now that she is convinced that Roland and Olivier really have gone to heaven and are waiting for her there. Both Aude's determination to join Roland and Olivier in heaven and the contrast between her public and private discourse are emphasized by the way the narrator recounts her final, private prayer to God: "le Segnor proie qe tot le mont fait a / qe mort li dogne, qe mot la desira. / A Oliver son frere s'en ira / et a Rollant, qe mervelles ama. / Aude se seigne et sa raison fina, / puis torne arere, son duel recommenza." [she prays to the Lord, who made all the earth, / That he grant her death because she so desires it. / To Olivier her brother she will go, / And to Roland, whom she loves in a marvelous way. / Aude crosses herself and finishes her speech, / Then she turns back and resumes her grieving.] (vv. 7225–30). Aude's death remains a joyful choice on her part, and her demonstrations of grief are a public performance that she can pause and resume at will: this passage ensures that

the audience is aware of that. Charlemagne and the other people present are persuaded by Aude's performance, however, which creates yet
another disjuncture between the audience and Charlemagne, affirmed
by the differing ways in which the two parties view the moment of Aude's
death:

> entr'als s'en est l'arme del cors sevree.
> . . . .
> Devant Jesu l'en ont la sus portee.
> Le rois l'esgarde, qide qe soit pasmee;
> quant la redrice, si l'a morte trovee.
> Lors recomence li deus et la criee.
>
> (vv. 7246–50)

["Between [angels][28] her soul is taken away from her body:
Before Jesus above they carried it.
The king looks at her, thinking she has fainted:
When he lifts her up, he finds her dead.
Then the grief begins anew, with cries.

As the audience watches Aude's soul being carried away to heaven, they
also witness Charlemagne's failure to see the same thing. As the first line
of this passage makes clear, the direct object *her* being used throughout
refers to two different entities: Aude's soul, now glorified in heaven,
and Aude's body, lying dead in Charlemagne's arms. For Charlemagne,
however, only the dead material entity is worthy of notice or comment,
and the emperor's renewed despair at this moment elicits another rebuke, this time from a member of Aude's own family, her uncle Girart:
"por amor Deu, laissez le duel ester! / . . . / car cist enpires nel pot plus
endurer." ["For the love of God, leave this grief be / . . . / For this
empire can no longer endure it."] (vv. 7284, 7287). As the narrator
implied in several earlier passages, Girart also now recognizes the damaging collective consequences of Charlemagne's grief, even though he is
more likely than anyone else to share Charlemagne's feelings at this
moment.

The effect of Châteauroux's expanded Aude episode upon other characters within the fiction, then, is to cause them to protest against Charlemagne's mistaken excesses of grief and the distortions of the truth
inpired by that grief, which are echoed by the learned clerk who instinctively adopts the same mistaken approach.[29] The Aude episode thus can
be read as the dramatization of informed and/or perceptive audiences

refusing to accept narratives in which they themselves would be incorporated into a self-deluding fantasy spun by a powerful person, whether that person influences the narrative as its author, its patron, or a subsequent performer/interpreter. In the closing lines of the text, the narrator of Châteauroux supports this rebellion against Charlemagne's narrative distortions by reminding the audience that they did nothing to protect Charlemagne from the ravages of his own grief. As Charlemagne's barons leave for their own lands after the execution of Ganelon, the narrator gives us a closing portrait of the emperor that is unique to Châteauroux (and Venice 7) within the Roncevaux tradition: "Li rois sospire, de Rollant s'est membrez; / et cil s'en tornent, s'avalent les degrez. / Et Charlle remest dolanz et abosmez." [The king sighs, he has remembered Roland. / And the others turn and go down the stairs. / And Charles remains, grieving and downcast.] (vv. 8195–97). This closing tableau quite literally shows Charlemagne's people moving on with their lives, while the emperor himself is immobilized with grief at the memory of Roland; unlike other Roncevaux narratives, Châteauroux does not consider Ganelon's execution to have been entirely successful in resolving the issues raised by Roncevaux, apparently because Charlemagne never formulated the right narrative through which to process the memory of Roland successfully.

Nor do any of the other versions (including Venice 7) convey the combined metatextual and religious content of the final lines of Châteauroux:

De cest romein nus n'en seit plus chantez.
Cil vus beneïe qi'n la crois fu penez
et au terz jor de mort resuscitez.
Deo gracias amen.
Explicit Roncisvali e de Rollant e
d'Oliver e de Aude.
                    (vv. 8199–explicit)

[Of this romance no one knows how to sing anymore [or no one can sing any more].
May he bless you who suffered on the cross
and on the third day was resurrected.
Thanks be to God Amen.
Here ends [the story] of Roncevaux and Roland and
Olivier and Aude.]

In fact, Châteauroux itself may be acknowledging the exceptional status of this passage in line 8199, which could be understood to assert that the lines that follow it are not included in any other version and/or that no contemporary author is fully capable of telling (or writing or performing) the Roncevaux story in the way that the Châteauroux author just did. In light of earlier scenes discussed in this chapter, it would make sense to understand the closing reference to Christ's death and resurrection, in combination with the peculiar formulation of the subject matter in the explicit (no other surviving version describes the Roncevaux *matiere* as the story of these three individual characters), as yet another mininarrative of Roncevaux. These lines can be read as an assertion that the story of Roncevaux, as exemplified by the experiences of Roland, Olivier, and Aude in Châteauroux, is really at its heart the story of receiving Christ's blessing and giving thanks to God for it. The fact that the narrator wishes for the audience to share the same blessing ("Cil vus beneie") suggests that this text was deliberately designed to convey a religious message that the author believed would be directly applicable to his contemporaries. The author may have considered it important to impress upon listeners the value of holy war for its own sake, as a form of service to God, for crusades to the Holy Land continued, albeit with ever-diminishing frequency and success, throughout the Middle Ages. Yet if that were the message of primary importance to the Châteauroux author, perhaps he would not have chosen to lavish so much attention on the episodes following the battles against Marsile and Baligant, which were both insistently critical of Charlemagne and suited for interpretation as literary commentary. In particular, if the narrator had wished to use this text as propaganda for a particular religious or political cause, it would not have served that interest to include the episode of a literate authority whose message to his illiterate audience directly undermined God's message as transmitted by a prophetic dream. And finally, the fact that Olivier's ultimate eyewitness statement about Roncevaux takes the form of oral discourse may reveal another reflexive dimension to the Aude episode in this version, a commentary on a particular contemporary Roncevaux narrative and/or upon thirteenth-century vernacular literature as a whole.

If the Roncevaux text contained in the Châteauroux version was composed at any time after 1200, it would already have become clear to its author that French literature was splintering into a number of styles and genres that contemporary authors viewed as distinct from and even in competition with one another. Most notably, this period is distinguished by the emergence of prose versions of *matieres* that were previously transmitted in the form of verse texts, a change of style that was thought to reflect the truthfulness of these narratives, since their authors no longer needed to distort their discourse in any way to make it fit into the constraints of rhyme and meter. The new prose format was often accompanied by an enhanced religious dimension for narratives whose religious significance had previously been vague or nonexistent. The proliferation of prose Grail narratives in the early thirteenth century is one of the best-known examples of this trend, but the Roncevaux *matiere* also appears in such a prose form at this early stage. Shortly after 1200, prose accounts supposedly narrated by the archbishop Turpin himself began to appear in Old French (the "Pseudo-Turpin Chronicles," which survive both in Latin and in Old French translations).[30] These texts represent a different approach to using character narration in written form as a tool to enhance the impression of the Roncevaux story as both true and doctrinally sound. Moreover, it would be fair to describe the Pseudo-Turpin narratives as "the story of Charlemagne" (a common Latin title for them is *Historia Karoli Magni et Rotholandi* or "the story of Charlemagne and Roland," and one Old French translation calls itself "l'estoire Charlemainne"), which would make them the complement to Châteauroux's self-description as "the romance of Roland, Olivier, and Aude." It is possible that the authors of the rhymed versions offered the scene of Olivier's miraculous speech within the fiction as a response to the choice on the part of the Pseudo-Turpin authors to move into prose narrated by an eyewitness in an effort to bolster the truth value of the story of Roncevaux. The narrators of the Pseudo-Turpin texts have a firm grasp on Christian doctrine and often incorporate religious commentaries into their narration, but one might say that in this scene from Châteauroux Olivier beats the Pseudo-Turpin narrators at their own game by offering an eyewitness account that contains a *purely* spiritual assessment of the lasting significance of the Battle of Roncevaux. This episode suggests that only a person who has already died and gone to heaven is capable of creating new and completely truthful discourse; all other new discourse that attempts to make truth claims for itself should be inherently suspect. By incorporating this metaliterary commentary into a rhymed literary text in the vernacular, in the form of spoken discourse within the fiction, the author of Châteauroux would be making this commentary about the relative value of vernacular prose texts as an outsider who had not embraced the new trend, but for the benefit of the same literary audience that was being targeted by it.

By contrast with the lofty ambitions of thirteenth-century prose writers, the virtue that Châteauroux seems to claim for itself is that of humility, through both its conservative rewriting strategy and its uncompromisingly religious perspective on the Roncevaux story. Instead of attempting to devise entirely new episodes or narrative strategies, it begins with episodes and even large chunks of written text that were already available and highlights selected aspects of that existing literary material for the spiritual and literary edification of its audience. By contrast with Charlemagne and the lying clerk to whom Aude turns for interpretative help, Châteauroux shows in these closing scenes that it is not attempting to reinvent the story of Roncevaux in an effort to influence the audience's interpretative process for the benefit of any self-serving human agenda. Instead, as in Olivier's speech when he returns from the dead, what Châteauroux wants most to impress upon its audience is simply the truth of Christian doctrine, which is also what Châteauroux understands as the essential lesson of the Battle of Roncevaux. The proof of Châteauroux's sincerity in privileging spiritual lessons over any political or literary agenda is that this text encourages the audience to detach from the primary narrator when it features within the fiction a manipulative storyteller in the form of the clerk of the Aude episode. This surprising move implicitly acknowledges that any literary text produced by human beings—even Châteauroux itself—should be read critically and that whatever wisdom literary works may contain must inevitably give way before the transcendent power of God's word and God's will. For all its differences from the Oxford *Roland*, then, Châteauroux does convey a similar closing message: that the proper attitude of a Roncevaux author is to emulate Roland's attitude of heroic self-sacrifice. For both of these authors, writing a new Roncevaux narrative was a metaliterary project and a heroic *geste*, and on both counts an enterprise capable of "improving all the time" by adding new layers of meaning to both the plot and the metaliterary message of "Roncevaux."

3 *Ronsasvals*

Distorted Discourse and Reliable Reception

This chapter focuses on the insights to be gained from the unusually prominent role devoted to character discourse in *Ronsasvals* as compared to the rest of the surviving Roncevaux textual tradition. I begin with an examination of the ways in which the characters in this Occitan text use both the vocabulary and rhetorical stances of Occitan lyric, gradually (or at times suddenly) redefining these traditional features by giving voice to them in a context of violent conflict and the mourning that results from it. In the second section, I trace Roland's heroic trajectory from an initial state of ignorant self-absorption to a final pinnacle of spiritual enlightenment. The agent of this transformation is Roland's grief at the loss of the rear guard, which instills in Roland a new humility and submission to the will of God as expressed through the events at Roncevaux. As I show in the third section, Charlemagne responds differently to his grief over the losses at Roncevaux, allowing it to immobilize him and eventually to push him into behaviors that are ineffectual, inappropriate, and even immoral. More explicitly than others in the surviving Roncevaux tradition, this text suggests that grief has this effect on Charlemagne because he has not repented of the sin of incest through which he fathered Roland. This reading relies on the medieval notion that behavior like Charlemagne's is a product of melancholy, or *acedia* (the sin of sloth), and that unconfessed sin is one contributing factor to that transgressive psychological and spiritual condition. In the context of this new characterization of Charlemagne, Aude's death becomes an act of self-sacrifice that jolts Charlemagne out of his rebellion against God and his circumstances. As in the Châteauroux version, however, Aude's death is also represented as the necessary, and therefore welcome, precondition to her reunion with Roland in the afterlife. At the end of the chapter, I emphasize the text's acknowledgment of its own generic hybridity, understanding it as a signal to audiences to reinterpret the traditional Roncevaux material in new ways. I then consider how the text's global signifying strategies support or undermine a potential reading of this text as a response to the Albigensian War, which probably occurred during or shortly before the text's composition.

About the Text

Ronsasvals, the only surviving Roncevaux narrative in Occitan, is contained in a single manuscript, along with another Occitan text set before the Battle of Roncevaux, which bears the modern title *Roland à Saragosse*. The two texts are followed by a register of the notary of the city of Apt (Provence) for the year 1398, which suggests the late date of execution for the manuscript. The original date of composition for *Ronsasvals* was probably in the first half of the thirteenth century, judging by its style and its references to (and at times citations from) twelfth-century Occitan lyric.[1] Its language is a peculiar form of Occitan that seems to have been influenced by Old French. The text contains a total of just over 1,800 lines, making it the shortest complete Roncevaux text that has survived. This modest length was accomplished in part through the omission of several major episodes contained in Oxford and Châteauroux, most notably the initial council scenes among the Franks and Saracens, the pursuit of Marsile's army, the battle against Baligant, and the trial of Ganelon. The text begins with the Battle of Roncevaux already underway and ends with multiple laments over those killed in that battle; thus it becomes an account of a disastrous defeat that throws all of France into a state of mourning from which it appears destined never to recover.

Several scholars have hypothesized that *Ronsasvals* was adapted from one of the rhymed Roncevaux texts in Old French or Franco-Italian.[2] The content of certain episodes in *Ronsasvals*, most notably the individual preparations of the twelve peers before the battle and the entire episode of Aude's death, resembles Châteauroux far more closely than the Oxford version. Furthermore, *Ronsasvals* shares with Châteauroux relatively frequent articulations of Christian doctrine, overt and at times lengthy references to biblical narrative, and an emphasis on submission to the will of God as the distinguishing factor among those characters who are portrayed as the most deserving of praise or blame.[3] Along with these thematic resemblances, however, it is important to note that the approach to rewriting exemplified by *Ronsasvals* is almost diametrically opposed to that of Châteauroux. Cesare Segre has used the Italian term *enucleazione* (enucleation) to describe the rewriting technique used in *Ronsasvals*, as well as in the two *Folies Tristan* of Bern and Oxford.[4] Reworkings such as these select certain episodes from an existing narrative tradition to recount as separate narratives, out of a desire not only for brevity but also for density of signification. Thus the selected episodes accentuate what the authors of these reworkings consider to be the most important issues of the larger narrative, to which they allude with brief summaries of pertinent events that they do not choose to narrate in full in the reworking. For *Ronsasvals*, the chosen episodes are those of the warriors' preparations for battle, the battle itself (with particular attention to Roland's death and including an appearance by Olivier's illegitimate son Galian), and laments over the dead by Charlemagne, the *jongleur* Portajoya, and Aude, whose death from grief concludes the narrative. Perhaps the most conspicuous omission from this account of the Roncevaux story is the betrayal and resulting execution of Ganelon, but Segre notes several short allusions scattered throughout the text to the betrayal itself, the logic behind it, and its anticipated punishment, concluding that by way of these references the whole narrative is present, but in a "virtual form."[5] Segre also points out that the choice of the Aude episode as one of the few privileged in this way by *Ronsasvals* may have inspired the later Spanish ballad "El Sueño de Doña Alda."[6]

Another distinguishing feature of *Ronsasvals* is its unusual emphasis on the expressed viewpoints of a relatively large number of minor characters. The text's first modern editor, Mario Roques, asserted that the presence of these characters was not a mere variation but a conscious and significant component of the text's design.[7] Roques consistently used theatrical vocabulary to describe the function of characters in *Ronsasvals*, ultimately describing the text as "a dramatic poem, much more than a *chanson de geste* or a story."[8] Most subsequent critics of *Ronsasvals* have hesitated to endorse Roques's characterization of the text as a drama given its form, which features a single narrator and division into laisses.[9]

Literary terminology aside, however, the unusually prominent place of character discourse and development in *Ronsasvals* has been one of the text's defining features in most of the discussions devoted to it since its first appearance in modern criticism. Perhaps the most unusual of these speaking characters is the *jongleur*, Portajoya, who pronounces a lament for the archbishop Turpin and then immediately falls dead from grief. As unique as this episode is within the Roncevaux tradition as a whole, it proves to be a logical extension of the consistent attention of *Ronsasvals* to ideas and stylistic traits characteristic of Occitan literary culture. This Occitan inflection to the narrative as a whole will be a primary focus of this chapter, since it has metaliterary implications and undoubtedly served as guidance for the text's reception by its intended audience.

What purpose might there have been for creating *Ronsasvals*, a version of the Roncevaux story in which Charlemagne's people never win a battle against the Saracens and spend much of their time in conflict with one another? Without a precise date of composition or any information about the text's author, the circumstances of its creation can only be guessed. The temptation to hypothesize is particularly strong, however, in light of the traditional crusading tone of the Roncevaux material and the chronological proximity of this text's composition to the Albigensian War (or "crusade")[10] of 1209–29. One starting point for interpreting *Ronsasvals* in that context, however, is to observe that it is unusually apolitical (or perhaps politically subversive). By omitting traditional post-Roncevaux events such as the revenge battle(s) against the Saracens, the punishment of Ganelon, and the endorsement of Charlemagne by divine messengers, *Ronsasvals* expresses a lack of faith or even interest in these traditional political remedies to the damage caused by the Battle of Roncevaux. Though there are exemplary individuals in *Ronsasvals*, the text ultimately stresses that it is dangerous to rely on human leaders and that trustworthy guidance comes from God alone. This shift of focus from collective political solutions to individual spiritual ones could express either an Occitan reluctance to validate the "French" emperor Charlemagne or a Northern attempt to alienate the Occitan-speaking audience from their political leaders who were resisting the "crusade" against the Cathar "heresy" in the South. Interestingly, then, another shift occurs in *Ronsasvals* that sets it apart from other surviving Roncevaux narratives. Charlemagne's people, still called "the Franks" *(Frances)* in *Ronsasvals*, are nevertheless portrayed as sharing a culture whose values and discursive strategies are rooted in the ideology of Occitan troubadour lyric. The most recent edition of *Ronsasvals*, which appears in one volume with the Occitan narrative *Roland à Sara-*

gosse, was entitled "*Le* Roland *occitan*" by its modern editors;[11] as this title suggests, these Occitan texts offer portrayals of Roland, and of other familiar French epic characters, that embody Occitan literary culture as well as the predominantly Northern tradition of the *chanson de geste*. *Ronsasvals* is not a text that merely happens to have been written in Occitan; it is a text that uses frequent and varied references to Occitan culture as a means of portraying the process through which such cultural identities are challenged by loss.

When I speak of "Occitan identity," then, it is in literary terms: medieval Occitan speakers shared a literary tradition that formed a part of their collective identity. On the other hand, though thirteenth-century speakers of Occitan may at times have defined themselves in opposition to their French-speaking neighbors to the north, they were not members of a single political entity but rather were divided into autonomous regions and city-states often in conflict with one another.[12] Given the many rifts among different regions of what is only called in retrospect "Occitania,"[13] I am not claiming the Occitan poetic tradition as the single source of "Occitan identity" for the real medieval inhabitants of the Occitan-speaking region. Within the fictional universe of *Ronsasvals*, however, Occitan poetic conventions play a fundamental role in the articulation of both personal and collective identity, which does constitute a redefinition of the fictional universe to make it resemble the audience's culture more closely. By representing Occitan identity as a state of mind rather than a real political status, *Ronsasvals* could circumvent the contemporary political minefield opposing North and South. Its characterization of Charlemagne's warriors as espousing Occitan values implicitly asserts that even the Franks (originally a Germanic people and thus normally considered one of the most prominent sources of Northern cultural values) could be, in a philosophical sense, the ancestors of the Occitan people. Yet again it is not entirely clear whether this cultural sleight of hand was meant to serve the interests of an Occitan author wishing to remake the Franks in the image of his own contemporaries or of a Northern author wishing to make a conciliatory gesture to the Occitan audience. The French-influenced linguistic forms of *Ronsasvals* could be an argument for the latter interpretation, but then again they could also be a product of the intervening steps of textual transmission between the text's original composition and its surviving late-fourteenth-century manuscript witness. Any historical interpretation therefore must be informed not only by the inconclusive codicological evidence but also by a close examination of the text's content and specifically of its unique revisions within the textual tradition as a whole.

As is consistently the case in the Roncevaux tradition, many of these revisions take the form of character discourse. In *Ronsasvals*, the rhetoric and vocabulary of the Occitan lyric tradition is clearly associated with the identity of those "Frankish" characters who are the most sympathetic and, after their deaths, the most to be mourned. Yet as these eloquent figures die off, communication becomes increasingly unreliable among the survivors. This crisis of communication adds a linguistic component to the damage caused by the Battle of Roncevaux: the loss of the society's heroes has the additional effect of alienating the survivors from one another. By evoking and then altering traditional features of Occitan poetic language, *Ronsasvals* makes of such linguistic and cultural corruption a metaphor for the way unity is damaged by a great communal loss such as the one suffered at Roncevaux. Although this metaphor would be meaningful only to those medieval Occitan speakers who were familiar with the Occitan lyric tradition predating this text, the language and rhetoric of *Ronsasvals* suggest that it was composed with that audience in mind. The emphasis *Ronsasvals* places in the post-Roncevaux scenes on the fragmentation of the sympathetic "Frankish" people, woven together with the tribute this text pays to Occitan literary culture, may indicate that *Ronsasvals* was designed to function as an appropriately complex meditation on the cultural impact of the Albigensian War, which may still have been under way at the time the text was composed. Yet even if one considers the "Frankish" society of *Ronsasvals* to represent contemporary Occitan society undergoing the effects of defeat and mourning, the text's ambiguous, love/hate attitude toward the "Frankish" society it portrays makes it difficult to ascribe to *Ronsasvals* a precise political agenda.

Its spiritual agenda seems relatively open as well: this text does not seek to elaborate upon particular theological issues, and it features, for example, a unique scene within the Roncevaux tradition in which a Saracen character prays to the Christian God over Roland's dying body. *Ronsasvals* systematically emphasizes the religious aspects of the Roncevaux story, a tendency that has prompted other critics to use the word *didactic* to describe the tone of this text.[14] It is important to stress, however, that *Ronsasvals* does not take a dry, detached view of the characters and situations it portrays; on the contrary, its "didactic" examples derive their effectiveness from the audience's emotional investment in the characters. The audience's sympathy is skillfully cultivated and guided throughout the narrative by the dual subtexts of Occitan cultural identity and individual Christian faith. Occitan culture does not receive a universally positive evaluation: only those characters who explicitly submit to God's will are ultimately endorsed by the text, while other characters are shown to belong to a society in decline. Although Roncevaux narratives always feature the conflict between Christian and Saracen, as well as messages and miracles from God, they usually portray the Christianity of the Franks as a collective trait. *Ronsasvals*, on the other hand, is dominated by a series of sympathetic characters who all struggle with their own sin and also seek to know God's will for them as individuals. *Ronsasvals* thereby dramatizes the division between those characters who see their primary identity as that of devout Christians and those characters who mistakenly consider their primary identity to be political and thus dependent upon secular leaders.

Charlemagne is an important character in *Ronsasvals*, but for most of the narrative he is incapable of leadership, by both secular and spiritual measures. To dramatize Charlemagne's failings, and fill the heroic vacuum created by his emotional abdication, the text widens its focus to offer audiences an interior view of several other individuals. One of the most obvious innovations of *Ronsasvals* within the French epic tradition is the way it highlights speeches and internal monologues by a variety of characters, some of whom appear only in this text; in the process, the text makes a prominent display of its characters' divergent perspectives at every stage of the plot's unfolding. *Ronsasvals* raises and resolves its central conflicts at the level of the characters' inner lives rather than focusing on the external consequences of their actions. This character development is personal in every sense: each character's inner struggle is different, and if readers are likely to view characters as individuals in this text, it is partly because of the many disagreements among them. This focus on the individual and the internal is usually associated with the medieval romance genre, as well as with lyric poetry, and might seem out of place in an epic narrative. Yet the personal character of *Ronsasvals* is entirely appropriate not only to its theme of individual salvation but also to a prevailing trend in thirteenth-century literature toward an individual and internal focus that would soon dominate lyrico-narrative genres such as the fourteenth-century *dits*. Moreover, this emphasis on personal discourse is a logical extension of the Roncevaux story's recurring theme of the cognitive and psychological value of verbal processing through individualized narrative performance: such processing was already present in the Oxford version but simply takes a more noticeable form in *Ronsasvals*. Finally, the importance of Occitan cultural identity to *Ronsasvals* explains why this text's innovations logically manifest themselves through monologues or verbal performances, a choice that maintains a metaliterary level of meaning through every episode in the narrative.

The Lyricized Rhetoric and Reception of Character Discourse

The most obvious evidence that Occitan lyric constitutes the characters' shared cultural heritage in *Ronsasvals* can be observed at the level of vocabulary: as I will show in my analysis of specific scenes, the significance of certain characters' speeches lies in their use and reuse, with revisions, of complex key words from troubadour poetry. In fact, troubadours' repeated use of these words gradually made their meanings so rich and complex that modern critics insist they are impossible to translate faithfully with a single term. Perhaps the most prominent example is the word *gauch* or *joya*, whose possible translations include happiness, fulfillment of aspirations, sexual pleasure, and poetic creation itself.[15] The word *amoros*, which can refer to someone who is in love or someone who is worthy of love, is used before the battle by Turpin to evoke one of the qualities to which the "Frankish" warriors should aspire: "So dis l'evesque: 'Aras es temps e sazons / com siam francs, savis es amoros'" [The archbishop said, "Now is the time and the season when we must be noble, wise and worthy of love"] (vv. 265–66). Similarly, the narrator later describes Saracen warriors with the epithet *l'envejos* [the jealous one] (vv. 547 and 1280), which in the Occitan lyric applies to the troubadour's enemies, the jealous husband or rival. These uses in a military context of the vocabulary normally associated with troubadour lyric show that, in this troubadouresque culture, the adjectives denoting a lover's attitude could be considered more generally positive attributes. The ability to love implied great virtue in every domain, including courage and skill in battle; jealousy, the quality Occitan lyric associated with an inability to love, could be considered as a generally negative attribute that implied a lack of all these important virtues. As Robert Lafont notes in reference to Turpin's prebattle speech cited above, the traditional epic imperative to state the moral superiority of one side over the other has passed through an Occitan filter in its articulation here.[16]

The use in *Ronsasvals* of multivalent terms whose richness had been developed by Occitan literary culture suggests that the most fruitful reading of *Ronsasvals* should take into account troubadour rhetoric as well as the subtleties of specific Occitan words. Indeed, my claim that certain *Ronsasvals* characters sound like troubadours is based on ways of signifying that go beyond mere word choice. Both the narrator and the characters in *Ronsasvals* use dense visual images in conjunction with words to convey nuances of meaning, a practice that also played an important role in the techniques of the troubadours. In her book on troubadour rhetoric, Linda Paterson confirms the importance of such dense images for both the composition and the reception of Occitan lyric by quoting from Geoffrey of Vinsauf's *Poetria nova* (c. 1210): "Let the craftsman's skill effect a fusion of many concepts in one, so that many may be seen in a single glance of the mind."[17] As I will show in specific scenes of *Ronsasvals*, the listener's reception of such dense images is more important in this narrative than the speaker's clever formulation of them. Correct interpretation affirms relationships between characters and even comes to be associated with general moral integrity, while misinterpretation and lying are signs of moral decline that recur frequently in the final section of the narrative. This notion that there is a moral component to the interpretation of a message, as well as its articulation, finds its roots in troubadour rhetoric: the villain of troubadour poems, the *lauzengier*, is often associated with real-life court gossips but may also represent people who twisted the poet's words in formal or informal transmission.[18] The Occitan lyric *topos* of the threat posed by people who misunderstand, particularly those who are incapable and unworthy of true love, leads to a rhetoric of secrecy and denial in many troubadour poems. Because of the threat posed by the *lauzengiers*, the poet-narrator could not take the risk, in public poetic discourse, of revealing the name of the person who inspired the poet's love. Because of a fear of rejection by this secret addressee, the poet-narrator also hesitated to give full voice to the emotional pain that had inspired the song.

This need for secrecy in the lovers' communication is usually stated outright, while what might be called the "rhetoric of denial" is most often an underlying emotional strain gradually revealed by the poem as a whole. The tension between the joy and the suffering resulting from love provides much of the dynamism of troubadour poetry and therefore is usually maintained throughout a poem rather than finding resolution. This tension places the poet-narrator in a position of repeatedly denying resentment toward the addressee who has not fulfilled his[19] desires: although both positive and negative feelings are necessary to maintain the emotional tension that animates the troubadour lyric, the poet-narrator often denies the negative as soon as he has articulated it. The resulting tone in many troubadour poems is one of submissive supplication occasionally interrupted by seemingly involuntary accusation. Once it had become a commonplace of troubadour poetry, this tendency toward inner conflict and the denial of feelings even took the form of inner dialogues that refracted the poet-narrator's voice into several quarreling voices. Sarah Kay has discussed this dialogue form at length, as evidence of the development of subjectivity in the Occitan lyric. Here are several lines from a poem by Peire Rogier, cited by Kay in three fonts to reflect the three discernible voices in conflict:

Dompn'ay. NON AY. *Ia.n suy ieu fis!*
NO SUY, QUAR NO M'EN PUESC JAUZIR.
Tot m'en jauzirai, quan que tir.
OC, BEN LEU, MAS SEMPRE N'A TORT.
Tort n'a? Qu'ai dig! Boca, tu mens
e dis contra midons erguelh.

I have a lady. NO I DON'T. *I'm sure of her!*
NO I'M NOT, BECAUSE I DON'T HAVE PLEASURE FROM
HER.
But I shall do so, in full, even though she makes me wait.
MAYBE YOU WILL, BUT SHE'S STILL IN THE WRONG.
In the wrong? What have I said? You are lying, mouth,
to speak such presumption against my lady.[20]

Here a troubadour dramatizes the traditional rhetoric of denial: the poet-narrator's voice is clearly fragmented into several conflicting voices, and the poet-narrator attempts to create an impossible distance from his own mouth by addressing it in the second person as if it were a distinct entity. Peire Rogier probably intended to create a comic effect by making the rhetoric of denial this explicit, but it is a joke that could have worked only if such a rhetoric were a widely recognized feature of previous troubadour poetry. Thus the recurring theme in *Ronsasvals* of denying the truth, a theme sometimes demonstrated by characters' complex rhetoric, may be seen as a commentary on the Occitan lyric tradition as well as an aspect of the plot of this specific narrative.

The last aspect of the Occitan lyric tradition that becomes a central preoccupation in *Ronsasvals* is a tendency toward self-absorption. The troubadours' isolation from the object of their desire, as well as their painstaking efforts to find the right words and images to describe their emotions, can make them seem endlessly fascinated by their own inner lives to the exclusion of all else.[21] Similarly, the principal weakness of several characters in *Ronsasvals* is the very fact that they see the situation only from their own point of view and that they cause damage by withholding crucial information from others. In the first part of the narrative, Roland gradually learns to shed this trait of self-absorption; on the other hand, this same trait later prevents Charlemagne from forming effective policy and impedes his ability either to express himself or to interpret effectively the words of others. These contrasting examples of diminishing and increasing self-absorption in Roland and Charlemagne provide a general comparative structure to the portrayal of these traditional protagonists that is unique to *Ronsasvals* and will thus provide an organizing principle for the specific passages to be analyzed in this chapter. As I will show with numerous examples, the speeches of other characters supplement and clarify these two contrasting portrayals, enhancing the audience's understanding of Roland and Charlemagne, of their society, and of the Occitan-inflected verbal rhetoric that characterizes that society in *Ronsasvals*.

As in the Oxford *Roland* and the Châteauroux version, the scenes in *Ronsasvals* recounting the horn debates, the Frankish laments over the dead at Roncevaux, and Aude's death serve as three structurally significant moments in the dramatization of the text's metaliterary message through character discourse. Of these, the second horn debate between Olivier and Roland in *Ronsasvals* provides the clearest example of the way Occitan lyric vocabulary, imagery, and rhetoric combine with traditional Roncevaux material to produce simultaneously familiar and surprising effects. Olivier's voice begins the following excerpt:

—Compans Rollan, yeu vos suy fin amayre;
ma fe vos plic per l'arma de mon payre
non amiey tant sor ni cozin ni frayre,
corna ton corn per l'arma de ton payre.
—Non plassa Dieu, lo sant glorios payre,
comenset dir lo duc Rollan de bon ayre,
que de mon corn yeu en sia cornayre
con fay aquel que del porc es venayre,
car le cornar non es mas de cassayre.
—Compans, se dis [Olivier], ja non tardaras gayre
que nos serem en Fransa ha ton repayre,
am ma seror Auda, de qui yest messennayre,
e vuelh que tengas ha ton plaser a fayre.

Cant aus Rollan de Bellauda parlier,
le cor li engrueyssa e vay li remembrier
de la Bellauda, sa seror d'Olivier,
cant ha Vienna l'espozet el gravier;
pueys si consira quar mort l'es a passier
e de Bellauda non aura joy entier.
Malmatin brocca dels esperons daurietz,
de tal vertut vay lo graylle sonier
que li aucels que l'auziron sonier,
la vos del graylle lur fes lo cor crebier,
e las venas del cor si van trenchier;
lo sanc del cor li vay per lo gravier.

(vv. 906–30)

["My friend Roland, I am a faithful and beloved friend to you; I pledge you my faith by my father's soul, I have never so loved a sister, cousin, or brother: sound your horn, by your father's soul!"

"May it not please God, the glorious, holy Father," began to say the noble duke Roland, "that with my horn I act like a bugler about this, as does a man chasing down a pig, for sounding a horn is no better than what a hunter does."

"My friend," said [Olivier], "now you will hardly delay, so that we might be in France, in your home, with my sister Aude, of whom you are the lord, and I want you to have her to do what pleases you."

When Roland heard talk of Belle Aude, his heart became heavy and he began to remember Belle Aude, the sister of Olivier, when he was betrothed to her in Vienne at the river's shore; then he considered that he would have to pass into death, and that he would not have the full joy of Belle Aude. He spurred Malmatin with his golden spurs, and he blew the horn with such force that, for the birds who heard it, the voice of the horn made their hearts burst, and the veins of the heart were severed; the blood from his heart fell onto the ground.]

Unlike other versions of the Roncevaux story, in which Olivier no longer wishes for Roland to blow the horn by the time he agrees to do so, *Ronsasvals* shows Olivier using a new rhetorical approach to change Roland's mind in their second debate: reverse psychology. In an earlier scene, Olivier already asked Roland to blow the horn (vv. 529–34), and Roland dismissed that suggestion in strong and prideful terms similar to those that he uses early in the passage cited above. Olivier then countered with a proverbial admonition against Roland's pride: "Dis Olivier: 'Compans Rollan, aujas: / ausir ay dir ha motz homes sennatz / que erguelh non es mas sobras gran foldat. / Ja non vos acorra, cant le dans es passatz.'" [Olivier said: "Roland, my companion, listen: I have heard it said by many wise men that pride is nothing more than great folly. It will no longer help you, once the damage has been done."] (vv. 535–38). In the second horn debate cited above, therefore, the audience understands that Olivier is suppressing his anger, or at least his disapproval, about Roland's continued refusal to sound the horn. Olivier's opinion has not changed in the second debate, but his rhetoric has. Instead of claiming (as he did in the Oxford *Roland*) that Roland's earlier refusals to blow the horn have convinced him that Roland should no longer have the right to marry Aude, in *Ronsasvals* Olivier unexpectedly refers to the happy future Roland will share with her. This speech borders on flattery: Olivier's image shows Roland not only as a survivor of Roncevaux but as master over everything upon his return, especially over Aude. Olivier's evocation here of the way in which Aude will "please" Roland is as erotically suggestive as was Olivier's rejection of Roland as Aude's future lover in the Oxford *Roland* ("you will never lie in her arms," Oxford v. 1721) and thus is a pointedly direct reversal of Olivier's previous stance elsewhere in the textual tradition. Indeed, Olivier's entire tone in this passage is pleading and conciliatory rather than critical and confrontational, as it was in other Roncevaux texts and even in the earlier horn debate from *Ronsasvals*. These aspects of Olivier's tone are anticipated by his opening line, in which Olivier refers to himself as Roland's *fin amayre*. This epithet brings to mind a frequently used medieval term for courtly love, *fin'amors*, but in the overall context it clearly does not indicate a romantic relationship between Roland and Olivier, since Olivier immediately speaks approvingly of Roland's future marriage to Aude. Instead, Olivier's self-description is characteristic of this text's thorough engagement with the vocabulary of courtly lyric: his use of the term *fin amayre* works as a dense descriptor of the profound (but asexual) love, respect, and self-sacrificing dedication that characterizes his friendship with Roland. Whereas the Olivier of past Roncevaux narratives appeared ready to terminate his friendship with Roland over the issue of sounding the horn, the Olivier of *Ronsasvals* uses this scene as an opportunity to reaffirm his commitment to their friendship, which he does with terms whose meaning has been enriched by their previous usage in Occitan literature.

For his part, Roland does not blow the horn because he is taken in by Olivier's inflated image of his future with Aude; on the contrary, Roland's emotional response makes it clear that he takes this speech in the ironic spirit in which Olivier meant it. Olivier's talk of Roland's future with Aude merely serves to remind Roland that the couple will have no future together, and that realization is enough to make him call out to Charlemagne. Roland's emotional investment in his marriage to Aude is demonstrated convincingly here by the fact that it is Roland's thoughts of Aude that become the immediate impetus for the horn call. The sound of Roland's horn signals a significant turning point in each Roncevaux narrative:[22] here it signals not only the end of Roland's hope of winning the Battle of Roncevaux but also the end of his hope of a future with Aude. The notion that the sound of Roland's horn is related to this significant emotional turning point, as well as to a turning point in the battle, is emphasized by the pitiful image of all the birds' hearts bursting from the loud noise, birds whose song of love was used frequently by the troubadours as an analogy for their poetry. The three uses of *cor* in this passage progressively attach to the word all its layers of meaning: the word first refers to the birds, whose hearts burst from hearing Roland's horn; then to Roland's own heart, whose veins experience physical damage from blowing the horn; and finally to "the blood from his heart" falling to the ground. The parallel between Roland's heart and those of the spontaneously dying birds offers an unusual impression of Roland as primarily a lover and/or a poet: Roland's premonition of his own death is marked by the end of the birds, which have been the symbol of a poet's inspiration in countless Occitan love songs. It is also important to note that Roland's emotional state and the horn call resulting from it are a response to an act of memory brought on by Olivier's discourse: when Roland hears Olivier speak of Aude, his mind returns to the moment of their betrothal, and that internal, cognitive move across the distance of time and circumstances succeeds in transforming Roland's attitude. In other words, the transformative effect of Olivier's discourse is caused by Roland's reception of his speech rather than inhering in the actual content of Olivier's arguments for sounding the horn. The dynamic between the two speakers is no longer that of a debate at all but rather that of a literary performance in which the fictional future recounted by Olivier moves his audience, Roland, not through direct intellectual persuasion but through personally engaged, creative reception. Furthermore, Roland responds to Olivier's rhetorical performance with a literary performance of his own in that the horn call expresses more than usual in this version of the familiar scene. When Charlemagne hears the horn, he correctly deduces not only that Roland is in battle but also that Ganelon's betrayal was the cause of the battle (laisse 25). Yet this insightful interpretation of Roland's circumstances nevertheless lacks an understanding of Roland's direct motivation for sounding the horn: Roland's thoughts of Aude provided that direct motivation, but they are missing from Charlemagne's subsequent reception of the horn call. Roland's sorrow over his lost future with Aude provides a surplus of meaning in this version that is narrated to the audience but withheld from the surviving characters within the fiction.

The reception of the horn call by Charlemagne does suggest a clear link between his cognitive processing and that of Roland because when Charlemagne hears the horn and Ganelon's denial of its meaning as a distress call, "l'ayga del cor li monta per lo vis" [the water from his heart ascended [and emerged] on his face] (v. 955). Charlemagne's spontaneous physical and emotional response to the horn call and to Ganelon's lies echoes not only the image of the blood from Roland's heart that falls to the ground twenty lines earlier but also Roland's own spontaneous tears upon witnessing the deaths of numerous fellow warriors in an earlier scene: "l'ayga del cors li cay per los huels amdos, / car anc non li remas mas .XXX. companhons" [the water from his heart falls from both his eyes, for now no more than thirty of his companions remain] (vv. 562–63). In both of these scenes, the protagonist's tears emerge first, followed by a speech explaining them, and the speech of each protagonist is focused on his sorrow for the sake of the other.[23] Charlemagne intuits that the warriors of the rear guard have all been lost, and he angrily blames Ganelon for betraying them; Roland claims that the sorrow he feels over the loss of the warriors of the rear guard is for the sake of their lord, Charlemagne, and his speech concludes with a proverbial statement that would be quite at home in a troubadour song: "Ben connosc aras e podem ho proyer / c'om non si deu trop en son gauch fisier" [I well know now, and we can prove, that one should not have too much faith in one's joy] (vv. 579–80).

As in several other scenes from *Ronsasvals*, including Roland's sorrowful thoughts of Aude, the term *joy* here has a meaning that is vague and variable but nevertheless crucial to the overall signification of the narrative. *Joy* might represent political or military confidence, sexual fulfillment, or the characters' anticipated existence in heaven after their deaths (v. 1270), but in all of these cases it represents a state that the characters in *Ronsasvals* repeatedly recognize as being denied to them in the fictional present and immediate future. Whatever the surviving characters do in the immediate wake of the losses at Roncevaux, they will have to do without the hope of regaining "joy" in their earthly lives. As we have seen, Roland and Charlemagne both realize this eventually, as evidenced first through their spontaneous tears "from the heart" and then through their speeches. What is interesting about the structure of *Ronsasvals* is that the two protagonists seem to be the last to realize that they are moving toward this joyless future, although they were the only characters in the narrative who received specific premonitions about the events to come and who thus might have acted to prevent them. The protagonists' self-absorption is emphasized by the relatively more expansive outlook of the other speaking characters, and it is primarily the text's audience that is encouraged to make that comparison. Speeches by other characters express earlier and more eloquently the perceptions that occur only belatedly to Roland and to Charlemagne, but the fact that these speeches cannot be heard by other characters within the fiction makes them available only to the audience. The audience's privileged access to the private speeches of several characters from *Ronsasvals* is a variation on the tradition in Roncevaux narratives of always granting the audience some form of information that is inaccessible to the characters within the fiction. In the absence of the initial council scenes and the scene of Ganelon's betrayal, which provided the audience's initial source of privileged information in both the Oxford and Châteauroux manuscripts, *Ronsasvals* nevertheless maintains this traditional narrative element by introducing new character speeches for the benefit of the audience alone. These speeches deserve closer scrutiny, then, not only because they provide interesting examples of character discourse within the Roncevaux tradition as a whole but also because they fulfill a narrative function for the audience that seems to have been essential to all Roncevaux texts.

The first of these speeches is uttered by the archbishop Turpin, whose role in the early scenes of *Ronsasvals* is that of both spiritual leader and leader of the rear guard. Indeed, Turpin is so favorably portrayed in these early scenes that Roland compares unfavorably with him. Roland is recognized as the military commander, but even in this area Turpin appears to have some authority: in laisse 6, the young warrior Navalier asks Turpin for permission to lead the charge in Roland's place, as if this were Turpin's decision to make. Roland appears at first to be naive in comparison to Turpin. While Turpin anticipates the outcome of the battle and the necessary spiritual preparations for it, Roland's perceptions seem limited to immediate physical realities. For example, Roland receives what is clearly an omen when his sword turns purple the morning of the battle, yet Roland only notes the exterior change without venturing to interpret its meaning (vv. 197–98). Roland then goes to observe the size of the enemy force from a hilltop but comments on what he has seen only when Turpin asks him about it (vv. 201–6). The necessity of Turpin's question suggests that the audience is actually seeing through Turpin's eyes: we watch Roland go up the hill and come down again, but the very hill Roland is climbing appears to obscure our vision of what lies beyond, just as it obscures Turpin's. Thus the narrator sets up an immediate identification of the audience with Turpin's point of view, both literally and figuratively, while the audience must observe Roland from an exterior, physical vantage point and rely on other characters as a source of information about him. As the conversation progresses, the audience is also granted access to Turpin's inner thoughts, access explicitly denied to Roland. When Roland comments that the Saracen army appears to be the biggest ever assembled and that it will be a very difficult force to fight, Turpin immediately rebukes him for this moment of doubt, saying that the Frankish warriors will strike down the Saracens easily. Roland, impressed by Turpin's boldness in both his preaching and his fighting, declares that he will ask Charlemagne to enlarge Turpin's land holdings as a reward when they return to France. Only the audience hears Turpin's startling response, which takes the form of a dramatic aside:

> L'arcivesque respont an cara mot ireya,
> tot suavet que el non l'entent mia:
> "Tot mi dares, quant yeu vos querray mia,
> ni non auras el bras Auda, ta mia,
> sor d'Olivier, ni l'auras espozeya.
> Ay! dousa jant de Fransa honoreya,
> anc non perdest tant de bona mayneya
> con ar perdres, don es descapdelleya,
> don mantas damas en seran corrosseyas,
> tantas pieuzellas en seran orfanellas
> e tantas donnas gentils veuzas clameyas.
> Amix Rollan, annas, si vos agreya,
> als jovencels que tant an desireya
> guerra e batalha que aras l'an trobeya:
> pos Dieus nasquet, non fon tant averseya."
>
> (vv. 227–41)

[The archbishop answers, his face showing his great distress, so softly that Roland does not hear him at all: "You give me everything, when I ask you for nothing, and you will not hold in your arms Aude, your beloved, Olivier's sister, nor will you have her as your wife. Oh! gentle people of France, a country so well honored, never before have you lost so many good men as you will lose now, by which loss you will be decapitated, and by which many ladies will be grief stricken, and so many young girls will be orphaned, and so many sweet ladies will be called widows. Roland, my friend, please, go to the young men who have so much desired war and battle, and tell them that now they have found it: since the birth of God, there never has been one so horrible."]

The narrator takes care to note that Turpin says this whole speech so softly that Roland does not hear it: Turpin's approach to leadership is to speak confidently in front of the men he leads, while privately anticipating the far-reaching consequences of defeat not only for the men going into battle but for the empire they have left behind and for all of human history. Turpin's use of the future tense implies that he is certain of the outcome of the battle and that he understands that it must be fought anyway; this is an attitude toward the battle expressed primarily by Roland in other Roncevaux narratives. Turpin's inaudible request that Roland warn the young and inexperienced warriors about the battle only serves to emphasize the futility of such a speech. Turpin's own silence is motivated by a sense that the battle to come is a manifestation of God's will, as was the "birth of God" in Christ with which Turpin's speech concludes. Understood from that perspective, Turpin's silence indicates that he is a willing sacrifice. The similarity between this prebattle speech by Turpin and Roland's private discourse before the battle in the Châteauroux manuscript reinforces the notion that *Ronsasvals* initially substitutes Turpin for Roland as leader of the rear guard.

In light of his understanding of the coming battle as a manifestation of God's will, Turpin devotes himself to preparing the men's souls for testing. Turpin is more interested in the effects of the battle on the spiritual well-being of individual characters than in military or political causes and effects, as is the text as a whole. Turpin spends the following scenes in nearly constant conversation with the warriors, giving several encouraging speeches, hearing their confessions, and even discussing their individual fates. Having been the only witnesses of Turpin's soliloquy, audience members are aware in these scenes of Turpin's true pessimism about the battle to come, yet the thoughts he voices aloud convey only encouragement and determination. As I noted earlier, Turpin's speeches show that the ideology developed in Occitan lyric poetry exerts an important influence over the Frankish characters: Turpin encourages the Franks not only by telling them that their entry into paradise is assured, as is traditional in Roncevaux narratives, but also by advising them: "de vostras amigas aras sias remembratz, / car qui ben fara, mot en sera amatz" [Now be mindful of your ladies, for whoever does well, he will be greatly loved for it] (vv. 503–4). For the men to whom Turpin speaks, the reward of being loved by their ladies is on a par with heaven, and Turpin does not shrink from including both possible rewards in his speech. Here Turpin tells the men they will be loved, just as he had earlier urged them to be worthy of love; in both cases, Turpin is urging them to honor their shared Occitan identity, rather than raising this question of romantic love for its own sake.

Turpin shows his balanced concern for both individuals and groups by giving a speech to the entire Frankish army in laisses 4 and 5, which he then follows with individual consultations in laisses 6 and 7. In this group of four laisses, Turpin's most frequent piece of advice is that the warriors repent of their sins. In laisse 5, he chooses as the scriptural lesson of his sermon Christ's teaching that when one refuses to minister to the needs of the most poor and wretched individuals on earth, one is in that moment forsaking Christ himself (Matt. 25:41–46).[24] By preaching on a biblical passage in which Christ urges his followers to act in accordance with their faith each time they encounter suffering, Turpin stresses individual responsibility for salvation and for true Christian identity while on earth. It is not enough merely to fight on the Christian side in this version of the Roncevaux story: each warrior is expected to fight in a spirit of sincere repentance and individual dedication to God. In laisse 7, the last in the series displaying Turpin's leadership qualities, the *Ronsasvals* poet offers an example of the ideal Frankish warrior in the young (and aptly named) Angelier. After Turpin has urged the entire Frankish army to have faith and repent, he turns to Angelier in private and asks him if he has repented and if he has dedicated himself to a lady. Angelier responds that his lady is none other than the Virgin Mary and that it is for love of her that he has become a knight. Turpin congratulates him on his choice but adds that Angelier must take care to keep his lady a secret inspiration: "mas non plassa ha Dieu, lo filh sancta Maria, / que lo sieu cors retraysses ha follia" [But may it not please God, the son of holy Mary, that you speak of her out of foolishness] (vv. 353–54). Here again it is easy to see the transfer of the troubadour ideal of discreet adoration not only into the epic but into its spiritual realm. Turpin does not disapprove of Angelier's concept of Mary as his lady but cautions him against voicing it in front of other people who might misunderstand Angelier's ideal.

Turpin is portrayed in *Ronsasvals* as a leader who is able to maintain a balance between his attention to the present and the future, the individual and the collective, earthly values as well as spiritual ones. In fact, Turpin's leadership might be summarized by one highly valued trait in Occitan culture, *mezura*, which denotes self-control on a personal level as well as a more general equilibrium in one's abilities, interests, and value to society.[25] The affiliation of Turpin with Occitan lyric is not limited to his vocabulary and subject matter; it is also signaled by his rhetoric, a deliberate silencing of both his own feelings and those of others. His deliberate substitution of positive, universally valued attitudes for negative personal feelings creates a similar tension to that of the rhetoric of denial that animates many troubadour songs. By showing the divide between Turpin's public and private speeches, the *Ronsasvals* poet chooses to portray from the beginning of the text a conflict between words and true emotions that was already inherent in the Occitan lyric tradition. In the context of the Battle of Roncevaux, however, the stakes of this conflict have been raised to a new height: Turpin's positive public words inspire the army representing an entire empire, and perhaps the entire Christian faith, while his negative private words portend the suffering not only of the person articulating them but of countless other individuals and groups.

Roland's Exaltation through Grief and Repentance

As I have already suggested, Roland's personality in the early scenes of *Ronsasvals* is far removed from the wisdom and balance shown in the same scenes by Turpin. When the Battle of Roncevaux begins, Roland's attention is devoted almost exclusively to the present moment and to the physical realm. Both the narrator and Turpin praise Roland's military prowess, while Roland is repeatedly shown as a physical presence, fighting furiously but speaking only to boast to his enemies of a supposedly imminent Saracen defeat. Roland's response to Olivier in the first horn debate reinforces this impression of him as prideful and overconfident, especially because the *Ronsasvals* narrator has already cited Roland's pride, along with Ganelon's betrayal, as a primary cause of the disaster at Roncevaux, which he describes as "aquel dia mal e fer e peyssant / que-ls vendet Gayne per l'erguelh de Rollan" [that evil and cruel and deadly day when Ganelon sold [the Franks] because of Roland's pride]

(vv. 82–83).[26] Here the narrator clearly states that Roland's pride was responsible for Ganelon's betrayal, as if that were common knowledge concerning the causes of Roncevaux; in reality, however, other texts of the Roncevaux tradition addressed the issue of Roland's pride primarily by making it an accusation of other characters against him, an accusation the narrators neither confirmed nor denied. Thus we might even say that the *Ronsasvals* narrator instills in the audience an initial prejudice against Roland, in comparison to the studied initial neutrality of the Oxford narrator and the pro-Roland rewritings of the early scenes of Châteauroux. Lest the audience forget the narrator's comment in their sympathy with Roland during the battle scenes, Olivier once again alludes to Roland's pride in the first horn debate, but with a tone of wise counsel rather than bitter reproach:

> Olivier venc, suau e amoros:
> "Bel compans senher, le reprochier es bons
> qu'ieu ay ausit comtar mantas sazons
> que ren non val cors que sia ergulhos,
> que gran erguelh ha mort Fransa e nos,
> e si avem perdutz ayssi mans companhons.
> Ilh son an Dieu el regne glorios
> e nos ayssi remasutz soffrachos.
> Ar si bastis un dol tant angoyssos
> que anc non cre plus salvage dol fos."
>
> (vv. 564–73)

[Olivier came to him, gently and lovingly: "Fair companion, sir, the reproach is right, that I have heard many times: a heart full of pride is worth nothing, for a great pride has killed France and us, and so we have lost many companions here. They are with God in the kingdom of glory and we remain here, suffering. Now a grief is being built that is so painful that I do not believe a more fierce grief has ever been."]

Here Olivier is described as "gentle and loving" despite his criticism of Roland. Olivier's mood seems to be one of resignation to his fate, for he speaks as if his own death had already occurred. His style of expression is also marked by his repetition of the pronoun *we*, a sign of solidarity with Roland that is usually lacking in Olivier's speeches about sounding the horn. Like Turpin, Olivier has now accepted his own inevitable death and begun to anticipate the consequences of the battle for

France, going so far as to say that the battle will kill France as a whole just as it kills her individual warriors. Olivier also shows an affiliation with Turpin by predicting the immense grief that will follow the Battle of Roncevaux, specifically saying that grief is being "built" as the battle progresses.[27] In contrast to Olivier's verbal description of the doomed rear guard, Roland's response to the same situation so far has been purely emotional and physical. In spite of his apprehension before the battle, Roland allowed himself to be reassured by Turpin's false predictions of victory; only now does Roland come to terms with the true gravity of his situation, a change in his attitude that is first marked by his tears. The narrator tells us that Roland's tears are caused by the loss of his comrades, but Roland himself says nothing at first. Thus the audience again must depend on another character's observation of Roland to gain an understanding of Roland's attitude: we see Roland's tears just as Olivier sees them, and the narrator then explains to us what they mean.

As soon as Roland does finally articulate his concern about the consequences of the battle for Charlemagne and for France, his attitude is immediately echoed and then transformed by his scout, Gandelbuon, whom Roland sends to estimate the size of the Saracen forces. This is another speech, like Turpin's, that takes the form of a dramatic aside, with a similarly pessimistic tone. When Gandelbuon first catches sight of the enemy forces, which he estimates to be sixty thousand strong, his dismay is similar to Roland's, but his attitude toward Charlemagne is accusatory:

> mas de ren alre del mont non ay dolor
> mas con de Karle, lo bon enperador,
> que ancuey perda l'estandart e la flor
> de dousa Fransa que li fazia honor.
> Cor aura mays de tant bons valedors
> com Karle pert ayssi per sa follor,
> car anc trames Gayne a l'amaysor?
> Dieus li confonda l'erguelh e sa ricor!
> Dos fils avia de ma gentil uxor:
> aquels comant a Karle mon senhor,
> mas non veyray lo mage ni-l menor;
> sant Michel angel lur doni per pastor.
> Dieus, fay los vieure an sens e an valor,
> que ancuey penray martire per t'amor.
>   (vv. 625–38)

[But I am saddened by nothing in the world so much as for Charles, the good emperor, who is losing today the standard-bearers and the flower of sweet France, who do him honor. When will there ever again be so many valiant men as Charles is thus losing by his folly, because he sent Ganelon to the Saracen leader? May God confound his pride and his power! I had two sons by my worthy wife whom I commend to my lord Charles, I will not see again the older nor the younger; I give them as a guide Saint Michael the angel. God, make them live with wisdom and courage, because today I will suffer martyrdom for love of you.]

Like Roland, Gandelbuon imagines the effect of the lost battle on his family members and on France first of all through Charlemagne, the emperor who is also his feudal lord and military leader. Yet by the end of his speech, he reaffirms his commitment to fight primarily for God and to follow the example of the saints by dying for his faith, sentiments that Turpin carefully instilled in the Frankish warriors. What is most unusual here, however, is Gandelbuon's strong condemnation of Charlemagne for having chosen Ganelon as his envoy to the Saracens and particularly the way this condemnation is bracketed by two acknowledgments of Charlemagne as a "good emperor" and as a lord who can be expected to take responsibility for Gandelbuon's orphaned sons. Gandelbuon's style of expression, like Turpin's, can be compared to that of the poetic voice in many troubadour songs: when in private, he allows himself to indulge in the expression of his negative feelings, but even then he surrounds that momentary lapse with positive rhetoric, as if to cancel it out. Gandelbuon also displays a level of insight comparable to Turpin's: he mentions Ganelon's betrayal as if it were an established fact at a point in the text where Roland has not yet acknowledged it. Gandelbuon's accusation against Charlemagne provides a good example of how the speech of minor characters conveys to the audience the potential rifts among members of Frankish society. Absent from the Oxford *Roland* and portrayed as a more docile messenger in the rhymed Roncevaux narratives and the *Pseudo-Turpin Chronicle*, Gandelbuon here expresses his own opinion in strong terms. While critics have debated about whether certain comments from the rear guard in the Oxford *Roland* should be read as accusations against Charlemagne, Gandelbuon's accusation in this scene is unambiguous. The fact that this curse comes from a relatively minor character gives it a unique power: other Roncevaux narratives prepared audiences to hear critical remarks from Olivier or Roland, but earlier narratives also prepared audiences to view the other warriors as one coherent group, "the Franks." This break from the usual consensus also implies Charlemagne's potential alienation from God in the perception of "the Franks": Gandelbuon's wish for God to strike back against Charlemagne's pride and power implies that Gandelbuon does not believe that Charlemagne is acting in accordance with God's will. Thus Gandelbuon's speech begins to change the audience's perception of Charlemagne in this text even before the emperor has appeared on the scene.

When Gandelbuon makes his report to Roland, he continues to isolate negative expression by surrounding it with encouraging sentiments. When Roland asks him straight out how many Saracens he saw, Gandelbuon's first response is: "Que voles qu'ieu vos diga?" [What do you want me to say to you?] (v. 646). Having signaled his reluctance to tell the unadulterated truth, Gandelbuon begins by urging the Frankish warriors to arm themselves immediately in the knowledge that when they die they will ascend to heaven because of their faith. It is only in the middle of his speech that Gandelbuon cites the actual number of Saracens he saw, sixty thousand, an astounding figure that he follows with a reminder that the Frankish warriors should be willing to die, since they are fighting for God and on the right side of the conflict. Most Roncevaux narratives feature some portrayal of the warriors' attempts to encourage one another even when the battle has become hopeless; what is different about that portrayal in *Ronsasvals* is that it is couched in the rhetoric of denial, with negative information embedded in the middle of the speech. In spite of Gandelbuon's rhetorical efforts, however, the numbers speak for themselves. At the end of his report, the other warriors are openly weeping; at the same time, however, they observe the traditional Occitan imperative to make an effort to mask their inner suffering with a joyful attitude (vv. 666–69).

In subsequent scenes from the battle, only Roland expresses his sorrow; in sharp contrast to his furious fighting on the first day of the battle, Roland's behavior on the second day is marked by periods of paralysis caused by his grief, a fulfillment of the conclusion to Olivier's gentle reproach (v. 573). In five consecutive scenes on the second day, Roland watches helplessly while Falsabroni, a single Saracen warrior, kills one after another of his closest friends. In fact, these five scenes of individual combat where the Franks are defeated seem to offer a deliberate parallel with five earlier scenes of triumphant Frankish combat. By this point, then, the expression of his emotions has become such a priority that the need to utter words of grief over slain comrades is preventing Roland from fighting effectively. Yet while the battle scenes show the weakening of Roland's famed military prowess, they ultimately pave the way for Roland's new spiritual development, and Roland's brief descent into despair is only a temporary stage preceding his eventual exaltation through personal faith. The grief stage will play a consistent role in the development of most of the characters featured from this point in the narrative until its conclusion. Although grief is an undeniably painful emotion, it also serves as a necessary signal to characters that a change needs to be made in their way of life. After this stage of mourning and meditation on the meaning of the Frankish deaths, Roland becomes ready to express a new attitude near the end of the battle, when he blows his horn to summon Charlemagne to the battlefield.

As we have seen, Charlemagne immediately deduces from the horn call that Roland and the rear guard are in dire straits; it is surprising, then, that he fails to initiate immediate action in response to Roland's signal. What is particularly damning about this is that Charlemagne admits that he has known the true state of affairs for several days because of a prophetic dream he had five days earlier after a conversation with Ganelon (vv. 942–47). In a medieval text, and particularly in a Roncevaux narrative, Charlemagne's clearly prophetic dream would have been understood as a message from God; as the Christian emperor, Charlemagne had the right and the responsibility to receive divine guidance directly. One might have more sympathy for Charlemagne's inaction if he did not understand this prophetic dream, since the dream was not explicit as to the direct cause of the threat to his empire, yet his immediate accusation against Ganelon upon hearing Roland's horn shows that he did interpret the dream correctly and nevertheless chose not to act upon it. Unfortunately, Charlemagne's tendency toward denial and inaction does not end when he hears the sound of Roland's horn. This initial example of Charlemagne's flawed leadership also shows that, even where Ganelon's guilt is concerned, Charlemagne has to be told what to do by his advisor Naime. It is Charlemagne who accuses Ganelon, but it is Naime who gives the pragmatic order that Ganelon be held prisoner; it is also Naime who insists that, should he be found guilty, Ganelon must eventually be drawn and quartered (vv. 968–74).

Charlemagne does not respond to this statement from Naime, and Ganelon's quick retort reveals both that he does not respect Charlemagne's leadership and that he is capable of using both religious and poetic rhetoric to serve his own ends:

> E fassa en Karle tot cant en poyra fier,
> qu'ieu non l'en blant lo valhant d'un denier,

car non m'espert per dich de lauzengier,
que ades seran li lial vertadier,
mal grat qu'en ayan li malvay messongier;
car anc non vi erguelh tant aut montier
que Dieu no-l fassa aytant bas trabuchier.
(vv. 983–89)

[And let Charles do everything he can, because I don't respect him even as much as a denarius is worth, for I am not disturbed by the words of the *lauzengiers*, because loyal people will always be truthful, in spite of the existence of malevolent liars; for I have never seen pride climb so high that God has not made it fall just as low.]

Ganelon's speech complicates the ongoing verbal references to the Bible and to Occitan culture in *Ronsasvals* because his condemnation of excessive pride echoes Turpin's speech before the battle: "e tuch siam lial e drechurier, / e non hi aya envejos ni parlier / que aus portar mal enveja a son pier, / car erguelh fay son senher trabuquier" [And let us all be loyal and upright, and let there be no envious or boasting men who would dare to harbor evil envy against their companions, for pride causes its lord to fall] (vv. 171–74). The idea of pride going before a fall comes from the Bible (Prov. 16:18) and thus was the common cultural property of everyone in the fictional universe and in the contemporary audience. Yet the fact that Ganelon's words are also a reference to Turpin's earlier speech would seem to associate Ganelon with the "loyal" rear guard and the ongoing theme of avoiding prideful actions. This scene therefore dramatizes the danger of taking a speaker's apparently wise words at face value. Putting these words in the mouth of Ganelon demonstrates that such apparent wisdom is susceptible to use for good or evil purposes, according to the intentions of the speaker. The parallel between the two men's words enhances the audience's understanding of the words rather than of the characters: the very fact that the audience already knows that Turpin is good and Ganelon evil is what makes this parallel startling and effective. Michael Riffaterre, in his description of medieval audience reception, points out that intertextual references are most effective when used in conjunction with "overdetermined" speech, giving the example of a pun on a proverb.[28] For a medieval Christian audience, few utterances could be as "overdetermined" as this passage from Proverbs; similarly, an Occitan literary audience would be quick to identify with the troubadour voice in the text, traditional enemy of the *lauzengiers*. Thus audience members initially would have been ready to discount anything Ganelon might say in this scene because of their knowledge about Ganelon from other Roncevaux narratives, but by the end of his speech they would have been jolted by Ganelon's lexical self-identification with the sympathetic voice of Christian, Occitan culture and perhaps specifically with the wise voice of Turpin. Ganelon's adoption of the voice of a troubadour narrator, and here specifically of Turpin, would seem to indicate that the audience should henceforth take care in judging characters who use Occitan vocabulary or rhetoric in unusual ways.

It emerges clearly from this confrontation between Ganelon, Charlemagne, and Naime that Charlemagne's silence has served Ganelon well. Ganelon despises those at court who advise Charlemagne because his plot could unfold successfully only in an atmosphere of silence and denial, the atmosphere that persisted until Roland's horn and Naime's accusations made themselves heard over Charlemagne's silence. Thus Ganelon's words open a fissure in the text's previous endorsement not only of troubadour vocabulary but of discreet silence and the rhetoric of denial. In this scene, Charlemagne's belated emergence from his period of denial proves that there is a high price to be paid for silence; by contrast, Roland's sounding of the horn proves that a true hero speaks out, even at the expense of his personal reputation, to ensure that crimes do not go unpunished. Ganelon's words also raise a new and troubling idea that will persist through the following scenes: that there can be a great deal of difference between one Christian and another. The notion that Ganelon would not measure up to the Christian ideal is hardly surprising, and in fact his traditional villainy is the very thing that causes discord between his words and those of the Frankish warriors at Roncevaux. Yet in later scenes this insincere parroting of religious discourse begins to leak into the speech of other Christian characters; if that speech, in turn, sounds familiar to the audience, it is in part because of this example set by Ganelon.

The sound of Roland's horn not only casts doubt on the cultural value of silence and denial but also summons another significant speaking character into the narrative for the first time: the young Galian, Olivier's son.[29] Galian's appearance is so abrupt and gratuitous that critics have offered the theory that the *Ronsasvals* author felt obliged to include Galian because he must have appeared in lost source texts but that the author could find no graceful way to incorporate him into the plot.[30] It is true that Galian's introduction into *Ronsasvals* is puzzling: he arrives during the last moments of the battle, meets his father Olivier at the moment of Olivier's death, and then is killed himself within a few hours. Yet I would argue that Galian must have had a function in *Ronsasvals* because of this text's dual tendency toward brevity and toward borrowing from diverse sources: it is unlikely that such a text would include anything out of blind adherence to a source. If *Ronsasvals* omitted scenes more commonly used in Roncevaux texts, such as the scene of Ganelon's punishment, it is fair to assume that Galian also would have been omitted if he had had no function. Perhaps, then, the fact that Galian is killed just a few hours after he arrives on the battlefield is meaningful in itself. For, as comments from both Roland and the narrator make clear, Galian represented a last false hope for the rear guard at Roncevaux. Galian himself appears from the first to be the embodiment of hope: for example, his opening words to Charlemagne display an outsider's naive belief that all the legends told about Charlemagne must be true:

> Gentil rey Karle, entendes mon semblant,
> grans es le pres que ha vostre cort s'espant;
> vostre pres sabon d'ayssi en Oriant,
> vostre pres sabon tro al solelh colcant,
> vostre pres sabon Sarrazins e Persans,
> car cor mirable e poder aves gran
> e sens antix vos an fach valer tant,
> car totz pres val per cels que valon tant
> e pos Dieu vol de tu que valhas tant
> que-l miels del mont tenes en ton comant,
> aujas qu'ieu suy ni que yeu vauc querent.
>
> (vv. 834–44)

[Noble King Charles, understand my way of thinking, great is the worth that emanates from your court; they know your worth from here to the Orient, they know your worth all the way to where the sun sets, they know your worth, both Saracens and Persians, for you have an admirable spirit and great power, and your ancient wisdom makes you so worthy, for all worth is measured against those who are as worthy as you, and since it is God's will that you be so worthy that you hold the greatest in the world under your command, hear who I am and what I have come to seek.]

The word that Galian so frequently repeats in this description of Charlemagne's reputation is *pres*, a key word in the Occitan lyric lexicon that is nearly untranslatable because it has been used in so many different contexts, all of them positive. The *pres* of a person represents the sum total of all of that person's good qualities, and is frequently used by troubadours to evoke the immense preciousness of a lady in the eyes of the poet, who claims to know not only her good qualities that are visible to everyone but also the true inner qualities visible only to the one admirer who appreciates her most. Thus Galian is paying the highest compliment to Charlemagne, but it is clear that this assessment is based on Charlemagne's reputation rather than on Galian's own knowledge of Charlemagne's character, an ironic nuance of the scene in light of the more personal established usage of *pres* in Occitan lyric. As soon as Galian has been knighted and sent to Roncevaux, Roland's horn is heard at the encampment, revealing to the audience, as we have just seen, the true deficiencies of Charlemagne's leadership.

When Galian arrives at Roncevaux with a group of one hundred Frankish warriors, he finds Olivier just in time to exchange a few words with him and then watch him be killed. This experience only galvanizes Galian's resolve to turn the tide of the battle, which he attempts to do with a short and fervent speech to his men: "Dis Galian: 'Ar es temps e sazons / que qui vol esser ha Dieu plazent e bon, / traya si enant, car es temps e sazons.'" [Galian said: "It is the time and the season when whoever wishes to be pleasing and good toward God must throw himself forward, for it is the time and the season."] (vv. 1069–71). Again, Galian's rhetoric is entirely positive, but his repetition of the phrase "es temps e sazons" links his speech to the deceptively positive rhetoric of the two previous encouraging speeches to the Frankish warriors by Turpin, who uses the same phrase in line 265, and by Gandelbuon, who uses it in line 665. Indeed, it is perhaps not coincidental that this phrase recurs regularly every four hundred lines, the steady increase of the Frankish body count making its ring more hollow with each repetition. This latest use of the phrase draws the audience's attention to the damage wrought by the passage of time: by the time Gandelbuon and Galian announce that "the time is right," the obvious reality is that it is already too late for the Frankish forces. The false hope offered by both Gandelbuon and Galian emphasizes the contrasting maturity and wisdom in Roland's evolving attitude toward the battle and each warrior's role in it. Just as Roland's decision to sound his horn changed the text's portrayal of the "season" at hand by silencing the singing birds of spring, Roland now offers a judicious correction to Galian's claim that the time is right for each man to fight his hardest in hopes of victory. After watching Galian throw himself back into the battle, Roland remarks: "Ben agra agut mestier / que Galian fos vengut en premier" [It really would have been necessary for Galian to have come at the beginning] (vv. 1052–53). In the next laisse, the narrator explicitly agrees with Roland's assessment at the moment of Galian's death:

Ben pot hom dir, si Galian hi fos
un pauc enantz de la mort dels barons,
ben leu non fora l'affar tan angoyssos.
Tant ha ferit Galian le barons
que si sinquen remas de companhons,
e pueys enantz que fos passat miey jorn,
del cor li part le fege e-l polmon,
e es remazut solet sus un erbos.

(vv. 1084–91)

[One can truly say that, if Galian were there a bit before the deaths of the lords, the battle could easily not have been so horrible. Lord Galian attacked so many times that few of his companions remained, and then before midday had passed, his heart was parted from his liver and his lungs, and he remained alone on the grass.]

The narrator's echo of Roland's words demonstrates a reversal in the initial relationship of Roland to the narrator and to the audience. At the beginning of the text, Roland could only be observed from the point of view of other characters: the audience could see Roland's physical movements but rarely heard him speak and occasionally depended upon explanations from other characters to understand his motives. Now Roland not only speaks but, like Turpin at the outset, expresses himself directly to the audience in a kind of soliloquy. The fact that Roland's sentiments are only afterward echoed in the narration suggest that his understanding of his situation has outpaced even that of the omniscient narrator. Another significant aspect of this comment from the narrator is its portrayal of Galian's death with graphic corporeality: the narrator stresses the physical details of Galian's body lying on the ground, his death unattended by anyone but the narrator and the audience. Galian is not a hero equivalent to Olivier and Roland, whose death scenes are always narrated with much commentary both from the narrator and from the heroes themselves; rather, Galian's death appears to represent the fulfillment of Turpin's early evocation of the young Frankish warriors who were so eager for battle and who could never hope to find a more horrible one than Roncevaux (vv. 239–41). Galian's death in the same battle as his father also emphasizes that both Roland and Olivier died without an heir to carry the heroic lineage into future generations. The fact that Galian is Olivier's illegitimate son sets up a parallel between him and Roland, who is explicitly presented as the illegitimate son of Charlemagne in this text.[31] Galian's faith in Charlemagne, as well as his determination to fight to the death, echoes Roland's point of view at the beginning of the text. Thus Galian shows what Roland's end would have been if he had not experienced the transformative effects of his grief: neither Galian's faith in Charlemagne nor his personal prowess ultimately does a thing to prevent his death or to advance the cause of France. Yet by the time Galian arrives, Roland himself has changed his priorities: although Roland does not abandon the battlefield, he now observes and evaluates the other warriors just as Turpin did before the battle.

Galian's brief appearance on the battlefield immediately after the sounding of Roland's horn might have served an additional purpose: that of substituting Galian and his band of one hundred men for Charlemagne and the entire Frankish army. The slaughter of Galian and his men might constitute another condemnation of Charlemagne's inaction: instead of going to Roncevaux himself, Charlemagne sent just enough men with Galian to increase the Frankish death toll without turning the tide of the battle. I would not suggest that Charlemagne deliberately caused the deaths of Galian and the Frankish reinforcements, but it is precisely his lack of conscious deliberation that caused him to keep the bulk of his army inactive at his encampment between Spain and France. Both the audible sound of Roland's horn and the rapid movement of Galian from the encampment to the battlefield demonstrate that the distance between Charlemagne and Roland would not have been impossible to cross; the fact that Galian's appearance becomes, ironically, the feeble response to Roland's call only serves to emphasize Charlemagne's negligence.

Roland achieves the full measure of his spiritual development in the last moments of his life, when he repents of all his sins in a fervent display of religious faith. Roland confesses his sins before death in many Roncevaux narratives, but nowhere else are these confessions as long and detailed as in *Ronsasvals*. The length of Roland's confession is a signal to the audience that this scene holds an important place in the narrative as a whole; the significance of this scene becomes clear when the audience observes that the sins Roland confesses are those common to all human beings:

ieu ay falhit, senher, en mos .v. sens:
yeu ay falhit amb aurelhas auzent
e ay falhit am los huels fals luzentz,
en esgartz orres es en laytz estamentz,
e ay falhit am mas narras sentent,
en malvays pens e yeu era consent,
e am ma lenga, am mas mans eyssament,
en mals parlars e en malvays contens,
en orres fatz e en tant fers contens.
Dieu, mia colpa de tan gran falhiment,
qu'ieu ay falhit vils e desconnoyssent;
e vos, senher, m'est humil e plazent,
e yeu ves vos fals e desconnoyssent;
en totz affars vos sui desconnoyssent:
en tantas guizas pequiey venialment;
de que no'm membra e de que suy sabentz,
de tot mi rent colpas e penedent.
(vv. 1332–48)

[I have sinned, Lord, through my five senses: I have sinned with the
hearing in my two ears, and I have sinned with the treacherous light
of my eyes, in impure gazes and vile attitudes, and I have sinned with
the smelling of my nose, in evil thoughts to which I agreed, and with
my tongue, and also with my hands, in evil talk and evil disputes, in
impure actions and in very fierce conflicts. God, *mea culpa*, for such
great sin, for having sinned like a man who is vile and ungrateful;
while you, Lord, were humble and kind toward me, I was false and
ungrateful toward you; in all things I was ungrateful to you: in so
many ways I have committed venial sins; for the ones I do not remember and for those of which I am aware, for all of them I admit my
guilt and I repent.]

The detail of this confession shows that Roland's repentance, and probably the topic of repentance in general, was unusually important to the
author of *Ronsasvals*.[32] By comparison, Roland's confession in the Oxford *Roland* merely alludes to a general category, "mes pecchez, des granz
e des menuz" [my sins, large and small] (v. 2370), leaving the precise
nature of those sins a mystery to the audience. Even in Roland's longer
religious speech in several versions of the *Pseudo-Turpin Chronicle*, the actual description of his sins is a most brief and general plea: "delivre la
moie ame de la voie d'enfer et me pardone, Sire, ce que je t'ai mesfet"

[deliver my soul from the way of hell and pardon me, Lord, for all the wrong I have done you].[33] Thus Roland's confession in *Ronsasvals* is not only a moment in which the hero humbles himself but a moment in which the audience hears Roland verbalize his most intimate perception of himself. This change in the nature of Roland's confession both emphasizes the importance of the act of confession and attributes to Roland a new heroism, built (or rather rebuilt, given Roland's well-established heroic status) upon the audience's understanding of a series of inner struggles over which he ultimately triumphs. Turpin's early insistence on individual repentance may have seemed only natural since it was spoken by a representative of the church; this theme can take on its full force for the audience only when it is acted out by the hero of the narrative. Roland is alone in this scene, not preaching before a crowd or serving as an example to his men of proper Christian conduct; instead, it is to the audience that Roland would seem to be serving as an example, both because there is no one else to observe him and because his words of repentance could so easily apply to anyone. While the medieval audience of *Ronsasvals* undoubtedly heard many sermons urging them to repent, this setting for the theme of repentance may have given it a particular resonance. Roland would be able to serve as an inspiration to audiences precisely because he is not infallible, because his wisdom and faith seem to develop before one's very eyes. In fact, Roland becomes a figure even more admirable than Turpin by the end of the Battle of Roncevaux: although Turpin advocated the confession of sins, the audience did not see him undertake his own confession so fervently as Roland does here. Thus, while Turpin offers wisdom to those around him, Roland puts these wise principles into practice, and the trajectory between the models offered by Turpin and Roland provides the most crucial development in this first half of the narrative.

The series of episodes culminating in Roland's confession shows, as a whole, that interiority has replaced the external political process as the method by which the audience apprehends the underlying tensions of *Ronsasvals*. There is no explanation of the cause of the battle in the opening scenes of the text; by the end of the battle, however, the audience understands that it was caused by Ganelon's betrayal, Roland's pride, and Charlemagne's folly in trusting the traitor. To reach this understanding, it is necessary to piece together the discourses of Turpin, Roland, Gandelbuon, and Charlemagne. By eliminating both Roland's contribution to the initial political debate and the battles that ultimately vindicate his point of view, *Ronsasvals* forces the audience to consider different evidence in order to understand Roland's situation and his response to it. That evidence, gleaned from the audience's new interior view of the hero, is significant to the overall meaning of *Ronsasvals*, to the text's very self-definition in relation to preceding Roncevaux narratives. Once the battle is over, there is very little additional action in the text; instead, the drama of these later scenes results from various characters' efforts to come to terms with the grief caused by the losses at Roncevaux. Thus interiority replaces action almost entirely as the narrative progresses toward its conclusion.

Charlemagne's Fall through Grief and Sloth

Just as Roland was the individual whose spiritual development served as the focal point for the first section of the text, Charlemagne becomes the focus of the post-Roncevaux section. This change in focus following the Battle of Roncevaux is typical of Roncevaux narratives, but what is unusual about the second section of *Ronsasvals* is that it is punctuated by Charlemagne's repeated failures to implement a concrete solution or even a more positive representation of events. This string of failures in public policy and communication is the external evidence of Charlemagne's developmental shortcomings: until the very end of the text, Charlemagne clearly does not know how to respond appropriately to the loss he suffered at Roncevaux. In comparison to his conduct in other Roncevaux narratives, what is perhaps most surprising about the Charlemagne of *Ronsasvals* is that he neglects the domain of justice (or revenge): he does not pursue the fleeing Saracens, nor does he undertake any additional battles to secure his hold on Spain or even consider trying Ganelon for his crimes. Instead, as is typical of characters in this narrative, Charlemagne operates through speech rather than action. Charlemagne's self-representation through speech may also be seen as a failure, however, because his vacillating statements reveal his faults much more than his strengths, particularly when his speech is contrasted with that of the characters around him.

In fact, the strategy for representing Charlemagne in *Ronsasvals* is precisely that of contrasting him with other characters who speak and act differently.[34] These potential comparisons of Charlemagne, both with other characters in the same text and with portrayals of Charlemagne from other Roncevaux narratives, create a number of unfulfilled expectations for the audience. In this way, the post-Roncevaux section of

Ronsasvals continues to engage the audience in the struggles of the protagonist, but now this audience engagement consists of a series of raised hopes and resulting frustrations. As Dominique Boutet observed in his comparative study of Charlemagne's portrayal in a large number of medieval French texts, it is usually Charlemagne whose actions at first appear extreme and illogical but are ultimately vindicated when they are proven to be the implementation of God's will for Christendom. Boutet takes as a primary example Charlemagne's insistence that the Frankish army continue to take on new military conquests, even when they are exhausted from previous efforts:

> The king often appears unreasonable and seems not to recognize the state of exhaustion his men are in: the war he wants to undertake appears to be a kind of self-extermination of the Frankish army. Nevertheless, the king's will corresponds well to his mission, while the apparent wisdom of his men conceals a resistance to their calling. For Charles, as for God, nothing is excessive, nothing is beyond measure when battling the Saracens. A sort of dialectic between what is and what appears to be sets up an opposition between two pairs: on the one hand, God and the king, and on the other, the king and his vassals. . . . The king, who is wrong from the point of view of the second pair . . . , is right from the point of view of the first pair, whose superiority is manifested clearly in the events that follow.[35]

Boutet's model of two groups with conflicting priorities, Charlemagne and God versus Charlemagne and his vassals, emphasizes the crucial role Charlemagne plays in guiding many *chansons de geste* toward a satisfying resolution in accordance with God's will. This observation concerning the literary tradition preceding *Ronsasvals* (Boutet's study covers the period from the earliest *chansons de geste* until the mid–thirteenth century) offers intertextual evidence of the radical innovation of the Occitan epic, for in *Ronsasvals* Charlemagne shows a desire to resign from both of the groups between which he usually negotiates. In the Occitan narrative of Roncevaux, Charlemagne attempts to forego both earthly leadership and spiritual communion; moreover, what efforts he does make in each domain are kept separate from the other, so that he vacates his role as mediator between God and humanity.

It is important to stress that *Ronsasvals* carefully reverses Charlemagne's traditional role rather than simply ignoring it: now it is Charlemagne who appears incapable of following God's will, while submission to God's will provides the primary motivation for the initially mysterious behavior of several other characters in the second half of the text. Still, seeing God's will as an alternative to the guidance of the emperor occurs only to a privileged minority of the characters because this relationship between God and individual vassals remains exceptional in *Ronsasvals*, just as Boutet has shown it to be in the *chanson de geste* tradition as a whole.[36] This aspect of the literary tradition preceding *Ronsasvals* gives a troubling sense to the intertextual void in this text, an absence of events that requires the preceding tradition in order to be perceived: Charlemagne's failure to respond to Roncevaux by leading his people into military retaliation, judicial proceedings, or even conversion of the Saracens to Christianity serves in turn as a barrier to his subjects' relationship to God. *Ronsasvals* thus reformulates the two groups Boutet identified as being central to the Carolingian epic: God is now joined with those who choose to follow God's will, a group of privileged individuals gradually gathering in heaven, while Charlemagne is now joined with the rest of Frankish society, which, in its state of alienation from both earthly and divine guidance, appears destined for a troubled future on earth.

Such alienation from God was an alleged consequence of unrepented sin in medieval culture, and evidence of Charlemagne's sinful nature appears in both obvious and subtle forms in *Ronsasvals*. In one of the few well-known scenes from this text, Charlemagne admits that Roland is his son as well as his nephew, since he was conceived through incest between Charlemagne and his own sister: "Bels neps, yeu vos ac per lo mieu peccat gran / de ma seror e per mon falhimant, / qu'ieu soy tos payres, tos oncles eyssament, / e vos, car senher; mon nep e mon enfant" [Fair nephew, I had you, through my own great sin, by my sister, and through my failing, so that I am your father, as well as your uncle; and you, dear lord, my nephew and my child] (vv. 1624–27).[37] In these lines, Charlemagne clearly identifies this incest as a "sin" and a "failing" on his part, while the juxtaposition of numerous words denoting the resulting relationships only serves to emphasize the disruption this sin caused in the natural order of things. Yet this admission of incest is not the only evidence that Charlemagne is a suffering sinner: *Ronsasvals* repeatedly reminds the audience of the emperor's sinful state by showing in Charlemagne's behavior more subtle signs of such suffering from sin.

Just as Roland's humble confession served as a positive example to the audience in that it could be imitated by anyone, Charlemagne's behavior can be seen as an index of well-known behaviors associated with unrepented sin in the Middle Ages and thus might be equally applicable to any audience member. Charlemagne's state of mind might be understood best when viewed as a manifestation of the medieval notion of *acedia*, or spiritual sloth. As Giorgio Agamben has pointed out, "sloth" has come to represent mere laziness in modern culture, but it was understood to be a grave sin in the Middle Ages, "the only one for which no pardon was possible."[38] In fact, since the thirteenth-century writings of Thomas Aquinas characterized *acedia*, along with envy, as "oppositis gaudio caritatis" (standing in opposition to the joy of love), [39] this state of sloth would be the precise opposite of *amoros*, the attitude advocated by Turpin and representative of the shared Occitan ideals of the "Frankish" warriors in *Ronsasvals*. In his detailed discussion of *acedia*, Aquinas stresses repeatedly that this is a misleading emotional state to which the sufferer wants to respond with denial, when in fact active resistance is the correct remedy. Aquinas carefully distinguishes between sorrow and *acedia*, which resembles sorrow but is really an attempt to escape from it.[40] It is understandable, then, that this spiritual state might both occur and pass undetected during a period of mourning such as the one that occupies the second half of *Ronsasvals*. Aquinas's description of the proper remedy for *acedia* helps to clarify the distinction between the normal grief of some characters in *Ronsasvals* and the transgressive *acedia* of Charlemagne: other characters in *Ronsasvals* respond to the same loss by turning toward God, and in comparison to them Charlemagne's behavior appears all the more clearly to be a turning away from God. In a summary of the thought of both Aquinas and Guillaume d'Auvergne, Agamben comments, "*[A]cedia* is precisely the vertiginous and frightened withdrawal . . . when faced with the task implied by the place of man before God."[41]

Hildegard of Bingen's description of a similar *melencolia*[42] suggests that it was a part of the original sin of Adam and thus that it is common to all humanity:

> Now, when Adam knew good and yet did evil by eating the apple, in the vicissitude of that change, melancholy welled up in him, which without the influence of the devil does not exist in human beings. . . . As a result, sorrow and despair welled up in him, since at Adam's Fall the devil kindled melancholy in him, which makes a man into a doubter or unbeliever on occasion. But because the form of man is fixed, so that he cannot rise above his limits, he fears God and is sad, and often in these circumstances he falls into despair, not trusting that God cares for him.[43]

This description of a melancholy initiated by the original sin of Adam includes three points that describe Charlemagne's behavior in *Ronsasvals*. First, Hildegard characterizes Adam's state of mind at the moment of sin as "knowing good and doing evil": as I will show, Charlemagne, similarly, describes what he should not do and then does precisely that.[44] A second point of comparison is that Adam's despair was inspired in him by the devil when he realized that he had committed sin; thus it was not God's punishment of Adam for that sin. Similarly, Charlemagne's state of sin-induced depression is related to his *anxiety* about the condemnation of God and man rather than resulting from actual condemnation. God's responsiveness to Charlemagne's prayers in *Ronsasvals*, in spite of Charlemagne's admitted state of sin, helps to clarify the text's message that Charlemagne's sin did not incur the wrath of God. Finally, Hildegard suggests that melancholy turns people into "doubters or unbelievers"; such a lapse in faith is not explicitly stated by Charlemagne but would help to explain Charlemagne's abdication of his customary role as the divinely chosen messenger to God's people. As with Adam, Charlemagne's relationship to God and to the realm over which he rules is transformed as a result of his sin; it is in that sense that Charlemagne can be said to be under threat of a "fall" in this Roncevaux narrative. Only in the very last lines of the text can the audience draw a conclusion about whether this is a fall from grace, like that of Adam, or a fall from the artificial heights of pride, as predicted by Turpin (and Ganelon) in the first section of the narrative.

In the final section of *Ronsasvals*, Charlemagne's failure as a messenger between the other characters and God is repeatedly shown at the level of speech. Charlemagne's conversations with other characters consist of a series of misunderstandings, both accidental and deliberate. In his communication with God, moreover, Charlemagne treats prayer as a matter of ritual rather than as a sincere request for guidance in making policy. Charlemagne can hardly be said to profess religious skepticism in *Ronsasvals*, but the final scenes of the narrative clearly show a struggle within Charlemagne between his beliefs and his fears, between his awareness of right and wrong behavior and his failure to implement the right and prevent the wrong from being carried out. Charlemagne's descent into *acedia* thus is not merely a negative portrayal of the emperor himself but rather an example for the audience of the potentially disastrous consequences of a state of being to which all human beings are susceptible in trying times. The fact that the *acedia*-stricken Charlemagne is the emperor of all Christendom provides an instructive moral portrait in two ways: it humanizes Charlemagne while simultaneously painting in broad and vivid strokes the consequences of this powerful individual's neglect of his relationship with God. What causes Charlemagne to turn away from God and to vacillate between potential policies is self-loathing rather than the pride that more often affects epic kings and heroes, yet the result is the same: alienation from God and fixation upon himself. If this self-loathing is viewed as a sort of pride in reverse, the connection between the text's two protagonists becomes more clear. Charlemagne is contrasted with Roland as a vivid counterexample: both men begin with a tendency toward denial, but grief eventually causes Roland to overcome his denial and turn to God, while grief combined with an awareness of his own guilt causes Charlemagne to attempt to prolong his denial beyond the appropriate grieving period. Indeed, Charlemagne can even be said to institute denial as an official policy when, upon his return to France after Roncevaux, he denies that Roland and Olivier were killed at all.

This second half of the text uses to full advantage the audience's awareness of other possible courses of action for Charlemagne, as if the audience were watching the emperor walk by a series of mirrors, each sending back a different reflection. The first such reflection is provided by the portrayal in the first half of the text of a Roland whose gradual realization and humble confession of his past wrongs provide an obvious solution to Charlemagne's troubled conscience. The unfolding of the post-Roncevaux section of *Ronsasvals* also plays upon intertextual reflections, tracing the outline of an intertextual void as Charlemagne neglects to initiate any of the reprisals against Ganelon and the Saracens that an audience familiar with Roncevaux narratives would be prepared to expect. Because the text depicts Charlemagne's inaction rather than simply different actions, no distraction is provided to interfere with the audience's intertextual memories of actions the emperor took in other Roncevaux narratives and thus could have taken in this one. Yet the reflective technique to which I will devote the most attention is that of comparing Charlemagne with other characters around him, particularly those who serve as messengers. To an even greater degree than in the first section, speech replaces action in the final scenes, as communicating the news of the deaths at Roncevaux becomes the only activity in which the Frankish survivors are engaged. Each successive messenger reveals a different aspect of Charlemagne's failure as a messenger between God and Christendom; at the same time, these other messengers showcase the new forms of communication that have become necessary in the post-Roncevaux era.

Since the final section of *Ronsasvals* is largely devoted to messengers, the beginning of this new section might be identified as the moment when Gandelbuon returns to Charlemagne's camp carrying a final message from Roland. Perhaps the most important aspect of this scene is that Gandelbuon, like Roland in his last confession, explicitly submits himself to God's will; because he and his horse are so badly wounded, they can make the journey only with God's help:

Pas davant autre la montanha perprant;
mas sos cavals es naffrat malamant,
non pot annar arreyre ni avant
. . . .
A ginolhons si gitet en orant
e preguet Dieu de bon cor fermamant:
"Bel senher Dieu, bel peyre omnipotant,
vos mi layssas vieure e aler tant
qu'ieu puesca far lo message valhant,
comtar ha Karle lo dampnage que prant.
Sancta Maria, prega en ton enfant,
dousa e pia, on joya si espant,
e tuch li angels que davant Dieu estan.
Bel senher Dieu, vera paterna gran,
m'arma vos rent e mon cor vos comant."
A petit pas la montanha perprant.
(vv. 1127–29, 1135–46)

[Step by step, he climbed the mountain, but his horse was so badly hurt that he could go neither forward nor backward. . . . He fell to his knees, praying, and asked God firmly and earnestly: "Good Lord God, good, all-powerful Father, let me live and go far enough that I might deliver this worthy message and tell Charles the loss he has suffered. Holy Mary, sweet and pious, where joy flowers, ask your child, and all the angels who are before God. Good Lord God, true and great Father, I surrender my soul to you and commend my heart to you." By small steps, he climbed the mountain.]

Gandelbuon's ability to continue his journey after spending this moment in earnest prayer may be seen as a miracle, if perhaps a subtle one; as this section of the narrative continues, God's responses to prayers will become increasingly evident. It is also appropriate as an introduction to this section of the narrative to observe that Gandelbuon's problem is that his immobility in an isolated location is preventing him from transmitting his message; as I will show in later scenes, Charlemagne attempts to create a permanent immobility in time and space as a way to avoid the responsibility of carrying the news of the Frankish deaths. As his earnest prayer shows, Gandelbuon is anything but reluctant to bring his message to Charlemagne: he realizes how important it is that Charlemagne face reality and accept the loss of the rear guard at Roncevaux.

When Gandelbuon delivers his message, his personal transformation is marked by an explicit change in his rhetoric: whereas his earlier speech to the Franks at Roncevaux had been couched in the rhetoric of denial, hiding harsh truths in the middle of a flood of encouragement, here he delivers a speech to Charlemagne in which he insists on telling the complete, unvarnished truth:

> Per ma fe, senher, ja celar non vos quier:
> si yeu vos mentia, non vos hi poyrias fizier.
> Rey emperayre, Dieus, que es drechurier,
> ti fassa esmenda e ti don alegrier!
> Malamens vey lo tieu poder bayssier;
> mort es Rollan e mort es Olivier,
> e la es mort Guizon e Berenguier,
> Turpin l'evesque e-l bon Gasc Navalier,
> Estout de Lingres e Estout Guilhalmier;
> mort son de Fransa trastuch li .XII. bier.
>
> (vv. 1180–89)

[By my faith, my lord, I do not wish to dissemble: if I lied to you, you would not be able to trust me. King emperor, may God, who is righteous, make reparations to you and give you joy! I see your power badly diminished; dead is Roland and dead is Olivier, and there lie dead Guizon and Berenguier, the bishop Turpin and the good Gascon Navalier, Estout de Lingres and Estout Guilhalmier; dead are all the twelve peers of France, without exception.]

The style of Gandelbuon's speech stresses the word *dead* and evokes the deaths of the twelve peers both individually and as a group. Gandelbuon explicitly states the importance he places on brutal honesty, a trend that continues as he transmits Roland's request that the bodies be buried immediately, lest they be eaten by scavenging animals (vv. 1196–98). At the end of his speech, Gandelbuon renounces knighthood and asks to receive communion (vv. 1199–1200); this conclusion to his message suggests an imminent change of state, either by dying or by assuming a new way of life. Whatever Gandelbuon intends as an alternative to knighthood, his repudiation of his status as a knight provides an immediate reversal of Galian's trajectory. Just a few scenes earlier, Galian was knighted by Charlemagne on his way toward Roncevaux; now Gandelbuon returns to Charlemagne's camp from Roncevaux and announces that he will no longer be a knight. This reversal may be seen as a move toward the unraveling of social cohesion: Gandelbuon's resignation alone would not undermine Charlemagne's military strength, but it does suggest the fragility of France's line of defense, which is founded on the service of a large group of individual vassals.

Charlemagne's chief advisor, Naime, seems to perceive this threat to social cohesion right away and responds with an effort to convince Charlemagne not to dwell on his grief, lest he provide a similarly discouraging example to the society he is supposed to lead. Naime is right to be concerned because Charlemagne's immediate reaction to Gandelbuon's report shows that this transformational effect of grief might easily spread to the emperor himself (vv. 1208–17).

Charlemagne's speech conveys his immediate perception of himself as having entered a state of grief marked by several symptoms of depression: suddenly Charlemagne feels physically unprotected, old, and too weak to eat. He no longer considers himself a warrior, and he dreads the possibility of another battle instead of seeing it as a way to make up for the deaths that caused his grief. Although Naime's concern for Charlemagne's leadership ability at this moment of crisis is certainly well founded, Gandelbuon is by far the more sympathetic of the two voices framing Charlemagne's reaction in this scene. For his part, Naime immediately urges Charlemagne to suppress his feelings, using a strange and unsympathetic logic (vv. 1218–27). This speech begins with the conventional wisdom that grief is useless, since it does not bring back the dead; however, Naime loses some of his dignity and credibility when he proposes the more bizarre notion that if people had two heads, perhaps our attitude toward losing one of them would be different. Mario Roques was also surprised by Naime's "mediocre arguments" in this scene and proposed that Naime was meant to provide some comic relief in several scenes of this exceptionally solemn narrative.[45] I believe that Roques was right to draw attention to Naime's many slips in judgment, major and minor, in the second half of *Ronsasvals*. I disagree with Roques, however, about Naime's comic value because Naime takes over Charlemagne's leadership role during the very moments when Naime's judgment is shown to be faulty. There is no official usurpation of the throne by Naime, but in the post-Roncevaux portion of the narrative Naime gives the orders while Charlemagne usually remains silent. For example, it is Naime, rather than Charlemagne, who gives the order to leave for Roncevaux just after he finishes his speech against grief: "'Mielher conselh que hom puesca donier / qu'en Ronsasvals annem lo camp levier / . . . / e siam la anuech al avesprier.' / Adoncs comanda tota l'ost as alier / en Ronsasvals per los mortz a serquier." ["The best advice that one can give is to go and set up camp at Roncevaux / . . . / and we will be there tonight at the hour of vespers." Then he commanded the whole group to go to Roncevaux to minister to the dead.] (vv. 1228–29; 1234–36). As in the earlier scene in which Charlemagne revealed his knowledge of Ganelon's treachery but then failed to give orders about how Ganelon should be treated, in this scene where Charlemagne is caught up in a grief-stricken reverie it is Naime who must give the orders so that the Frankish army can respond to the news as soon as possible.

In a second speech against grief, Naime expresses himself more like a troubadour. In this scene, the author returns to a use of Occitan lyric style that strikes a discordant note: Naime's speech is obviously grounded in the Occitan lyric tradition, but Naime fails to observe the proper balance and control (*mezura*) in his choice of words. The narrator already reveals a touch of contempt for Naime in the introduction to this speech: "Nayme comensa lo libre dels sermons . . ." [Naime starts in on the book of sermons . . .] (v. 1245). The idea that this is a "sermon," but one preached "by the book," seems to characterize Naime as a person who unthinkingly repeats proverbial truths from his culture as if they were profound words of wisdom. An excerpt from Naime's "sermon" will reveal his flair for Occitan lyric style:

> Doncs qui sens pert per perdre non es prous,
> E qui vol esser suau ni amoros,
> Creyre deu hom so que dis Salamons
> C'om non gauzisca trop sos gautz delichos
> Ni de son dol non sia trop doloyros,
> car trop deliech non es trop plazer bons
> car trop deliech ten dan motas sazons.
> Dieu, proar puesc per autres e per nos
> que non pot esser dengun trop saberos,
> e qui vol vieure, sie dous es amoros
> qu'en pas sostenga sos afars mals e bons.
>
> (vv. 1251–62)

[Thus he who feels lost because of loss is unworthy, and he who wishes to be sweet and full of love must believe what Solomon said, that one must not enjoy too much the delights of his joys, nor be too grief-stricken because of his grief, for excessive joy is not good, nor excessive pleasure, for too much joy very often leads to pain. God, it can be proved by others and by us that for no one should there be too much joy, and whoever wants to live, he should be sweet and full of love, so that he may weather with serenity both his bad and good experiences.]

Naime's call for *mezura*, the Occitan ideal of balance and self-control, is matched by his polished style: phrases like "pert per perdre non es prous" and "de son dol non sia trop doloyros" show a poet's care in combining words and sounds with artful echoing effects. In the following lines, however, Naime's troubadouresque description of love and moderation as one's ideals in life is perhaps too readily echoed by his description of heaven: "Que adoncs aurem vera dilection, / Tota plendansa d'entier gauch amoros" [Then we will have the true pleasure, all the fullness of the complete joy of love] (vv. 1268–69). The sexual edge to Naime's vocabulary[46] in this description of heaven pushes this speech toward the category of blasphemy, in contrast to Turpin's careful distinction in earlier scenes between using the vocabulary of love to describe earthly experiences and using the vocabulary of Christ himself to describe one's passage into the afterlife. Turpin also explicitly admonished the knight Angelier not to use the language of courtly love to speak of his devotion to the Virgin Mary in public. Roland's confession provided another earlier example of the proper association of lyric vocabulary with religious faith: the very purity of the qualities admired by troubadour poets was proven in Roland's speech by their association with his faith in God. Naime's second speech against grief therefore demonstrates the danger of misusing the vocabulary of the Occitan literary tradition after earlier scenes in the text demonstrated responsible uses of that vocabulary. The message seems to be that there is nothing wrong with the words themselves but that the unthinking transfer of the vocabulary of troubadour lyric to every domain, including the spiritual, leads people to speak in potentially sacrilegious terms. The balance, or true *mezura*, in the speeches of Turpin and Roland resulted from these heroic characters' more profound understanding both of troubadour rhetoric and of the qualities to be sought in communion with the divine.

Ronsasvals creates a structural parallel between the scenes of Roland's death and of Charlemagne's reception of the news of his death. The order is not chronological (the death and then its announcement) but comparative: Charlemagne's limited perception of Roland's death as a personal and political loss is subsequently answered by a depiction of Roland's actual death scene as an experience of spiritual transcendence. In the same moment that Charlemagne begins a downward spiral into *acedia*, Roland rises above his sins and the pain of his earthly life. In fact, Roland's death scene in *Ronsasvals* brings to mind Christ's crucifixion to an unusual degree; though several critics have pointed to a possible parallel between Roland and Christ in other Roncevaux narratives, the *Ronsasvals* author goes to great lengths to make this comparison clear at a visual level. After Roland's confession, at the moment of his death, two Saracens arrive: Alimon, a hostile Saracen who delivers the killing blow to Roland with a lance, and then Falceron, a good Saracen who cradles Roland's head in his lap and prays that the Christian God will have mercy on Roland's soul (laisses 35–36). As Robert Lafont notes in his commentary on this scene, the author offers in the two Saracens a parallel to the two thieves between whom Christ was crucified, a parallel then strengthened by Roland's wounding with a lance.[47]

Just moments after Roland's death, Charlemagne arrives at Roncevaux, and his first response upon discovering the Frankish dead is that of a generous leader and devout Christian. Before uttering words of personal regret, Charlemagne offers a prayer asking God to receive the souls of the twelve peers, a prayer the narrator once again connects to the crucial theme of individual salvation:

Ar fes preguiera Karle mayne aytals,
perque Rollan degues a Deu ir sals
e l'arcivesque e-l barnage rials,
on foron dich li set gauch principals
que per nos ac li mayre esperitals,
qu'el mont non es pecayre tant mortals,
que si los dis cascun jorn a son laus,
que a la fin non pogues esser sals.
                    (vv. 1451–58)

[Then Charlemagne said this prayer, so that Roland should go to God a saved man, along with the archbishop and the king's barons, in which were said the seven principal joys that the holy Mother had for our sake, because there is nowhere in the world such a mortal sinner who, if he says them every day to her glory, cannot in the end be saved.]

Here the narrator explicitly states what was implicit in the scene of Roland's confession: this prayer said within the narrative can also be used outside it, for it will help anyone who prays it to reach salvation. As the articulator of this prayer, Charlemagne gains a spiritual endorsement in this scene and shows that he is capable of communicating with God when he so chooses. Yet Charlemagne then adds: "Si com vos est veray Dieu e lials, / clardat vos quier, que non vos demant als" [Since you are the true and loyal God, I ask you for light, because I ask you for nothing else] (vv. 1487–88). Charlemagne's prayer for light causes the sun to remain immobile for a period of three days, during which the Frankish army also remains immobile, in a vigil several commentators have characterized as "ritual" or "ceremonial." As Lafont observed, this three-day waiting period after Roland's death might be another signal of Roland's connection to the crucified Christ (who was resurrected on the third day following his crucifixion), this vigil thereby transforming the battlefield into a sacred space.[48] Yet while this reverence for the dead is certainly appropriate, the "and nothing else" with which Charlemagne ends his prayer would have reminded the audience of other Roncevaux narratives in which Charlemagne's prayer for extended light instead served his purpose of pursuing the fleeing Saracens. Here, in what is perhaps the most striking change *Ronsasvals* makes to the Roncevaux plot, there is no further contact between the Franks and the Saracens, or any additional appearance by Ganelon. Although this immobility at the military and political levels of the plot was ultimately an authorial decision, Charlemagne is the only character within the fictional universe who could have led the other characters into action. If Charlemagne's prayer for the light to be extended can be seen as an intertextual reference to the epic tradition in which the emperor served as the messenger of God, we might also observe that it is Charlemagne, not God, who makes a change to that tradition here: God performs the same miracle in response to Charlemagne's prayer, but Charlemagne uses this miraculous extension of time for a different purpose, imposed inaction rather than action against the Saracens.

Charlemagne's discovery of Roland's body after the initial mourning period prompts him to make a speech of lamentation that lasts for the next six laisses. Although obviously an acknowledgment of Roland's death, Charlemagne's lament simultaneously expresses his reluctance to acknowledge that the passage of time must resume after Roncevaux, a reluctance shown in his words and also in his refusal to assume his rightful leadership position. Charlemagne's prayer before the vigil was explicitly praised by the narrator, but Charlemagne's lament is clearly transgressive, most obviously because it culminates in his admission of the grave sin of incest. I call this an "admission" rather than a "confession" because Charlemagne's speech is addressed to the dead Roland rather than to God; Charlemagne is not repenting of his sin but citing it as the cause of his unusually strong feelings of loss after Roland's death. This admission of sin, in contrast to Roland's solitary scene of repentance, is not an effort by Charlemagne to seek redemption but rather an expression of his desire to privilege his personal bond with the dead and even to reveal his sin to the other Frankish warriors surrounding him.[49] Charlemagne's lament plays an important role in placing his portrayal along the continuum of speaking styles so important to this narrative. His lament is not an uncontrolled emotional outburst but instead follows very closely the form of the traditional Occitan lyric lament. Gabrielle Oberhänsli-Widmer has documented carefully the styles of lamentation associated with different periods and genres within medieval literature; according to her research, Charlemagne's lament in *Ronsasvals* is more typical of the Occitan lyric genre than of the French epic tradition, in which Charlemagne also frequently laments the loss of Roland and the rear guard.[50] Whereas laments in the early *chansons de geste* were spoken by characters who were socially equal or superior to the deceased and emphasized the consequences of this death for the country or clan as a whole, the laments of the troubadours tended to be narrated by a social inferior or dependent of the deceased and emphasized the personal qualities of the dead man and the consequences of his death for the speaker. As Charlemagne's unusual admission of incest makes clear, the bond between Charlemagne and Roland is more personal than political in *Ronsasvals*, and Charlemagne's attitude toward Roland is dominated by this blood tie rather than by Charlemagne's role as Roland's king and feudal lord.

Charlemagne's lament follows the form, as well as the content, of the Occitan *planh* but departs from it, significantly, in the closing lines where Charlemagne admits to his sin of incest. The structural importance of Charlemagne's admission of sin can be observed by comparing this lament to the Occitan pattern described by Oberhänsli-Widmer: (1) the poet announces his intention to stop writing because of the death of his patron (in lines 1522–26, Charlemagne announces his desire to be made mute so as to avoid telling the news of Roland's death); (2) the deceased is lamented primarily for his generosity, as well as for more general personal qualities indicated by words like *pretz* or *valor* (vv. 1533–36, 1550–54, 1565–68); (3) the speaker declares that the morality of the world has declined with the loss of the example provided by the deceased (vv. 1546–49, 1611–19); (4) the poet addresses Death, who becomes the primary enemy of the mourning world and who therefore is sometimes called a *lauzengier* (vv. 1530–31, 1545–46, 1611–12); and (5) the poem ends with a prayer for the deceased. This last stage of the *planh* marks Charlemagne's departure from his model: a prayer to St. Michael appears at the end of one laisse (vv. 1582–83), but the lament then resumes in the next laisse, moving to the level of personal details. Here Charlemagne recalls the day he knighted Roland and then throws Roland's sword into a nearby lake, thereby guaranteeing that no future warrior may replace Roland as the bearer of Durendal. This gesture is a memorial to Roland's superlative heroism, but by the same token it expresses Charlemagne's pessimism about the future of France: by expressing so strongly his grief for Roland as an individual, Charlemagne also conveys a certain disregard for his people, who have been so well protected by Durendal and who will continue to require protection in the future. This gesture of personal grief leads naturally into the last passage of Charlemagne's speech, in which he reveals the incest by which Roland was conceived. Even within the literary form he has chosen to use, then, Charlemagne's expression of his feelings is transgressive: beyond the point where his lament should have ended, Charlemagne continues to express his desire to dwell on the past and to deny the prospect of future Frankish heroes after Roland. Once again, the author draws the audience's attention in this scene to the idea that the Occitan lyric tradition is not the appropriate vehicle for all types of expression: Charlemagne's adherence to the *planh* model is not appropriate to his station and substitutes conventional emotions for spontaneous personal expression. Although Charlemagne's use of this poetic persona might be credited with lending elegance to his expression, it also creates a certain cognitive dissonance for the audience, particularly when Charlemagne employs the standard *planh* theme of the generosity of the deceased. By aligning himself with the traditional troubadour narrator, Charlemagne places Roland in the role of his patron, thus reversing the traditional relationship between Charlemagne as lord and Roland as vassal.

Distorted Rhetoric, Reception, and Recontextualization

In accordance with the habitual practice in *Ronsasvals* of comparing the protagonist to other characters in order to emphasize the protagonist's strengths and weaknesses, the potential characterization of Charlemagne as a troubadour during his lament is enhanced by the immediate entrance of an actual troubadour character. In the next scene, the *jongleur* Portajoya follows Charlemagne's *planh* with his own lament over the body of Turpin. Portajoya's lament provides an explicit reminder of the conventionality of Charlemagne's *planh*: it is comparatively short and does not follow the same catalog of sentiments. Portajoya's lament takes its overall structure not from literary tradition but rather from the notion that both Turpin's life and his death were expressions of God's will:

> anc non poc Dieus plus duramant raubar
> que-ls miels del mont n'a fach am si menar;
> e fes que savi, car volc asi triar
> los miels des segle, mas vos degra layssar.
> Aquest dampnage non pot nuls homs pensar,
> e car m'aven contra razon parlar
> . . . .
> Don arcivesque, ben puesc dir e retrayre
> que gran legor pres Dieu en vos a fayre,
> que art vos det, engienh de ben a fayre
> e sobre tot el vos fes de bon ayre.
> {break between laisses}
> Don arcivesque, vos que ha fach montar
> lo vostre pres e l'a fach aut pujar
> c'om non pot trop vostra lauzor lauzar,
> lenga non ho pot dire ni dengun cor pensar
> la gran bontat que Dieus vos volc donar.
>
> (vv. 1636–41, 1646–54)

[Never could God more severely deprive us than by having the greatest man in the world led to him; and he acted wisely, since he wanted thus to distinguish the greatest in this earthly life, but he should leave you here. No man can conceive of this loss, and thus I must speak against reason. . . . Lord Archbishop, I can well say and report that it was a great moment when God created you, for he gave you talent, the desire to do good, and above all he made you part of a good lineage. Lord Archbishop, he made your worth rise and he made it climb high, so that no one could exaggerate in glorifying your glory, there is no tongue that could say nor any heart understand the great goodness that it was God's will to give you.]

While Portajoya's lament could not be confused with a prayer, he does maintain a constant focus both on God and on Turpin. Charlemagne expressed a desire to remain silent, while simultaneously narrating a long poem in conventional troubadour style; Portajoya describes himself as speaking "contra razon," which does not express precisely the same sentiment. It would not be inconceivable to translate the line in which Portajoya describes his own speech as "I must speak against conventional poetic form," or even "I must speak against speaking," since the Occitan word *razo(n)* was used to denote not only the mental capacity of reason but poetic expression itself.[51] By saying that he is speaking "contra razon," Portajoya thus could be acknowledging his departure from, or even his rejection of, the usual *planh* form. This interpretation is supported by the lines in which Portajoya claims that Turpin's death represents an extraordinary loss, one that goes beyond the capacities of any poet or poetic form.

Portajoya's speech does show agreement with Charlemagne in one sense, however: he emphasizes that the death of a loved one should cause all activity in the surviving world to be forever altered, or even to cease (vv. 1654–58). Portajoya then puts those lines into practice by suddenly falling dead. Both Portajoya's presence in the text and his surprising death are innovations that contribute to the ongoing commentary in *Ronsasvals* on the text's own transfer of Occitan lyric conventions into an epic context. Portajoya's speech distinguishes him from the traditional troubadour narrator in an ironic way: first-person troubadour narrators often predict an imminent death from a broken heart, but the real-life troubadours evidently lived to write again. When the troubadour enters the epic universe of *Ronsasvals*, the end of the world he describes so conventionally actually becomes a reality (the "chanson de *geste*" being a "song of things *done*"); even a troubadour can expect his words to have real consequences in this epic universe. While Portajoya's death provides the ultimate affirmation of his sincerity, it may also be seen as a betrayal of him by previously stable lyric conventions, now destabilized by their relocation into the epic. Like the birds killed by the sound of Roland's horn, the real troubadour Portajoya cannot survive in the new fictional universe defined not only by the losses at Roncevaux but also by the tendency to act out in events what had been mere expressions of emotion in the Occitan lyric tradition. After Portajoya's death, a transitional laisse recounts Charlemagne's order that the bodies of the twelve peers each be returned to his own country for burial, a movement away from the site of Roncevaux that leads the narrative directly to the scene of Aude's death. The carefully articulated change of the narrator's focus from Charlemagne to Aude at this moment appears to acknowledge Aude herself as the final resting place for the text's continual movement between hopes and frustrations during the scenes of Charlemagne at Roncevaux: "Huemays layssem lo perdre que grans es, / car qui contava lo dapnage cal es, / non es nuls homs que azemar o pogues. / Ar parlem de Bellauda an son jent cors cortes." [From now on, let us leave behind this loss, which is great, for whoever would tell of such a harm, there is no man who could estimate it. Now let us speak of the beautiful Aude, with her noble, courtly person.] (vv. 1696–99). Of course, the transition from Portajoya's death to the Aude episode is also a smooth one in that Aude dies in the same spontaneous way as Portajoya, with an unusually strong emphasis on the contributing factor of character discourse in this version.

The first function ascribed to Aude in *Ronsasvals* is that of representing all the grieving women of France: the connection between Aude and faceless groups of grieving women was made as early as Turpin's monologue in the third laisse. Grieving women also appeared in Charlemagne's lament for Roland: Charlemagne mentioned twice the daunting prospect of telling the news of Roland's death to the women of France (vv. 1516–20 and 1539–43) and added that he would like to be struck mute so that he would no longer have to repeat this terrible news (vv. 1522–26). While Turpin seemed to feel pity for the grieving women at home in his speech early in the text, Charlemagne imagined the same women with apprehension: "Cant mi veyran las donnas ses duptansa / e diran mi per lur bona amistansa: / 'On es Rollan ni-l barnage de Fransa?' / E yeu diray que mort es ses duptansa; / partra mi lo cor, cant n'auray renembransa." [When they see me, the ladies surely will say to me because of their good affection: "Where is Roland and the barons of France?" And I will say that he is surely dead; my heart will desert me when I remember it.] (vv. 1516–20). Charlemagne's repeated concern about grieving women in the middle of his lament may have been an ironic reference to the lament tradition in the early French epics, in which the mourner worried that the death of a great warrior leader would cause the rebellion of enemy peoples;[52] here those rebellious enemy peoples have become the women of France, an irony stressed by Charlemagne's own admission that the women would be motivated by "good affection." Charlemagne himself also explains that the women of France constitute a threat to him because they would remind him of Roland's death.[53] As shown first by Charlemagne's reluctance to pay attention to his prophetic dream concerning Ganelon's betrayal, one of Charlemagne's primary shortcomings in *Ronsasvals* is his refusal to face the truth; this quality resurfaces when he faces the task of announcing the deaths of the twelve peers upon his return to France. In fact, his lament, with its resentment of the women who would ask about Roland, already suggested Charlemagne's intention to deny Roland's death even to himself. Aude's realization of the text's anticipation of the reaction of groups of faceless women is one cause of other critics' perception of her as a character inappropriate to an epic text, a stereotypical courtly lady with no function other than that of triggering the audience's sympathy.[54] Aude's introduction into the narrative almost explicitly encourages this conventional perception in that she first is used as a symbol for all Frankish women and then, when she finally enters the scene, is depicted visually as a typical heroine of a *chanson de toile*.[55] In accordance with the narrative's depiction of Portajoya, however, these generic roles for Aude are set up only to be transformed when she is finally allowed to speak. Aude becomes the primary threat to Charlemagne in the final scenes of *Ronsasvals* because she represents Charlemagne's own conscience, his own awareness that his state of denial is wrong. Thus even Aude's "generic" role as a woman in a state of grief, without any consideration of her as an individual, contributes to maintaining the audience's suspense about the consequences of Charlemagne's *acedia*.

Yet Aude is also an individual, whose own state of grief makes her not only a threat to Charlemagne but a double for him, as Charlemagne himself suggests at the moment of Aude's death: "'Ay! Dieus,' dis Karle, 'ar vey mon dol doblier'" ["Oh God!" said Charles, "now I see my grief double"] (v. 1792). Like Gandelbuon, Portajoya, and, of course, Roland, Aude provides a counterexample to Charlemagne in the way she handles grief: *Ronsasvals* devotes several scenes to describing the process whereby Aude, unlike Charlemagne, deliberately chooses to face the truth of Roland's death. Throughout these scenes, as in the rhymed Roncevaux texts, it appears that God wishes Aude to know the truth, while the human characters around her seek refuge in denial. Aude is first made aware of her loss by a prophetic dream, which she asks a group of ladies for help in interpreting (vv. 1710–21). In spite of the dream's terrifying imagery,[56] the other ladies assure her that it is a good omen, a dream sent by God to tell Aude that Roland and Olivier will soon return from the war. Ironically, the ladies are right in relating this dream to the return of Roland and Olivier, though they will return dead; they appear to be correct, as well, in interpreting this dream as a message from God, an interpretation the author encourages by way of the ladies' explicit statement. Just as Aude finishes narrating her dream, a passing pilgrim informs her that Roland and Olivier are dead, adding that, unlike Charlemagne, he intends to carry the news to all of France:

> An grans jornadas suy vengut esforsant
> e iray m'en en Fransa la valhant
> aols novas dir a cels que la estan.
> Ve vos Karle mayne an trastot son borban;
> e an enpres entr'els un covinant
> que-ls cors en porton an joya e an burban,
> que per Belauda non mostron dolor gran.
>
> (vv. 1739–45)

[Traveling long days, I have come at a strenuous pace and I will go into worthy France to tell the news to those who are there. Here comes Charlemagne with all his pomp; and they have made an agreement among themselves that they will carry the bodies with a great show of joy, because for the sake of Belle Aude they will not show their great grief.]

In just a few lines, this anonymous pilgrim reveals everything: the deaths of Roland and Olivier, the plan of Charlemagne and his men to hide the truth from Aude, and the pilgrim's own determination to bring the news to the families of the dead warriors as soon as possible, motivating him to travel even faster than the emperor himself. The audience knows nothing about this man except that he was on a pilgrimage when he heard the news of Roncevaux; this one fact about him might therefore be all the audience needs to know. The person who is dedicated to revealing the truth is also dedicated to his religious faith and thus would be a suitable messenger from God to Aude. Here we see a sudden multiplication of messages from God to Aude, once it has become clear that God's usual messenger to France, Charlemagne, is determined to remain in a state of grief-inspired *acedia*.

Ronsasvals

The plan to bring false news to Aude provides the final stage of Charlemagne's ongoing struggle with *acedia*, for the narrator immediately makes clear that this plan is really Naime's idea, against which Charlemagne protests rather feebly. Here the established leadership conflict between Naime and Charlemagne, which began with the issue of expressing or suppressing grief, has escalated: Naime is now more confident than ever in issuing orders, even orders that go against Charlemagne's wishes:

> Am las paraulas ve vos Karle lo bier,
> Lo dol que mena non pot res azimier;
> Mot lo confortan sieu baron cavallier:
> "Rey emperayre," dis Nayme de Bavier,
> "Per amor Dieu, sest dol layssas estier;
> Fazes los graylles e las trompas sonier,
> Si que non puesca dols en ellas intrier,
> Per la Belauda que devem tenir chier."
> "Per ma fe," dis Karle, "aysso non si deu fier
> A menar joya cel que'l cor non ha clier."
> Ar fan per l'ost trompas aparelhier:
> Tal mena gauch que ha gran consirier.
>
> (vv. 1747–58)

[Meanwhile, here is Lord Charles; the grief that he feels cannot possibly be measured; his noble knights comfort him very much: "King emperor," says Naime the Bavarian, "For the love of God, you must leave this grief behind; have the bugles and trumpets sounded, so that no grief can enter into them, for the sake of Belle Aude, whom we should hold dear." "By my faith," said Charles, "this must not be done, for someone to behave joyfully who does not have a light heart." Now the troops make their trumpets ready: in this way he behaves joyfully who has great cares.]

The narrator ironically emphasizes Charlemagne's alienation from his men by introducing Naime's curt demand that Charlemagne silence his grief with the line "His noble knights comfort him very much." Naime's fear of that grief, and most likely of his own as well, is expressed eloquently by his order that the trumpets be sounded quickly before grief creeps into them and takes them over. Naime is able to give this order against Charlemagne's wishes because Charlemagne's resolve to do what he knows is right has weakened since his speeches at Roncevaux. When he first contemplated the questions of the grieving women of France, Charlemagne clearly stated that it would be wrong to lie in his response but that he worried about the personal consequences of telling the truth: "E yeu diray, que non poyray mentir, / qu'en Ronsasvals lo covenc a morir." [And I will say, because I will not be able to lie, that he was forced to die at Roncevaux] (vv. 1539–43). In the time it has taken to move from Roncevaux back into France, Charlemagne's *acedia* has progressed to such an extent that he can no longer live up to his own expectations for himself as a leader: although he protests against Naime's policies now, he makes no effort to contradict Naime's orders to the men who are supposed to look to Charlemagne for leadership. When Charlemagne eventually utters the lie himself, Hildegard's characterization of the sinful aspect of grief is fulfilled: knowing what is right and still doing what is wrong.

Aude, who has been made aware of Roland's death and of Charlemagne's plan to conceal it from her, does not show her grief when Charlemagne and his men arrive. She pretends at first not to know anything, but when Charlemagne concocts a story about Roland and Olivier being away on amorous adventures, Aude reveals that she knows about the deaths of the twelve peers. Then, surprisingly, Aude claims that she thinks it best to suppress one's grief at such a time: "E per aysso non devem dol menier, / Car per dol far non vey ren gazanhier: / Temps es de perdre e temps de conquistier" [And we should not show our grief over this, for I have never seen anything gained through grief; there is a time to lose and a time to gain] (vv. 1768–70). Aude's cool verbal assessment of the situation echoes Naime's earlier discouragement of mourning behavior not only by quoting his phrase "nothing to be gained through grief" but by alluding to frequently cited verses from Ecclesiastes, thus making of her speech another "book of sermons" like Naime's. Aude concludes her speech by anticipating and accepting in advance Charlemagne's offer of a new husband to replace Roland; in an aside, however, she lets the audience know that she could never agree to such an arrangement: "Pues dis soau: 'Non plassa al drechurier / Que homs de carn aya mays de mi joya entier!'" [Then she said softly: "May it not please the Righteous that a man of flesh ever take his full pleasure with me!"] (vv. 1773–74). Aude then demands to see the bodies of Roland and Olivier, lies down beside Roland, and dies instantly.

Although shorter here than in most of the French versions (ninety-one lines), the portrayal of Aude's death from grief in *Ronsasvals* manages to make of her a central figure within the narrative as a whole. The conflict between seeking and evading the truth in the Aude episode from *Ronsasvals* not only intensifies the audience's awareness of Charlemagne's responsibility for Aude's death but also reveals the crucial role played by Aude in the text's depiction of Charlemagne's "fall." The question of Aude's marriage to another man after Roland's death provides a bridge between personal relationships and public roles that echoes the issues involved in Charlemagne's descent into *acedia* and its potentially disastrous consequences for his empire. Charlemagne's conflict with Aude reflects his own inner conflict: just as Aude is torn between her personal loyalty to Roland and her duty to marry and carry on her lineage (a duty of utmost importance in the universe of the medieval epic), Charlemagne is torn between remaining in his private role of grieving for his dead son and taking on his public role of leading his empire into an active response to the Battle of Roncevaux. This parallel between Aude and Charlemagne also hinges upon the theme of messengers in this section of the text, for the issue of Aude's marriage was already raised by the message Roland sent to Charlemagne via Gandelbuon.

Roland's concern about how Aude might be treated after his death prompted him to send Gandelbuon as a messenger to Charlemagne in the last moments of the battle. Yet in his report to Charlemagne, Gandelbuon took it upon himself to alter Roland's message in a specific way, as a comparison of the two messages will show. Here is the message Roland dictated to Gandelbuon on the battlefield:

> portas m'a Karle lo message valhant,
> que prenna Auda am son clar vizamant;
> an si la tenga com pros donna valhant,
> com fay le poms dins lo fruchier semblant:
> may non veyra Olivier ni Rollan;
> e totz los cors que soterrar fassan,
> que lops ni cans non los an devorant;
> corps ni voutours, ni aucels cayronant.
>
> (vv. 1117–24)

[Carry this precious message to Charles for me, that he should take care of the fair Aude and keep her in the style of a noble and worthy lady, just like an apple tree in an orchard: she will never see Olivier or Roland again; and [tell him] to have all the bodies buried, so that neither wolves nor dogs may eat them, nor crows nor vultures, nor carrion birds.]

and here is Gandelbuon's transmission of the message:

Per mi vos mandan Rollan e Olivier
que la annes per los cors soterrier,
e prennes Auda am son viage clier
c'ami fin captenga la donna per amier,
com fay le poms el servador fruchier;
mays non veyra dengun dels .XII. biers.
Annas la, senher, si-ls feytes soterrier,
que lops ni voutres non los puescan mangier,
corps ni voutors ni aucels caronnier.

(1190–98)

[Through me, Roland and Olivier ask that you go there to bury the
bodies, and that you take charge of the fair Aude in such a way that a
true lover may care for the lady out of love, just as a servant takes care
of an apple tree in an orchard; she will never again see any of the
twelve peers. Go there, my lord, and have them buried, so that neither wolves nor vultures may eat them, nor crows nor vultures, nor
carrion birds.]

While Gandelbuon carefully transmits the portion of the message involving the burial of the Frankish dead, complete with the list of animals
that might eat any bodies left above ground, he takes it upon himself
to change significantly the portion of the message involving Roland's
wishes for Aude's future. Roland's version of the message implies that
Charlemagne should provide for Aude himself, thereby excusing her
from the need to marry, yet Gandelbuon explicitly states that Roland
and Olivier wanted Aude to marry someone else, with whom she might
find true love. By introducing the character of the true lover who would
behave toward Aude like a servant, and by reinforcing that message with
Olivier's authority as one of Aude's guardians until her marriage, Gandelbuon does much to miscommunicate Roland's last request. Yet this
distortion of Roland's message is coherent in its harmonious combination of Aude's public and private responsibilities. By stressing the
servant role of Aude's future husband, Gandelbuon's interpolation follows the courtly tradition, according to which the most desirable fate for
a woman is to be served by a worthy lover; his introduction of Olivier
into the message acknowledges that this prospective marriage would be
a public affair as well and thus that her guardian's consent would be
crucial.

Though coherent, Gandelbuon's interpretation of Roland's message is superficial and one might even say conventional: he takes into account only generic literary and social roles, rather than the feelings of the individuals involved. By looking more deeply into the repetition of Roland's message, and especially of its vivid images, within the space of seventy lines, one may perceive Roland's words at a far more personal level: they express his underlying anxiety about the prospect of Aude's marriage to another man. Roland's message contains two major elements in two vivid images: that Aude must be cared for, like an apple tree in an orchard, and that the bodies must be buried, lest wild animals eat them while they are left visible and unguarded. Although the two actions to be undertaken are quite different, the two images used to describe them fit together: Aude must be cared for like a tree whose fruit is meant for the orchard's owner and should be guarded carefully so that no fruit will fall to the ground to be eaten by scavengers. This underlying message may explain why Roland took the time to list so many ferocious, scavenging creatures: they stand in for the opportunistic men from whom Charlemagne should protect Aude. If Roland transmitted to Charlemagne his wishes for Aude's protection in the form of an image, rather than spelling it out for him in words, it may be precisely because it was an important and private message. It would sound arrogant to some if Roland stated clearly before the entire Frankish army that a noble lady such as Aude should be forever treated as his widow even though the two had never consummated their marriage.

Gandelbuon's change to this important message, and Charlemagne's resulting failure to interpret it correctly, call into question Charlemagne's customary portrayal in the Roncevaux tradition as a good interpreter of the messages Roland leaves behind at the moment of his death. As several critics have noted with reference to the Oxford *Roland*, one of the unique characteristics of the Charlemagne-Roland relationship in that text is that Charlemagne is capable of interpreting the underlying meaning of both verbal and nonverbal messages from Roland: Roland's careful arrangement of objects and bodies in the last moments of his life was meant as an encoded message for Charlemagne, which Charlemagne then interpreted perfectly.[57] The presence of an underlying message in this scene from *Ronsasvals* would therefore represent only a slight embroidery upon the existing Roncevaux tradition. The change is, however, significant with reference to the text's overall contextualization in relation to the Occitan lyric tradition. By conveying his hidden message to Charlemagne through the juxtaposition of two seemingly unrelated verbal metaphors, rather than through an arrangement of physical bodies and objects on the battlefield, Roland communicates in a way similar to that of a troubadour and might even said to be constructing a message in the *trobar clus* style, which often consisted of creating meaning through the comparison of things that are customarily unrelated or opposed (here, a battlefield strewn with corpses and an enclosed apple orchard).[58] The transmission of Roland's message confirms the conventional troubadour notion that words spoken in public are a dangerous form of private communication, yet at the same time an irresistible one for a poet who has no opportunity to speak to the poem's addressee in person. Like the troubadour who addresses his poetry to a lady to whom he is never allowed to speak in private, Roland must resort to the imperfect medium of metaphor because he will have no further opportunity to speak to Aude or to Charlemagne. As in the earlier scene of Portajoya's death, the transmission of Roland's message shows once again that in the action-oriented epic universe Occitan lyric conventions gain a concrete dimension that makes the articulator of his feelings in turn the victim of that articulation.

Charlemagne's exchange with Aude provides his final opportunity in the text to rise above his penchant for denial by telling the truth to Aude and thus acknowledging the end of denial and the resumption of time with a real grieving process. The careful preparation for Charlemagne's lie in several earlier scenes maximizes its impact as a sign of Charlemagne's refusal to transcend his state of *acedia*: this preparation is evident not only in Charlemagne's own repeated admission that lying about Roland's death would be wrong but also in the parallel drawn between Gandelbuon and Charlemagne in the scene in which the lie is actually uttered. Aude's reception of Charlemagne is similar to Charlemagne's earlier reception of Gandelbuon: both ask where the members of the rear guard are, and both caution the person arriving not to lie (vv. 1174–79, 1760–62). Thus Charlemagne's lie to Aude can be linked to Gandelbuon's misinterpretation of Roland's message for Charlemagne, and Charlemagne fulfills Gandelbuon's earlier statement that a messenger who lies cannot be trusted. If Charlemagne reprises Gandelbuon's role as the untrustworthy messenger in this scene, Aude nevertheless does better than Charlemagne at the task of interpretation: not only does she refuse to believe the false message she has heard, but she also appears to understand Roland's wishes, even though no trace of his message remains in this parallel messenger sequence. It appears that true love has created a meeting of the lovers' minds that makes reliable verbal transmission unnecessary.

Aude's refusal to accept any husband other than Roland, and her prayer that God preserve her from such a fate, make of her death a sacrifice for Charlemagne's sinful state of *acedia* in this Roncevaux narrative, just as Roland's death has been interpreted as a sacrifice for Charlemagne's sin of incest by commentators on the Oxford *Roland*.[59] Aude's death is sacrificial in the sense that it compensates for the spiritual failings of another person. In this version, Aude does not fall dead at the first mention of Roland's death; instead, the unfolding of this scene in *Ronsasvals* separates the announcement of his death from the scene of her death to stress that the direct cause of Aude's death is her exchange with Charlemagne. Like every major event in the text, Aude's death can be seen as an expression of God's will, for Charlemagne's discussion with Aude has been anticipated in the text as the final test of his denial, and was also prefigured in Aude's prophetic dream. In the dream, Aude's death was caused by a ray of fire that entered her mouth and burned her heart. This image corresponds well to the conditions in which her death eventually comes to pass: once Aude has said that she will accept another man as her husband (hence the focus on her mouth), her desire to remain faithful to Roland demands that she die. Yet her death is not entirely tragic, for it may well be that Aude already anticipates a better life after death, as was stated more clearly in the Châteauroux version. Aude's narration of her dream ("when I was dead, I woke up") suggests that her continued life on earth is really the nightmare from which she needs to be awakened. If it is God's will for Aude to die, as the miraculous nature of her death suggests, this is not a way of punishing Aude but rather a reward for Aude's fidelity to Roland. This interpretation can be supported by the strong suggestion that the lovers will be reunited in heaven. Aude refers to Roland as her "husband" (v. 1787), an idea that might be at work even in the moment when Aude evokes her future marriage: "Am que Dieu vuelha las lurs armas salvier, / vos mi podes autamens maridier" [Provided that God wishes to save their souls [the souls of Roland and Olivier], you can give me a high marriage] (vv. 1771–72). Perhaps Aude's agreement to a "high marriage" refers not to social status but to spiritual transcendence: by refusing to be united with a "homs de carn" [man of flesh] (v. 1774), Aude leaves open the possibility of being united with Roland, a man who has transcended the flesh. The narration of Aude's death also confirms this interpretation of a continued union between the lovers. Aude's death in *Ronsasvals* is from a heart that not only breaks but "bursts" (v. 1790); Aude is thereby linked to the birds whose hearts burst when Roland blew his horn, a moment in which some veins in Roland's heart were also said to have "burst" (vv. 926–30). As we have seen, this previous scene marked the moment when Roland gave up on his future with Aude on earth, yet his final message to Charlemagne, implying that Aude should remain faithful, suggests that he shares her hope for this marriage in the afterlife. Thus the words used in Aude's death scene bring together the recurring themes of God's will and of love as it was expressed in the Occitan literary tradition. Aude's miraculous death makes clear that the *fin' amors* so prized in Occitan literary culture could receive God's approval, under the same conditions that Turpin had imposed on Angelier's choice of the Virgin Mary as his lady: that the relationship remain subservient to a reverence for God, rather than becoming an object of worship in itself.

If Aude's death is both a spiritual union with Roland and a sacrifice necessitated by Charlemagne's state of *acedia*, the closing lines of the text suggest that her death has not been in vain. In the moment when Charlemagne recognizes that his own grief has been "doubled" by Aude's death, her death puts an end to his period of denial and stubborn inaction. Once Aude has died, Charlemagne finally completes the grieving process he suspended at the end of the three-day vigil at Roncevaux, and the narration of this process in the very last lines of the text stresses that Charlemagne has taken back from Naime his rightful role as the political and spiritual leader of his society:

"Ay! Dieus," dis Karle, "ar vey mon dol doblier."
"Rey emperayre," dis Naime de Bavier,
"fe que deves, layssas cest dol estier;
fatz los amdos portar al monestier."
Aqui fes Karle cappellas aparelhier;
quatre .XX. preyras hi fes Karle pauzier:
per las lurs armas devon tostemps cantier.
Adoncs fes Karle moynes e monestier,
fes soterrier la donna e-l cavallier.
E-ls gentils cors ha fach totz enbalcemier,
pueys cascun fes en sa terra portier.

(vv. 1792–1802)

["Oh God!" said Charles, "now I see my grief doubled." "King emperor," said Naime of Bavaria, "by the faith you owe, leave this grief alone; have both of them carried to the monastery." There Charles erected chapels; eighty priests Charles established there, who were to pray constantly for their souls. Then Charles created monks and monasteries, he had the lady and the knight buried. He had all the noble bodies embalmed, and then he had each one carried back to his own land.]

These closing lines of the text show the resolution of the true threat put forward by this Roncevaux narrative: a threat posed not by the Saracens and Ganelon, all of whom remain free and unpunished in this closing scene, but by the immobilization of France and the *acedia* of its leader. The insistence on Charlemagne's agency in these last lines, this list of things he orders to have done, conveys that he has taken the lead in the one area he most dreaded before: the public commemoration of what he previously perceived as his own private loss. Naime's last order to Charlemagne only serves to emphasize Charlemagne's resumption of his spiritual responsibilities, "the faith that he owes." This phrase, in turn, echoes Olivier's first plea to Roland to blow his horn to summon help from a higher authority (v. 529), a piece of advice Charlemagne now follows in his attention to strengthening the church; in a small way, it is suggested here that Charlemagne will now lead according to his newly restored faith and no longer according to his pride, as Roland did in the early part of the battle.

Although most of the specific comparisons between Roland and Charlemagne in *Ronsasvals* serve to show the differences between the two leaders, one can perceive in the final scene that their paths have been parallel all along. The consistent focus on the inner struggles of the protagonists ultimately builds the very plot of *Ronsasvals* around a notion that seemed only an aside or afterthought in other Roncevaux narratives: that the battle against the Saracens is, more than anything, a symbol for every Christian's battle against sin. This theme is not unique to *Ronsasvals* but does become a uniquely dominant theme of the Occitan version, crowding out other elements of the Roncevaux material that might have obscured it, such as the post-Roncevaux battles against the Saracens or the punishment of Ganelon. Having organized (or omitted) the events surrounding Roncevaux so that every tension in the text would have a spiritual component, *Ronsasvals* is able to close on a note of spiritual resolution even after leading the audience through one unresolved tension after another, right up to the text's final lines.

The spiritual resolution *Ronsasvals* offers to the tensions of the Roncevaux tradition reprises a trend common to the thirteenth-century epic and romance traditions: a preoccupation with the end of time. Boutet emphasizes the universality of this theme in the conclusion to his study on Charlemagne and Arthur: "Rather than speaking of the degradation of the royal image, we therefore should describe a change in the perception of the king's condition, a crisis in the *representation* of kings, which becomes a kind of symbol of humanity's finitude. . . . [S]ociety appears no longer to aspire to anything but its sublimation in death, conceived as a kind of assumption."[60] As I have shown, *Ronsasvals* is a text built on numerous representations of individuals: its epic, universal quality lies in the link between these individual characters and humanity as a whole, a link forged by the applicability of the characters' experiences to those of any member of the contemporary audience. The fact that Charlemagne is depicted in this text primarily as a sinful man, and that he views himself in those humble terms, is therefore not a sign that this text seeks to belittle Charlemagne but rather that it seeks to redefine him according to the mentality of thirteenth-century culture.[61] *Ronsasvals* connects Charlemagne's sinful human state to this contemporary mentality of humanity moving toward its end by dramatizing Charlemagne's attempt to stop the passage of time permanently after Roland's death. Members of Charlemagne's society, particularly Aude, also follow the pattern observed by Boutet by seeking an "assumption" into heaven. The closing lines of the text provide relief by suggesting that Charlemagne is fulfilling his spiritual duties; they do little, on the other hand, to indicate the continuation of historic time after Roncevaux. The burial of Roland and Aude may be seen as a resolution of sorts, after the importance of burying the dead was stressed so many times in earlier scenes, yet at the same time Charlemagne is sending out embalmed corpses to every region of his empire, so that the text closes on an image of death and fragmentation. It would not be out of the question, then, to interpret Charlemagne's empire at the end of *Ronsasvals* as nearing the end of its earthly existence but offering the prospect of eternal salvation for the righteous. Even the narrator's closing prayer encourages this interpretation, since it expresses the hope that the text's author and/or scribe will be among the saved in heaven ("Qui scripsit scribat, semper cum Domino vivat" [May the one who wrote this write, and live with the Lord forever] (vv. 1803–4).

Reworking as Renewal

If unity is the mark of the traditional French epic, multiplicity can be seen as the distinguishing feature of *Ronsasvals*, where a variety of characters offer conflicting impressions of the events and their meaning as they unfold. This multiplicity is also evident in the text's clear references to a variety of medieval genres and literary conventions, which are combined with one another in surprising ways at several introductory or transitional moments. This deliberate generic hybridity serves as an introduction to the text in its opening lines, where a traditional lyric evocation of spring is interrupted by the entrance of a galloping Saracen warrior: "So fon el mes de may quant la verdor resplant, / en prima vera quant renovella l'an / per miey la prieyssa venc .I. Sarrazin brocant" [It was the month of May when the greenery is resplendent, in the spring when the year is renewed; from among the crowd a Saracen came galloping] (vv. 1–3). These lines are appropriately placed at the beginning of the text, since the theme of spring appears in the opening lines of many Occitan songs; here, however, they also serve to characterize in an unusual way the historicity of epic poetry. It represents a significant change that the spring being evoked here is a season in the far-distant past, for in many troubadour poems spring provided the immediate stimulus for writing: like the birds around them, poet-narrators were inspired to sing because spring is the season of love. Since the *Ronsasvals* poet cannot claim to be directly inspired by spring greenery that flourished centuries in the past, this evocation of spring serves instead to efface the distance between the past moment and the present act of narration. The verb *renovella* indicates that time is meant to be understood as cyclical here, years being "renewed" with each spring just as the epic is renewed with each retelling. The two present-tense verbs encourage audiences to view this concept of cyclical time as an inherent feature of reality: history is renewed regularly by literary narratives just as the green grass and leaves reappear each spring. In these first few lines, both the lyric and epic genres are evoked and then transformed: the audience sees a pastoral spring scene, the indication of a lyric opening, which is then abruptly interrupted by a galloping Saracen, an indication that the narrative is actually set in the epic universe. Yet this Saracen is shown as an individual riding outward from the middle of a crowd, giving audiences an immediate visual representation of the narrative's overall tendency to allow individuals to emerge from the groups portrayed by previous epic narratives. Both the preparations among the warriors and these literary allusions emphasize that the first laisse of Ronsasvals functions as a shorthand preface to the text, an opening that explains, as do many others in medieval literature of all genres, what kind of narrative the audience is about to hear.[62]

This unusual exposition of the text is, in turn, redefined at the start of the third laisse, where this lyric/epic setting is replaced by a lyric/religious setting:

So fon de may an la gran matineya,
que-l solelh lus e debat la roseya
e-ls auzelletz cantan per l'encontreya,
un martz matin per bona destineya,
el temps que fon la Santa-Cros passeya
ans Pandecosta, cant canta la copeya.
Turpin l'evesque ha la messa canteya;
le duc Rollan l'a de cor escouteya.

(vv. 177–84)

[It was in May, in the late morning, when the sun shines and disperses the dew and the birds sing in the countryside, a Tuesday morning by good omen, in the time when the feast of the Holy Cross had passed and before Pentecost, when the lark sings. The bishop Turpin sang the mass; the duke Roland listened to it wholeheartedly.]

Like the first line of the poem, the first line of the third laisse states that the action takes place in the month of May; in this passage, as in the first lines of *Ronsasvals*, May is first described in lyric terms, with the mention of singing birds. Yet the liturgical calendar is now integrated into this conventional evocation of spring, and the archbishop Turpin is said to sing the mass just as the birds sing in the fields. Then Roland, the character already known to the audience as the hero of the Battle of Roncevaux, is named as the audience for Turpin's singing. As a result of this interplay of literary conventions, Turpin appears to be at once a priest and a troubadour, while Roland seems at once a parishioner and the audience for a troubadour's song.

In the closing scenes of *Ronsasvals*, as well, conventional genres are referenced by the narration, only to be undermined by the unfolding of the plot. The clearest example is the scene in which Aude first appears (laisse 45): as I have noted, this scene has been viewed as an example of the *chanson de toile* genre, beginning with an evocation of spring and the familiar tableau of ladies talking and arranging their hair. Aude's ladies in waiting are given names, but names (Aisselenette and Aibelina) whose frequent use in a variety of medieval texts labels them, and the entire scene, as the epitome of established literary convention.[63] For a while the *chanson de toile* unfolds as expected: the ladies discuss the return of Aude's lover from the war, and just then a messenger appears to bring news of the awaited return; this messenger, of course, is the pilgrim whose announcement of Roland's death disrupts the conventional tableau as rapidly as it had been sketched out. Just as the Saracen galloped into the spring meadow at the beginning of the text, the pilgrim's arrival disperses the *chanson de toile* setting by disrupting its expected conclusion. Yet even before the pilgrim's arrival, it is possible to observe the combination of certain epic elements with those of the *chanson de toile*. Aude is sitting "in the shade of a green pine" [ha l'ombra d'un vert pin] (v. 1702) and is surrounded by "more than twelve ladies" [e d'autras donnas plus de .XII. entorn si] (v. 1705), a combination that brings to mind Charlemagne's position when he holds his councils in the *chansons de geste*, surrounded by the twelve peers and other members of his army.[64] This parallel is strengthened when Aude asks her ladies to "counsel" her about the meaning of her dream (v. 1720), particularly because Charlemagne, too, is famous for having prophetic dreams. Finally, the two named ladies in waiting are described as the daughters of specific Frankish warriors (vv. 1704, 1722), just as individual members of the Frankish army are described by their family lineage. I have already shown that Aude is Charlemagne's double in the final scenes of the text, at the same time that she plays the role of the lady to Roland as knight ("fes soterrier la donna e-l cavallier" [he had buried the lady and the knight], v. 1800); the earlier scene's use of conventional language from both the *chanson de toile* and *chanson de geste* genres helps to prepare the audience for Aude's complex role in the following scenes.

In all of these examples, the audience watches literary conventions being disassembled and recombined, as if the narrator were taking the narrative apart and displaying its mechanisms, deliberately breaking the illusion of a coherent reality that is caused when audiences' genre-based expectations are instead confirmed. Just as implicit comparisons to other characters amplify Charlemagne's portrayal throughout the second half of *Ronsasvals*, these implicit comparisons between the poem itself and its multiple literary sources emphasize the radical reframing of the Roncevaux story that takes place in this poem. These generic disruptions at the surface of the text, that is, in the language and images that cause the text to signify within multiple literary contexts simultaneously, encourage the audience to shed the habit of literary reception according to established conventions. Yet this practice of disrupting literary conventions is not merely an attention-getting device: it announces not only *that* this narrative is unusual but also *how* it is unusual.

By revealing its own mechanisms, this Roncevaux narrative dismantles the illusion of providing a self-contained textual reality through the seamless, universalizing strategy that many critics have observed at work in the Oxford version.[65] Conversely, here the border between the textual universe and the real-life experience of its audience becomes permeable, as when Charlemagne's prayer is recommended to any audience member who wishes to find salvation (vv. 1456–58). This destabilization of literary conventions is not a matter of literary virtuosity, not merely a way to adapt old material to new tastes; rather, it advocates a new kind of literary reception. In harmony with the text's explicit theme of troubled communication, the unexpected interplay of literary conventions, particularly in sections that serve as introductions,[66] gives the impression of a narrative that repeatedly reintroduces itself to the audience, as if to convey a willingness to start over as many times as necessary in order to be properly understood.

Yet at every level of *Ronsasvals*, the responsibility for successful communication is placed on the person who hears the message even more than on its articulator; it can be said of both the text's protagonists, Roland and Charlemagne, that they are misled not so much by the words of others as by their own refusal to understand. The test of Roland's interpretative skills comes when Olivier puts before him the impossible image of a happy future with Aude, an appealing falsehood that Roland is nevertheless able to see through. Though Charlemagne at first does not want to believe in his prophetic dream's announcement of his betrayal by Ganelon, he also refuses to believe Ganelon's scornful but reassuring interpretation of Roland's motives for blowing his horn. It is interesting that this scene includes Ganelon's one appearance in this text and that it is the traitor who offers the most explicit commentary on speech and interpretation. When accused of betraying the rear guard, Ganelon retorts that this accusation is the work of the *lauzengiers* among Charlemagne's men (vv. 985–87). Ganelon's simplistic way of interpreting people matches a frequent observation in modern criticism about characters in the medieval French epic: that they are either all good or all bad, since they are portraits of virtues or vices in human form. For example, François Suard states this view in his basic introduction to the *chanson de geste* genre: "Like all the other characters in medieval literature, but perhaps to a greater degree, the epic character is a type, that is an exemplary figure made up of virtues and vices linked to the system of representation used by the author or of the group for whom he was working. The type is thus opposed to any individualizing procedure."[67] While this observation is true of some *chansons de geste*, the "individualizing procedure" that Suard describes as opposed to the goals of the *chanson de geste* is nevertheless a guiding principle of *Ronsasvals*, a choice appropriate to a text that uses the subversion of genre-based expectations as one of its narrative strategies. This is a narrative about personal transformation, an experience shown in great detail for the heroes, Roland and Charlemagne, but also to some extent for other individual characters such as Gandelbuon and Portajoya. In *Ronsasvals*, no character's personality is fixed, and it is the struggle of virtues and vices within each character, rather than the battle against outsiders, that provides the central conflict upon which the narrative is built. *Ronsasvals* encourages audience members to exercise their own judgment in every scene in order to construct a coherent reading out of the diverse collection of voices, genres, and sympathies that animates the text from beginning to end. *Ronsasvals's* reinterpretation of Roncevaux as a metaphor for individual spiritual crisis goes hand in hand with this active, discerning audience reception, which it not only encourages through its narrative techniques but also models through the characters' reception of each other's discourse within the fiction. Thus it is precisely by encouraging audiences to question the apparent, received meaning of the Roncevaux story that this Roncevaux text conveys its didactic implicit message that individual audience members should attend to their own spiritual development, "commemorating" Roland's heroism each time they confess their own sins and show evidence of sincere repentance.

Having examined in detail the functioning of both the primary narration and the discourse of characters in *Ronsasvals*, a return to the issue of historical context is in order. Yet what I have observed about the reworking of the Roncevaux material through transformed character discourse in this text does not, in my estimation, lead to a conclusion about whether *Ronsasvals* expresses the viewpoint of one side or the other in the Albigensian War. When I first studied *Ronsasvals*, I saw it as an Occitan author's tribute to the independent Occitan political and cultural identity that was on a course for annihilation in that war. Furthermore, I read the successful communicative strategy of distorted discourse between sympathetic characters (Olivier and Roland, Roland and Aude) as a representation within the fiction of the author's own narrative strategy: incorporating into a Roncevaux narrative both a glorification of Occitan culture and a harsh critique of Charlemagne (a symbol of the contemporary French kings) and of religious hypocrisy. This strategy could have been a way of circumventing the literary censorship that accompanied and followed the Albigensian War in some parts of Occitania. Rather than composing a forthright *sirventes* against the French invaders, I believed, this author chose the vehicle of a Roncevaux narrative to convince censors that this text was traditional, religiously orthodox, and pro-French. For Occitan readers, however, this version of the Roncevaux material could have functioned as did the distorted discourse within its fictional universe: announcing to the initiated (as did Olivier's discourse to Roland about Aude) that it meant the opposite of what it appeared to mean.[68] I have lost confidence in this explanation over time, however. I was taken to task for the censorship hypothesis by an anonymous reviewer when I attempted to publish an article including it. Literary censorship occurred only in the Languedoc, protested the reviewer, and the survival of a number of virulent *sirventes* from that period attests to its limited effectiveness as well as its limited scope. Furthermore, the Occitan-speaking population was not unified as one political entity at that time or, indeed, at any time, so the annexation of the Occitan region to France, which was not complete until the late thirteenth century, may not have been perceived as a great tragedy by its contemporary inhabitants. In all likelihood, their most universal shared emotion would have been relief at the cessation of armed hostilities at the war's end. Finally, as I had seen myself from the first, this text's entire approach to reworking tends to undercut the validity of such a simple "us versus them" mentality.

It is my reading of *Ronsasvals* as a full member of the Roncevaux textual tradition that must prevail here, causing me to conclude that the purpose of this text was not to advocate any one political viewpoint but, on the contrary, to encourage its audience (an audience quite possibly undergoing or recovering from the ravages of war) to read critically and to respond thoughtfully to the universal relevance of this story's themes and tensions. The brilliance of *Ronsasvals* as a Roncevaux narrative is that it applies to the Roncevaux material selection criteria radically different from those of the Oxford *Roland* and far more interventionist than those of the Châteauroux version, while at the same time it can be said that the central themes and tensions it privileges were already present in those other verisions, at least in potential form. *Ronsasvals* in no way violates the essential spirit of the Roncevaux tradition but rather liberates the central themes of the Roncevaux material (pride, grief, sin, self-expression) from the constraints imposed by the complete Roncevaux plot as preserved by the longer surviving redactions. *Ronsasvals* embodies the notion that "Roncevaux" might have had a meaning for medieval audiences that went beyond crusading, the feudal system, political maneuvering, an inherent endorsement of France and its dynastic ancestors, or even a collective struggle of good versus evil. Instead, *Ronsasvals* situates the struggle of good versus evil within each human heart, while also validating the bonds of loyalty and affection that may persist, unbreakable, between one human heart and another beyond the reach of verbal distortions or even of death.

4

Galïen restoré

Rewriting and Reception as Remembrance

The three main sections of this chapter examine three facets of the stated aim of the late fifteenth-century version of *Galïen restoré*: to remedy its audience's "forgetfulness" of the example provided by the heroes of Roncevaux. This was a complex enterprise because the author's approach to reworking the Roncevaux material in this new narrative was to incorporate into it a new hero in the person of Galien, Olivier's illegitimate son, who survives the Battle of Roncevaux and goes on to become emperor of Constantinople. As several modern medievalists have said, and as the text itself seems to recognize in several passages, this preservation of older epic material in a text featuring a new hero generated some dissonant effects. That very dissonance, however, constantly reminds the audience of the persistent presence of the older material alongside the new. Indeed, I show that the global signifying strategy of this text is to emphasize the interplay between old and new material in this text rather than to join the two in a seamless new product. In the first section of this chapter, I address the issue of why *Galïen restoré* should be categorized as a Roncevaux narrative, though only certain elements of the Roncevaux plot are included in this version, interspersed among and often overshadowed by other episodes starring Galien. This approach to reworking reveals which persistent problems in the Roncevaux plot were considered by this author to be in need of resolution, even though the author chose to transmit faithfully other unpleasant episodes, such as Ganelon's betrayal and the deaths of Roland, Olivier, and Aude. In the second section I focus on the narrative voice and techniques of this version, which affirm consistently that Galien is the predestined hero of this text, only to turn against Galien out of loyalty to the old heroes during the scenes recounting the Battle of Roncevaux and its immediate aftermath. The narrative voice validates Galien warmly as long as he is a naive boy in search of his father but critizes Galien and then attempts (unsuccessfully) to eliminate him from the narrative once he becomes the only survivor of the Battle of Roncevaux and begins to accomplish heroic feats that threaten to obscure the heroism of Olivier, Roland, and Charlemagne. In the third section, I provide a detailed analysis of the antiquated linguistic forms used in this text, arguing that the author used this old-fashioned language deliberately and selectively as a strategy for simultaneously reinforcing and calling into question the notion that Galien was worthy to take his place as a great epic hero beside his glorious ancestors from the earlier Roncevaux tradition. Throughout the chapter, I argue that this text's tribute to past literature also represented and underlined in numerous ways the extent of the temporal and cultural distance it was allegedly attempting to span.

About the Text

Scholars have applied various forms of the title *Galien(s) (li) restoré(s)* to a group of narratives in which both the adventures of Olivier's son Galien and the Battle of Roncevaux hold a prominent place, so that the multiple Galien texts form a textual tradition unto themselves. This group includes not only the fifteenth-century verse version I will discuss in this study but also several distinct fifteenth- and sixteenth-century prose versions in manuscripts and printed editions. This Galien textual tradition resembles the Roncevaux tradition in that, on the one hand, the texts share so many plot elements that it is easy to think of them as a unified group while, on the other hand, the relatively minor variations between texts reflect significantly different narrative priorities. Therefore it is possible to view these texts as different versions of what is basically the same story or as the same collection of events told from fundamentally different perspectives. By adopting the second viewpoint and exploring in depth the unique perspective of one Galien text, I hope to prove that much still remains to be discovered in texts such as this one, which have been viewed by previous critics as mere copies or corruptions of other contemporary texts bearing similar titles and of the earlier medieval texts with which they share certain characters and plot elements.

The single text to which I devote this chapter will be called *Galïen restoré* throughout. I use this title to refer to the Galien story contained in the fifteenth-century Cheltenham manuscript and therefore entitled *Le Galien de Cheltenham* in its most recent edition.[1] The actual manuscript is now owned by the Department of Special Collections at the University of Oregon (shelfmark CB B 54), but it is named for the collection of Thomas Phillipps of Cheltenham, England, to which it once belonged. This anonymous manuscript is one of several that insert the Galien story into a larger cycle of narratives featuring epic heroes from the Monglane family; in this manuscript, the entire cycle consists of the texts *Hernaut de Beaulande*, *Renier de Gennes*, *Girart de Vienne*, *Galïen restoré*, and the *Chronique de Saint-Denis*. What is unique about this version of *Galïen restoré*, compared to other surviving Galien texts, is that it is written in verse form and divided into rhymed laisses. This choice of form proclaims a nostalgia for literature of earlier periods that is also represented by this text's peculiar mix of Old French and Middle French linguistic forms. This linguistic hybridity has made it difficult to use the language of the manuscript to assign its original provenance to any particular region,[2] though the linguistic forms do indicate that the composition of this particular version coincides with the date of the manuscript, around 1490.[3]

The plot of this text contains a series of distinct episodes, some unique to the Galien narrative and others drawn from the larger tradition of medieval epic, most notably the events of the Battle of Roncevaux. I will provide a brief list of major episodes here; summaries of the story in a more thorough, narrative form are available elsewhere.[4] *Pilgrimage to Jerusalem* (vv. 1–276): Charlemagne and the twelve peers make a pilgrimage to Jerusalem and return to France carrying a number of holy relics, which protect them from attacks during the journey. Upon their return, they decide to go into Spain to avenge Marsile's slaughter of two French commanders, Basin and Basile, as well as the men stationed in Spain with them. *Birth and Childhood of Galien* (vv. 277–890): The narrative leaves Charlemagne in order to tell the story of the birth of Olivier's illegitimate son, Galien, to Jacqueline, daughter of the emperor of Constantinople. Although *Galïen restoré* does not recount how Galien was conceived, the earlier medieval narrative *Le Pèlerinage de Charlemagne à Jérusalem et à Constantinople* tells the story of Olivier making an epic boast (*gab*) that he could have sex with the emperor's daughter one hundred times in one night. Although Olivier was unable to follow through more than a few times, the emperor's daughter obligingly claimed that he had, thus sparing Olivier from death.[5] This episode was presented as comic in the *Pèlerinage*, which is probably why *Galïen restoré*, a text that treats Galien's complex family relationships with great seriousness, skips over this ribald episode. Instead, this text begins its account of Galien's life with a scene of Jacqueline giving birth alone in the woods, having been banished from Constantinople by her father. Two fairies arrive to give special powers to the child Galien and to predict his future accomplishments; he is then brought up by Jacqueline at the home of her uncle. At the age of fourteen, Galien is presented to his grandfather at Constantinople; then, having learned the identity of his father, Galien departs in search of Olivier. *Preparations for Roncevaux* (vv. 891–1900): The narrative returns to Charlemagne to recount the familiar circumstances of Marsile's offer of peace, the councils, Ganelon's betrayal, and the departure of the rear guard for Roncevaux. Galien arrives shortly afterwards, clashes with Ganelon, and then leaves for Roncevaux himself. The narrator recounts the beginning of combat at Roncevaux, followed by the sounding of Roland's horn. *Galien at Roncevaux* (vv. 1901–3501): Upon his arrival at Roncevaux, Galien engages in a long and eventually victorious combat with the supernaturally strong Saracen Pinart. In a weakened state, he calls for and receives help from the six remaining members of the twelve peers. After introducing himself to Olivier, Galien sees his father die and then fights fiercely alongside Roland. By the time Charlemagne arrives at Roncevaux, Galien is the only survivor. *Monfusain and Constantinople* (vv. 3502–4028): Galien conquers a Spanish castle, Monfusain, and immediately marries its princess, Guimarde. He then returns to Constantinople to defend his mother in a judicial combat against her brothers; victorious, Galien then becomes the new emperor of Constantinople. *Baligant Episode* (vv. 4029–4682): Charlemagne summons Galien to help his army resist the attack of Baligant's immense army; after Galien singlehandedly rallies the exhausted French warriors, Baligant requests a resolution by single combat with Charlemagne, which Charlemagne wins. *Conclusion* (vv. 4683–4911): Galien returns home to his castle at Monfusain. Charlemagne delivers the news of the deaths at Roncevaux to Aude, who quickly dies of grief. After Ganelon's trial and conviction, the traitor escapes briefly, thereby forfeiting his right to judicial combat, and then is soon caught and executed.

Galïen restoré as a Roncevaux Narrative

The narratives featuring Olivier's son Galien became the most widely circulated versions of the Roncevaux legend in the fifteenth century and therefore the first to appear in printed editions. Different versions of the Galien story continued to circulate in print well into the nineteenth century, while the medieval Roncevaux narratives that had not made the transition into print dropped out of circulation. The rediscovery of the Oxford *Roland* in 1835 caused an abrupt reversal of fortune: nineteenth-century medievalists soon selected it as the most important Roncevaux narrative and relegated the Galien texts to the category of obscure, minor works. In spite of the central role of the Galien texts in carrying the Roncevaux story to readers for at least four hundred years, these texts were then depicted as inauthentic accounts of the events at Roncevaux because of the claim of originality and authenticity that generations of scholars have made for the account contained in the Oxford version.

The Galien narratives not only kept the story of Roncevaux alive during the period when most other Roncevaux narratives had been lost but also reminded French audiences of the multiple virtues that earlier medieval texts had ascribed to Charlemagne.[6] This function was significant, for by the fifteenth century, when the surviving Galien texts were written, this positive portrayal of Charlemagne had become the exception rather than the rule in the most French epic narratives. The French versions of the *Pseudo-Turpin Chronicle* were still circulating but generally were incorporated into compilations of historical texts.[7] David Aubert's *Croniques et conquestes de Charlemaine* (1458), similarly, does not appear to have been written with a popular audience in mind. In an article on French epic texts of the fourteenth and fifteenth centuries, William Kibler suggested that the Galien texts were the only Roncevaux narratives reaching a wide audience at that time, though not the only narratives featuring Roland, Olivier, and Charlemagne.[8] The popular *Fierabras* painted a particularly heroic portrait of Olivier but was far less flattering to Roland and Charlemagne. The two other late medieval

French epics that Kibler documents as having enjoyed a lasting popularity equal to that of the Galien texts, *Huon de Bordeaux* and *Renaut de Montauban* (also known as *Les Quatre fils Aymon*),[9] featured plots in which a tyrannical Charlemagne unjustly persecuted a sympathetic young hero. The Galien texts therefore played an important part in the cultural history of France, serving as a perpetual reminder of the heroic nature both of the emperor Charlemagne and of the warriors who had sacrificed themselves for him at Roncevaux.

The Galien texts have attracted more interest than most other late *chansons de geste* because their plots include the Battle of Roncevaux, yet for the same reason they have disappointed critics who believed that the Battle of Roncevaux should be the most important event in their plots. When critics do not find in the Galien texts a plot unified by events directly related to the Battle of Roncevaux, as are the plots of other Roncevaux narratives, they tend to assume that the texts' unifying factor was meant to be the hero Galien himself. There are a number of good reasons for this assumption, the most obvious reasons being that Galien occupies more textual space than any other character and that he is credited repeatedly as a divinely appointed savior both to his own family and to the victorious Charlemagne. Even the brief summary of Galien's adventures offered above suggests how important he is to *Galïen restoré* and also how extensively his adventures dovetail with the episodes of the traditional Roncevaux plot. Galien becomes the hero of the traditional battle scenes as well as of new episodes entirely focused on him, tracing an impressive heroic trajectory from unknown outsider to emperor of the East and powerful ally of Charlemagne.

As a way to describe both the character Galien and the structure of the Galien narratives, Jules Horrent used the metaphor of a keystone,[10] which is particularly apt given the manner in which *Galïen restoré* was composed. Like a keystone, Galien himself was the last element to be added but also the element that kept the rest of the structure standing: *Galïen restoré* borrowed its main episodes from the existing tradition of Roncevaux narratives and then made Galien such an integral part of those episodes that the basic coherence of the text would come to depend upon his continued participation. On the other hand, Galien's very existence was dependent upon material from source texts, since he was created as a literary character only after his conception had been recounted in the *Pèlerinage de Charlemagne*. A significant choice on the part of all the Galien adaptors was to explain, and in some cases to retell, the circumstances of Galien's conception, showing that they could document his literary as well as physical genealogy.[11]

Given Galien's central heroic role in this narrative, Horrent certainly was not wrong to say that he is its protagonist. Yet, as Horrent's own comments about the Galien textual tradition make clear, ascribing this role to Galien does not account for some important aspects of the Galien narratives' structure and purpose. In spite of the thoroughness of Horrent's study of the different Galien narratives, his emphasis on the plots of these narratives tends to obscure the larger principles motivating and guiding their narration. My point of strongest disagreement with Horrent and other earlier commentators concerns the idea that the Battle of Roncevaux becomes just another episode when it is combined with many others in the eventful Galien narratives.[12] Past critics conflated cause and effect in their perception of this text's brand of literary adaptation: they observed that Galien was a prominent participant in the Galien narratives and then concluded that the texts' creation was motivated by a desire to incorporate Galien into the Roncevaux matiere and turn him into its most prominent figure. There is no doubt that Galien acts as an epic hero in the texts that now bear his name, but I would emphasize that, in *Galien restoré* at least, this was merely the effect of a process of literary adaptation whose priorities remained quite similar to those of past *chansons de geste*. *La Geste de Monglane* as a whole is devoted to Galien's paternal ancestors, and the narrative recounting Galien's adventures maintains that same focus: Galien is the successor to Olivier on both a physical and a literary level, since both he and his story continue after Olivier's death at Roncevaux. To allow this epic of the Monglane family to end with the death of Olivier, possibly the family's most famous member, would have run counter to the compilation's overall agenda of portraying the triumphs of succeeding generations. Olivier's heroic feats at Roncevaux could hardly be left out of the story of the Monglane family, but it would have been awkward for Olivier to survive the battle in this new epic cycle when his death had become an important part of the epic tradition; moreover, a conventional Roncevaux narrative largely devoted to Roland and Charlemagne would have seemed out of place in the Monglane cycle. Galien therefore becomes the protagonist of the narrative in which Olivier's death occurs, but Galien's most important contribution to *La Geste de Monglane* as a whole is that, unlike his father Olivier, he survives the Battle of Roncevaux and fathers a son to continue the heroic line. Although Galien's son is not actually born within the narrative time of this text, the son's future existence as an epic hero in his own right is so important that it is explicitly announced to the audience twice (vv. 3523–25 and 4708–10).

Galien's story was dictated by Olivier's literary past, and Roncevaux holds the central place in both. The need for a member of the Monglane family to survive Roncevaux justified Galien's presence in the narrative, rather than Galien's participation in the battle justifying the inclusion of Roncevaux within what would otherwise be the story of Galien alone. Even Galien's apparently unrelated post-Roncevaux adventures at Monfusain and Constantinople are in fact directly caused by the immovable object that was Roncevaux for medieval literature because in both episodes Galien fills voids left by Olivier's inevitable death. Two possible disappointments associated with Olivier in the earlier epic tradition were his failure to father children and his controversial affair with the daughter of the emperor of Constantinople as told in the *Pèlerinage de Charlemagne;* the character Galien took care of both issues at once. Therefore, if Galien rides out to conquer his future wife's castle in Spain immediately after Roncevaux, the urgency of his accomplishing this minor adventure is related to the narrative's larger agenda of ensuring that the family line continue (in contrast to the way in which Roland and Olivier usually die in Roncevaux narratives without leaving a child behind). If Galien then immediately sets out for Constantinople, it is not because of any ambitions Galien has to take over as emperor but rather because his mother Jacqueline needs a champion in a judicial combat, a responsibility that rightfully belonged to Olivier from the moment he spent the night with Jacqueline in the *Pèlerinage de Charlemagne*. When Olivier's importance to the overall agenda of *Galïen restoré* is fully taken into account, the plot line no longer appears chaotic: everything in it is organized around the Battle of Roncevaux and its consequences, both for Olivier's family and for Charlemagne.

The importance of Roncevaux to the plot of *Galïen restoré* has been largely assumed and defended by past critics, rather than proven with specific evidence, because of the importance of the Oxford *Roland* to modern medievalists. The relationship of *Galïen restoré* to Oxford has been cited as past critics' primary justification for studying this late epic in the first place, and the issue of what Roncevaux might have meant to *Galïen restoré*'s own creator has been entirely overlooked. In fact, when past critics adopted a defensive tone concerning the importance of Roncevaux to the Galien plot, what they seemed to be defending Roncevaux against was the Galien plot itself: because their perception of Roncevaux was dictated by the vision set forth in the Oxford *Roland*, these critics considered the Galien texts to be Roncevaux narratives that had been invaded and overtaken by a new and inferior hero. One recurring comment in past studies was that the idea of Galien's adventures was a good one but that in the surviving texts later medieval adaptors were overly interested in Galien himself and therefore did not harmoniously integrate him into the Roncevaux plot.[13] Even Jules Horrent, who studied the entire Galien textual tradition and thereby showed it the respect of careful scrutiny, held onto the notion of a lost original version of the story that would have been better than all of its descendants: "A poem such as the one conceived by the creator of *Galien* attested to an undeniable power of invention on his part. To be sure, it is not lacking in imaginative variety. . . . But often its features remain coarse, its plan uncertain, its innovations unfortunate. Partial defects of an artistic realization that is not always equal to its inspiration. But such as we may imagine it, the original *Galien* is far from being a mediocre work."[14] Subordinating all the surviving Galien texts to a hypothetical common source has been a consistent feature of the early studies of the Galien tradition and has been an obstacle to further study. Horrent's suggestion that we look beyond the concrete evidence provided by the surviving texts in order to *imagine* the good qualities that an earlier version might have contained does much to explain a basic flaw in his study: his focus on the events that appeared in multiple texts (the legacy of the "original *Galien*") ultimately blurred his perception of each individual surviving text.

Horrent carefully specified differences between individual surviving texts when it came to events; his plot summary is a masterpiece of concise clarity in which he documents each episode as it appears in at least four different versions.[15] Yet Horrent's approach to the overall structure and narrative style of these different versions was to measure for each text the thoroughness with which its narrator recounts the common events shared by all the texts, so he found "inconsistencies" in nearly every version. In his comments on the structure of *Galien restoré*, Horrent assumed that the goal of this version was to promote the achievements of Galien but then wondered why the plot did not have Galien finish his days in Constantinople, where he held the most power.[16] When discussing a printed version in prose, Horrent asserted that, in the text's extreme tendency toward brevity, one could perceive a deliberate effort to limit the story to the adventures of Galien. Yet Horrent noted that it is during the scenes at Roncevaux, the scenes in which Galien is not the only hero present, that the otherwise rapid narration of this version slows considerably: "The prose adaptor is more involved when he begins to recount the Battle of Roncevaux: *here is his true subject*. Then details do not scare him. In fact, he is quite generous with them" (emphasis added).[17] When he considered the prose version in manuscript 3351 of the Bibliothèque de l'Arsenal, Horrent was baffled by the narrator's priorities, remarking that this version "drags where one would prefer to speed up, and races on where one would prefer to linger!"[18] After making only passing comments on the narrative techniques of specific versions, comments that showed that the narrators were not working according to the goals he had ascribed to them, Horrent returned to the notion with which he had begun. In spite of the structural and stylistic differences among the different versions, Horrent concluded that the goal of all the adaptors had been that of bringing Galien to the fore while making Roncevaux and its traditional heroes recede into the background.

Reading the Galien narratives as attempts to downplay the importance of the Battle of Roncevaux in French literature runs directly counter to the goals that the narrator of *Galien restoré*, at least, explicitly announces at the beginning and end of the text. In the first laisse,[19] the narrator recounts the betrothal ceremony of Roland and Aude, a transitional event marking the resolution of the conflict between Roland and Olivier that was a major theme of the *Girart de Vienne* section directly preceding *Galien restoré* in the Cheltenham manuscript. The narrator then introduces the *Galien restoré* section by suggesting that the bond between Roland and Olivier was the real basis for the greatness of France and that the widespread contemporary forgetfulness of their good example has been as damaging as Ganelon's betrayal:

> Leur compaignie fut une amour sans muance,
> Depuis en tous estas ourent telle oubliance
> Que dedens Rainchevaulx en print Gannes vengence;
> Car au roy Marsillon les vendi sans doubtance,
> Dont encore vault pis le royaume de France.
> S'ilz eüssent vescu en leur bonne esperance,
> De ça mer ne de la ne feust que une creance.
>
> (vv. 12–18)

> [Their friendship was a love without change.
> Among all levels of society there was such forgetfulness
> Since Ganelon took revenge for it at Roncevaux;
> For to King Marsile he sold them without fear,
> And because of this the worth of the kingdom of France has decreased.

If they had lived according to their good hope,
On this side of the sea and on the other there would have been only
one faith.]

This passage is metatextual in that it offers the narrator's judgment, in retrospect, of the most lasting significance of the events following this structural juncture in the manuscript. By talking about what has happened "since" Roncevaux, the narrator assumes a vantage point beyond the temporal limits of the text at hand. From this privileged perspective, the narrator implicitly imperils the positive thrust of the Galien story about to be told by saying that the deaths of Olivier and Roland resulted in the ultimate failure of France to promote Christianity throughout the world. The foreboding in this passage is related not merely to Roncevaux, an event to follow within the narrative, but to the fate of the contemporary "kingdom of France," which is depicted as still suffering from the loss of its heroes at Roncevaux long ago. If France has declined in worth since Roncevaux, the narrator intones, this decline should not be blamed on Roland and Olivier; on the contrary, their friendship offered the model that could have saved France if readers had followed their example. What is most interesting here is that it is not the fictional characters but the contemporary inhabitants of France, as well as the entire audience for the Roncevaux *matiere* (because of the universal "forgetfulness" of Roland and Olivier's example), who are considered responsible for this ultimate failure of France and of Christendom. This implied accusation against the audience seems at first an unusual introduction to the text. While many medieval narratives open with an attempt to convince the audience that listening will be worth their while, this narrative opens with an insinuation that, by listening to this Roncevaux narrative, audience members may do penance for their past neglect. This neglect, the audience's "forgetfulness," probably referred to the virtual disappearance of the Roncevaux legend from fifteenth-century popular literature.

Strange as it seems in comparison to most medieval addresses to audiences, this narrative commentary does resemble the opening passages of the Oxford *Roland* or *Ronsasvals* in that it reminds audience members that this is a story to which they should pay close attention because it has been designed specifically for them. Like the "nostre emperere" of Oxford's first line, or the evocation of spring with which *Ronsasvals* begins, the opening remarks of the *Galïen* narrator indicate more clearly than ever the function of this Roncevaux text as a commentary on its contemporary literary and social context and the critical role of audience reception in realizing the instructive potential of this commentary. The central issue of the narrator's address to the audience is still that of identification with the fictional universe, but here audience members are supposed to listen not because they perceive the fictional characters to be like themselves but because they mistakenly perceive the characters to be unlike themselves and thus irrelevant. The declining worth of contemporary France alleged by the narrator had an obvious historical basis of direct concern to the audience: the hope of spreading Christianity to both sides of the Mediterranean had been tarnished by the fall of Constantinople to the Turks in 1453, but in the following decades Charles VIII still had hopes of reclaiming Jerusalem and Constantinople for Christendom.[20] The narrator's reproach against contemporary audience members may have been meant, therefore, as a challenge to goad them into supporting these planned campaigns.

This connection between the narrative at hand and the plans of Charles VIII for a Christian reconquest of the Holy Land would also explain why this passage about the role of the audience's forgetfulness in quenching the hope of spreading the Christian faith is immediately followed by a reminder of Charlemagne's successful pilgrimage to Jerusalem. This episode demonstrates how much a great Christian king can accomplish when God endorses his projects and how misguided it is for his people to balk at supporting such projects. In the Jerusalem episode, the narrator takes advantage of every opportunity to portray Charlemagne as a superlative Christian hero. Upon arriving in Jerusalem, Charlemagne sits on the throne of Christ, at the same time humbly thanking God for granting him a miraculous entry to the place (vv. 70–77). On the return trip to France, the relics Charlemagne carries allow him to cross rivers without a boat and to heal the crippled and the blind in Christlike fashion (vv. 136–41). When Charlemagne and the twelve peers are then ambushed by five thousand Turks, Roland, Olivier, and Ogier prepare to fight, while Charlemagne and Naime instead pray to God to intervene. In his argument for fighting the Turks, no matter how severely the French are outnumbered by them, Roland not only opts for a military solution but disparages the power of prayer: "'Priez tant que vouldrés,' s'a dit le duc Roulant, 'Car ja n'en prieray fors m'espee trenchant'" ["Pray as much as you would like," thus said Duke Roland, "For I will not pray about it, except with my sharp sword"] (vv. 191–92). Of course, it is Charlemagne's way of faith that prevails: by a miracle, the Turks are turned to stone (vv. 206–17). Again, Roland's reaction to this miracle shows that his faith is far weaker than the emperor's: although Roland knows that Charlemagne has been praying for divine intervention, his first thought upon seeing the Turks turned to stone is that it must have been the work of the devil (vv. 208–9).

This episode establishes Charlemagne's power and piety from the beginning of the text, which not only would have flattered a French king who viewed himself as a new Charlemagne but also would have counteracted the negative portrayals of Charlemagne in other contemporary epic texts. Even within the Roncevaux tradition, it was unusual to begin with such a strong endorsement of Charlemagne as a spiritual leader. Although the Oxford *Roland* acknowledges Charlemagne's greatness in its opening line, neither that text nor other previous Roncevaux narratives offered episodes that justified the emperor's heroic reputation before the battle put it in jeopardy. Moreover, Charlemagne is the only heroic figure in these opening scenes of *Galïen restoré*: in other Roncevaux narratives, Roland was the one member of Charlemagne's council who wanted to continue fighting in Spain until the Christians could conquer it entirely, but in *Galïen restoré* he appears to join the rest of the French in resenting even the initial mission to Spain to avenge the thousands of French warriors already killed there. There is a clear contrast in the final scene of the Jerusalem episode between Charlemagne's polite request for advice and the French warriors' resentful reaction (vv. 234–48).

Arriving at the end of an episode glorifying Charlemagne, the French lords' resentment of the upcoming Spanish campaign is portrayed as the most significant problem threatening an emperor who has been validated in every other respect. This episode shows the audience that Charlemagne himself is strong, just, and pious but that he is burdened with a group of nobles who are prideful and lacking in resolve. The negative portrayal of Roland and Olivier in this episode might appear to contradict the narrator's opening assertion that these two set the ultimate standard for heroism, but actually this shift in perspective serves the narrator's differing purposes in the two scenes. In the narrator's metatextual address to members of the audience, the emphasis was on their failure to learn from past literary examples, and the view of Roland and Olivier in that passage was global and retrospective, referring to the two heroes' overall contribution to French epic literature. In the Jerusalem episode, the narrator's purpose is to show an initial problem within this specific fictional universe that will be solved in the remainder of the narrative. This problem is twofold: first, the Saracens have slaughtered the warriors Charlemagne stationed in Spain under the command of

Basile and Basin, so Charlemagne promises to avenge them upon his return from Jerusalem (vv. 21–37). Yet the lack of support for the Spanish campaign among Charlemagne's lords then raises a second problem: the Jerusalem episode as a whole is meant to persuade the audience that Charlemagne's initial problem is not only the Saracen threat but also the selfishness of his own men. This problem of the weak support for Charlemagne among his nobles will be resolved in two ways by the events that follow in the narrative. First, the sacrifice of the twelve peers at Roncevaux more than compensates for their initial protests against pursuing the Spanish campaign. This solution has limited value as an inspiring projection of the contemporary audience into the text, however, because so many French warriors die at Roncevaux. *Galïen restoré* therefore offers in the young Galien a less intimidating model of heroic loyalty to one's king. In addition, Galien creates a physical bridge between the contemporary audience and the historically distant Roncevaux story because he allows for the continuation of Olivier's heroic lineage; with this adjustment to the Roncevaux story, French nobles of the fifteenth century can more readily imagine themselves as descendants of the great heroes of Roncevaux.

Taken together in a logical series, then, the first several scenes form a preface meant to prepare audiences to understand the rest of the narrative within a context relevant to their own situation. The narrator's opening comments to the audience announce that this is a Roncevaux narrative written in response to the audience's forgetfulness of their own history. As is characteristic of Roncevaux narratives, the first scenes then establish a connection between this specific audience and the characters in the fictional universe: the Jerusalem episode reminded contemporary audiences that they were ruled by a divinely supported Christian king in a world where Christians were being attacked from all sides. Though the challenges facing them might appear overwhelming, as in the case of the ambush of Charlemagne by five thousand Turks, the Jerusalem episode as a whole suggests that they can prevail through loyalty to their king and trust in God. All that is lacking at the end of this preface is the French lords' own resolve to support their king. Since the lords remain unconvinced by Charlemagne's leadership at the end of the preface, it serves as a logical preparation for the following episodes, in which both Roland and Galien gradually learn to assume their proper roles as supporters of Charlemagne.

Roncevaux narratives frequently showed an initially proud Roland attaining a new level of humility, and the stages of that process in *Galïen restoré* are more obvious than ever, since Roland's pride initially is also more evident in this narrative than ever before. The extreme pride Roland displayed during the Jerusalem episode resurfaces again during the council scenes, when he smugly announces to Ganelon that he nominated him for this dangerous mission as revenge for Ganelon's previous nomination of Roland for a similar mission. The narrator then adds, disapprovingly, "Mais on voit bien souvent tel se cuide venger, / Qui son dommaige encroist et le fait aproucher" [But one quite often sees that he who thinks he is taking vengeance increases his own suffering and draws it nearer] (vv. 1157–58). This is not only an explicitly negative judgment of Roland's attitude but one that implies that the Battle of Roncevaux served as Roland's personal chastisement. The idea that Roland has a great deal to learn in this narrative is reinforced when Roland first realizes that the Saracen attack represents a betrayal by Ganelon. Although the council scene made it clear that Roland resented Ganelon, in this scene he reacts with shocked grief rather than anger: "Et quant Roulant l'a oui, adonc va lermoiant, / Ne fut pas pour paour, pas ne s'aloit doubtant, / Mais pour la fauceté Guanelon le tirant. / 'Ha, parastre!' dit il, 'que j'ay le ceur dolent.'" [And when Roland heard this, tears sprang to his eyes; / this was not because of fear, he was not starting to worry, / but rather for the falseness of the stubborn Ganelon. / "Oh, stepfather!" he said, "I have such a grieving heart."] (vv. 1702–5). These remarks suggest that Roland believed that even Ganelon would never go so far in pursuing a personal vendetta. Roland's new realization about the dark side of human nature then causes him to encourage his men with a speech articulating what he believes are the most lasting positive human values, the love of God and of one's lady:

Aions fiance en Dieu, le pere royamans!
Car ceulx qui hui mouront sur la gent nonsachant,
Il vivront lassus au trone suffisant.
De rien qui soit au monde, ne vous voit remembrant,
Fors d'acquerir l'amour qui sans fin est durant!
Olivier, beau compaigns, venés avant,
Tenés vous pres de moy, ne m'alés eslongnant,
Et pensés a l'amour que vous desirés tant,
Jacqueline la belle qui a le doulz semblant,
Monstrés pour son amour a paiens fier semblant,
Et j'en monstreray pour vostre seur autant,
Car ja homs n'est hardis s'il n'a vray ceur d'amant.
(vv. 1717–28)

[Let us have faith in God, the royal Father!
For those who will die today alongside the ignorant pagans,
They will live above, before the all-sufficient throne.
Of nothing in the world should you be mindful ["remembering"],
Except of acquiring that love which endures without end!
Olivier, fair companion, come forward,
Stay close to me, do not go far from me,
And think of the love which you so desire,
Jacqueline the fair who has such a sweet face,
For love of her, show to the pagans a proud face,
And I will show the same love for your sister,
For no man is ever brave unless he has the heart of a true lover.]

This speech is one of the few passages from *Galïen restoré* that has already become famous, because here Roland seems to be a warrior inspired by love, a depiction of him that contrasts rather strongly with the Roland of the Oxford version. It is more significant within the immediate narrative context, however, that Roland is thinking in this passage about someone other than himself. Having glimpsed the true depths of Ganelon's selfishness, Roland reacts by turning away from his own selfish perspective and instead viewing himself as a participant in relationships with God and with other human beings, both the men he is leading and the woman he loves. It is also interesting, in light of the narrator's opening comments, that Roland speaks specifically to the issue of what his men should "remember" during the battle (v. 1720), what they should hold consciously in the forefront of their minds. Just as the narrator suggested to audiences that they should remind themselves actively of past heroic examples, here Roland suggests to his men that they should strive actively to inspire themselves with thoughts of their own ideals, both religious and secular. In spite of the narrator's momentary disapproval of Roland in the early scenes of *Galïen restoré*, then, Roland does share the narrator's own perspective in later scenes, as he often does in other Roncevaux narratives.

In this version of the Roncevaux story, as in others, Roland refuses several times to sound his horn to summon help from Charlemagne; what is slightly different about this feature of the story in *Galïen restoré* is that it is the rear guard as a group, rather than Olivier personally, who try to convince him to do so (vv. 1698–1701, 1709–10, 1830–31, 1865–68). This change creates a mental image of Roland resisting the group consensus, not just the advice of one friend; it eliminates the personal antagonism between Roland and Olivier and instead offers an image of Roland alone against the entire rear guard. In this, Roland is not following his own advice to his men or the example provided earlier by Charlemagne: he is not mindful of the will of God for him in this situation. Instead, Roland relies on his own evaluation of the physical reality of his situation, maintaining that Charlemagne is too far away to hear the horn call (vv. 1832–35, 1869–70). Yet here again, as with Roland's earlier realization of the extent of Ganelon's perfidy upon seeing Marsile's assembled army, it is a negative visual tableau that changes Roland's mind by teaching him a painful lesson. The sight of his many slain comrades is shown to be the immediate impetus for Roland's horn call (vv. 1881–83). Seeing Olivier mortally wounded soon afterward also impels Roland to use prayer in a seemingly hopeless situation, as Charlemagne did from the beginning of the narrative:

> "Ha, compaings!" dit il, "je prie au roy Jhesus.
> Qui pour les pecheurs fut en la croix pendus,
> Que la vostre ame soit en la glo[i]re lassus."
> Il regarde son sang qui du corps est issus,
> Oncquez mais en sa vie il ne fut si confus.
>
> (vv. 1949–53)

> ["Oh, my friend!" he said, "I pray to Jesus the king,
> Who for sinners was hanged on the cross,
> That your soul might be received above in glory."
> He looks at the blood which has come out of the body,
> And never before in his life has he been so troubled.]

In all of these examples, the narrator emphasizes that the events at Roncevaux cause Roland to behave differently because they inspire in him a level of pain that he has never experienced before. This is a possible interpretation of Roland's portrayal in other Roncevaux narratives, especially in *Ronsasvals*, but Roland did not change a bit in the Châteauroux version, and many commentators on the Oxford *Roland* consider his character to be fixed throughout that text as well. In *Galïen restoré*, however, Roland's learning experience is contrasted with the distinctly different style of personal development that characterizes the young hero Galien.

Although different from that of Roland, Galien's learning process is strikingly similar to that of the romance hero Perceval, whose passage from ignorance to worldliness to holiness remained a consistent feature of his depiction in the many medieval French texts in which he appeared. Like Perceval, Galien is the son of a great knight he has never met, and he is raised in a remote land. Like Perceval, Galien begins his quest by making contact with various relatives and demanding to be knighted by the king. Like Perceval, Galien displays unusual and occasionally humorous behavior because he is an outsider; at the same time, both heroes have been predestined for specific future accomplishments of benefit to the entire kingdom. There is one significant difference between Galien and Perceval, however: Galien has an uncanny knowledge of the literary tradition preceding the text in which he appears, while Perceval often has trouble interpreting even his immediate circumstances. Later medieval Grail texts such as the Didot-*Perceval* show Perceval needing increasingly explicit instruction in order to pursue the Grail quest successfully; Galien, by contrast, understands perfectly the place he is meant to hold in the fictional universe, as if he had prepared for his performance in this text by studying past epic texts. Indeed, Galien's process of learning could be described as one of textual remembrance, a far less painful learning method than Roland's and a particularly appropriate one for this "forgetful" audience to witness. In addition to these two differing portrayals of heroic development, a third narrative strand completes the plan behind *Galien restoré*: Charlemagne is portrayed throughout the narrative, and particularly in its opening and closing scenes, as an infallible Christian emperor who has already learned Roland's lesson in humility and therefore can harness Galien's talents for France without allowing the young hero to threaten his authority. *Galien restoré* manages to incorporate all the traditional events of a Roncevaux narrative into an optimistic context in which the issue of Charlemagne's guilt is never raised and the prospect of a triumphant France is revealed to the audience from the beginning. It is appropriate that this last medieval Roncevaux narrative ends in a lasting peace, whereas the ending of the Oxford *Roland* suggested that the struggle against non-Christians would continue forever, and the ending of *Ronsasvals* left even the struggle against Marsile unresolved. The unusual finality of the resolution to *Galien restoré* is made possible by the text's uncompromising faith in three of Charlemagne's personal strengths that have been established by earlier medieval literary and historical texts: his piety, his military might, and his ability to administer justice.

Horrent viewed the early scenes of *Galien restoré* as incoherent, but his hypothesis that the redactor felt obliged to follow the order of scenes from a lost source text does not help readers to understand the text's own narrative logic.[21] On the contrary, the hypothesis of lost source texts amounts to a dismissal of narrative logic in favor of narrative happenstance. In this case, a closer examination reveals that the narrator of *Galïen restoré* was following a coherent logic: the Jerusalem episode serves as a separate but related preface to the rest of the narrative. This preface emphasizes the qualities that Charlemagne's lords (who will be represented both by Roland and by Galien) will need to develop as the narrative progresses. Just as the narrator's comments about the lasting example of Roland and Olivier were meant as a transition between *Girart de Vienne* and *Galïen restoré*, the narrator's comments in laisse 13, following the Jerusalem episode, create a transition between the earlier laisses, meant as a preface, and the main text that follows. Laisse 13 does not continue recounting events in chronological order, as did the eleven laisses preceding it; instead, it summarizes past events and announces upcoming events. Furthermore, the style of this summary conveys additional information about the priorities of the text as a whole and therefore serves as a guide to the audience. A close examination of this transitional laisse will therefore provide an overall framework within which to interpret the events that follow in the main body of the text as well as the way in which they are told.

In lines 270 through 276, the narrator restates what the audience has just heard: that Charlemagne has assembled his lords for an attack on the Saracens in Spain. Here, however, the narrator places this campaign in a larger religious, historical, and literary context by appealing to the audience's established intertextual memory of Charlemagne:

> L'emperiere de France son bernaige assembla,
> Au plus tost qu'il pot en Espeigne ala
> Pour payens en chacer qui lors estoient la;
> Il n'a yci personne, s'en lui science a,
> Qui n'ait ouÿ parler ens ou temps de pieça,
> Que [Charlemainne] fu l'omme que Dieu crea,
> Que pour guerroyer payens plus son corps travailla.
> (vv. 270–76)

> [The emperor of France assembled his lords,
> And he went into Spain as soon as he could
> To drive out the pagans who were there at that time;
> There is no one here, if he has any knowledge,
> Who has not heard it said of him for a long time,
> That [Charlemagne] was the man that God created
> Who worked hardest to fight off the pagans.]

Although the narrator has just demonstrated Charlemagne's exceptional status as a Christian hero, these lines support that portrayal further by reminding the audience of the entire literary tradition standing behind it ("There is no knowledgeable person who has not heard it said . . ."). This remark pushes into the ranks of the uninformed any audience member who does not accept Charlemagne as the greatest defender of Christendom who ever lived and therefore serves as a catalyst to the audience's memory of the larger epic tradition. In fact, this reminder of the larger epic tradition is well placed, since the audience must rely on their knowledge of past literature to understand the following lines:

Et en tant comme il fut en Espaigne de la,
La fille du roy Hugon d'un enffant acoucha,
Que le conte Olivier en son corps engendra.
Quant [Charles] l'emperiere qui France gouverna,
Retournoit du sepulcre ou Dieu resucita,
Lui et les XII pers que avec lui mena.
Mais ains qu'elle acouchast moult de painne endura,
Car hors de Costentin son pere la chaça.

(vv. 277–84)

[And during the time when he was in Spain,
The daughter of King Hugues gave birth to a child,
Which Count Olivier had implanted in her body
When [Charles], the emperor who governed France,
Was returning from the sepulchre where God rose from the dead,
He and the twelve peers whom he brought with him.
But before she gave birth, she endured much pain,
For her father had banished her from Constantinople.]

This allusion to the circumstances of Galien's conception conflicts with the events that were just recounted in the Jerusalem episode: here the narrator claims that Charlemagne and the twelve peers stopped in Constantinople during the return trip from Jerusalem, even though that stop was not mentioned in the version of events that the narrator has just finished telling. To understand who "le roy Hugon" was and why he banished his daughter from Constantinople for becoming pregnant with Olivier's child, the audience would have to be familiar with *Le Pèlerinage de Charlemagne*, or perhaps with an earlier version of *Galïen restoré* that included the Constantinople episode. For audience members who did not know the story of Galien's conception from an earlier text, this summary would be both confusing and frustrating, since it says just enough to let them know that they have missed what was a deliciously scandalous episode in Olivier's life. This sketchy allusion to Galien's textual as well as physical sources makes it clear from an early stage that this narrative is meant for audiences with active intertextual memories.

Laisse 13 closes with a summary of Galien's role in the narrative, a summary that suggests that the audience should judge Galien's importance by the service he will eventually provide to Charlemagne, Roland, and Olivier:

> Mais l'enfant Galïen, si com vous orrés ja,
> Ce fu cellui qui [Charles] si bien reconforta
> Quant Roulant et son pere Olivier s'i fina
> Quant a Rainchevaulx fut ung jour qui passa,
> Dont la mort des barons toute France troubla.
> Mais l'enfant Galien tant fist et pourchaça
> Qu'i[l] vint a Rainchevaulx et son pere trouva,
> Ainsi que je diray qui taire se vouldra.
>
> (vv. 288–95)

> [But the child Galien, as you will soon hear,
> Was the one who comforted Charlemagne so well
> When Roland and his father Olivier died
> As it came to pass one day at Roncevaux,
> The lords whose deaths upset all of France.
> But the child Galien accomplished and strove so much
> That he came to Roncevaux and found his father,
> As I will tell whoever wishes to be quiet.]

The repetitive structure of this passage implies that it should be understood in two parts: both sentences beginning with "Mais l'enfant Galïen . . ." announce Galien's future actions, but the first sentence describes his overall achievements, while the second sentence introduces directly the pre-Roncevaux portion of the narrative that begins with the following laisse. The relationship between these two statements about Galien's future emphasizes once again that this laisse as a whole has a transitional, metatextual perspective, according to which Roncevaux is the context for the narrative as a whole. Galien's other significant adventures, taking over the castle of Monfusain and winning the crown of Constantinople, are omitted here to emphasize that this is a Roncevaux narrative and that Galien is meant to occupy a supporting role within it.

Before Galien is introduced into the text, therefore, the audience has already heard twice that Roncevaux is the most important event in the story and that Charlemagne, Roland, and Olivier are the most important characters. This global view is restated in the closing lines of the text, where Roncevaux, Roland, and Olivier are described as the real subject matter of the narrative, even though the adventures of Galien and Charlemagne have occupied far more space within it:

> Seigneurs, ouy avez bien et veritablement
> Les fais de Rainchevaulx et le commencement,
> La venüe Roulant et d'Olivier le gent,
> Temps est que je define ce livre a present,
> Tous ceulz qui l'ont ouÿ, gart [Dieu] d'encombrement
> Et les vueille sauver lassus ou firmament!
> Si fault de Rainchevaulx tout le definement,
> Paradis nous doint Dieux qui fist le firmament! Amen.
>
> (vv. 4904–11)

> [Lords, you have heard well and truly
> The events of Roncevaux and their beginning,
> The coming of Roland and the noble Olivier,
> It is time that I finish this book now,
> All those who have heard it, may [God] protect them from harm
> And may he wish to save them above in heaven!
> Here ends all the resolution of Roncevaux,
> May paradise be granted to us by God who made the heavens!
> Amen.]

Both the opening and closing lines of *Galien restoré* suggest that preserving the memory of Roncevaux, rather than promoting Galien, is the primary goal of the narrative. While the narrator criticized the forgetfulness of contemporary audiences with regard to Roncevaux in the first laisse, in this closing passage the audience is praised and Roncevaux is depicted as entering into an eternal life analogous to the paradise envisioned for the human narrator and audience.[22]

Remembering and Forgetting as Strategies for Heroic Action, Retelling, and Reception

A passage near the end of the Baligant episode in *Galïen restoré* represents within the fiction the complex role played by Galien in the narrative's agenda of preserving the memory of Roncevaux and the heroes who were killed there. When Galien falls into a faint because he has lost so much blood, his great-uncles Ernault and Emeri, thinking he is dead, begin to grieve over him: "'Haa, sire nieps!' dit il, 'Or nous est retournés, / Le deul de vostre pere est par vous oubliés'" ["Oh, lord nephew!" he says, "Now it is coming back to us, / The grief for your father is forgotten because of you"] (vv. 4649–50). Galien's apparent death reminds his uncles of their grief for Olivier, whom Galien's heroic exploits have temporarily overshadowed in their minds. Galien's apparent death not only compounds the grief they feel but, more precisely, allows their memory of Olivier's death to be reawakened, only to be overshadowed again by their more immediate grief for Galien. Present loss leads to a memory of past loss, which then recedes again behind the vividness of the present loss. This episode suggests the most appropriate role for Galien, as well as for the text in which he appears: Galien is a living memorial to Olivier just as *Galïen restoré* is a literary revival of Roncevaux. The apparent function of the new generation is to remind contemporaries of past generations, but since the success of both the hero and the text have the potential to overshadow the ancestors to whom they were created to pay tribute, both hero and text have to be sacrificed to some degree in order to ensure that these ancestors will still remain in view and in memory. Collective memory is a delicate and cyclical phenomenon of loss and recuperation.

Just as Galien can be perceived on occasion as overshadowing his elders, the text as a whole compromises its own identity in an attempt to disguise itself as an earlier medieval narrative. The fact that this attempt is perceptible proves that it was not entirely successful: if *Galïen restoré* had succeeded in masquerading as an older text, even modern medievalists might have been fooled. In their very failure as convincing disguises, these aspects of the text demonstrate that its nostalgic mentality, like the rewriting techniques that shaped its characters and events, is rooted in the basic tension between the desires to emulate and to transform its literary sources. It is important that this deliberate nostalgia of

.

Galïen restoré be recognized so that the narrative's success can be evaluated according to the degree to which it achieves its own goals, rather than according to the degree to which it actually resembles earlier medieval narratives. Both the lasting appeal of this story to popular audiences of the fifteenth to nineteenth centuries and the repulsion it has inspired in nearly all the scholars who have studied surviving medieval versions of it can be explained by viewing this as a work of medievalism, a literary genre dear to many modern readers but irritating to many professional medievalists.

My claim of fifteenth-century medievalism in *Galïen restoré* may sound anachronistic to readers who believe that medievalism could not have existed before the Middle Ages was recognized as a distinct period of history, and one that had already ended. Yet such strict notions of periodization have been called into question by many medievalists in recent decades, and my interpretation of *Galïen restoré* as a case of medievalism provides evidence of the practical applications of that shift in perception, for it explains features of the text that simply do not make sense in any other context. *Galïen restoré* appears to have deliberately emphasized its "old-fashioned" traits so that they would be recognizable as such to its fifteenth-century audience. That *Galïen restoré* imitates earlier narratives only selectively is obvious from one's first glimpses of the text, and nineteenth-century medievalists were disoriented by this startling experience. In fact, the harshest critic of the Galien texts also offered an inkling of their unusual position within literary history. Although he thought that the first Galien texts had been composed in the thirteenth century, Léon Gautier still repeatedly used the word *modern* to express the nature of their faults: "The subject matter of Galien, although modern, was quite beautiful. . . . Unfortunately, neither the author of the verse version from the thirteenth century nor, even more so, the prose authors of the fifteenth were of the stature to do justice to such a subject. This work offers in reality all the characteristics of decadence. . . . The romance of Galien is completely fantastical; it was not even founded upon a legendary tradition. Everything in it is dictated by convention; everything in it is false. It is a true 'romance' in the most modern and in the worst sense of the word."[23] Gautier's reference to "decadence" in this passage will sound familiar to anyone who has worked with French literature of the late Middle Ages: this label was applied routinely in Gautier's time to many texts written in the fourteenth and fifteenth centuries. Similarly, it is not unusual to hear medievalists of his generation bemoan the loss of the "original" and therefore superior source texts that they believed had preceded those texts that actually survived.

Although these aspects of Gautier's commentary are typical of scholars of his generation, they are also significant to study of the Galien tradition, since they helped put an end to the continuous transmission it enjoyed until specialists of medieval literature came along.[24] What is perhaps most informative about Gautier's commentary is its ambivalence. Gautier notes that the Galien texts are full of medieval literary conventions; on the other hand, he claims that the story is not based on a "legendary tradition" (an assertion that distances the Galien texts arbitrarily from the Roncevaux legend) and thus that everything in it is "false." Considering *Galien restoré* as a work of medievalism helps to identify some legitimate sources for the discomfort Gautier and others have expressed concerning the "modernity" or "inauthenticity" of the Galien tradition: they were not wrong in saying that the Galien texts did not measure up to the usual standards for earlier medieval literature because even the Galien narrative tradition seems to have recognized itself as unusual.

Whatever the exact meaning Gautier had in mind when he applied the term *modern* to the Galien textual tradition, he was right to observe that at least one version of the Galien story, *Galien restoré*, conveys an awareness that earlier medieval literature could no longer be reproduced with complete faithfulness. Though the fifteenth-century audience for *Galien restoré* would not have thought of it as "modern" or "postmedieval," the Galien story clearly contained something new that made it more appealing to that audience than the earlier narratives that scribes had ceased to copy and circulate. The Galien texts generated such an enthusiastic response, in fact, that their popularity lasted well into the sixteenth century.[25] Because of their continued circulation in early printed editions, the Galien texts continued to be reprinted in a variety of forms and contexts through the nineteenth century, by which time they were usually presented as adventure stories for children, a status that may have contributed to the scorn felt toward them by adult scholars of that era. I believe that one factor contributing to the fifteenth- and sixteenth-century success of *Galien restoré* was that it captured the ambivalent attitude of its audience toward the literature of the increasingly distant medieval past. Because this text dramatized the distance between itself and the earlier medieval texts that had inspired it, readers of later periods (who felt even more distant from the medieval literary context) could still appreciate it; on the other hand, the author's obvious desire to project the text into this distant past expressed the anxiety that accompanies an awareness of historical change. In fact, the notion that such a mentality of historical transition plays a crucial role in the narrative is supported by the reissue of a version of the Galien story as part of the *Bibliothèque universelle des romans* in the latter part of the eighteenth century, another period when French readers seemed aware of a coming change but could not have identified its exact nature. Fifteenth-century intellectual conflicts in France between self-identified groups of "ancients" and "moderns" show a contemporary awareness of an awkward transitional trend, as do the efforts of other thinkers to reconcile the ideas of the two groups in order to avoid an intellectual schism as painful as the religious schism in which France had played a central role in preceding centuries.[26]

The literature of fifteenth-century France has been studied somewhat less than the religious and philosophical debates of the time, but what is widely known about it attests to the tension of "old versus new" in the literary realm as well. François Villon has been characterized by generations of scholars as the first "modern" poet, yet he used conventional medieval literary forms and themes as the context for much of his work. Alain Chartier's "La Belle Dame sans Merci" was a commentary on medieval poetic conventions as well as on one specific interaction between a lady and her suitor. The debate within the poem found an echo in real life when Chartier was summoned to defend this controversial poem before the "Court of Love," a formal arena for literary debate as well as a nostalgic attempt to revive earlier medieval values of chivalry known to the participants mainly through earlier literature. The fifteenth-century "Querelle de la Rose" pitted against each other critics and defenders of the thirteenth-century continuation of *Le Roman de la rose* by Jean de Meung; this literary debate led to more wide-ranging consideration of gender relations in contemporary texts such as Martin Le Franc's pro-woman *Champion des dames* or the misogynistic *Quinze joies de mariage*. All these examples point toward a conscious emphasis on the relationship between past and present literature on the part of fifteenth-century authors and readers: the texts of the time reflected upon past literary works and themes, and the writers debated about how to define themselves in relation to each other and to this ever-present context of past literature. Earlier medieval literature had already become a separate corpus to which new literary authors compared their works: the most famous of fifteenth-century poems and narratives no longer portrayed themselves as copies or adaptations of earlier medieval legends but at the same time required the implicit presence of earlier medieval literature to complete their meaning. Written down in the late fifteenth century, the Galien text in the Cheltenham manuscript fits perfectly into this cultural chronology, though other critics have argued that the text was merely copied, not composed, at that late date.

Viewing *Galïen restoré* as an early participant in the enterprise of medievalism helps to explain why it shares as many features with early medieval texts as it does with its chronological contemporaries. In a commentary on the shortcomings of one medievalist's view of medievalism, Domenico Pietropaolo proposes a fundamental shift to be made in the traditionally retrospective delineation of historical periods: "History understood as and through recollection fails to see the present as a futural dimension of the objective past or as an evolutionary consequence of the past."[27] Literary recollection across a temporal distance certainly plays a part in *Galïen restoré*, but it is also helpful to apply to this text Pietropaolo's notion of continuity (i.e., the present as located along an evolutionary time line beginning in the past) as a way to gain a different understanding of its notion of the relationship between past and present. Similarly, an editorial introducing the second volume of *Studies in Medievalism* provides some helpful distinctions between different forms of diachronic *imitatio*. In this introductory overview of the field, medievalism is said to appear in three different forms: survival, revival, and re-creation. Survival is defined as the attitude of postmedieval people toward artifacts created during the Middle Ages that continue to exist beyond that period, revival as the effort of postmedieval people to actually produce the same kinds of artifacts or customs as in the Middle Ages, and re-creation as the practice of using medieval materials in a way not meant to be authentic but rather to project contemporary concerns onto the past setting, often through humor or satire.[28] These three elements provide a good framework for my discussion of the medievalism of *Galïen restoré* because all three are traits of this text. Indeed, a significant aspect of my analysis is the tension created by the coexistence of recollection and continuity in the text, which one could describe as combined revival and survival resulting in an overall effect of re-creation. These categories of medievalism allow for a basic revision in the traditional depictions of fifteenth-century literature, since they suggest that the continuity of literary themes and styles throughout the Middle Ages can be seen as a series of conscious historical stances, rather than as a mere sameness that sought to ignore or resist the passage of time. Continuity is not sameness but growth: in Pietropaolo's words, continuity sees the present as "an evolutionary consequence of the past," and thus change is an integral part of continuity, just as it is integral to biological evolution. It is important to note, however, that my understanding of "evolution" in late medieval literature does not correspond to "survival of the fittest": literary texts written later in the Middle Ages are neither inherently inferior nor inherently superior to earlier medieval texts. In fact, I would prefer to discard the notion of "survival" altogether where literature is concerned. *Survival* empowers the historical narrative of newly dominant ideologies sweeping away the old, making the continued existence of certain cultural features appear surprising and exceptional. *Continuity* acknowledges that ideological clashes are certainly real but not so all-encompassing as the master narratives of academic disciplines make them appear; this term also suggests that features that carry over from one cultural context to another are consciously maintained because they satisfy real cultural functions or because they provide a counterbalance to the potential excesses of newly dominant ideologies. When one views fifteenth-century literature as the adaptation of earlier medieval literature for the purpose of analyzing the contemporary state of literature, supposedly stagnant imitation shows itself to be observant, self-aware historical and literary analysis; this tendency toward comparative analysis in late medieval literature would be entirely appropriate to an age of lively intellectual debate. As is appropriate to a work of medievalism, *Galïen restoré* maintains a consistent tension between stability and change, continuity and recollection.[29] This view of *Galïen restoré* as animated by a deliberate tension between past and present, remembering and forgetting, is applicable to its form, its narrative strategies, and even its linguistic forms.

The very fact that this late-fifteenth-century text was written in rhymed laisses is indicative of a desire to set itself apart from contemporary epics and to associate itself instead with those of the earlier Middle Ages. The opposite mode of literary adaptation, replacing verse narratives with prose reworkings, not only was the dominant trend during this period of French literary history but actually was represented by many authors as a necessity for sociolinguistic or even moral reasons. For centuries, prose had been increasingly perceived as the form in which truthful and legitimate works were written, while verse was associated with fantasy and impiety. By the fourteenth and fifteenth centuries, prose was considered superior to verse for practical as well as ideological reasons: authors claimed that it was easier for contemporary audiences to understand. For example, a prose reworking of *Guillaume d'Orange* expressed this view as if prose were inherently more clear than verse: "[A]y entrepris de translater et rediger ceste presente hystoire de rhime ancienne en prose en plus cler et entendible langage que ladicte rime ne porte" (I have undertaken to translate and compose this formerly rhyming story into prose, in more clear and intelligible language than rhyme can bear).[30] Note how easily the phrase *rhime ancienne* is inserted into this sentence: while in this context the author was speaking literally about adapting a former verse text into prose, verse was also generally viewed as antiquated during this period of narrative production. Even this author of a rhymed *chanson de geste* recognized that the verse form led inevitably to distortions of truth: "Nus hom ne puet chançon de jeste dire / Que il ne mente la ou li vers define, / As mos drecier et a tailler la rime" (No one can say a *chanson de geste* without lying where the line ends, in arranging the words and in carving out the rhyme).[31] Thus the choice of prose or verse for a fifteenth-century narrative was a way to guide its reception: at a time when nearly everyone opted for prose, to choose verse for *Galïen restoré* would have been to make a strong statement that this epic narrative should be read differently from others of its time.[32] The choice of verse conveyed the impression that this text was not to be taken as truth: its literariness was considered a more important aspect of its identity than was its historicity or even its potential to appeal to the largest possible audience. In other words, the form of *Galïen restoré* deliberately announced to its audience an intention to examine the literary issue of portraying the past rather than an intention of portraying the past faithfully.

Galïen restoré appears at first to be a mere compilation of earlier medieval texts, and its rhymed form contributes to this impression of extreme literary conservatism. On the other hand, its ambivalent portrayal of Galïen's heroism at various points in the narrative makes of the entire text an elaboration upon its complex view of the "old versus new" literary tension it shared with other texts of its time. Thus *Galïen restoré* is hardly the anomaly it has been called; on the contrary, the text can be seen as an effort to work through at all levels (form, plot, narration, and language) the period's literary preoccupation with the proper relationship of new texts to those of the past. In the following pages, I demonstrate how this relationship between past and present is dramatized metaphorically by the narration of Galïen's adventures, particularly by the way in which the narrative voice shifts its sympathy from Galïen to the more traditional characters (Roland, Olivier, and Charlemagne) in the scenes during and immediately after the Battle of Roncevaux. In the final section of the chapter, I will demonstrate how these same narrative tensions are reinforced by the selective use of antiquated linguistic forms in such scenes.

The metatextual narrative frame of audience "forgetfulness" already cited from the opening and closing lines of the text provides an introduction to the evidence I present in the following pages: the narrator's comments here suggest that Roncevaux was a literary inheritance worthy of a strenuous preservation effort because it was a source of collective memory. The narrator's lesson in these addresses to the audience is that forgetfulness of Roncevaux leads to real-life ruin, while being reminded of Roncevaux (or providing that reminder as the narrator) prepares one to enter paradise. Galien's behavior in the sections of the text devoted to him shows that he is the embodiment of this program of active remembrance as a remedy for collective self-forgetting. Indeed, the appeal of Galien might be understood best if he is considered to be the personification of remembrance. Galien makes more sense as a personification than as a person: his behavior is somewhat erratic and his thought processes are almost entirely hidden from the audience, so that he does not demonstrate the kind of observable moral development typical of many medieval heroes. Unlike Roland and Olivier, Galien does not engage in long monologues analyzing the various situations in which he finds himself; instead, Galien's opinions and plans usually appear in the form of sudden, full-blown solutions to problems. This is possible for Galien because he is guided by an ancestral (and therefore literary) memory of astounding accuracy. Since the audience observes Galien from the moment of his birth, we cannot assume that his behavior is motivated by past experience; instead, the behavior of the young and inexperienced Galien can be explained only by his imitation of literary models. Galien remains an entertaining figure through his many adventures in the early section of the text because his behavior is both surprising and familiar: surprising because the audience has no knowledge of his inner thoughts and feelings, yet also familiar and successful because he is always following literary precedents.

The most significant example of Galien's use of literary precedent is his apparently intuitive knowledge of the circumstances of the Battle of Roncevaux and of his own predestined role in that battle. For example, Galien vows to help his father in battle before he even discovers his true identity. When asked who his father is, Galien replies:

"Ne sçay," dist Galïen, "foy que doy saint Amant,
Oncques ne vy mon pere en jour de mon vivant.
Mais se je le sçavoye en nul païs manant,
Feust a mort ou a vie, je [l'iroye] querant;
Et s'il estoit en guerre ou en estour pesant,
Mais que on me prestast une espee trenchant,

Tant ferir y voulroye et arriere et avant,
Envers ses ennemis je lui seroye aidant."
(vv. 471–78)

["I do not know," says Galien, "by the faith that I owe to Saint
Amand,
I have never seen my father in my life.
But if I knew that he was in any country,
Whether alive or dead, I would go looking for him;
And if he was in a war or a difficult battle,
As soon as someone gave me a sharp sword,
I would want to strike there, behind and before him,
so that I would be helping him against his enemies."]

Of course, these are the exact circumstances in which Galien does eventually meet his father: he finds Olivier in a foreign country, in the midst of a difficult battle, and he joins the fight against Olivier's enemies using a sword recently given to him. Though in this early passage Galien has only a vague intuition about Olivier's plight and about the literary tradition of which he is a part, his perception of his circumstances sharpens later, when he meets Ganelon at Charlemagne's camp. When Galien introduces himself as Olivier's son, Ganelon demands that he give up his fine horse, which he considers too good for a bastard to ride. Having been insulted in this way, Galien does not respond with immediate indignation but instead asks Ganelon's name, as if to compare the man's behavior to what he already knows about a villain he might encounter in Charlemagne's retinue. When he hears that it is indeed Ganelon who has insulted him, Galien announces that he knows of the evil lurking under Ganelon's elegant appearance:

Qui bien voit vo viaire et vostre barbe meslee,
Mieulx semblés estre faulx que chevalier d'espee;
Je vouldroie gaiger sus ma teste couppee,
Ja de vous ne sera bonne chançon chantee,
On parle[ra] de vous jusques a la mer salee.
(vv. 1573–1578)

[To whoever sees your appearance and your gray beard
You look more like a false man than a knight with a sword;
I would like to wager on my own severed head,

That never will there be a good song sung about you,
There will be talk about you all the way to the salty sea.]

Galien's description of Ganelon's apparent but misleading dignity strengthens the impression that the young hero suspects Ganelon's "false" nature because he has access to inside information about the traitor. The last lines of Galien's speech allude to Ganelon's literary reputation, another hint that Galien has formed his opinion of Ganelon on the basis of a knowledge of past literary texts. Galien claims later that his grandfather Regnier warned him to avoid Ganelon (vv. 1598–1601), but that warning did not appear in the earlier scene between Galien and Regnier; instead, this claim might have been an attempt to account for Galien's uncanny prescience by claiming a mundane source for his negative opinion of Ganelon. Yet even if the audience is meant to assume that Regnier really did warn Galien about Ganelon in an unnarrated portion of their conversation, Galien's next words provide the most surprising evidence yet of his portrayal as possessed of intertextual knowledge and memory: "Faictes moy chevalier! Pour Dieu vous en prion, / Puis iray a l'encontre Olivier le baron, / Qui dedens Rainchevaulx acent Marsilion; / Je me doubte forment de mortel traïson." [Make me a knight! By God I ask this of you, / And then I will go to meet Lord Olivier, / Who is waiting for Marsile at Roncevaux: / I strongly suspect a deadly betrayal.] (vv. 1604–7). Galien describes Olivier as awaiting Marsile at Roncevaux, even though the names "Marsile" and "Roncevaux" have never before been mentioned in his presence. He also alludes to a betrayal, and in the context of this conversation about Ganelon the implicit accusation against Ganelon immediately registers, causing the traitor to flush with rage and to threaten Galien with bodily harm (vv. 1608–10). All in all, the confrontation between Galien and Ganelon suggests that the young outsider recognizes the traitor because he already knows about his misdeeds through earlier Roncevaux narratives: only such intertextual knowledge would account for his specific reference to Roncevaux.

Galien's intertextual awareness may have struck a delightfully familiar chord with the audience, who resembled Galien in that they entered the fictional universe of each Roncevaux narrative already knowing its most significant characters and events. By the same token, however, Galien's intertextual advantage could have made his adventures boring if it had caused him to pursue the most appropriate solution to every problem, having heard it all before. Heroes of past medieval narratives, such as Galahad in *La Queste del Saint Graal*, had demonstrated the inherent weakness of plots built around an ultimate success that the audience knows from the beginning to have been predestined. Galahad might have been the most successful participant in the Grail quest, but it was up to the other characters in that narrative to maintain the audience's sense of sympathy and suspense. Galien provides a more appealing model of the predestined hero because he chooses his actions not by infallible instinct but by selective memory and analogy. In his confrontation with Ganelon, for example, Galien appears to be following a predetermined course of events, which initially makes him appear wise, mature, and infallible. When Ganelon makes a physical threat against him, however, Galien loses his temper and oversteps the boundaries of the role delineated for him by the narrative. Having been threatened with an eventual beheading, Galien draws his sword and nearly cuts Ganelon's head off then and there, and it takes four French warriors to hold him back (vv. 1608–17). Galien makes another attempt on Ganelon's life after the Battle of Roncevaux, and he is again prevented from completing his blow because this death for Ganelon would violate the established textual precedent: Charlemagne's lords pull Galien away from Ganelon, saying, "Il mourra d'aultre mort en fine verités" [He will die by another death, in truth] (v. 3461). The "other death" to which Ganelon is doomed, of course, takes place in the traditional closing scene to the Roncevaux plot. In this particular case, Galien's failure to follow textual precedent might have made his connection to the audience particularly pronounced: one of the frustrations of the Roncevaux audience is that of knowing who the traitor is and nevertheless being forced to watch Ganelon's betrayal unfold in spite of a number of moments in which it might have been prevented or at least mitigated. Just as audiences watching horror movies today occasionally shout out warnings to the characters about to become victims, the contemporary audience for *Galïen restoré* could see in the new young hero the dramatization of their own desire to use their knowledge of the Roncevaux plot to prevent some of the suffering it inevitably held in store.

In addition to his ancestral, intertextual memory, Galien is guided by an intratextual precedent: in the scene of Galien's birth, two fairies offer a sketch of the events to come by making specific predictions about Galien's future achievements. These fairies have been sent by God (vv. 328–30) to give Galien the precise supernatural gifts he will need in order to face the challenges to come in this narrative. Although other commentators have considered the fairies to be a fanciful flourish, out of place in the solemn context of a Roncevaux narrative, actually these messengers make sense within the logic of the narrative as a monument to textual remembrance: the fairies articulate God's will in the form of a statement that Galien can "remember" at the appropriate time. In fact, the fairy Galienne announces that her presence at Galien's birth is meant to become a lasting verbal memory: she demands that Galien be named for her, "afin que sa mere que orendroit voyon / Lui souviengne de nous quant nous departiron" [so that his mother whom we see here / will remind him of us once we have departed] (vv. 339–41). The fairies give Galien extraordinary strength and even invulnerability, announcing that he cannot be killed in combat or "by treachery" and that he will heal from any wound within three days (vv. 331–36). They also announce that he will be emperor of Constantinople and a "duc de renom" (v. 337), setting the stage for Galien's future rise to positions of power in France and Spain. Finally, the fairies make an announcement that echoes the narrator's summary of Galien's most significant future accomplishment. The fairy Esglentine begins:

"Et quant les XII pers seront a mort finé,
Tant fera cest enfant a son branc aceré,
Que [Charles] l'emperiere et tout l'autre barné,
Sera par cest enfant de la mort respité."
"Ma seur," dist Galienne, "vous avez bien parlé,
Puisque restor[er]a Charles et son barné,
Des gens sera nommé Galien Restoré."
(vv. 351–57)

["And when the twelve peers will be killed,
So much will this child do with his steel blade,
That [Charles] the emperor and all the other lords
Will be by this child rescued from death."
"My sister," said Galienne, "you have spoken well,
Since he will restore Charles and his lords,
By people he will be called Galien Restoré."]

Galien will not only "comfort" Charlemagne (as the narrator has already said in lines 289–90) but actually save him and all of his lords from death. This prediction expands upon the function the narrator has assigned to Galien but also confirms the overall limit the narrator has placed upon Galien's heroism: in spite of the many other glorious accomplishments they predict for Galien, the fairies ultimately confirm the narrator's statement that what is most heroic about Galien is his support of Charlemagne in the post-Roncevaux episodes. Again, as with the nostalgic language of this text, the fairies' speeches provide a surprising new example of an established tendency of the Roncevaux textual tradition: that of character discourse to reinforce certain metatextual or metaliterary implications of the primary narrator.

The fairies describe their verbal predictions repeatedly as "a gift" (vv. 311, 312, 323, 325, 343, 344); this singular gift is the fairies' verbal articulation of Galien's multiple personal qualities and future achievements. What the fairies give to Galien is a personalized narrative that, along with those provided by previous epics featuring Olivier, offers Galien a complete guide for his future behavior. Galien's unique heroic quality is the ability to remember and act upon this announcement of his destiny even though he heard it moments after his birth, a time that is normally inaccessible later in life through a conscious effort of memory. Although the fairy Galienne stressed how important it was for Galien's mother to remind Galien about what the fairies said, there is no evidence that she does so or recounts the incident to any other character. What Galien knows about the fairies' visit, therefore, seems to be available to him only by means of his unusual heroic memory. Galien's apparent ignorance of his own name provides a concrete example of a piece of the fairies' discourse that is activated only by the hero's memory at the appropriate predestined juncture in the narrative. Galienne links Galien's name to memory when she first pronounces it, and Galien's name continues to play that role later in the text when it is pronounced by the narrator and by other characters with narrative functions. The full name given to Galien by the fairies and used at his baptism, Galien Restoré, appears relatively rarely in the text but has been a recurring concern of previous critical studies of it. Certainly the modern connotations of the epithet *restoré* seem appropriate to the hero of this narrative about literary revival and memory. Moreover, Peter Dembowski's detailed examination of Galien's name argued that a desire for an uncompromisingly epic past led the author of *Galïen restoré* to offer a new explanation of Galien's name that would be more in keeping with its modern meaning: by emphasizing that *restoré* refers to Galien's future support of Charlemagne and his lords after Roncevaux, *Galïen restoré* takes the focus off the fact that the hero of the text was named for a female fairy (the first meaning of *Galïen restoré* actually was that the young hero represented a new Galienne).[33] Since the name itself has been studied in some detail already, with conclusions that amply support the point that it corresponds to the narrative's larger goal of literary revival, I will turn here to the question of how the name is used within the text.

With the exception of three instances, to which I will return, the full name Galien Restoré is used only by the narrator. In fact, the rare appearances of his full name seem to serve as a narrative mnemonic device to remind the audience of Galien's glorious future exploits during moments when something appears to put his future success in doubt. Each time the narrator refers to him as Galien Restoré, the audience is reminded of the fairies' explanation of the name: Galien will be the one to save France after Roncevaux, no matter how unlikely that might appear at the moment. Examples of this use of "Galien Restoré" as a comforting reminder begin with the first threat Galien faces upon leaving Constantinople in search of his father. After his treacherous uncles have finished making their plans to kill Galien in an ambush, the narrator exclaims, "Or veuille Dieu garder Galïen Restoré!" [Now may God protect Galien Restoré!] (v. 570). It is appropriate that this appeal includes the epithet given to Galien by the fairies, since the fairies said that Galien would never be killed through treachery (v. 332); thus the epithet serves as a reminder that the uncles' plan can never succeed. Indeed, this reminder seems to work at once on the narrator, who abruptly stops fearing for Galien's safety and states that the uncles' plans are doomed to failure:

> La mort de Galien ont ensemble juré;
> Mais ne fut pas ainsi comment l'ont devisé,
> Bien leur venist autant, ja n'en feussent meslé.
> {break between laisses}
> Galien Restoré, que Dieu puisse beneir,
> De Constantin le noble s'on ala departir.
> (vv. 575–79)

[Together they plotted the death of Galien;
But it did not happen the way they planned it,
Good would have come to them, if they had never undertaken this.

Galien Restoré, may God bless him,
From Constantinople began to depart.]

This first departure is interrupted by the attempted ambush, but after Galien defeats the uncles and their men, the narrator again uses his full name to conclude the episode in which it has played an important part: "Au roy Hugues s'en part Galien Restoré" [From King Hugues Galien

Restoré takes his leave] (v. 778). Thus the name is used at the introduction of the threat and again at the moment of the threat's resolution.

The narrator uses Galien's full name in a similar way during his combat with the Saracen Pinart. When Galien knocks Pinart off his horse, Pinart reminds Galien that he must treat him fairly, since Pinart did not kill Galien when he first found him asleep in a field. Although Galien agrees that the Saracen could have killed him ("'Tu diz voir,' ce respont Galien Restoré," v. 2424), the narrator's use of his full name here reminds the audience that, in truth, Galien could not have been killed in this way because the fairies said that he could not be killed through treachery or, for that matter, in any war (vv. 333–34) or single combat (vv. 345–46). When Galien wins the combat by killing Pinart, the narrator again uses his full name, as if to emphasize that this victory has been a foregone conclusion (v. 2683). Yet this victory itself puts him in danger, since it causes Pinart's men to attack him as a group. When they cut Galien's staff out of his hand, he worries that his sword will do no good against them, since it was ineffective against the supernaturally invulnerable Pinart. Both the narrator and the audience understand that Galien's anxiety that all the Saracens may have impenetrable skin is ridiculous, however, and by using Galien's full name to introduce this worry, the narrator widens for the audience's benefit the ironic distance between Galien's actual situation and his mistaken perception: "Galïen Restoré va grant deul demenant / Pour l'amour de son baston c'om luy ala couppant" [Galien Restoré begins to feel great sorrow / For the love of his staff that they cut away from him] (vv. 2722–23). The narrator uses Galien's full name again later in this scene when the last six living members of the rear guard ride out in response to his cries for help ("Ces VI contre les trente ont tost esperonné / Pour secourre l'enffant Gualien Restorré," vv. 2809–10). Here the name appears in conjunction with Galien's ancestral verbal memory, since he summons the French warriors by shouting "Monjoie!" and "Saint Denis!" (v. 2759), significant expressions that Galien probably knows from past French epics, since he was not raised in France and has not yet fought among the French in the present narrative. Although they are all mortally wounded already, the six remaining peers feel compelled to respond to Galien's use of the French war cries and of the individual names of Roland and Olivier (v. 2760). This is a situation in which Galien's behavior might seem inappropriate: he is endangering the greatest heroes of France when they have already been pushed to the limits of their endurance. The narrator's use of Galien's full name therefore reminds the audience in this tense situation that his actions after the Battle of

Roncevaux will make up for any danger he might seem to be bringing to the rear guard at the moment; helping Galien is in the best interest of the six remaining peers as defenders of France.

After this initial meeting, however, the scenes depicting Galien at the Battle of Roncevaux feature a temporary shift in his portrayal. At Roncevaux Galien no longer instinctively understands how to behave appropriately in order to achieve everything he desires; the distances between him and the traditional Roncevaux characters embody the tension inherent in the narrative's attempt to tell simultaneously the unhappy story of the rear guard's slaughter and the upbeat story of Galien's success. Because Galien has such a firm grasp on the memory of the fairies' prediction of his future success, he cannot interact effectively with Roland and Olivier, who have an equally firm conviction of the fact that they are about to die. The moment when Galien and Olivier meet at Roncevaux just before Olivier's death has been viewed, even by generally hostile critics, as the most compelling and worthwhile scene in the Galien texts; it also contains one of the most striking instances of simultaneous change and stability in all the surviving Roncevaux texts. Although Galien's goal in riding to Roncevaux was to bring Olivier back to marry his mother, the narrative does not allow for such a radical change to Olivier's established fate: Galien has been characterized by critics as a hero who succeeds in everything he does, but his first and most personal quest to reunite his parents remains forever unfulfilled. For his part, Olivier shows himself to be tragically unaware of his son's glorious destiny as predestined savior of France, though the audience can be sure of Galien's future success after having heard it predicted numerous times early in the text. Addressing the absent Charlemagne, during his speech to Galien, Olivier implies that the emperor is even now marching toward a country turned upside down by Ganelon's betrayal: "Roy qui en France viengne, si hault ne la tendra, / Comment l'avés tenue, car en temps qui venrra, / Tel par paix l'a amee qui a mort la herra / Et tel l'a honnouree qui la defoulera" [Whatever king who may come in France, he will not maintain it so highly / As you have maintained it, for in the time that is coming, / He who loved her in peace will hate her in death / And he who honored her will cast her down] (vv. 2923–26). The audience knows that Olivier's version of both the present and the future in this passage is incorrect: France will not be dishonored but instead strengthened as a result of Galien's future exploits if the confident earlier pronouncements of the narrator and the fairies are fulfilled. Because Olivier's fate remains the same as it was in past Roncevaux narratives, he has no way of knowing that his own son's heroism will alter the fate of France; because the audience does know that France ultimately will weather the current crisis, both the audience and Galien are somewhat distanced from Olivier's perspective.

Roland, too, contemplates with traditional pessimism both his own future and that of France. Grief has such a grip on Roland by the time Galien meets him that he believes he will die of it (vv. 2987–89). Roland's bleak vision of his future precedes and therefore nuances the following scene in which Olivier and Roland agree that Roland and Galien are to be companions in battle from now on. It is fairly clear that Roland says this only to please Olivier, since both of Roland's statements about his partnership with Galien contain important conditions: ". . . tant que mon corps durra, / Ne pour mort ne pour vie je ne te fauldray ja!" [. . . As long as my body lasts, / Neither in death nor in life will I fail you!] (vv. 3004–5) and ". . . se j'ay bien, il aura" [Any good that I have, he will have] (v. 3014). The style of Roland's speech, like Olivier's, serves to heighten the drama of this poignant scene for the audience member, who knows very well that both traditional heroes will die by the end of the battle. The first of these statements ("as long as my body lasts . . .") is weakened by the established fact of Roland's imminent death, while the second statement ("any good that I have, he will have") takes on an ironic twist soon afterward, when Roland fails to pass on to Galien his sword, Durendal. The interaction between Galien and Roland after Olivier's death consists of a series of scenes in which the two heroes fail to work together or communicate effectively. This rift between the two reaches its height when Galien returns to Roland after having singlehandedly driven off a group of Saracens and accuses him of not living up to his earlier agreement to act as Galien's companion in battle.

"Haÿ, sire Roulant!" dit Gualien le fier,
"Je vous vi a mon pere jurer et fiancer
Que ne me fauldriés pour les membres trencher,
A icestui besoing vous voy trop esloingner."
Haa, Dieu! pour quoy le blasme Gualien le guerrier,
Quand Roulant se mouroit, se puis bien tesmongner?
(vv. 3112–16)

["Alas, lord Roland!" said Galien the proud,
"I saw you swear and vow to my father
That you would not fail me even if your limbs were cut off:
From this duty I see you withdrawing too much."

Galïen restoré

237

Oh God! why is the warrior Galien blaming him,
When Roland was dying, as I can well attest?]

The narrator's interjection here shows sympathy for Roland and disappointment with Galien: although the narrator praised Galien and promised his future success in the early scenes of the text, here the narrator
chides Galien for his lack of sensitivity to Roland's condition. Here a
tension implicit in the basic agenda of the text reaches a breaking point.
Since the scene of Galien's birth, the narrator has maintained faithfulness both to the Roncevaux tradition and to the glorification of the
Monglane family; now the narrator faces a meeting of two heroes representing these two traditions, in which one must necessarily overshadow
the other by surviving the battle in which the other one will die. The
narrator projects the frustration of this situation onto Galien, criticiz-
ing him even though Galien is only remaining true to his proper role in
the fictional universe: Galien cannot understand Roland's death as inevitable, since he believes that he is there to help prevent it.

If the narrator is frustrated by this situation, Roland appears to take
great offense at Galien's remarks: his only response to Galien's com-
plaint is to begin trying to destroy his sword Durendal, a traditional part
of his death scene. Yet here Roland's attempt to destroy Durendal has
added significance: Roland is refusing to pass it on to Galien, although
earlier in the battle he has specifically prayed for a worthy French knight
to inherit it: "Or suis je trop dolent que Sarrasin felon / Auront [ja]
Durendal a leur devisïon. / Pleut a celuy Dieu qui souffrit passïon / Que
ung chevalier de France si l'eut en son giron, / Si en trenchat la teste au
conte Guanelon." [Now I am excessively aggrieved that the evil Saracens / Will have Durendal to do with as they please. / May it please that
God who suffered the Passion / That a knight of France have it at his
side, / So that he might cut off the head of Count Ganelon.] (vv.
2235–39). The idea that Galien could have been this worthy French
knight[34] was underlined by Galien's arrival at Roncevaux immediately
after Roland spoke those words (vv. 2241–42). Moreover, Roland's specific desire that the imagined heir to Durendal use the sword to cut off
Ganelon's head would have sounded familiar to the audience, who had
already witnessed Galien's attempt to do just that when he first met Ganelon (vv. 1604–17). Yet even if these earlier clues failed to indicate to
the audience that Roland's desire to destroy Durendal represented a
personal rejection of Galien, this troubling point is made clearly as the
scene progresses. When Roland realizes that he cannot destroy Durendal himself, he throws it into a nearby stream, praying to God to keep

the sword out of the hands of the unworthy: "Vray Dieu, ung don vous pri, par la vostre bonté. / Que jamaiz n'ait ce branc homme de mere né, / S'il n'essauche autant saincte crestienté / Comment j'ay [fait] . . ." [True God, one boon I ask of you, by your goodness: / That no man born of woman ever have this sword / If he does not serve holy Christendom as much / As I have . . .] (vv. 3134–37). When Galien returns and asks to borrow Durendal, having lost his own sword in the battle, it is already too late; as Roland explains to Galien, "trop avés demouré" [you have tarried too long] (v. 3147), a statement that seems to mean that the sword would have been available if Galien had returned sooner but that might also imply Roland's displeasure with the idea that Galien will outlive him at Roncevaux. Galien does not manage to recover Durendal from the stream, although it is easy to imagine a different outcome for this series of events: the sword could have risen out of the stream of its own accord, or Galien could have reached in blindly and grasped the hilt on his first attempt. Instead, as André Moisan has pointed out, Galien loses some dignity in this scene by actually wading into the stream and searching unsuccessfully through water clouded by the blood of dead warriors.[35] In fact, Roland's prayer requests a divine judgment between the two heroes, and the judgment appears to be that Roland is a greater Christian hero than Galien. Just as Galien's initial entry into the Roncevaux scene appeared to be a direct response to Roland's prayer for a worthy French knight to inherit his sword, Galien's unsuccessful effort to regain the sword here appears to be a response to Roland's revised prayer that the sword go only to a knight as great as Roland himself. Rather than a judgment against Galien, however, the disappearance of Durendal makes more sense, within the narrative as a whole, as special praise for Roland. Given Galien's eventual role as savior of France, and more specifically God's direct intervention on Galien's behalf during his battle against Burgualant (vv. 3891–3906), there is ample evidence after this scene that Galien is, in fact, as great a Christian warrior as he needs to be. Yet by denying Galien the privilege of inheriting Durendal, this narrative proclaims its fidelity to another familiar principle of the Roncevaux narratives: that Roland is irreplaceable. By raising the possibility that Roland's sword might pass to Galien, and then refusing to allow that transfer to take place, *Galien restoré* pays tribute to this traditional element of the Roncevaux story.[36]

The resistance of the Roncevaux scenes to compromising Roland's irreplaceability for the sake of enhancing the symbolic portrayal of Galien's success provides an example of what Peter Haidu has described as the resisting "fragment" in medieval textuality. Because medieval texts are made up of material from earlier sources, whether written or oral, Haidu sees their transplanted parts as leading a double life: they are meant to have one meaning in the text at hand, but they still carry with them the associations they had in previous texts.[37] It would be easy for a reader of *Galïen restoré* who was unfamiliar with other Roncevaux narratives to view the scenes at Roncevaux merely as one small part of a larger narrative about Galien; yet even for such a reader, the pessimistic perspectives of Olivier and Roland and the quarrel between Roland and Galien draw attention to themselves because of their contrast with the harmonizing approach of *Galïen restoré* as a whole. This contrast in perspective is a direct result of the "fragmentary" nature of the Roncevaux sequence, in Haidu's sense. Because they had had such a full intertextual life before their reincarnation in *Galïen restoré*, the scenes at Roncevaux simply could not be changed in certain respects, not within a text that had declared itself to be a preservation of the Roncevaux tradition. The intact Roncevaux "fragments" remain as a testimony to the greatness of past Roncevaux narratives, which Haidu has described as the crucial function of all such fragments for medieval textuality: "As fragment, the fragment always recalls its anterior status: refusing present integration, it does so in the name of an earlier totality, its originary status, more worthy of respect, more valorized than the present. The fragment . . . is always returning. It is the creature of the eternally desired return to its anteriority, in order to affirm its fragmentariness, its lost integrity. Negation of totality, the fragment is nonetheless a form of cathexis on totality, the totality of origins, of genealogical integration, a cathexis on totalities that have become impossible."[38] This description of the meaning of the medieval textual fragment helps to explain the way in which the clash of perspectives in the Roncevaux scenes, and particularly Roland's refusal to allow Galien to inherit Durendal, simultaneously resists and reaffirms the overall program of *Galïen restoré*. This is a narrative about the need for new generations of French audiences to remember the role of their unchangeable past in forming a stable collective identity to rely on in the present. In the Roncevaux scenes, the narrative thus demonstrates its adherence to its own ideological rules: just as Durendal eludes Galien's grasp, the episode of the Battle of Roncevaux is shown here to be out of the reach of this literary adapter, in spite of significant changes made to other scenes surrounding the battle.

The crucial role of *Galïen restoré* in continuing the Roncevaux textual tradition is represented at the end of the Battle of Roncevaux by another scene in which the name Galien Restoré plays an important role. Upon meeting the six remaining peers on the battlefield, Galien introduced himself merely as Olivier's son, without using even the name Galien; Roland and Olivier therefore address him merely as "ami" during the battle scenes that follow (vv. 2876, 2895, 3147). Just before his death, however, Roland looks up to heaven, sees God and Saint Michael looking down at him (vv. 3164–66), and addresses a series of final prayers directly to them. The narrator makes it clear that for this moment Roland has simultaneous access to the heavenly and earthly realms: after he sees into heaven, the narrator remarks that at the same time Roland is listening to the sounds of the ongoing battle (vv. 3177–78). From this unusual vantage point between eternal and temporal perspectives, Roland prays that Galien will live long enough to tell Charlemagne what has happened at Roncevaux: "Et vous donnés tant vivre Gualien Restorré / Qu'il ait a mon oncle nostre angoisse conté" [And grant that Galien Restoré lives long enough / that he tells my uncle about our suffering] (vv. 3173–74). Roland attempts to communicate the circumstances of the battle to Charlemagne in every Roncevaux narrative, an attempt that represents one aspect of Roland's newly expanded perspective on his own role in the battle and in its transmission as a narrative of lasting significance for France. *Galien restoré* offers Roland's uncanny knowledge of Galien's full name as a reworking of his attempt to communicate with Charlemagne that is particularly appropriate to this version of the Roncevaux story.

While Roland acknowledges in the last moments of his life that Galien has an important role to play in the post-Roncevaux fictional universe, the primary narrator seems to resist that predestined reality as the text continues. The narrator's addresses to the audience after the Battle of Roncevaux make it clear that the narrator expects this new section of the text to be dominated entirely by Charlemagne, as was characteristic of earlier Roncevaux narratives. The narrator seems to anticipate that Galien's role in the rest of the text will be minimal, restricted to "comforting" Charlemagne, as the narrator stated rather vaguely at the end of the preface. In reality, however, Galien still has a significant contribution to make during the upcoming battle against Baligant: to save Charlemagne and the French from death, as the fairies announced more precisely. A close examination of this transitional section of the text will show that tailor-made character discourse had to be used as an alternate form of narration to straighten out this discrepancy between the earlier predictions made about Galien by the narrator and by the fairies. This narrative struggle can be glimpsed in the awkward transitions between

laisses 131–32 and 132–33, two passages following the Battle of Roncevaux in which the narrator tells the audience to listen carefully and then
announces a change in the focus of events. At the end of laisse 131, the
narrator expresses an intention to leave the subject of Galien in order
to tell the story of Charlemagne's revenge against Marsile and Baligant.
Having described Galien's conquest of the Spanish castle of Monfusain
and his marriage to the beautiful Saracen princess Guimarde, the narrator hastens to announce that the two eventually have a son who becomes a great epic hero in his own right.[39] This continuation of the
Monglane line seems to the narrator to be a fitting end to Galien's role,
and thus the narrator concludes:

> Gualien Restorré qui no loy exaussa,
> Fut pere [de] Maillart, n'en doubtés ja,
> Le compagnon Logier qui maint mal endura.
> Mais de ce me tairai, dire me convendra
> Ainsi que Marsilles Charles tost le [chassa],
> Jusquez en Sarragoce et le siege mit la,
> Et comme le roy Balingant le vint combatre la,
> Corps a corps en bataile Charles le conquesta,
> Ainsi que vous orrés qui taire se vouldra.
>   (vv. 3523–31)

> [Galien Restoré, who upheld our law,
> Was the father of Mallart, have no doubt of that,
> The companion of Lohier who endured much pain.
> But about this I will be silent, for I need to tell
> How Charles soon chased Marsile
> All the way to Sarragossa and besieged him there,
> And how King Baligant came to fight him there,
> In hand-to-hand combat Charles defeated him,
> As you will hear, whoever wishes to be quiet.]

This passage announces the closure of Galien's story in several ways:
first, the full name Galien Restoré is used, as is often the case when the
narrator is making reference to Galien's fulfillment of his predestined
role. The association of Galien's full name with the future birth of his
son, who is to become the hero of another epic, suggests that the son
represents Galien's final contribution to the restoration of France, in
the form of another physical and literary generation of Galien's heroic
line. In addition, this passage also contains stylistic markers of its func-

tion as the preface to the Baligant episode. The repeated phrase "Ainsi que" is used in a similar way as the repeated phrase "Mais l'enfant Galïen" in laisse 13: the first occurrence of the phrase introduces a summary of all the events to come, while the second occurrence serves as an announcement to the audience that the detailed narration of these events is about to resume.

All of these stylistic features of the passage at the end of laisse 131 suggest that the narrator meant this attempted closure of the Galien episode in earnest. At the end of laisse 132, however, Charlemagne has barely had time to besiege Marsile's fortress when the narrator announces that the rest of this story will have to be told later because Galien has received a message that his mother is in trouble in Constantinople. The narrator repeats the same phrase from the end of laisse 131 to announce to the audience this new change of focus at the end of laisse 132: "Ainsi que vous orrés . . ." (v. 3549). These traditional marks of orality are important because laisse 133, which shows the apparently unexpected arrival of his mother's messenger as well as the entire dialogue between the messenger and Galien, immediately turns this supposed orality against the narrator. Just after the narrator uses an address to the audience to put Charlemagne at the center of events, a messenger within the fictional universe announces a new Galien-centered episode too compelling not to be told. This move and countermove bring to the level of the primary narration the established strategy in this text of creating comic effects through characters whose behavior is simultaneously familiar and surprising. The messenger's intervention is surprising in that it conflicts with what the narrator has just announced as the next event to be told, yet the very device of the unexpected messenger was a traditional one in medieval narratives. The identities of both the messenger and the person who sent him remain a mystery in this passage: it would be logical to assume that Jacqueline sent the messenger, but the narrator says later that Jacqueline would not have wanted Galien to endanger himself on her behalf (vv. 3707–10). If the messenger was not sent by Jacqueline, then, it is surprising that he uses Galien's full name, since the only people in the fictional universe who know it are the fairies, Jacqueline, and the archbishop who baptized Galien. Like the scene in which Roland used Galien's full name as a part of his prayer that the Battle of Roncevaux be remembered, this scene in which the messenger overrides the narrator's announced agenda therefore represents an exceptional transgression of the usual boundaries of the fictional universe in the interest of the larger purposes of the narrative. The use of the

name Galien Restoré in this scene, following upon the narrator's vacil-
lations in the previous two laisses, conveys to the audience that there is
an underlying plan in this narrative that is greater than the narrator realizes. Tracing the uses of Galien's full name that follow will show the
continuing trajectory of the narrative shift caused by the messenger's
intervention at this juncture, a trajectory that will point the way toward
the extratextual source of this intervention.

It is the narrator who next utters the name Galien Restoré, yet the result is a further continuation of the Galien story in spite of the narrator's declared intention, once again, to end it. Galien wins the crown of
Constantinople through a judicial combat that proves his mother's in-
nocence in the murder of the emperor Hugues and therefore also proves
his uncles' guilt and disqualification as heirs to the throne. Galien then
brings his mother back to his castle at Monfusain to meet his wife. With
the Constantinople episode concluded so satisfactorily, the narrator
once again assumes that Galien's story has reached its end. The narrator
therefore announces a shift back to the story of Charlemagne, but not
before another message has made its way into the narration:

> Guimarde leur fit feste et moult grant amitié,
> Sa dame festia, honneur lui a porté.
> Lors print ung messaiger Gualien Restorré,
> A Charles l'a tramis et si lui a mandé,
> S'il a mestier de lui, qu'il ait tantot mandé.
> Or vous lairrons de lui . . .
>
> (vv. 4002–7)

> [Guimarde welcomed them with very great affection,
> Her lady she celebrated, and showed honor toward her.
> Then Galien Restoré took a messenger,
> And sent him to Charles, to inform him
> That if he needed him [Galien], he should send for him right away.
> Now we will stop telling you about him . . .]

Again, the use of the full name Galien Restoré suggests that Galien's
message to Charlemagne, saying that he will be available to support the
French emperor if the need should arise, is part of his predestined restoration of France. And indeed, this message allows Galien to return to
the narrative immediately to support Charlemagne, in spite of the narrator's announcement that Galien will no longer appear in the story.
Just a few lines later, Charlemagne does send for Galien when he hears

that Baligant will be coming into Spain with a large army (vv. 4013–17). Yet the narrator does not appear to be pleased with this second unexpected reintroduction of Galien, and makes a futile attempt to resist it:

Seigneurs, or entendez, pour Dieu de majesté.
De Gualien lairrai ycy dorennavant,
Dirai de [Charlemainne], le fort roy combatant
Comment se combati au fort roy Balinguant,
Et a Marsilion, le cuvert mescreant,
Qui issi de Sarragoce avec maint Persant.
Toulx feussent desconfiz, Bavier et Alemant,
François et Burgongnons, Angevins et Normant,
Se Dieu et Gualien ne les feut secourant.

(vv. 4029–37)

[Lords, now listen, for God in majesty.
I will leave the story of Galien from now on,
And I will tell about [Charlemagne], the strong fighting king
How he fought against the strong King Baligant,
And against Marsile, that lowly unbeliever,
Who came out of Sarragossa with many Persians.
They all would have been defeated, Bavarians and Germans,
French and Burgundians, Angevins and Normans,
If God and Galien had not been there to help them.]

The narrator's exasperated interjection, "pour Dieu de majesté," ends the first line of the laisse, but the rest of the laisse uses the -ant rhyme scheme instead of rhyming with its ending sound é, as if to mark the narrator's outburst as transgressive. And indeed, in spite of the narrator's initial protestations to the contrary, the last lines of this laisse indicate not only that the audience will hear more about Galien but that he will be the hero of the upcoming battle, saving Charlemagne's army from otherwise certain death.

The narrator's repeated vacillation about whether Galien will continue to participate in the narrative is caused by the narrator's memory of previous Roncevaux narratives (intertextual literary precedent) and the narrator's forgetfulness of what has already been predicted about Galien's future exploits in the present narrative (intratextual literary precedent). The narrator's tendency to privilege intertextual over intratextual literary precedent is shown to be mistaken: only a harmonious blending of both will produce a satisfactory result. The Baligant episode

as a whole continues to follow this rule of blending intertextual and intratextual source material. In these scenes Galien brings military support so crucial that Charlemagne might have been defeated without it,
just as the fairies had predicted. At the same time, the way in which
Charlemagne's traditional single combat against Baligant is told re-
freshes the audience's impression of the French emperor's independent
sovereignty. Combined with the punishment of Ganelon that follows,
the battle against Baligant offers a closing portrayal of Charlemagne as
strong, pious, and just: the same positive portrayal that dominated the
Jerusalem episode with which the text began. These closing episodes
therefore emphasize that the support of strong allies like Galien is crucial to the king's success but also that no such ally could rival the king's
might.

Although the French are ultimately victorious in the battle, Galien
arrives at a point when it appears as if Baligant's army will carry the day.
Just before Galien arrives, Charlemagne makes a speech that emphasizes
his great need for Galien's support:

> De Sarragoce issi a force et bandon,
> Bien estoient X mile, sans nombre de garson.
> Et quant [Charles] le vit, se fist grant marrison,
> A ses barons a dit: "N'aiés ja suspeçon,
> Oncquez ne les doubtés, s'il sont tel foison!
> Ne sçavons ou tourner s'a l'oriflambe non;
> Trop est loing Gualien, ja secours n'y auron."
> Françoiz ont respondu: "Or soit chascun preudon!
> Ja pour doubte de mort le champ ne guerpiron."
>   (vv. 4154–62)

> [From Sarragossa they emerged in great force,
> They were easily ten thousand, without counting the squires.
> And when [Charles] saw this, he began to feel a great concern,
> And to his barons he said: "Do not ever doubt,
> Never fear them, even if they are so numerous!
> We know of nowhere to turn but to the oriflamme;
> Galien is too far away, we will never have help from him."
> The French responded, "Now let each man be brave!
> We will never leave the field for fear of death."]

This speech constitutes a literary allusion that is at once intertextual and
intratextual, since it shows the state of mind shared by the French war-

riors before Galïen's arrival to be strikingly similar to that of the rear guard at the Battle of Roncevaux, both in this text and in other Roncevaux narratives. Galïen has taken Charlemagne's place in this scene as the powerful leader who represents for the beleaguered French warriors their only hope of survival and victory, but in the same situation where Charlemagne traditionally failed to arrive in time to rescue the French warriors, Galïen now succeeds by arriving at just the right moment: "La faulsist nos François en l'eure mourir, / Quant Gualïen voient hors du vaucel issir" [There our Frenchmen were about to die at that hour, / When they see Galien emerge out of the valley] (vv. 4214–15). Again, this description of the suspenseful circumstances of Galïen's arrival would be likely to bring to mind the usual series of events at the end of the Battle of Roncevaux, in which Roland dies just moments before Charlemagne arrives. Although the timing here is still close, the reinforcements arrive just in time instead of just barely too late. The fact that Galïen's perfectly timed arrival represents the salvation of France is confirmed when Galïen delivers an encouraging speech in which he finally suggests that he has remembered his full heroic name. At the end of a long speech in which Galïen vows to avenge the death of Olivier, he concludes: "Mon nom veul exaucer, plus cy ne veul demourer" [I want to live up to my name, I do not want to tarry here any longer] (vv. 4230–31). This intention to fulfill the meaning of his name must mean that Galïen has remembered the assignment he received at birth, to restore power to the French in a way that will make up for the losses at Roncevaux.

It is not merely Galïen's arrival that completes his mission, of course: Galïen's amazing military prowess in the battle itself is what allows for the French victory. Soon after entering the battle, Galïen starts fighting hand to hand with Baligant himself, which causes the entire battle to be reoriented around this pair:

Ung capple ont commencié si fort et si pesant,
Que je cuide que Balinguant fut a tart reppairant.
Quant paiens sont venus a esperon brochant,
Marsilles et les siens qui lui sont secourant

. . . .
Et d'aultre part est venu [Charles] le roy puissant.

Pour aider Baliguant vindrent paiens le cours,
Et François d'aultre part pour Gualïen le doulx.
                    (vv. 4305–08, 4311–13)

[They began a combat so strong and so strenuous
That I believe that Baligant was retreating at last.
When pagans came in at full speed ["applying their spurs"],
Marsile and his men, who were coming to his aid
. . . .
And from the other side came Charles, the powerful king.

To help Baligant the pagans came running,
And the French from the other side for the good Galien.]

Galien becomes the rallying point for the French here, and it is clear
that he nearly defeats the Saracen leader. When Galien tears down the
Saracen standard, therefore, Baligant stops the battle to propose that he
and Charlemagne settle the conflict by single combat. This series of
events suggests that Baligant believes that he can defeat Charlemagne
but that he cannot defeat Galien. Even Naime, Charlemagne's closest
advisor, seems to agree with Baligant when he suggests that the emperor
choose Naime, Ogier, or Galien as his champion instead of fighting
Baligant himself. In his reply, Charlemagne seems to understand that
this combat is his chance to prove that, while he may need help from his
lords, he does not need a champion to preserve his empire for him:
"Ou je le conquerray, sachés par verités, / Ou en champ m'occira, car
n'en seray sevrés" [Either I will defeat him, know this truly, / Or he will
kill me on the field, for I will not be dissuaded] (vv. 4404–5). With this
statement, Charlemagne sends an important message to his lords: for
the sake of France, he is willing to subject himself to the same dangers
that his men have faced in defense of his empire. Charlemagne is suggesting here that it is through taking such risks that an emperor proves
himself worthy of the great power he holds, which is nearly a reversal of
the famous viewpoints expressed by characters in the Oxford *Roland* concerning the roles of lords and vassals.[40]

Like Galien's arrival, Charlemagne's single combat represents a simultaneous intertextual and intratextual reworking of existing material.
The combat was a feature of most past Roncevaux narratives and thus
would be an expected part of this new version; what is particularly interesting about it, however, is that it bears a striking resemblance to Galien's
earlier single combat at Constantinople. As if to draw the audience's attention to this intratextual parallel, the narrator addresses the audience
before the combat begins, alerting them to the exceptional feats of courage to be heard in the following scenes: "Seigneurs, or entendés, pour
Dieu de majestés, / Et vous orrés bataile de grant fiertés. / Ains tel es-

tour ne fu de deulx roys affermés, / Ainsi que vous orrés, se je suis escoutés." [Lords, now listen, for God in majesty, / And you will hear of a battle of great valor. / Never has there been such a struggle between two strong kings, / As you will hear, if I am heeded.] (vv. 4413–16). The narrator stresses that this combat is worthy of the audience's attention because it is unprecedented. While it is indeed rare in medieval literature to witness such a combat between two kings, this combat nevertheless has a precedent even within this text. With only the names and a few other words changed, the narration of Charlemagne's combat with Baligant (vv. 4512–4620) is nearly identical to the earlier narration of Galien's combat with Burgualant at Constantinople (vv. 3762–3906), including the rhyme scheme in which the respective laisses were composed, a choice that suggests that the author planned to create this parallel. A few lines from each will demonstrate the extent of the resemblance between the two scenes. First, from Galien's combat:

> Or sont les vassaulz ou meileu de la place,
> Apuiez aux escus, n'y a cil qui n'ait place
> Tainte de sang vermeil, au champ en pert la trace.
> Quant furent refreschis, chascun d'eux se rambrace;
> Burgalant sault em piedz, long fu comme une estaiche.
> Et Galien sault sus, son hëaume relace.
> Burgualant vit l'enfant, moult forment le menace,
> En sa main tint l'espee, plus noire que n'est glace,
> Galien Haulte-Clere, plus trenchant que n'est hache.
>
> (vv. 3848–56)

[Now the vassals are in the middle of the field,
Leaning on their shields, there is not one of them who has a place that is not
Colored red with blood, on the field the trace of it is lost.
When they were rested, each of them rearms himself;
Burgualant jumps to his feet, tall as a stake.
And Galien jumps up, and refastens his helmet.
Burgualant sees the youth and threatens him in very strong terms,
In his hand he held a sword, blacker than ice,
and Galien [held] Haulte-Clere ["High-Bright"], sharper than an axe.]

Now, from Charlemagne's combat:

Or furent les deulx vassaulx en mi la place,
Apuiés aux escus, n'a cellui qui n'ait place
Tainte de sang vermeil, n'a cellui a qui ne paire place.
Quant il sont rafreschiz, chascun d'eulx se rebrache,
Balinguant sault en piés, long fu comme une attache.
Charlemaine sault sus, son hëaume relache;
Balinguant vint vers [Charles], fierement le menace,
En sa main tint l'espee plus clere que n'est glace;
Et [Charles] tint Joieuse plus trenchant que n'est hace.

(vv. 4576–84)

[Now the two vassals were in the middle of the field,
Leaning on their shields, and there was not of them who had a
single place that was not
Colored red with blood, nor one who had not met his match.
When they are rested, each one rearms himself,
Baligant jumps to his feet, he was as tall as a spike.
Charlemagne jumps up, and refastens his helmet;
Baligant came toward [Charlemagne], and proudly threatens him,
In his hand he held a sword brighter than ice;
And [Charlemagne] held Joyeuse, sharper than an axe.]

The fact that the narrator uses the same words in both scenes creates an implicit comparison between the two heroes that the narrator could have avoided by making different word choices: combat scenes can be quite repetitive and formulaic in medieval literature, but the resemblance between these two is too close not to have been deliberate. In fact, the narrator's use of four verbs of listening in the four-line introduction to Charlemagne's combat (vv. 4413–16) may be an attempt to draw the audience's attention to this intratextual resemblance. This apparently deliberate parallel between the two combats of Galien and Charlemagne also deserves closer scrutiny because Horrent has shown it to be an area of inconsistency in his own reading of *Galïen restoré*. In addition to pointing out the similarity between these two scenes, Horrent showed through a comparison with other versions of the story that the author of this version in the Cheltenham manuscript took particular care to place Galien's combat in Constantinople before Charlemagne's combat with Baligant, whereas in other versions it had appeared afterward.[41] Horrent saw this choice as part of a larger structural plan to keep all of Galien's adventures together and then to conclude the narrative with scenes depicting Charlemagne's ultimate triumph over the Saracens and Ganelon. At the same time, this plan appeared strange to Horrent because of Galien's domination of all the other parts of the narrative before the battle with Baligant: "Why diminish in this way a hero that one wants to magnify? Adaptors have their reasons that art does not know. I would not be surprised if our man was refusing to make of Galien a competitor for Charlemagne."[42] This implied and then refused competition between Galien and Charlemagne seemed peculiar in the context of Horrent's reading of *Galïen restoré* as the story of Galien, but it makes perfect sense in the context of a narrative designed to showcase both the significant contributions that can be made by allies to a powerful French king and also the king's ultimate sovereignty in spite of such alliances. As is characteristic of Roncevaux narratives, *Galïen restoré* raises a potential threat to French unity by presenting Baligant's perception of Galien as a more powerful opponent than Charlemagne, only to neutralize that threat immediately by proving that Charlemagne has earned his great power. The fact that Charlemagne's combat comes after Galien's is also significant in the context of this narrative's emphasis on remembering and restaging textual precedents: the combat against Baligant gives the narrator an opportunity to restage Galien's combat, inscribing Charlemagne's name where Galien's used to be. After this scene in which Charlemagne is systematically substituted for Galien within a specific context, it becomes clear during the closing scenes that Charlemagne has also taken over Galien's larger role as primary hero of the narrative.

One of the odd features of *Galïen restoré*, when it is viewed as a narrative designed to promote Galien, is that the triumphant young hero is absent from the scene of Ganelon's punishment, with which the problem of Roncevaux is resolved and the narrative concluded. Galien not only had an obvious reason to want revenge against the traitor responsible for his father's death but even made two attempts on Ganelon's life earlier in the text. Why, then, does Galien return home without seeing Ganelon punished? One reason is that, as a survivor of the Battle of Roncevaux, Galien enjoys the unprecedented privilege of returning home to his family, a heartwarming note with which to initiate this most happy of endings to the Roncevaux story. On a practical level, Galien's family is staying at his castle in Spain at the conclusion of the battle against Baligant, so he would have to go out of his way to witness Ganelon's punishment in France. More importantly, however, Galien continues to serve Charlemagne by holding newly conquered Spain after the departure of the French emperor, as is clear in Galien's final dismissal from the narrative:

Puis [Charlemagne] dit a Gualien: "Aler vous en fauldra,
Pour guarder vostre terre et decha et dela."
. . . .
Le païs tint en paix et sa terre guarda.
Or vous lairrons de lui, plus on n'en parlera;
Car depuis ot ung filz que Guimarde porta,
Dont le vaillant Maillart issi, n'en doubtés ja.

(vv. 4699–4700, 4707–10)

[Then [Charlemagne] said to Galien: "You must go,
To guard your territory both here and over there."
. . . .
He [Galien] maintained peace in the region and guarded his
own land.
Now I will leave his story, we will not speak of him anymore;
For afterward he had a son that Guimarde carried,
From whom came the worthy Mallart, have no doubt of that.]

As is typical of this narrative's intratextual repetitions, these last lines
repeat the earlier address to the audience (vv. 3523–26) in which Galien's future exploits were summarized with the apparent intention of
leaving them out of future scenes. It is clear here that Galien fulfills his
duty to guard Charlemagne's land as well as his own (v. 4707), as Charlemagne's "both here and there" requested. The final words exchanged
by the two emperors express a mutual respect that is implicitly confirmed by Galien's very absence from Ganelon's trial: in his combat
against Baligant, Charlemagne proved himself to be a capable emperor
whom Galien could trust to carry out a fitting punishment for the
traitor.

The version of Ganelon's punishment in *Galïen restoré* places an unusually strong emphasis on the notion that Charlemagne has become
the primary hero of the text in these closing scenes. As is traditional,
Charlemagne is opposed to holding a judicial combat to decide Ganelon's guilt, but for once in the Roncevaux tradition Charlemagne has
his way in this matter. After Charlemagne asserts that there would be no
"reason" for having such a combat (v. 4845), Ganelon proves him right
by running away before the combat can begin. While Ganelon's temporary escape at this juncture appears in other Roncevaux narratives as
well,[43] in those cases the judicial combat on his behalf still took place
after his recapture; in *Galïen restoré*, his escape attempt convinces everyone
that he is guilty and that no combat is required to convict him of the

crime. Charlemagne's accusation against Ganelon is vindicated by popular acclaim rather than by the surprise victory of his young champion Thierry; this change keeps Charlemagne firmly in the heroic position, reaffirming the message of Charlemagne's combat against Baligant. Charlemagne does not need a young champion to fight in his place, nor is a judicial combat required to prove that his accusation against Ganelon is just. Ganelon's punishment is the last event in the narrative, followed only by the narrator's closing comments describing the narrative as having told the story of Roncevaux. Just as that closing address to the audience reprises the narrator's opening comments about the audience's forgetfulness, the last scene within the fictional universe reprises the portrayal of Charlemagne from the Jerusalem episode, with which narrative time began in this text. It is Charlemagne who dismisses the rest of the characters before the narrator's final comments, so that he is the last fictional character to leave the narrative: "Charles donna congié a trestoute sa gent, / En long temps ne fist puis aucun hastivement" [Charles dismissed all of his people; / And for a long time afterward he did not undertake another conflict] (vv. 4900–4903). This harmonious ending, in which lasting peace and justice are restored to France through an unproblematic cooperation between Galien and Charlemagne, certainly appears to make up for the French defeat at the Battle of Roncevaux. In a sense, the new alliance with Galien as emperor of Constantinople allows Charlemagne to gain the world in exchange for the loss of Roland and the rear guard.

Anachronistic Language as a Stylistic Strategy

Several modern commentators have agreed that the linguistic forms used in *Galïen restoré* are strange, but disagreement has already emerged about whether that strangeness should be perceived as meaningful. Peter Dembowski has pointed out general stylistic traits of *Galïen restoré* that are more characteristic of twelfth-century *chansons de geste* than of most fifteenth-century reworkings (such as the use of binomial constructions and traditional hemistich-formulas) and has cited several specific examples of linguistic inconsistencies in *Galïen restoré* that reveal the author's conscious attempt to give the text a nostalgic flavor.[44] The unusual mixture of old and new linguistic forms in the Cheltenham manuscript has also been studied by Giuseppe Di Stefano, though in a different context.[45] Di Stefano saw this manuscript as a typical example of the transitional state of French in the fifteenth century rather than as a deliberate attempt at reinventing for literary purposes the Old French forms that had already disappeared from common usage. Yet Di Stefano's study provides an important insight into the style of the manuscript because he stresses the pragmatic aspect of its inconsistent use of Old French forms: as Di Stefano illustrates with numerous examples, the Cheltenham manuscript often used these forms in places where it would otherwise be impossible to maintain the meter or rhyme of a given line. By combining the insights of Dembowski and Di Stefano with a close reading of key passages from *Galïen restoré*, I have discovered that the author did not use equal doses of "old language" in every scene but rather systematically associated these linguistic forms with the text's young hero, particularly in scenes where Galïen initiates or strengthens relationships with the traditional Roncevaux protagonists Charlemagne, Roland, Olivier, and Aude. Like its form, then, the nostalgic language of *Galïen restoré* provided a clear signal to its contemporary audience of its own conscious examination of the relationships between the literary past and present. As "strange words" of a new kind, the unusual linguistic forms of this text renew the tendency of all Roncevaux texts to draw the audience's attention to discourse in order to offer consistent metaliterary commentary at that level of the narration.

Di Stefano makes it clear at the outset of his study that he does not consider the Cheltenham manuscript's unusual linguistic features to have been a deliberate invention of the author. In fact, he states that he chose this manuscript precisely because he believed that it was the product of a popular author who would have been incapable of manipulating the language: "The very mediocrity of the texts allows one to analyze certain phenomena from a point of view that is purely linguistic rather than stylistic."[46] As part of the justification for the linguistic interest of a study on a manuscript that Di Stefano considers otherwise lacking in literary value, he adds that a poet whose work is not considered high art must be careful to make his style easily understandable.[47] It is this point that provides the guiding principle for Di Stefano's comments throughout the essay: in his view, the author of the Cheltenham manuscript used Old French forms alongside those of Middle French only when they would not interfere with comprehension for a contemporary audience.

Di Stefano's study focused on the manuscript's inconsistent use of definite articles and other markers of the Old French system of noun cases indicating grammatical subjects and objects. The definite article *li* provided an audible signal of the subject case in Old French but would have served no purpose in the French normally spoken and written in the fifteenth century: by that time, the case system had already been eliminated from common usage. Where *li* in Old French had served to mark either a singular or plural masculine noun in the subject position, Di Stefano found in the Cheltenham manuscript a number of examples of singular subjects introduced by *le* and plural subjects by *les*, as in modern French. The article *li* still existed alongside *le* and *les*, but only in two positions. The first use of *li* was before a subject following its verb, as in the line "Quant de Monglenne yssirent li IIII damoysel."[48] In this line, *li* introduces a plural noun (*damoysel*) that does not look plural to the modern eye: the author used the appropriate Old French form for a plural subject but made sure that the audience would understand this noun as plural by associating it with the number four. The second use of *li* was before a noun beginning with a vowel sound, as in the line "Li hostes s'est assis et l'ostesse plaisant" (v. 349), in order to add an extra syllable. Yet the form *l'*, which in this line is used with a feminine noun, could also be used in the same manuscript with a masculine noun, as in the line "L'oste se departy de l'ostel a itant" (v. 2506). A comparison of lines 349 and 2506 shows that the final *s*, which in the Old French system had indicated a singular subject, was properly maintained in the line using *li* and left out in the line using *l'*. Di Stefano also found a striking example of the final *s* being used even without a preceding *li*: "Oncle estoit a Millon a la chiere hardi / Et oncles a Ernault, dont je vous signefie" (vv. 2691–92). Here there are no definite articles before the two forms of *oncle* that refer to the same person, yet *oncle* appears beside *oncles* because the final *s* provides an extra syllable in the second line that was not needed in the first. Di Stefano also observed that the author of the Cheltenham manuscript invented by analogy forms that had never existed in Old French, such as the singular subject *barons*: "Et Garin son frere qui tant est noble barons" (v. 1645). Where in Old French, the regular pattern had been *ber* for a singular subject and *barons* for a plural object, the author chose to ignore *ber* in favor of *barons* because this line appears in a stanza based on the final sound *-ons*. The author invented this singular subject form *barons* by logical analogy, adding a final *s* to the singular object case form.

These examples and others in Di Stefano's study indicate that the author of the Cheltenham manuscript understood the proper functioning of the Old French case system but felt free to manipulate it when necessary to maintain the rhyme of a laisse or the meter of an individual line. In fact, Dembowski has proposed that the Cheltenham author "must

have had in front of him a text of (an) older version(s), for hardly anyone in the 15th century could have been capable of reproducing so many
features of OFr."[49] Yet even if the Cheltenham manuscript's Old French
forms were copied from an earlier manuscript, now lost, it is remark-
able to what extent the fifteenth-century author or scribe was able to
adapt the Old French case markers to prevent confusion or frustration
among contemporary audiences. Di Stefano's study shows that the author usually provided supporting clues to help the audience to absorb
the meaning of the antiquated forms, as in the case of the logical pair "li
oste . . . et l'hostesse": such stylistic interventions reveal an active and
conscious effort to maintain the old alongside the new. Like the choice
of verse form, this effort at maintaining Old French linguistic features
adds an additional global meaning to the narrative: in every scene of the
narrative, the anachronistic language provides a reminder of elapsed
time. The Old French forms suggest a continuity with past literary traditions but simultaneously mark the distance between the fifteenth century and the period centuries earlier when the French *chansons de geste*
were first written down.

One of Di Stefano's primary points is that Old French case markers
were used in this manuscript only where they would assist the author in
maintaining the meter and rhyme necessary to a verse text. The widespread dominance of prose over verse in fifteenth-century French literature might seem to justify Di Stefano's implication that it was the
author's lack of poetic skill and/or experience that led to this manipula-
tion of articles and endings throughout the manuscript. Yet this assertion becomes more difficult to accept when the antiquated style of the
Cheltenham *Geste de Monglane* author is compared to that of François
Villon, who was probably a contemporary and who was undoubtedly a
poet of immense and varied talents. In one of the ballads inserted into
Villon's *Testament* (vv. 385–412), Villon writes in what appears to be a
flawed rendition of Old French. Indeed, Clément Marot, who published an edition of Villon's works in the sixteenth century, could easily
recognize this poem's unusually antiquated style and therefore gave it
the name "Ballade en vieil langage françoys." One stanza will be enough
to provide numerous examples of this style:

Voire, ou soit de Constantinobles
L'emperieres au poing dorez,
Ou de France le roy tres nobles,
Sur tous autres roys decorez,
Qui pour ly grant Dieux adorez

Batist esglises et couvens,
S'en son temps il fut honnorez,
Autant en emporte ly vens![50]

In several lines of this ballad, Villon uses incorrectly the definite article *li*, as in the line "Qui pour ly grant Dieux adorez" (v. 397). Here *li* precedes a singular noun in the object position (after the preposition *pour*), where in Old French it would have introduced a subject. A case-inflected plural ending is then added to the past participle *adorez*, though it modifies the same singular object, *Dieu*. Villon used case-inflected participles several times to maintain a rhyme scheme in *-ez*, sometimes correctly, as in the line "Sur tous autres roys decorez" (where *decorez* modifies *roy tres nobles* in the preceding line, a singular subject with an *-s* ending), and sometimes incorrectly, as in the line "L'emperieres au poing dorez" (where *dorez* modifies the singular object *poing*). It appears that in Villon's ballad, Di Stefano's observation about late medieval poets holds true once again: they were willing to use Old French case markers inconsistently to preserve a rhyme scheme. Yet this comparison of the style of the Cheltenham poet with that of Villon's ballad shows Di Stefano's analysis to be overly simplistic: if the inconsistent use of Old French case markers is viewed merely as a stylistic crutch for late medieval authors unaccustomed to writing in verse, what are we to make of their use by Villon, a widely acknowledged master of French verse? Villon's ballad, like *Galïen restoré*, uses anachronistic language to emphasize the theme of the passing of time; this analysis is clearly applicable to Villon's ballad, since it is one of the most famous meditations on the past in all of French literature. Furthermore, this ballad is just one of a whole group of poems on the theme of the passing of time in one section of Villon's *Testament*: it is preceded by ballads devoted to famous ladies and knights of the past and followed by a ballad narrated by an old woman remembering her youth. In this context, it is quite likely that Villon's "Ballade en vieil langage françoys" deliberately falls short of grammatical perfection in order to portray the passing of time in the very fabric of the ballad, its "old language."

In a work on the morphology and syntax of Middle French, Christiane Marchello-Nizia commented that this ballad by Villon, "where the forms of the subject case, sometimes outlandish, are rarely used correctly, is only one more proof, if such was needed, that the system of declension no longer had any relevance (at least in the grammatical domain) for the writers, scribes and readers of the fifteenth century."[51] In my own remarks on the language of *Galïen restoré*, I will elaborate on

Marchello-Nizia's parenthetical suggestion that such an imperfect attempt at using older language forms in the fifteenth century might have had a purpose that lay outside the grammatical domain. My analysis of the text's language shows that it follows the same trend as the narration of the events of the text: anachronistic style is first used to imply that Galien was a character as authentically old as Roland, Olivier, and Charlemagne. Then during the Roncevaux section, anachronistic style is used instead as a resisting fragment that emphasizes the rift between new and old heroes as well as new and old events. Finally, during the battle against Baligant, parallel constructions are multiplied to a dizzying degree, underscoring the emergence in that scene of the cooperation between Galien and Charlemagne that resolves many of the narrative's most significant tensions.

In several early scenes of the narrative that recount Galien's quest to find Olivier, "old language" is used to describe the young hero, particularly at moments when his relationship to Olivier is under discussion. When Galien leaves Constantinople, for example, Jacqueline gives Galien a ring by which Olivier is meant to recognize him as his son: "Et veci ung annel que jadis m'a donné" (v. 556). The very object that symbolizes Galien's connection to Olivier retains an antiquated ending, for the Old French singular accusative form *annel* had been replaced by *anneau* by the fifteenth century;[52] the word *jadis* further emphasizes the past-present literary and familial relationship represented by the ring. Similarly, Aude uses an antiquated phrase to describe the extent to which Galien resembles his father. When she first sees Galien, Aude says to Regnier: "Venu est Olivier, ve le ci a bandon" (v. 822). Normal fifteenth-century usage had eliminated *ve le ci* in favor of *veci* + object, the form that appears almost everywhere else in the *Galïen restoré* portion of the Cheltenham manuscript.[53] *Ve le ci* is a form not only antiquated but far more emphatic than the alternative *veci* in its portrayal of Galien as a person in whom one can actually see Olivier (literally, "see him here"). When Regnier agrees that Galien greatly resembles Olivier, Galien states in antiquated language that Olivier must be his father, since Jacqueline "N'ama oncq en sa vie nul homme se lui non" (v. 843). This construction, *ne . . . se . . . non*, was changed in the fourteenth century to *ne . . . se non* (giving, in the case of this line, "nul homme se non lui"), and no longer appeared in the sample of fifteenth-century texts studied by Marchello-Nizia.[54] Jacqueline's continued faithfulness to Olivier is logically consistent with the scenes between Olivier and Jacqueline in the earlier medieval *Pèlerinage de Charlemagne* but had not actually been portrayed by an earlier text; this simultaneously emphatic and antiquated line provides linguistic support to the idea, crucial to this narrative's legitimation of Galien, that Jacqueline's love for Olivier was rooted in earlier medieval tradition and had never wavered.

The repeated use of the term *damoisel* to refer to Galien is another technique for ensuring that the young hero would appear to fit into the traditional epic context during the scenes in which he is introduced into the narrative. This title still existed in the fifteenth century, though it was used only for the highest nobility, denoting young men who had not yet been knighted. Yet occurrences of the word that have been cited in dictionaries show a steady elimination of the *–el* ending;[55] in *Galïen restoré*, by contrast, the word has either this outdated *–el* ending or, more rarely, an ending reminiscent of Old French case markers. For example, the first appearance of this word ("A Damas fut nourris le gentil damoyseaulx," v. 413) sets the rhyme pattern for an entire laisse in *–aulx*, an ending that, like the *–el* ending, has been characterized as exceptional and antiquated for the fifteenth century.[56] Although the Old French forms are not used consistently in this line (the *x* ending suggests the Old French nominative case, but the matching subject case article *li* does not appear with it), this placement of *damoyseaulx* at the beginning of the laisse is important because it suggests that Galien himself generates this string of old-fashioned endings, as if special antiquated terms were needed to describe him. Moreover, this laisse interpolates a carefully timed reminder that Charlemagne, Roland, and Olivier were fighting the Saracens in Spain during Galien's childhood:

A Damas fut nourris le gentil damoyseaulx,
Endementres que [Charles] estoit a Rainchevaulx
Qui forment guerroy[oi]t les payens desloyaulx,
Et Roulant son nepveu, le nobile vassaulx,
Et le conte Olivier qui fu franc et isnaulx.
Et Galïen son filz qui estoit jeunes et baulx
A Damas chascun jour montoit sur los chevaulx
Et les esperonnoit contreval les carreaulx,
Tant qu'il faisoit yssir le sang a grant ruisseaulx.
De chevaucher estoit si preuz et si isnaulx
Que chascun prioit Dieu qui le gardast de maulx.
(vv. 413–23)

[At Damas the noble youth was raised,
While Charles was at Roncevaux,
Who was making war strongly against the disloyal pagans,

Galïen restoré

And Roland his nephew, that noble vassal,
And the count Olivier, who was noble and agile.
And Galien his son, who was young and handsome,
At Damas each day used to ride horses
And spur them in the sides,
So much that he made great rivers of blood run out.
He was so worthy and skilled at riding
That everyone prayed to God that he be kept from harm.]

The rhyme scheme and the parallel structure ("Et Roulant . . . Et le conte Olivier . . . Et Galïen") implicitly compare Galien to Charlemagne and Roland as well as to his father, Olivier, with whom Galien shares the antiquated adjective *isnaulx*.[57] In addition to the antiquated language, the inaccurate assertion here that Charlemagne was in Roncevaux at this time (he was, instead, conquering cities all over Spain) serves to place all four heroes in the context of a larger literary past, rather than in a moment consistent with the parameters of the fictional universe. Roncevaux must be evoked here not only because it fits into the rhyme scheme but because it is the ultimate setting for traditional epic literature. The end result is that Galien, even as a young child, is depicted as an epic hero alongside the traditional threesome of Charlemagne, Olivier, and Roland. This impression is confirmed at the end of this passage, when the people watching the boy Galien practicing his riding skills pray to God to keep him from harm, just as the narrator does later while recounting the exploits of French warriors on the battlefield.

The term *damoisel* appears several times as the term used by people who do not yet know Galien's true identity. For example, Olivier's father Regnier uses it to ask Galien's name ("'Damoysel,' dist le duc, 'comment avez a nom?'" v. 826); there it has an old-fashioned sound but not an appropriate Old French vocative ending. When Galien arrives at Charlemagne's camp, the term *damoisel,* as well as the antiquated pronoun and adjective *cil,*[58] is used repeatedly instead of Galien's name because the scene is told from the point of view of Charlemagne, who does not know Galien's identity. The following excerpt from this scene shows antiquated vocabulary in italics, with references to Galien italicized and underlined:

La se *deduit* le roy aulx chevaliers puissans.
Ung pou aprés disner, *se dit le rommans,*
Luy vint ung <u>*damoisel*</u> qui moult estoit plaisans,

Monté *sus* ung cheval qui beau fut et serrans.
. . . .
Et quant <u>*cil*</u> vit le roy qui la estoit sachans,
Du cheval descendi, si le *baille* a deulx sergans.
Quant Charles voit <u>*celuy*</u> qui la fut descendans
Et la grant beaulté dont fut fait son *semblans,*
Luy souvint d'Olivier qui tant fut combatans.
"Nayme," dit le roy, "or soiés regardans
Ce noble <u>*damoisel*</u> et bien considerans,
Mieulx resemble Olivier que *rien*[59] qui soit vivans!"
"Sire, vous dictes *voir!*" dit Naymes le vaillans.
"Or le faictes venir," dit le roy *suffisans,*
Adonc fut amené le <u>*damoisel*</u> plaisans.

Seigneurs, <u>*cil damoisel*</u> dont je fais mencïon
Fut le filz Olivier, Galïen *ot a nom.*

(vv. 1510–13, 1517–29)

[There the king with the noble knights amused himself.
A little after dinner, so says the romance,
There came to him a youth who was very attractive,
Mounted on a horse that was beautiful and well trained.
. . . .
And when this youth saw the king who was so wise,
He got down from the horse, and handed it to two servants.
When the king saw the one who was dismounting there
And the great beauty that made up his appearance,
He remembered Olivier, who had fought so much.
"Naime," said the king, "now take a look at
This noble and attractive youth,
He looks more like Olivier than anyone else alive!"
"My lord, you speak truly!" said Naime the brave.
"Now have him come over," said the strong king,
And so the attractive youth was led over.

Lords, this youth whom I mention
Was the son of Olivier, his name was Galïen.]

Like the passage recounting Galïen's childhood training to be a knight,
this passage in which Galïen is introduced into Charlemagne's court
places the event in the larger context of the literary past, this time by

using the phrase "se dit le rommans" to evoke the authority of an earlier source text. The use of antiquated vocabulary links Galien to Charlemagne throughout this passage: both men are described in old-fashioned terms, and the pair of demonstrative pronouns *cil* and *celuy* encode proper Old French usage as well as parallel structure into the moment when they first catch sight of each other ("quant cil vit le roy . . . descendi" and "Quant Charles voit celuy qui la fut descendans").[60] The narrator's use of *cil damoisel* to introduce Galien to the audience at the beginning of the next laisse reinforces the impression that Galien belongs at Charlemagne's court, situated in the literary past, and the traditional epic formula "Galïen ot a nom" projects even the audience's point of reference for the character, the now-familiar name Galien, into the established epic context.

The repeated use of *damoisel* in the passage above once again has an old-fashioned sound but does not observe the rules of Old French, according to which *damoisel* would be used as a singular object, while an alternate form with an ending in *s* or *x* would be used as a singular subject. Instead, in the passage above, *damoisel* is used as an object in line 1523 but as a subject in lines 1512, 1527, and 1528. Old French case endings are also ignored in two other instances later in this scene, when Charlemagne addresses Galien directly with this title but both times fails to use a marked vocative form ("'Damoisel,' dit le roy, 'comment est vostre nom,'" v. 1542; "'Nennil,' [li] dit le roy, 'mon gentil dancillon,'" v. 1555). What is particularly interesting about this neglect of case endings on the part of Charlemagne and the narrator is that in the very next laisse Galien shows a surprising knowledge of the Old French vocative form and even of the French epic tradition. When Galien asks Ganelon's name, Ganelon replies, "J'ay nom Guanelon" (v. 1572); without missing a beat, Galien then begins a tirade against Ganelon with the proper Old French vocative form of his name, Guanes (v. 1573). Galien's linguistic mastery is strongly emphasized by the fact that Ganelon specifically tells Galien what to call him but that Galien calls him something different in the very next line; moreover, Guanes was not a common name outside the realm of epic literature, as were other vocative forms of names such as Charles. If Galien knows the vocative form corresponding to "Ganelon," these lines imply, it is because he is actually a knowledgeable insider in the epic literary context, rather than the newcomer and outsider he might at first appear to be. Thus the antiquated vocabulary and grammatical forms in the section of the text introducing Galien repeatedly emphasize the young hero's connection to the established epic tradition.

It is Galien's use of a formulaic expression from traditional epics that leads directly to his meeting with Olivier. When Galien is surrounded by Saracens after his combat with Pinart, he calls out for help, hoping that Olivier and Roland will hear him: "Se vous feussiés en vie, sain et sauf et entier, / Vous me secourissiés selon le mien cuidier" (vv. 2762–63). Galien's distress call ends with an epic formula, "selon le mien cuidier" [by my way of thinking], that is particularly significant because of its cognitive meaning: if Roland and Olivier do not respond, this disappointment will change Galien's entire notion of the heroes of the rear guard, his way of remembering them. Olivier uses the same expression in his attempt to convince Roland to join him in defending this stranger. Having recognized the horse Galien was riding as one that used to belong to him, Olivier concludes, "Et croy qu'il m'appartient selon le mien cuider" [And I think that it belongs to me, by my way of thinking] (v. 2796). Thus Olivier's recognition of Galien as his son is reinforced by the traditional epic language both characters share at this important moment in the narrative. Moreover, antiquated language punctuates the entire section of the text recounting the Battle of Roncevaux in ways that emphasize this event's emotional impact as well as its long textual history. For example, Gondrebeuf's announcement of Roland's death to Charlemagne ("Mort est vo niepz que vo corps tant ama," v. 2135) is linguistically conservative in several respects. The word *niepz* is the most strongly marked, since it represents the nominative half of the Old French pair *niés/neveu*,[61] "restoring" an etymological *p* (based on the Latin *nepos*) that had not been there in French before. Second, the singular possessive adjective *vo* was a rare form for the fifteenth century,[62] but it is used twice in this line. Finally, this use of *corps* also seems outdated: it could be used in Old French to refer to a person as a whole, as well as to a person's physical body, and in this instance it appears to be part of a traditional epic formula deliberately used for its old-fashioned sound. This line marks one of the most significant turning points in the Roncevaux plot, and the retention of antiquated language here emphasizes the connection of the present narrative to the many Roncevaux narratives that have preceded it. Specifically, this line also emphasizes the long-standing and unchangeable fact of Roland's death, an element of the plot that I have identified as central to the entire structure of *Galïen restoré*.

The expressions used in the Roncevaux section to talk about time itself tend to have an antiquated ring, particularly when they are used by Roland and Olivier to describe the future they will not live to see. For

example, when Olivier addresses the absent Aude in the speech he pronounces before dying, he uses the phrase "d'oresmes en avant" (v. 2960)
to talk about Aude's life after his death, even though the one-word form
dorenavant had been in common usage since the early fourteenth century.[63] Similarly, Roland declares that he will die "ançoiz que la nuit
voie" (v. 2987); *ainçois que* was an expression that had fallen out of use by
the end of the fourteenth century.[64] The mixture of antiquated form
and future meaning emphasizes Roland's ambivalence when he tells
Galien that he will not let him down but will continue to fight alongside
him: "je ne vous fauldray més" (v. 3055). The expression *ne . . . més* was
rare for the fifteenth century, when several more current synonyms were
available,[65] but it was appropriate to a situation in which Roland was
making a promise in words that went against his destiny; much as Roland might try to rise above his predestined circumstances, his language
links him to the earlier medieval literature in which his fate has been
permanently recorded. A few lines later, a linguistic reminder of Roland's literary past, and even of his imminent death, appears in the same
line with the narrator's assertion that Roland is determined to ride back
into battle: "Roulant, le niepz Charllon, ne s'i voult atarger" (v. 3067).
The first half of this line was a well-worn epic formula, and one that
used two words clearly marked by Old French noun cases (*niepz*, subject
case, and *Charllon*, object case with genitive meaning). In addition, *niepz*
is a word that is always associated with Roland's death in this text (see
earlier occurrences in lines 1338, 1852, 2135), and thus it is as if Roland were already dead but still trying to ride into battle, a linguistic depiction of the growing tension in this scene that soon reaches its height
when Galien reproaches Roland for not fighting harder and the narrator in turn reproaches Galien for his failure to understand that Roland
is mortally wounded.

As I discussed in the last section, Roland's sword Durendal comes to
symbolize the ways in which Roland and Galien both win and lose in this
conflict between them: lost in the bloody river, Durendal is stuck in a
literary past that is inaccessible to Galien, and several lines use antiquated language to emphasize the deliberate rift maintained between
the literary past and present in this scene. If read in terms of Old French
grammar, the line in which the river is first described suggests that it
suddenly appeared and filled with blood as an answer to Roland's prayer
that Durendal not fall into unworthy hands: "Devant lui venoit courre
ung grant risel et lé, / Venu y est le sang et vermeil et becté" [In front of
him a large and wide stream started to run, / and blood came into it, red
and cold] (vv. 3138–39). *Venir a* + infinitive indicated the start of an ac-

tion in Old French,[66] and though there is no *a* following *venoit* in this line, it is unclear what other function *venoit* would have here: if the river had been there the whole time, *couroit* alone would have been sufficient to describe it. The idea that the river was created as a resting place for Durendal, symbol of the untouchable earlier epic tradition, is reinforced by the antiquated form of the word, *risel*. An echo of the sword's inaccessibility as part of the unchangeable past is once again heard in the text when Galien finds himself alone after all the other French warriors are dead and remembers that he has no sword with which to defend himself if the Saracens should return: "Pourpenssé s'est l'enfant qu'il n'a point de branc" [The youth bethought him that he had no sword] (v. 3201). *Se pourpenser* was one of the words that Froissart seems to have considered outdated in the late fourteenth century,[67] while *enfant* emphasizes Galien's youth, both physical and literary. Thus the language provides audible support to the rift that appears here between Roland and Galien and between old and new literature.

In the passage recounting Roland's death and Charlemagne's ride toward Roncevaux, a steady stream of antiquated words attests to the present text's faithfulness to the way in which this scene had been told in past texts:

Quant Roulant fut assiz *delés* le conte Olivier,
Afleby fut forment, ne peut *més chapploier*;
Roulant a escouté, si a *ouÿ noiser*,
Tant cheval *ot* hennir et tant paien crier,
"Heë, Dieu!" dit Roulant, "beau pere droicturier,
Tant comment j'eüsse armes et me puïsse aider,
Ne venissent paiens a qui Dieu doint encombrier!"
Roulant *lieve* sa main, son *chief* print a saignier,
Puis a prins III *peulx* d'erbe et se va *commicher*.
L'ame part *a bandon* de Roulant le guerrier,
Les angres l'emportent, a Dieu le vont p[or]ter;
Et Gualien *remaint illec* tout effraier,
Le jour prent a declin, si prent a *anuiter*.
Et Charlles chevauchoit *et o lui si guerrier*,
A temps *cuide* venir au secours sans targer.

                                   (vv. 3175–89)

[When Roland was seated beside the count Olivier,
He was very much weakened, he could no longer fight,
Roland listened, and he heard noises,

He heard many horses whinnying and many pagans shouting.
"Oh, God!" said Roland, "beautiful and just heavenly Father,
As long as I have weapons and can defend myself,
May the pagans not come, whom God should hinder!"
Roland raises his hands, his head began to bleed,
Then he took three blades of grass and began to eat them.
The soul freely left Roland the warrior,
The angels carried him, they went to carry him to God,
And Galien remained there, very afraid,
The light started to fade, it began to be night,
And Charles was riding, and with him his warriors,
He thought that he could come in time, without delaying.]

In fact, it seems significant that the only lines in this passage without antiquated language are those that make reference to God, as if to imply
that God alone can watch over one generation after another without
being affected by the passage of time. The phrase "et o lui si guerrier"
(v. 3188) has been identified as a traditional epic formula,[68] and it is repeated with variations ("et o lui si princher," v. 3248; "et o lui si guerrier," v. 3250) as a way of emphasizing Charlemagne's established and
eternal military might in the scene in which Charlemagne and his men
pursue the Saracens.

I have already described how the battle against Baligant restages intertextual and intratextual material to highlight the harmonious partnership between Galien and Charlemagne, a partnership that allows for the
"restoration" of France. In laisse 146, the narrator uses traditional linguistic cues to indicate that this is a new episode that begins a section of
the text in which Charlemagne will be the protagonist. Having just acknowledged in the previous line that Galien will be the deciding factor
in the French victory in the upcoming battle against Baligant, the narrator emphasizes with traditional language that Charlemagne nevertheless is the hero of the episode as a whole. Laisse 146 starts with an
evocation of spring ("Se fut ay moys de moy, qu'il fit seri et bel" v. 4038),
a traditional mark of beginnings in medieval literature, and is further
marked as a beginning in that it recounts the French army's preparation
before a battle. In addition, each line ends with the sound *el*, usually
caused by using the antiquated form of a noun or adjective (*bel, nouvel,
mantel, jouvencel, chatel, loiel, isnel*, etc.). These nouns and adjectives
strengthen the impression that Charlemagne and the French warriors
other than Galien (who is absent from this scene) are at home in this
deliberately antiquated literary setting. In the following laisse, in which

Charlemagne encourages his men to fight with the memory of their forebears in mind, the rhyme -our is often maintained by using plural nouns without s endings, as was appropriate for plural subjects in Old French;[69] moreover, these are reinforced with the appropriate Old French article li (li grant et li minour, v. 4060; li prince et li contour, v. 4061; li cuvert vanteour, v. 4067; li pluseour, v. 4073). The repeating rhymes of both laisses proclaim the reorientation of the narrative toward the past literary tradition that revolved around Charlemagne, as do the remaining events in Galïen restoré. The preceding sections of the narrative, including the Roncevaux section, shifted literary tradition by placing the focus on Galien and his family; now the language works together with the narrator's interventions in an attempt to shift the focus back to Charlemagne. The emperor fulfills his role as the representative of the collectivity when he reminds his army and the audience in his speech that all of his men, not just Galien, had an "ancessour" (v. 4066) killed in the Spanish campaigns. The almost entirely correct use of Old French endings to maintain the rhyme during this speech (the only exception in this laisse is "Charles l'empereour," line 4064, which mixes subject and object endings) reminds the audience of Charlemagne's long-established authority in epic literature at the same time that his leadership of the army affirms his authority within the fictional universe. Thus the language and content of these laisses preceding the Baligant episode already begin to convey the widening scope of the text's perspective, which is no longer focusing on the fates of the individual heroes but now explicitly addressing the significance of this story for all of France, past and present.

Since the Charlemagne-Galien cooperation is a strong theme of this section of the narrative, it is worth taking note of one specific term, li per ("the peers," as in Charlemagne's twelve peers), which is used in its antiquated form during the scene in which Galien wins the crown of Constantinople. Both before and after Galien's combat, "li per" (properly used as a plural subject) provide important support to Galien's cause, just as the twelve "peers" of France formed the core of Charlemagne's support throughout the earlier epic tradition. Before the combat, the army standing by to fight, if necessary, against the men loyal to Galien's uncles included "li per qui s'afichent forment / De guarder le champ bien et loialment" [The peers who affirm strongly / that they are guarding the field well and loyally] (vv. 3660–61). While the identity of these "peers" is unclear at first, it seems later that this group must give its consent before Galien can become emperor: "Et les bourgois l'enmainent ens ou palais licé, / Trestous li per s'accordent que il soit couronné" [And the people of the city bring him into the walled palace, / All of the peers agree that he should be crowned] (vv. 3971–72). Although the term *per* was used in a variety of contexts in medieval literature, its most obvious connection within a Roncevaux narrative would be to Charlemagne's twelve peers, a connection emphasized by the use of its most antiquated form, including the article *li*. This usage emphasizes that Galien's empire will replicate Charlemagne's, making Galien a double for Charlemagne who will handle his new responsibilities in a familiar and therefore trustworthy way. The idea that Galien has his own "peers" affirms his restoratory function: although Charlemagne's twelve peers have been killed at Roncevaux, Galien's peers still remain and are now loyal allies of France.

Language again supports this parallel between Galien and Charlemagne after Galien's entrance into the battle against Baligant: the wording of this passage features a recurring parallel structure, which is particularly dense in the passage where Baligant decides to challenge Charlemagne to a combat because Galien proves to be unbeatable:

> Grans coups y se donnent, ne se vont espargnant,
> Mais les haubers leur sont *deffense et guarant.*
> Les lances font voler par esclas ens au champ,
> Ung capple ont commencié *si fort et si pesant,*
> Que je cuide que Balinguant fut a tart reppairant.
> Quant paiens sont venus a esperon brochant,
> Marsilles et les siens qui lui sont secourant,
> Et furent XII mile hardis et a merveilles combatant.
> La fut recommencé li estour *fort et grant,*
> Et d'aultre part est venu [Charles] le roy puissant.
>
> Pour aider Baliguant vindrent paiens le cours,
> Et François d'aultre part pour Gualïen le doulx;
> Moult avoit Gualïen *grant ire et grant couroulx,*
> *Grant fut la bataille et pesans li estours,*
> Qui il peut consuïr, moult est son terme cours.
> Occiz leur a *ung roy et ungs admiratour;*
> Mais plus seuffre de coups que ne feroit ungs ours.
> Balinguant escria qui fut *crains et iroulx:*
> "Par Mohom! il me semble qu'il me va a reboulx."
>
> (vv. 4302–20)

[They give each other great blows there, without sparing themselves,
But their hauberks are a defense and protection to them.
They make their lances fly in pieces onto the field.
They have begun a battle so strong and so painful,
That I believe that Baligant would have have returned home later.
When the pagans came, digging in their spurs,
Marsile and his men who were there to help him,
And there were twelve thousand, strong and fighting marvelously.
There the battle began anew, great and strong,
And from the other side came Charles, the powerful king.

To help Baligant the pagans came running,
And the French from the other side for the gentle Galien;
Galien had a great anger and a great rage,
Great was the battle and the fighting painful;
Whomever he pursues, his life span is very short.
He killed from among them a king and an emir,
But he suffers from blows more than a bear would.
Baligant cried, who was afraid and angry:
"By Mohammed! It looks to me as if the tide has turned against me."]

The italicized phrases show several variations on such parallel structure: binomial expressions (as in line 4303), pairs of adjectives (v. 4305), and parallel phrases made up of adjectives and nouns together (vv. 4314–15). While the Baligant episode contains several other examples of parallel structure,[70] it seems that a conscious effort was made to create linguistic pairs in this particular passage. The reason for this density of parallel structure is that here Galien and Charlemagne are facing Baligant as a team, in contrast to the Oxford *Roland*, for example, where Charlemagne and Baligant were depicted as the two sole leaders of their respective armies. The doubling of words and phrases emphasizes in language what is happening in the narrative: two characters are occupying the same heroic space as leaders of the French army, just as two words are being used to describe the same thing. While the use of such parallel structure is common in the medieval *chanson de geste*, the particular examples that appear in this passage show a coexistence of old and new language that indicates a conscious effort to capitalize on the effect of this traditional technique. Perhaps the oldest use of such parallel structure in Old French was in binomial expressions pairing a Latinate word with a Germanic word to ensure that listeners from every background would understand; this phenomenon persists here in the case of "deffense [Latinate] et guarant [Germanic]." In an updating of this use of parallel structure for practical, linguistic reasons, "Grant fut la bataille et pesans li estours" pairs an antiquated term *(li estours)* with a term in current usage *(la bataille)*, so that the old word will be understood as a synonym for the current word. In the early lines of this passage, the repeated technique of using two words or phrases to refer to the same thing emphasizes both that the style of the narration sounds authentically epic and that the doubling itself is purely redundant. The last two examples in this passage break that pattern, however, in that they put two different things into a parallel structure: after Galien kills "ung roy et ungs admiratour" (two different people) on the Saracen side, Baligant feels "crains et iroulx" ("afraid and angry/sad"). This moment turns the tide of the battle and of the narrative: when Baligant realizes that he is starting to lose the battle, he challenges Charlemagne to single combat, thereby choosing to focus on one French leader and force the other into inactivity. The passage thus reveals an awareness of how parallel structure was used to resolve linguistic ambiguity in the oldest French texts and how it might be used to resolve the "old versus new" linguistic ambiguity particular to this text; this conscious use of parallel style then is expanded to mark the moment of Baligant's consternation, when discordant pairings replace the pattern of harmonious redundancy established in the earlier lines.

All of the above examples demonstrate that *Galïen restoré* consistently used "old language" to reinforce in the very fabric of the text the complex relationships between the old and new literary material out of which the text was built. This use of language was therefore not an involuntary, authentic trait of fifteenth-century popular literature but instead a deliberate stylistic medievalism. At both the narrative and linguistic levels, *Galïen restoré*'s literary nostalgia was made up of carefully balanced proportions of remembering and forgetting.

A Happy Ending by an Author in Mourning

In the ending to *Galïen restoré*, the narrator validates the fictional representatives of the contemporary French king (in the form of Charlemagne) and of the contemporary French lords willing to support him (in the form of Galien) but is unwilling to do so at the expense of the traditional heroes of the rear guard at Roncevaux. As the narrator's closing comments remind potentially forgetful audience members, this is the story of Roland and of Roncevaux. I would suggest that what "Roncevaux" really means here is not the actual Battle of Roncevaux but rather the literary mission that always characterized Roncevaux narratives: to use an old story for the purpose of addressing the concerns of both the contemporary audience and contemporary literature. It is no accident that the narrator concludes with a reassertion of the notion that this is primarily a Roncevaux text, for the resonances of "Roncevaux" ultimately mitigate the occasional earlier tensions between the story of Galien and the parts of the plot featuring the traditional Roncevaux heroes. If the narrator had omitted Galien from the portion of the text following laisse 131, as the narrator initially announced, presumably the result would have been a traditional Roncevaux ending, without the added episodes of Galien becoming emperor of Constantinople and then supporting Charlemagne in the battle against Baligant. What these two added episodes have in common is that they are the events of the greatest relevance to the contemporary historical context and therefore the ones that audiences particularly needed to notice and remember.[71] If the audience, like the narrator in this instance, forgot the example provided by the adventures of Roland *and* of Galien, this successful resolution would not have been possible. Galien's method for achieving the long-desired unification of East and West has all the ease, simplicity, and magic that usually accompanies literary representations of wish fulfillment; during Galien's many adventures in this text, he incurs minimal losses and enormous gains as a result of his singleminded dedication to living up to his responsibilities. The narrative as a whole therefore suggests, again through magical thinking, that the French nobility actually will end up, not sacrificing, but instead benefiting, if they support the king's new military campaigns. This historical relevance explains why so much attention is devoted in this narrative to the adventures of Galien, in spite of the narrator's opening and closing remarks insisting that Roncevaux is its most important event.

At the same time, as we have seen in the previous chapters, "Roncevaux" also consistently represents collective loss and the need to overcome threats to the ongoing commemoration of that loss. Just as Roland's death at Roncevaux is often shown to stir up immense grief in all of France, past and present, the author of *Galien restoré* seems to want to alert fifteenth-century French audiences to the grief they should have been feeling over the disappearance of most of the earliest French literary texts. For as much as this text, like the hero Galien, strives to make up for the absence of its ancestors, it also appears to recognize that there are certain ways in which it cannot. Through its nostalgic form, language, and narrative strategies, *Galïen restoré* represents, among other things, vernacular literature's recognition of its own limitations. After centuries of expansion for this literary domain, which viewed itself as new all along, *Galïen restoré* consciously looks backward and mourns the loss of many early French texts along the way, losses it represents as the product of audiences' "forgetfulness." In spite of its overall optimism, *Galïen restoré* acknowledges a discomfort with the changes and resolution it has brought to the Roncevaux plot by retaining a deliberately "fragmentary" textuality (to use Haidu's term once again), ambiguities and apparent contradictions that indicate the continued presence of past texts not forgotten in the creation of a new narrative.

Conclusion

Roland's Heart and "Roncevaux"

Preservation and Transformation

When Charlemagne leaves the battlefield at Roncevaux in the Oxford *Roland*, he carries with him the hearts of Roland, Olivier, and Turpin, wrapped in silk inside a white marble sarcophagus (laisse 213). This act of corporeal transformation for the purpose of preservation is accompanied by no explanation from the narrator, either because its meaning would have been obvious to contemporary audiences or because this was another instance of mysterious behavior on the part of a character that was offered as a catalyst to the audiences' own interpretative process. As we have seen, similarly unexplained moments elsewhere in the Oxford *Roland* include several episodes that can be interpreted as reflections upon the Oxford author's literary project and that of the contemporary audience: Roland's emphatic submission to the *geste*, Ganelon's false narrative about Roland and the apple, and Aude's death. Eugene Vance has ascribed a similarly metaliterary meaning to the enclosure of the heroes' hearts in a white marble reminiscent of Greek or Roman monuments: "In wishing to endow his moment of loss with the same monumental glory previously reserved for heroes of earlier empires, Charlemagne is also reviving a relationship between history and writing that had been essentially Roman and classical." Vance then adds, "[T]his textualization of vernacular poetry is a perfectly tangible equivalent of a shift in attitude toward monumentality that occurs within the story of the poem when Charlemagne displaces Roland as the central hero."[1]

Vance's commentary here captures two ideas that have been central to my analysis of the Oxford *Roland* and of all the Roncevaux texts: first, that events within the fiction tend to dramatize in a visual and audible form the artistic and cultural tensions inherent in the project of the Roncevaux redactors; and second, that these dramatizations return frequently to the point that every act of textual preservation simultaneously effects a transformation in the Roncevaux material and in the available contexts for its reception. As I stated at the start of this book, the dramatization of the retelling and reception of Roncevaux narratives by characters after the Battle of Roncevaux within the fiction was treated by nearly all the redactors as the most appropriate place in which to exert their own transformative influence over the Roncevaux material and its future reception. After the close examination of many of those individual transformations in the preceding chapters, it is possible now to draw some comparative conclusions about what common qualities can be found in these diverse accounts of the Roncevaux material, and thus about what the label "Roncevaux" meant to medieval authors and audiences.

Returning to the Oxford *Roland* and the "tangible" and "monumental" qualities that Vance ascribed to its dramatization of Charlemagne's first act of memorialization of the battle and its heroes, my study allows us to add to this analysis that the global attitude of the author toward the poem also privileges these two qualities. Just as the white marble resting place for the heroes' hearts serves as a concise symbol for Charlemagne's desired form of transmission and reception of the news of the battle, I have argued that Roland's sword Durendal can be interpreted as a symbol for the unchanging *geste* contained within the poem at hand. Moreover, these two objects representing the poem and its sources and aspirations have a reciprocal relationship: both contain corporeal relics of Christian martyrs, but the sarcophagus is the ultimate symbol of stasis, an object designed for contemplation from a distance, while the sword is the ultimate symbol of action and historical change, an object designed for the most strenuous use in close combat. Since this poem heralded the transfer of the orally transmitted Roncevaux material into the fixed form of the written text, the proper representation of this complex project required both the contemplative, monumental stasis of the sarcophagus and the miraculous, transformative dynamism powered by the relics within Durendal's hilt, in cooperation with the succession of living heroes whose fingerprints had marked that hilt and then faded away.

If we compare these symbolic objects from the Oxford *Roland* to their equivalents in the other texts included in this study, the specific literary agenda of the Oxford *Roland* can be seen to diverge markedly from those of the other surviving versions, but what all the Roncevaux texts have in common is the impulse to insert the Roncevaux story into a larger literary and cultural context that is different every time. I argued in the first chapter that the implicit literary agenda of the Oxford *Roland* was both to comment upon the entry of the Roncevaux material into written form and to preserve the traditional authority of the *geste*, which Oxford represents specifically as a spiritual and a factual authority, the capacity to correct misunderstandings and enlighten the ignorant. Although the Châteauroux version affirms many of the readings found in Oxford, and seems to convey a generally conservative interpretation in its early sections, its closing scenes repeatedly undermine the notion that written texts are the best place to invest spiritual or even factual authority.

For the Châteauroux author, as demonstrated by the episodes we have already seen from the final section of the text, spiritual and factual authority are one and the same, and such authority is not most reliably transcribed in or later derived from books because books are the products of unreliable human agents. Similarly, Châteauroux's treatment of Durendal and of the corpses of the Roncevaux heroes strengthens this notion of a fundamental split between material forms and the transcendent spirits that animate them but do not permanently reside within them. Whereas the Roland of Oxford carefully arranges his dying body so that it shields Durendal after he realizes that he has not been granted the power to destroy the sword, the Roland of Châteauroux throws Durendal into a deep, foul, poisonous fountain, where it will remain until the end of time (vv. 4116–28). That is one way to keep the sword out of the hands of the unworthy, but it is a method that would seem to debase the sword itself (not to mention the relics within it, which are still there [laisse 242]). Yet the last line of this passage alludes to the end of time, which, within a Christian context, is the moment when the things of earth will be "freed from corruption" and the souls and bodies of the faithful redeemed and glorified (Rom. 8:18–25). Interestingly, the Châteauroux narrator claims to have heard about this fate for Durendal in local oral lore, which the narrator represents as reliable (indeed, he calls this oral source a *guarant*): "La gent del reigne en trai vos a garent: / cil nus ont dit, se l'estoire ne ment, / q'encor i est, por voir certanement, / et esera deci au feniment" [The people of that area I can cite to you as a reliable source: they told us, if the story does not lie, that it is there still, truly and certainly, and will be there from now until the end of time] (vv. 4125–28). Thus the local oral tradition not only preserves accurately the facts about what became of Durendal but also understands those facts within the orthodox framework of Christian universal history.

As we have seen in the chapter on Châteauroux, the Aude episode in this version dramatizes a similar fate for the bodies of Roland and Olivier. When Aude finally sees Roland's corpse, the narrator emphasizes its pitiful materiality, Roland's flesh having turned black in some places and white in others (v. 7082). In vain, Aude begs the dead Roland to speak to her (vv. 7088–89). Not only has Roland's heart not been encased in a sarcophagus, but his entire body, which was carefully embalmed in Oxford, here appears to be on a normal course toward decomposition. Just as Charlemagne's careful preservation of the bodies in Oxford corresponded to his desire, and probably that of the author, for material preservation of the Roncevaux story in a beautiful, monumental form, Charlemagne's relative negligence of the heroes' corpses in Châteauroux corresponds to the emperor's introduction of self-serving narrative corruption into the account of Roncevaux that he is trying to circulate in this version. The parallel between the bodies and the text at hand is completed, of course, by the brief resurrection and speech of the dead Olivier, which occurs only when an angel leans down from heaven in response to Aude's prayer: "Li verais Deus la pucele n'obile, / car li sanz angles, a sa voiz esbaudie, / joste Oliver s'apoia les l'oïe. / Lores paroles comme si fust en vie." [The truthful God does not forget the maiden, / for the holy angel, gladdened by her voice, / leans down next to Olivier's ear. Then he speaks as if he were alive.] (vv. 7182–85). If this representation of the heroes' respective corpses symbolizes the author's attitude toward the text of Châteauroux, that attitude is one of combined humility and reverence, viewing the text as a mere material thing, subject to corruption when entrusted to the care of flawed human agents, but also capable of being filled with spiritual power and meaning in the presence of the right audience: Aude specifically asks to be alone with the corpses, and presumably they would have spoken to her only under those conditions. This representation of Aude's privileged communion with the dead Olivier therefore does not merely criticize Charlemagne's narrative representation of Roncevaux but also excludes him from this text's scene of successful, spiritually enlightened, oral transmission. One possible implication of this variation is that the retelling and interpretation of legends such as that of Roncevaux were not the exclusive domain of learned men and their patrons, and perhaps even that the legends had been corrupted through their recent passage into that domain. In comparison with Châteauroux, then, the Oxford *Roland*'s metaliterary message appears relatively prideful and even suspect.

The fate of Roland's heart in *Ronsasvals*, as we have seen, was to leak water and blood during key moments of personal grief and transformation: when he witnessed the deaths of his closest companions on the battlefield and when he blew the horn out of despair over the battle and his forfeited future with Aude. Charlemagne addresses Roland's heart at one point during his lament, equating it with his entire person—"Ay! valentz cors, bel neps" [Alas! valiant heart, fair nephew] (v. 1614)—showing that this text repeatedly represents Roland's heart as the essence of the hero, a body part with intellectual, emotional, and spiritual power. This was, of course, the same meaning attached to Roland's heart by the Oxford *Roland*, which is why that text dramatized its preservation. After Roland's death, however, all that we hear about his body was that it was carried back to his own land, like those of all the twelve peers (vv. 1692–95). At the moment of Aude's death, however, Roland's body and heart play an important role. Aude lifts the veil covering Roland's body and demands the right to "embrace my husband" for the first and last time (vv. 1784–87). This embrace turns out to be the means of Aude's suicide, however, because "tant fort estrenh lo cors del cavallier / que-l cor del ventre si vay tot esclatier; / l'arma s'en vay que non poc plus estier" [she embraced so tightly the body of the knight / that the heart in the body broke all into pieces; / her soul goes away, because it can no longer remain there] (vv. 1789–91). Line 1790 would logically refer to Aude's heart and Aude's body, but in my translation I maintain an ambiguity of the original language, in which possessive adjectives are not used with parts of the body; it is possible, then, that the heart breaking to pieces is Roland's, Aude's, or perhaps both simultaneously. This variation on the scene of Aude's death implies that neither her heart nor Roland's could have been preserved because the circumstances of her death destroyed the structural integrity of the lovers' hearts. Perhaps, then, *Ronsasvals* was emphasizing that textual preservation is an inherently virtual medium: what is being preserved in a textual narrative is only the memory of the person, not the person's actual essence (as the sarcophagus of the Oxford *Roland* suggested).

As is typical of *Ronsasvals*, its depiction of the fate of Durendal after Roland's death dramatizes Charlemagne's willful refusal to dissociate

Roland the man from either his material trappings or his role as the emperor's protégé. In accordance with Charlemagne's generally melancholic (in a Freudian sense) response to Roland's death, he fixates on the sword and on his own agency rather than Roland's, remembering how he knighted Roland with the sword and gave it to him, but also mentioning one of the prominent enemies whom Charlemagne himself had killed with Durandal before passing it on (laisse 44). Charlemagne then concludes, "Pres anc nuls homs aytant angoyssos dan / qu'ieu pert l'espeya e pert vos eyssamant? / Fon anc nuls temps caytieu que perdes tant? / Rendes la mi, si vos ven ha talant!" [Did any man ever suffer such a horrible loss / as I, losing the sword and losing you as well? / Has there been at any time a miserable man who lost so much? / Give it back to me, if you are willing!] (vv. 1597–1600). Charlemagne takes Durendal out of Roland's dead hand, which resists giving up the sword, and the text leaves open a doubt about whether the dead Roland would have chosen to give up the sword even to Charlemagne: "Del ponh la trays al palaÿn Rollan: / non fon nulh autre que penre l'auzes anc, / que ayssi s'en desfendia com si fos vieu estant" [From the fist of the knight Roland he drew it: / no other would ever have dared to take it, / for he defended against it so much, as if he were still alive] (vv. 1601–3). These lines say, not that Roland would not have given Durendal to anyone else, but that no one else would have dared to take it from him; perhaps the implication here is that Charlemagne violated the dead Roland's wishes by taking the sword, which is not surprising given the self-centered rhetoric with which Charlemagne prefaced this gesture. Charlemagne then throws Durendal in a lake, from which it never again emerges, saying directly to the sword that now it will no longer accomplish brave exploits or do any harm (v. 1607). Charlemagne seems to intend this gesture as a tribute to Roland's greatness, for he also says to Durendal, "mays non vos aura nuls homs que valha tant" [never again will any man have you who is as worthy] (v. 1606), but this same line betrays Charlemagne's refusal to continue in his role as a leader of great warriors. In light of my reading of Durendal as an avatar of the poem itself in the Oxford *Roland*, it is possible to interpret Charlemagne's gesture in *Ronsasvals* as a representation of this author's project of rewriting the Roncevaux story from start to finish: instead of retaining recognizable chunks of previous Roncevaux texts (analogous to the relics contained in Durendal), as the Châteauroux author did, *Ronsasvals* dispenses with the material form of the textual tradition in order to generate a Roncevaux text entirely from abstract memories of the story and a relatively new conception of its essential meaning. In the context of Char-

lemagne's transgressive, self-centered grief, however, the potential pit-
falls of this approach emerge more clearly in this scene than its
advantages. Another possible reading, then, within the Occitan cultural
context, might be that Charlemagne's forcible reappropriation of Durendal from an unwilling Roland, after the emperor claimed that the
sword originally belonged to him, is a dramatization by an Occitan
author of the contemporary phenomenon of literary material passing
from Occitan into Old French. This happens most famously in the domain of lyric poetry, but some modern scholars believe that the Roncevaux material first circulated in an Occitan version, only later being retold farther north. None of this can be proven, but my point here is that
these possible readings of this scene in *Ronsasvals* come to mind only
through comparative study of multiple Roncevaux texts.

Certainly Roland's resistance to passing Durendal on to Galien in
Galïen restoré, which I interpreted in the previous chapter as a sign of the
text's resistance to the idea of equating Galien fully with the irreplaceable Roland, only strengthens this potentially metaliterary reading of
the Durendal scene from *Ronsasvals*. Furthermore, *Galïen restoré*'s emphasis on Roland's emperiled position as the focal point of the Roncevaux narratives, and customarily the primary source of messages directly
from the battlefield, takes another form not previously mentioned in
my analysis of *Galïen restoré*. When Roland realizes that the rear guard
cannot prevail over Marsile's forces, he sends Gondebreuf (this text's
analogue to the Gandelbuon of *Ronsasvals*) back carrying messages for
Aude and for Charlemagne. Gondebreuf delivers the message to Charlemagne but makes no effort to carry Roland's message to Aude, even
though it was the first one Roland dictated to him (laisses 85, 89,
170–72). As in Châteauroux and *Ronsasvals*, then, this detail of *Galïen restoré* conveys the notion that narratives about Roncevaux are susceptible
to suppression and distortion, no matter how reliable their original
source might have been. Interestingly, then, this skepticism about the
possibility of flawless transmission of the Roncevaux story is one of the
most consistent characteristics of the surviving Roncevaux textual tradition. The Oxford *Roland* comes closest to entertaining the possibility
of flawless transmission, but its recurring focus on Ganelon's unreliable
narration and its naive reception still retains that theme in one of
its more palatable forms, even as Oxford dispenses with other forms of
this theme, most notably those featured in the more extensive, anti-
Charlemagne Aude episodes of multiple rhymed versions.

In this study I have devoted particular attention to such metaliterary
readings of the Roncevaux material because they are one of the most

distinctive products of comparative study of multiple Roncevaux texts. Although such interpretations cannot be offered or accepted as definitive facts emerging directly from the textual evidence, some of these interpretations are considerably strengthened when they are borne out by a preponderance of textual evidence drawn from multiple Roncevaux texts that are otherwise dissimilar in many ways. I have devoted the earlier chapters to documenting the specific similarities and differences among four particular Roncevaux texts and to constructing readings from these comparisons that highlight the particular contributions of each of these texts to the Roncevaux textual tradition as a whole. All of that material contributes to our understanding of what "Roncevaux" meant to medieval authors and audiences: not only the account of that battle but also the accompanying account of how the battle and its heroes would be represented and remembered afterwards. In these final lines, however, I would like to return to the basic term "Roncevaux," in an effort to consider what made that term the one chosen by medieval authors for the purpose of summarizing this large and complex oral and textual tradition for their audiences.

As we have seen, the term "Roncevaux" (valley of thorns) refers to the episode in the literary legend in which hawthorn bushes grew out of the corpses of the Saracens, as a way to distinguish them from the French corpses (e.g., Châteauroux laisses 333–34). These bushes have two supernatural characteristics: first, they have no flowers, only thorns; second, they are remarkably hardy, since they are said in thirteenth-century accounts to still be visible to pilgrims on the road to Compostela five hundred years after the battle. These thorns, of course, represent God's discernment between French and Saracen and, in a larger sense, God's perfect discernment in all matters. By the same token, the thorns represent the faulty judgment of the Saracen dead: from the medieval Christian perspective of the Roncevaux texts, these people made the wrong choice and entrusted themselves to the wrong divine protector, to multiple gods who did not even exist.[2] Thus in one sense, "Roncevaux" is a term denoting interpretations in conflict, and the lasting traces on earth of both human folly and divine wisdom. This inherent connotation of discernment among conflicting human interpretations already has a clear relevance to literary transmission, especially transmission in the form of frequent reworking, which characterized the Roncevaux material in both its oral and written medieval forms. The other basic meaning of "Roncevaux" was the battlefield and the battle fought upon it. Located in an inhospitable, mountainous border zone, the battlefield at Roncevaux has an essentially liminal character, making it an appropriate representation of change itself, a psychological space in which one is aware of being midway between two different states of being. Without knowing every detail of the provenance of the manuscripts included in this study, I have been able to identify aspects of the historical context of each version that correspond to such a transitional cultural state. But then, human individuals and cultures are nearly always in transition, as one senses in every moment of life but realizes with particular clarity when considering particular events retrospectively. Thus regarding Roncevaux narratives as stable monuments to past or future glory certainly captures one aspect of this transitional mentality successfully, but it does not do justice to the surviving Roncevaux texts' collective anxiety and individual insights about that enterprise. Nor does the traditional view (based on one interpretation of the Oxford *Roland* alone) that Roland is the hero of this legend because his unchanging character personifies an unwavering certainty of the Roncevaux legend about its intended meaning. On the contrary, a reading of the four Roncevaux texts in this study shows that Roland may be the character who changes most from one version to another. Thus, in its miraculous continuity ("valley of thorns") and in its irresolvable multiplicity ("interpretations in conflict"), "Roncevaux" and the bloody battlefield it brings to mind is a particularly appropriate label to have given to this narrative tradition, which expresses the precious, ephemeral nature of individual human beings as well as humanity's collective impossible dream of understanding and preserving flawlessly the self-knowledge generated by the explosive interactions among them.

Notes

Introduction

1. "Etre médiéviste c'est, au plus vrai, prendre position sur la C[hanson de] R[oland]." Bernard Cerquiglini, "Roland à Roncevaux, ou La Trahison des clercs," *Littérature* 42 (1981): 40.

2. Even Ramón Menéndez Pidal, one of the scholars who has done the most painstaking, detailed research on the Oxford *Roland*, argued for the relatively marginal place of the Oxford *Roland* within the Roncevaux tradition of its own time, asserting this well-informed position against the prevailing opinion of critics in the 1950s: "On croit que la version transmise par le prétendu Turold marque un point de perfection; c'est elle qui a créé le premier chef-d'oeuvre. Ensuite, il a dégénéré au cours de ses remaniements; antérieurement, il n'avait pas d'existence en tant qu'oeuvre littéraire. Mais la vérité est que la version d'Oxford tient peu de place dans les succès, éclatants et continuels, obtenus par la *Chanson de Roland*." Ramón Menéndez Pidal, *La* Chanson de Roland *et la tradition épique des Francs*, trans. I. Cluzel, 2nd ed. (Paris: Picard, 1960), 466.

3. Douglas Kelly, *The Art of Medieval French Romance* (Madison: University of Wisconsin Press, 1992), 312.

4. For artistic representations of the Roncevaux story, see Rita Lejeune and Jacques Stiennon, *La Légende de Roland dans l'art du Moyen Âge*, 2 vols. (Brussels: Arcade, 1960). On the "Olivier-Roland" baptismal records of the early eleventh century, see the discussion and bibliography in Paul Aebischer, *Préhistoire et protohistoire du* Roland d'Oxford (Bern: Éditions Francke, 1972), 108–9.

5. Jules Horrent, *La* Chanson de Roland *dans les littératures française et espagnole au Moyen Âge* (Paris: Belles Lettres, 1951). Even this book tended to assume

the inherent superiority of the Oxford *Roland* over the later manuscripts, however. As Simon Gaunt remarked in his study of one of the later manuscripts: "Horrent is disparaging about the rhymed *Roland* and . . . his purpose is to demonstrate the excellence of the Oxford *Roland*." Simon Gaunt, *Gender and Genre in Medieval French Literature* (Cambridge: Cambridge University Press, 1995), ch. 1, 295 n. 8. Fortunately, the prospects for today's medievalists studying the post-Oxford French and Franco-Italian manuscripts have just improved with the recent publication of a series of new critical editions of them: *La Chanson de Roland, The Song of Roland: The French Corpus*, ed. Joseph Duggan et al., 3 vols. (Turnhout: Brepols, 2005), henceforth referred to throughout this book as *French Corpus*.

6. By far the most comprehensive description of the modern reception and editing history of the Oxford *Roland* can be found in Joseph J. Duggan, "General Introduction," in *French Corpus*, 1:5–38. For a less detailed overview, see Andrew Taylor, "Bodleian MS Digby 23," in *Textual Situations: Three Medieval Manuscripts and Their Readers* (Philadelphia: University of Pennsylvania Press, 2002), 26–70. On nationalistic aspects of *Roland* reception, see Joseph J. Duggan, "Franco-German Conflict and the History of French Scholarship on the *Song of Roland*," in *Hermeneutics and Medieval Culture*, ed. Patrick J. Gallacher and Helen Damico (Albany: SUNY Press, 1989): 97–106, and Hans Gumbrecht, "'Un souffle d'Allemagne ayant passé': Friedrich Dietz, Gaston Paris and the Genesis of National Philologies," *Romance Philology* 40 (1986): 1–37. On the attitudes of nineteenth-century medievalists toward late medieval epic, see Robert Francis Cook, "'Méchants romans' et épopée française: Pour une philologie profonde," *Esprit Créateur* 23.1 (1983): 64–74, and William Kibler, "Relectures de l'épopée," in *Au carrefour des routes d'Europe: La Chanson de geste*, ed. François Suard (Aix-en-Provence: Publications du Centre Universitaire d'Etudes et de Recherches Médiévales d'Aix, Université de Provence, 1987), 1:103–27.

7. One can find such commentary in an introductory overview of the *chanson de geste* genre for a literary encyclopedia, for example: "The title *Chanson de Roland* will be used in this essay to refer to the entire complex of medieval works, those written in French and those translated into other languages, relating Roland's actions at the Battle of Roncevaux." Joseph J. Duggan, "The *Chanson de Roland* and the *Chansons de Geste*," in *European Writers*, vol. 1, *Middle Ages and Renaissance: Prudentius to Medieval Drama*, ed. W. T. H. Jackson (New York: Scribners, 1983), 89.

8. Paul Zumthor, *Essai de poétique médiévale* (Paris: Seuil, 1972), 73.

9. Any discussion of the status of textual "variants" in the modern study of medieval literature should recognize the effort of Bernard Cerquiglini to document and to change entrenched attitudes with his book *Éloge de la variante: Histoire critique de la philologie* (Paris: Seuil, 1989).

10. This is a prominent instance of what Stephen Nichols has termed "the touchstone approach," after Matthew Arnold's notion of "touchstones," iso-

lated masterpieces used by modern readers to represent the entire culture of a given period. Nichols's critique of Arnold states, "The fracturing effect of the touchstones approach disrupts the symbolic matrix in which the historical context unfolds. There can be no textual problematic, no abstract model of contextuality in the Arnoldian method because the narrative has been dismantled." Stephen G. Nichols Jr., "Remodeling Models: Modernism and the Middle Ages," in *Modernité au Moyen Âge: Le Défi du passé*, ed. Brigitte Cazelles and Charles Méla (Geneva: Droz, 1990), 52.

11. The importance of narrative to psychology has long been recognized; see, for example, Theodore R. Sarbin, "The Narrative as a Root Metaphor for Psychology," in *Narrative Psychology: The Storied Nature of Human Conduct*, ed. Theodore R. Sarbin (New York: Praeger, 1986), 3–21. Within medieval literary criticism, Peter Haidu has recently asserted that "narrative remains an essential mode by which men and women apprehend and constitute their being, their desires, the meanings with which they surround their lives and constitute their subjectivity." Peter Haidu, *The Subject Medieval/Modern: Text and Governance in the Middle Ages* (Stanford: Stanford University Press, 2004), 95. He documents how this process works in twelfth-century romances, those of Chrétien de Troyes in particular; I see the thirteenth-century Roncevaux texts as engaged in the same project, perhaps bearing in mind some of the same romance intertexts that Haidu examines in this chapter of his book.

12. "Paien unt tort e chrestïens unt dreit." *La Chanson de Roland*, ed. Ian Short (Paris: Librairie Générale Française, 1990), v. 1015. All subsequent citations from the Oxford *Roland* will be taken from this edition, unless otherwise noted. All English translations are my own.

13. Some examples of such studies include Peter Haidu, *The Subject of Violence: The* Song of Roland *and the Birth of the State* (Bloomington: Indiana University Press, 1993); Alexandre Leupin, *La Passion des idoles: Foi et pouvoir dans la Bible et la* Chanson de Roland (Paris: L'Harmattan, 2000), chs. 3–5; Karl-Heinz Bender, *König und Vasall* (Heidelberg: C. Winter, 1967); Dominique Boutet, "Les Chansons de geste et l'affermissement du pouvoir royal (1100–1250)," *Annales* 37 (1982): 3–14; David Douglas, "The *Song of Roland* and the Norman Conquest of England," *French Studies* 14 (1960): 99–116; Robert Eisner, "In Search of the Real Theme of the *Song of Roland*," *Romance Notes* 14 (1972–73): 179–83; Albert Gérard, "L'Axe Roland-Ganelon, valeurs en conflit dans la *Chanson de Roland*," *Moyen Âge* 75 (1969): 445–66; Hans Erich Keller, "The *Song of Roland:* A Mid-Twelfth Century Song of Propaganda for the Capetian Kingdom," *Olifant* 3.4 (1976): 242–58.

14. This is the term used by twelfth-century author Jean Bodel to describe the many Old French narratives set during the reign of Charlemagne, of which the Roncevaux texts are a cohesive subcategory. Bodel uses this term in the prologue to his own Charlemagne narrative, *La Chanson des Saisnes*, alongside two other categories, "la matiere de Bretagne" (Arthurian legends) and "la matiere de Rome" (now called the *romans antiques*).

15. Benedict Anderson, *Imagined Communities: Reflections on the Origin and Spread of Nationalism* (London: Verso, 1983).

16. Robert Siegle, *The Politics of Reflexivity: Narrative and the Constitutive Poetics of Culture* (Baltimore: Johns Hopkins University Press, 1986), 2. Siegle's introduction also disparages the association of reflexivity or metaliterarity only with modern and postmodern literature, on the principle that "reflexivity is a basic capability of narrative exercised in every period, historical schematizations notwithstanding" (3).

17. A sampling of explicits to Roncevaux manuscripts will illustrate this point more precisely, indicating how different medieval authors described their own texts: "liber tocius Romani roncivalis" [the book of the whole romance of Roncevaux] (Venice 4); "Roncisvali e de .R. e d'Oliver et de Aude" [about Roncevaux and Roland and Olivier and Aude] (Châteauroux); "Le livre des XII pairs" [the book of the twelve peers] (Cambridge); "li chançons des XII combatants . . . la desconfite de Roncevauz" [the song of the twelve combatants [and of] the defeat at Roncevaux] (Lyon); "Les fais de Rainchevaulx et le commencement" [the deeds of Roncevaux and their beginning] *(Galïen restoré)*. See Bibliography for details about these manuscripts and their modern editions.

18. The complex signification of "Roncevaux," within the Oxford *Roland* and medieval literary culture generally, as well as in the context of the medieval pilgrimage route to Compostela, is documented and analyzed at length in Stephen G. Nichols Jr., "Roncevaux and the Poetics of Place/Person in the Song of Roland," in *Romanesque Signs: Early Medieval Narrative and Iconography* (New Haven: Yale University Press, 1983): 148–203. Interestingly, in the opening to this chapter, Nichols devotes particular attention to character discourse and its reception by an analytical implied audience, citing these as distinctive narrative aspects of the Oxford *Roland* within its contemporary literary context: "Now the uniqueness of the Oxford *Roland*, and its excitement, stems precisely from the fact that it forces the characters to discover and predicate for themselves the valence of the action they undertake; and it permits them to question and make mistakes. By the same token, it encourages the audience to participate in the same dialectic, to take sides with and against the characters and their positions" (149). This view of narration and reception in the Oxford version was unusual at the time when Nichols's book was first published, but it has been affirmed by many recent studies and is fundamental to my analyses of all the "Roncevaux" texts, for I see narrative and its reception as an essential aspect of the literary entity "Roncevaux" for medieval authors and audiences.

19. In *Ronsasvals*, for example, two potential remedies to this narrative problem ultimately fail to alter it in the slightest. First, a group of fresh warriors rides out from Charlemagne's camp to Roncevaux during the battle, but these reinforcements are too few, and they are rapidly struck down alongside the rear guard, merely serving to increase the final death toll. Second, Roland sends a messenger to Charlemagne with news of the battle, but only after everyone but himself has already been killed; this messenger announces only the deaths re-

sulting from the battle (the same evidence that Charlemagne and the Franks will soon witness for themselves), supplying no other firsthand details about what he saw while the fighting was still under way. *Ronsasvals*, laisses 22, 26–29, in *Le* Roland *occitan*, ed. Gérard Gouiran and Robert Lafont (Paris: Christian Bourgois, 1991). All subsequent citations will be taken from this edition.

20. The Battle of Roncevaux is based on a real event that took place in August 778, in which local Basques ambushed the rear of Charlemagne's army as they went through a narrow pass in the Pyrenees. Many summaries and detailed source studies of this historical event are available; one of the most concise and informative summaries can be found in Eugene Vance, *Reading the Song of Roland* (Englewood Cliffs, NJ: Prentice-Hall, 1970), Appendix II, "The Historical Event," 96–99. Two helpful historical and source studies are those of Menéndez Pidal, *La* Chanson de Roland, and Aebischer, *Préhistoire et protohistoire*.

21. Perhaps the most influential statement of this point of view was the one offered by Erich Auerbach in his essay "Roland against Ganelon," in *Mimesis: The Representation of Reality in Western Literature*, trans. Willard Trask (Princeton: Princeton University Press, 1953), 96–122. Another frequently cited source is R. Howard Bloch's characterization of the dynamics of Old French epic language, which also includes a helpful sampling of earlier studies on that topic. Yet Bloch's extended discussion does acknowledge some examples of linguistic disjunction in epic texts. In fact, he puts his finger on a key to the functioning of language and character narration in the Roncevaux texts when he discusses linguistic integrity as the *ideal* of the epic and "recuperation" as its strategy for coping with transgressions against that ideal. R. Howard Bloch, *Etymologies and Genealogies: A Literary Anthropology of the French Middle Ages* (Chicago: University of Chicago Press, 1983), 100–108.

22. Examples include Leupin, *La Passion des idoles*; Michelle Warren, "The Noise of Roland," *Exemplaria* 16.2 (2004): 277–304; Sharon Kinoshita, "'Pagans are wrong and Christians are right': Alterity, Gender, and Nation in the *Chanson de Roland*," *Journal of Medieval and Early Modern Studies* 31 (2001): 79–111; Joseph Long, "'Cest mot mei est estrange . . .': La Belle Aude and the Irreducible Difference of Words," *Nottingham French Studies* 38 (1999): 114–19. Earlier examples of approaches to the Oxford *Roland* as a deliberately ambiguous text include Nichols's comments on character discourse and audience reception in "Roncevaux"; William Paden, "Tenebrism in the *Song of Roland*," *Modern Philology* 86.4 (1989): 339–56; and Joseph Duggan, "Ambiguity in Twelfth-Century French and Provençal Literature: A Problem or a Value?" in *Jean Misrahi Memorial Volume: Studies in Medieval Literature*, ed. Hans R. Runte, Henri Niedzielski, and William Hendrickson (Columbia, SC: French Literary Publications, 1977), 136–49.

23. Haidu does use a semiotic approach in this book and in several other pieces of his work, but in the introduction to his book he also comments upon the limits of the "analytical tool" provided by narrative semiotics and upon the complexity of a text's process of cultural signification (*Subject of Violence*, 10–11).

24. Sarah Kay, *The Chansons de Geste in the Age of Romance: Political Fictions* (Oxford: Oxford University Press, 1995), 5. See also her discussions of the influence of Bakhtin and Jameson on her approach to twelfth- and thirteenth-century texts, 4–6 and 11–14.

25. Ibid., 13.

26. As Nichols put it, "[W]hen the author permits the personae to play a greater role in the discourse, then uncertainty, doubt, error, in short, all the natural conditions with which humans generally relate to the wor(l)d must be inscribed in the text" ("Roncevaux," 149).

27. Modern readers tend to think of a particular story as being defined by certain characters and events, but the corresponding medieval term *matiere* also included distinctive elements of style, as Douglas Kelly noted in his study of the term, "*Matiere* and *Genera Dicendi* in Medieval Romance," *Yale French Studies* 51 (1974): 147–59, esp. 152.

28. Two such charts can be found in Raoul Mortier, ed., *Les Textes de la Chanson de Roland* (Paris: Éditions de la Geste Francor, 1940), I:viii–ix, and Cesare Segre, ed., *La Chanson de Roland: Édition critique*, 2nd ed. (Geneva: Droz, 2003), 16.

29. Boutet affirms that medieval *chansons de geste*, in particular, were composed to be heard and interpreted in this way, with unique features inserted into conventional scenes in order to attract the audience's attention and engage them in revising the standard interpretation of those scenes by making sense of the newly incorporated material. Dominique Boutet, *La Chanson de geste* (Paris: Presses Universitaires de France, 1993), 145–46.

30. See, for example, Walter Ong, *Orality and Literacy* (New York: Routledge, 1982), 41–42, 48, 60.

31. Michael Riffaterre offers an interesting portrayal of this kind of medieval reception in his article "The Mind's Eye: Memory and Textuality," in *The New Medievalism*, ed. Marina Brownlee, Kevin Brownlee, and Stephen Nichols (Baltimore: Johns Hopkins University Press, 1991), 30–44.

1. The Oxford *Roland*: *La Geste* and Reliable Rewriting

1. Charles Samaran, ed., *La Chanson de Roland: Reproduction phototypique du manuscrit Digby 23 de la Bodleian Library d'Oxford* (Paris: Société des Anciens Textes Français, 1933). For digital facsimile, see "Early Manuscripts at Oxford University," http://image.ox.ac.uk (accessed September 26, 2006).

2. For documentation of this controversy, and of many details concerning the manuscript and its modern reception, see Taylor, "Bodleian MS Digby 23," 26–70. (On the question of manuscript dating, see 223–24 n. 61.) A more thorough description of the manuscript, its text, and its scribe can be found in Ian Short's introduction to his edition of the text ("The Oxford Ver-

sion") in *French Corpus*, vol. I, pt. I, 13–107. A complete account of the text's modern reception and editing history can be found in Joseph Duggan, "General Introduction," in *French Corpus*, 1:5–36.

3. The text contains 3,995 lines of actual text, but most modern editions give 4002 as the last line number because of an editorial convention of assigning line numbers to several lines in the text that are believed to be missing.

4. For the supporting evidence for the earlier date, see Taylor, "Bodleian MS Digby 23," 37; for the later date, see Short's introduction to "The Oxford Version," *French Corpus*, vol. I, pt. I, 14–20, esp. 18.

5. Short states with confidence that "the Insular provenance of the script [is] confirmed not only by palaeographic but also by graphemic analysis" (introduction to "The Oxford Version," *French Corpus*, vol. I, pt. I, 20). Taylor notes that for French scholars with a nationalist agenda "[i]t is a singular embarrassment that the earliest written version of France's national epic survives in a manuscript copied by an Englishman in an Anglo-Norman dialect" ("Bodleian MS Digby 23," 63).

6. Duggan provides descriptive details about all modern critical editions in "General Introduction," *French Corpus*, 1:5–36.

7. For the most thorough discussion of the formulaic composition of the Oxford *Roland*, see Joseph Duggan's *The Song of Roland: Formulaic Style and Poetic Craft* (Berkeley: University of California Press, 1973), as well as the documentation provided in his *A Concordance of the* Chanson de Roland (Columbus: Ohio State University Press, 1969). A more recent study on this topic is Edward Heinemann's *L'Art métrique de la chanson de geste: Essai sur la musicalité du récit* (Geneva: Droz, 1993). An influential study on the general topic of oral composition was Albert Bates Lord's *The Singer of Tales* (Cambridge, MA: Harvard University Press, 1960).

8. Short considers formulaic composition so central to the Oxford *Roland* that he uses it as a criterion for determining whether the Oxford scribe copied a given line accurately from the source. See Short, introduction to "The Oxford Version," *French Corpus*, vol. I, pt. I, 47ff.

9. Eugene Vance, "Roland and Charlemagne: The Remembering Voices and the Crypt," in *Mervelous Signals: Poetics and Sign Theory in the Middle Ages* (Lincoln: University of Nebraska Press, 1986), 51–85, 57.

10. We do not know who the author of Oxford was, or even if it was an individual or a group. Instead of using the term *author* and the singular masculine pronoun *he*, then, it might be more accurate to speak of "the author function" and to use the pronoun *it*. My resistance to doing so, and the old-fashioned (or even sexist) sound of my *he*-inflected discourse in discussing the "Oxford poet," should be understood, above all, as the result of my core belief that poems are produced by people, who carry out their various "functions" with their own glorious human idiosyncrasies. Moreover, as in the context of the discussion where this note appears, what often concerns me about the Roncevaux authors was the way in which they might have perceived and been perceived by the other

human participants in the literary field of their own time. Authorial presence was far more pronounced in medieval literary transmission than it is today, making the notion of an "author function" in some ways anachronistic in a discussion of medieval literature. On the issue of using gender-marked pronouns for anonymous authors, I have opted to use *he* for all of the anonymous authors included in this study primarily because that remains the official unmarked singular pronoun of the English language, and also because medieval audiences almost certainly imagined authors and narrators as male unless they had been informed to the contrary. It may well be, however, that some medieval texts do not specify their authors because they were women concerned that their gender might prejudice audiences against them.

11. See Taylor's discussion of M. B. Parkes's analysis of the bookhand in "Bodleian MS Digby 23," 38. But in the introduction to his edition ("The Oxford Version"), Ian Short emphasizes the mediocrity of both the manuscript and the scribe, disparaging what he sees among modern editors of the text as "the progressive sanctification of every letter and squiggle that came from the modest, sometimes clumsy, pen of the Anglo-Norman scribe who copied it into a modest, if not downright shabby, book sometime between the 1140s and the 1170s" (*French Corpus*, vol. 1, pt. 1, 43). He also gives an overview of the scribe's idiosyncracies and shortcomings (82–83).

12. Taylor, "Bodleian MS Digby 23," 42.

13. In fact, Charlemagne combines a future-tense scenario and an imperative in his offer to Roland, marking this as a strong statement of his intended policy concerning the rear guard: "Demi mun host vos lerrai en present. / Retenez les; c'est vostre salvement!" [Half of my force I will give you as a gift. / Keep them with you; it is your salvation!] (vv. 785–86).

14. Reflected, for example, in Gérard Brault's English translation ("I'll do no such thing, I'll be damned if I'll act unworthily of my family!"), which takes this interpretive tradition into account without an explanatory note in either his edition or its accompanying volume of commentary. Gérard Brault, ed., *The Song of Roland: An Analytical Edition*, vol. 2, *Oxford Text and Translation* (University Park: Pennsylvania State University Press, 1978), 51.

15. Karl Uitti, "'Ço dist la geste': Reflections on the Poetic Restoration of History in *The Song of Roland*," in *Studies in Honor of Hans-Erich Keller: Medieval French and Occitan Literature and Romance Linguistics*, ed. Rupert Pickens (Kalamazoo, MI: Medieval Institute Publications, 1993), 1–27.

16. Ibid., 10.

17. Ibid., 10–11.

18. Ibid., 16–17.

19. Ibid., 18.

20. My focus on grammar, and particularly on verb tense switching, in a number of passages from the Oxford *Roland* was certainly influenced at an early stage in my research by my study of Suzanne Fleischman's book *Tense and Narrativity: From Medieval Performance to Modern Fiction* (Austin: University of Texas

Press, 1990), in which she frequently cites and discusses examples of verb tense usage by the characters of the Oxford *Roland*. Yet when I tried recently to locate specific examples used both by me and Fleischman, I found only one (see n. 45). I can only conclude that her book taught me to read in a certain way that has since become automatic; certainly that level of influence deserves at least this general citation and the general recommendation that her book be consulted by anyone with an interest in medieval narrative.

21. Uitti even uses an expression here, *re-live*, that realizes the literal potential of the literary notion of "revival": "For Thierry to remember Roland is to re-live him, that is, to serve Charles as Roland had and to keep Roland alive. Thierry's story is enmeshed in Roland's story, and, it must be said, the converse is equally true" (Uitti, "Ço dist," 17).

22. Vance, "Roland and Charlemagne," 51–52.

23. Ibid., 58.

24. Although Vance omitted from his own citation the line about pagans being wrong and Christians being right, I include it for reasons that I will explain more fully with reference to the horn debate between Roland and Olivier: the inherently transgressive status of the Saracens, because of their refusal to believe in God, is the reason why the Battle of Roncevaux becomes an episode in the ongoing *geste* of Christendom. Roland's personal heroism is genuine and conscious, as the other lines of this passage suggest, but I believe that he is also convinced that he becomes the hero of this episode of the Christian *geste* not simply because of his own exceptional military prowess but more importantly because God chose Roland as the living manifestation of the *geste* for this particular time and place. In so doing, God redeems Ganelon's selection of Roland for a higher purpose, in accordance with the spirit of Joseph's forgiveness of his brothers for their abusive treatment of him: "You intended to harm me, but God intended it for good to accomplish what is now being done" (Gen. 50:20, NIV).

25. "[H]éros de l'oralité, qui vit (comme un poète) au centre d'une collectivité." Eugene Vance, "Roland et la poétique de la mémoire," *Cahiers d'Études Médiévales* 1 (1974): 103–15, 107.

26. Haidu also cites this passage, but for the purpose of emphasizing its legal and political implications, explicitly cautioning modern readers not to understand it as "a moral tale within another moral tale" and choosing not to explore it as an independent Roncevaux narrative (*Subject of Violence*, 158–59).

27. My translation here acknowledges the feudal sense of *amur*, the reliable bond between a good vassal, his lord, and his lord's other vassals. This feudal sense is warranted here especially because Ganelon had explicitly renounced his *amur* for Roland after being nominated for the mission to Marsile (v. 306).

28. For a detailed consideration of the meaning of "traïsun," see F. R. P. Akehurst, "Murder by Stealth: *Traïsun* in Old French Literature," in Pickens, *Studies in Honor*, 459–73, esp. 464.

29. Pickens, "Roland's Apple: Truthful and Untruthful Discourse in *la Chanson de Roland*," in Pickens, *Studies in Honor*, 73–80, 77–79. See also Brault, *Song of Roland*, 1:141–44, and Tony Hunt, "Roland's 'Vermeille Pume,'" *Olifant* 7 (1979–80): 203–11.

30. It has been estimated that 40 percent of the Oxford *Roland* consists of direct discourse between characters. Wolfgang van Emden, *La Chanson de Roland*, Critical Guides to French Texts (London: Grant and Cutler, 1995), 102. Van Emden continues to stress the importance of character discourse and the responsibility of the audience for proper judgment of the characters on the basis of their discourse throughout his introductory comments on the poetics of the text, 101–4. See also Marie-Thérèse de Medeiros, "Temps de l'histoire, temps du récit dans la *Chanson de Roland*," *Le Moyen Âge* 88 (1982): 5–28.

31. Pickens, "Roland's Apple," 80.

32. Ibid., 79.

33. Leupin's reading of Oxford comes very close to this Ganelonesque possibility in that he sees the text's Christian imagery as not only insincere but diabolical, since he believes that it (like many other aspects of the text) is intended to signify by *inversio*: implying the opposite of what it appears to mean on the surface. Leupin, *La Passion des idôles*, 157–60.

34. van Emden, *La Chanson de Roland*, 101.

35. Most translations of line 179 do not stress Ganelon's personal agency as I do here. For example, Ian Short's modern French translation reads, "alors commence ce conseil de malheur"; Gérard Brault's English translation reads, similarly, "Now begins the council that went wrong" (Brault, *Song of Roland*, 2:13). It seems significant to me, however, that *le conseill* is marked as a noun in the object case rather than the subject case, so that the only available grammatical subject for both *cumencet* and *prist* in line 179 is the *Guenes* of line 178.

36. Pickens, "Roland's Apple," 77–79.

37. Also cited in Haidu, *Subject of Violence*, 161.

38. Uitti, "Ço dist," 18.

39. Medeiros considers whether the characters' pronouncements about the future should be considered as narrative "prolepses" in Genette's terms and concludes that they should not, precisely because they are unreliable: "rien ne garantit leur réalisation, à la différence des interventions du narrateur qui sait ce qui va arriver. . . . Les prolepses . . . apparaissent donc comme liées au statut du narrateur" ("Temps de l'histoire," 9).

40. Furthermore, as Rupert Pickens has noted, the issue of unreliable discourse already emerged in the preceding scene of the Saracen council: "The very first exchange of discourse among characters portrays the deliberate fabrication of a Saracen lie meant to deceive the Christian emperor (laisses 2–4)." Pickens, "Roland's Apple," 73.

41. This would be true in any case, but Robert F. Cook has pointed out that Marsile's chosen date of Michaelmas for his promised arrival in France to be baptized a Christian suggests his intention that Charlemagne not discover Mar-

sile's treachery until a date too late in the fall for Charlemagne to attempt an immediate recrossing of the snow-covered Pyrenees. Robert F. Cook, "Roncevaux symbole de la nécessité," *Olifant* 8 (1981): 352–66.

42. In truth, of course, even Charlemagne cannot be certain of future events. Yet as Suzanne Fleischman emphasizes at the start of an entire book on the future tense, what the future tense communicates most fundamentally is the *"speaker's conviction"* about what will happen in the future. Suzanne Fleischman, *The Future in Thought and Language: Diachronic Evidence from Romance* (Cambridge: Cambridge University Press, 1982), 21 (emphasis in the original). In the context of Charlemagne's council, then, each speaker who uses the future tense is conveying the fact that his own conviction about the future is one in which his own agency, rather than that of Charlemagne or the collectivity, is at the center of his concerns.

43. Medeiros notes that here, as in the narrative as a whole, "L'événement passé n'est donc pas phénomène isolé, accident de l'histoire perdu dans sa contingence: il est indice de vérité, leçon pour le présent, exemple" ("Temps de l'histoire," 15).

44. Long, "'Cest mot mei est estrange.'"

45. Fleischman's analysis of the grammar of this passage concluded that "[i]n the last verse of this passage [v. 2413], the summative result clause in the PS [passé simple] coupled with the preceding clause of external evaluation . . . [is] a stark interruption (boundary) in Charlemagne's anguished *planctus*, underscoring the finality and senselessness of the massacre of his men" (*Tense and Narrativity*, 161–62).

46. This phrase appears several times in the portion of the poem devoted to the Franks' futile attempt to reach Roncevaux in time to support the rear guard (v. 1806, v. 1840), even at the otherwise thrilling, hopeful moment when Marsile's men flee the battlefield at the sound of Charlemagne's approaching army (v. 1913).

47. See, for example, Haidu, *Subject of Violence*, 131–32.

48. For example, this scene can be found in the Châteauroux-Venice 7 version, vv. 6198–6209. In Duggan's notes to this passage in his edition, he explains that "Roncevaux" was a folk etymology and that the name was actually derived from the Basque name for the site (*French Corpus*, vol. 2, pt. 3, 509–10).

49. Haidu also analyzes the parallel structures linking these scenes (*Subject of Violence*, 83–84).

50. Vance also notes this parallel between Olivier's reasoning here and Ganelon's in the council scene: "Pour Olivier (comme pour Ganelon, mais pour des raisons différentes), le signifié peut être *dans* le signifiant" ("Roland et la poétique," 112). This semiotic phrasing corresponds to Vance's larger argument that for Roland, as for the poem as a whole, there is a necessary distance between signifier and signified, "une dialectique où le présent est aperçu

comme une absence, et où un être ou un objet absent est invoqué et commémoré comme une présence" (108). It is both in this semiotic context and in the context of Roland's intentionally exemplary heroism as an aspect of the larger *geste* of Charlemagne that Vance cites the contrasting line from Roland's initial speech in the horn debate, "Ben devuns ci estre pur nostre rei" [We really must be here for our king] (v. 1009) (112).

51. Several points of view on this question are summarized and then explored in further detail by Gérard Brault, "*Sapientia* dans la *Chanson de Roland*," *French Forum* 1 (1976): 99–118. See also June Hall McCash, "'Scientia' and 'Sapientia' in the *Chanson de Roland*," *Mediaevalia et Humanistica* 11 (1982): 131–47.

52. Howard Bloch also devotes particular attention to the relics in Durendal as a symbol of historical continuity in *Etymologies and Genealogies*, 103–14.

53. Haidu offers a number of translations of this line (*Subject of Violence*, 180).

54. Short, *Chanson de Roland*, 258–59, n. to line 4002.

55. See especially Haidu's chapter "The Semiotization of Death," which analyzes this scene in detail, beginning with Haidu's assertion that Roland "transforms himself into a complex sign" when he arranges his body before dying (*Subject of Violence*, 18).

56. Vance, "Roland and Charlemagne," 65.

57. *Recrëant* is a difficult term to translate into the terms of a modern, secular culture. It literally refers to the sin of apostasy, "believing again" in the sense of renouncing traditional beliefs and taking on new ones. It is also used in Old French texts as a more general insult, particularly for non-Christians (those who never espoused Christian beliefs in the first place) or for cowards (people who were unable to live up to the models of bravery that were prevalent in their society). Its use here to describe Ganelon seems particularly appropriate, since it describes negatively what Ganelon offered as his own defense at his trial: the fact that Ganelon turned against his feudal lord and kinsmen at a particular moment because of a threat to his own safety. Its implications of a negative "newness" would also make it an appropriate term to describe vernacular authors who did not respect the letter or the spirit of the *geste* in their literary reworkings.

2. The Châteauroux Version: Retelling as Redemptive Reception

1. All of the information about the Châteauroux and Venice 7 manuscripts that I include here comes from Joseph Duggan's introduction to his new edition ("The Châteauroux-Venice 7 Version" in *French Corpus*, vol. 2, pt. 3, 13–110). I am grateful to Professor Duggan for making this introduction and the texts available to me in electronic form before their publication. In this chapter I cite from the text of the Châteauroux version (alone), which Duggan

includes as Appendix B (pp. 531–807) after his edition combining readings from both manuscripts. The joint edition has improved readings in comparison to the Châteauroux version alone, but in this book my methodology demands that I restrict my analysis to the content of only one version at a time. For occasional cross-referencing, I have also used the edition of Mortier, *Les Textes de la Chanson*, vol. 4, which is flawed in many ways but which was the only available edition of Châteauroux until very recently.

2. Duggan, "The Châteauroux-Venice 7 Version," in *French Corpus*, vol. 2, pt. 3, hereafter referred to as "C/V7."

3. Paris appears to be missing pages at the beginning, while Cambridge is more likely to owe its "late" start to a deliberate compositional strategy. The case of Lyon is complex, since that version begins with a twelve-line introduction to an entirely different narrative, followed abruptly by the initial lines of the Roncevaux narrative, which are marked in a number of ways as an intentional starting point, although they recount the start of actual combat, omitting all the scenes before that point. This relatively belated beginning is consistent with the overall character of the Lyon version, which has a tendency to condense and summarize passages that are far longer in the other rhymed versions. In his introduction to his edition of Lyon ("The Lyon Version"), William Kibler affirms, "The codicological evidence . . . all indicates that this manuscript is complete as it has come down to us, with no missing leaves or textual lacunas" (*French Corpus*, vol. 3, pt. 6, 17). Kibler adds on the following page that "what is 'missing,' I believe, has been deliberately suppressed" (18).

4. A detailed concordance of laisses for all of these versions, compiled by Karen Akiyama, is included in *French Corpus*, vol. 1, 41–124, and provides a helpful introduction to the textual tradition for readers who are unfamiliar with the rhymed texts.

5. In his *stemma* of the surviving Roncevaux versions, Cesare Segre confirms both the relative chronological closeness and the perceptible independence of composition of the five separate rhymed versions (Châteauroux and Venice 7 being considered as two copies of the same source). He shows Venice 4 as having been composed at an earlier stage, between the composition of Oxford and of the other five rhymed versions, though it survives only in a fourteenth-century manuscript. The other five rhymed versions he lists on the same chronological level, yet as separate witnesses. See Cesare Segre, *La Chanson de Roland*, 2nd ed. (Geneva: Droz, 2003), 16.

6. "For us the texts are artifacts; in the Middle Ages they illustrated stages in a dynamic process of social and moral reflection elaborated in textual commentary and correction" (Kelly, *Art of Medieval French Romance*, 312).

7. See the longer examination of these distinctions in my Introduction, pp. 14–15.

8. Duggan discusses this in the introduction to his edition of C/V7, 36–39.

9. Specific line references are provided by Duggan in the introduction to his edition of C/V7, 45. See also the discussion of this issue in Joseph J. Duggan, "L'Épisode d'Aude dans la tradition en rime de la *Chanson de Roland*," in *Charlemagne in the North*, ed. Philip Bennett, Anne Cobby, and Graham Runnalls (Edinburgh: Société Rencesvals British Branch, 1993), 273–79.

10. Duggan credits scribal error for the variation in linguistic forms because the Italianate forms are not consistent between the lines of Châteauroux and Venice 7 that consist of the same transcribed Old French words. This seems to have been one of Duggan's reasons for assembling a composite edition drawn from both versions: in this way he could use the most accurate linguistic forms from each version, resulting in a consistently comprehensible text for modern readers. See the introduction to Duggan's edition of C/V7, 55–57.

11. All citations and line numbers are from Duggan, *French Corpus*, vol. 2, pt. 3, Appendix B, unless otherwise noted, and all English translations are my own.

12. On my unusual translation of this line, see ch. 1, n. 35.

13. Duggan and Mortier correctly indicate that Venice 4 contains the same material in the same order in its laisses 10–11, but it is worth noting that these laisses of Venice 4 are considerably shorter and simpler: they summarize the most pertinent content of Oxford without maintaining its stylistic integrity as Châteauroux does to a greater extent.

14. Duggan's transcription of Châteauroux includes "Mas ne dist autre outrage" as part of Roland's quoted speech rather than ascribing it to the narrator, as Mortier did in his edition of Châteauroux (*Textes de la Chanson*, vol. 4, v. 331). This is a matter of editorial judgment, since quotation marks are not present in the manuscript at all. I will note, however, that Duggan chooses as his reading in the composite C/V7 edition the wording "Mes ne dite autre outrage!" which would seem to be an accusation against Charlemagne if we understand *dite* as a second-person plural imperative. Thus the two ways of construing this passage offer us the choice of perceiving a milder Roland deliberately projected by the narrator or of perceiving a prideful Roland whose interjection also criticizes Charlemagne's discourse with the quite serious Old French term *outrage*. Ultimately either reading affirms the general direction I see for the reworking of this scene that is unique to Châteauroux (and to some extent Venice 7 as well). This laisse in Venice 4 (17) follows exactly the wording of Oxford, which emphasizes Ganelon's status as Roland's stepfather, a consideration that Châteauroux omits.

15. Some of the most prominent studies of the "démesure" question include Alfred Foulet, "Is Roland Guilty of *Desmesure*?" *Romance Philology* 10 (1956–57): 145–48; Pierre Le Gentil, "À propos de la démesure de Roland," *Cahiers de Civilisation Médiévale* 11 (1968): 203–9; Jean-Charles Payen, *Le Motif du repentir dans la littérature française médiévale* (Geneva: Droz, 1968), 108–37; William Kibler, "Roland's Pride," *Symposium* 26 (1972): 147–60; Larry Crist, "À propos de la desmesure dans la *Chanson de Roland*: Quelques propos (démesurés?)," *Olifant* 1

(April 1974): 10–20; Robert Francis Cook, *The Sense of the* Song of Roland (Ithaca: Cornell University Press, 1987), esp. text and notes to chs. 2 and 3, where Cook includes a fairly exhaustive inventory of studies related to this issue.

16. Duggan offers this possibility in his note to line 455 in his edition of C/V7, while also acknowledging that this change would represent a misreading of this speech as the probable invention of Ganelon in Oxford and V4.

17. The prayers of the Châteauroux characters, particularly Roland, Charlemagne, and Ganelon, have been documented, compared, and presented in a helpful table by Leslie C. Brook, "Expressions of Faith in the Rhymed Versions of the *Chanson de Roland*," in Bennett, Cobby, and Runnalls, *Charlemagne in the North*, 145–56. Brook does not ascribe much interpretative significance to these prayers, however, considering them primarily as a stylistic feature (155).

18. Mortier and Duggan both indicate in their editions an overall resemblance between laisse 66 of Châteauroux and laisse 61 of Oxford because Roland's accusation against Ganelon is included in the conventional episode where he accepts the symbolic tokens of his leadership of the rear guard, the wording of which is similar to Oxford and V4; Roland's explicit accusation against Ganelon does not appear in this scene from either of these other versions, however. The only other surviving version that includes it is the far later Cambridge, but it is worth noting that Roland's accusation provides the starting point for the Cambridge version in that it appears in the first laisse of that text, a positioning that may have resulted from the inadvertent loss of earlier laisses in the transmission of the Cambridge version or that may have been a deliberate compositional choice on the part of the author. Wolfgang van Emden, the editor of the version of Cambridge included in *French Corpus*, gives detailed codicological evidence that could support the theory of either deliberate or accidental omission of the earlier laisses (vol. 3, pt. 5, 25–26).

19. The Paris version devotes its opening laisses to the moment when Roland goes up to the hilltop to pray and parallels Châteauroux closely thereafter.

20. This passage appears twice in laisse 164, vv. 2664–66 and 2670–72. In all likelihood, the repetition represents simple scribal error. In light of other subtle rewriting strategies in Châteauroux, however, it is possible to wonder whether this repetition might have been deliberate: this is one of Olivier's most pessimistic statements, and it is phrased in the markedly worldly language of economics, putting it into sharp contrast with Roland's more spiritually minded statement in the following laisse.

21. Or perhaps, if *e* is construed as *en,* as Duggan suggests it should be, the translation would be "As clerks find it in books of sermons."

22. With the exception of the Lyon version, which omits the Baligant episode but then generally parallels Châteauroux from the defeat of Saragossa through the end of the text.

23. Duggan, note to line 6007 of his edition of C/V7.

24. Although this miracle does not occur in the Oxford version, the use of the name "Roncevaux" in that text suggests that this episode did exist in the pre-Oxford oral tradition. Duggan notes that the name "Roncevaux" was originally a folk etymology for the Basque place name. (See Duggan's edition of C/V7, note to line 6198.)

25. Then "fresh, green" plants also miraculously grow over the Christian bodies on the ground. Duggan's edition of C/V7 indicates that these are hazel bushes, which may be the reading in Venice 7; in Châteauroux, what is said to be "growing among the graves" are "les tonbes" ("tombs" or "tombstones"), which is a confused reading not worthy of direct citation here.

26. The most extensive psychoanalytic interpretation of Aude's dreams is found in Jann Matlock, "The 'Clear Visions' of 'la Bele Aude': Dream Form and Function in *La Chanson de Roland*," *Pacific Coast Philology* 15 (1980): 35–44. See also Duggan, "L'Épisode d'Aude," and Kay, *Chansons de Geste*, 209–11.

27. This tendency of the Châteauroux prayers to reference pertinent biblical narratives was also noted several times by Brook, "Expressions of Faith."

28. Duggan's edition of C/V7 supplies a line (7430) that is missing from the Châteauroux manuscript, which explains that angels carry Aude away.

29. Duggan has also observed a continuity between the misinterpretation of the clerk and the specific form taken by Charlemagne's lies to Aude in the following scene ("L'Épisode d'Aude," 276).

30. A useful description of the emergence of the Old French Pseudo-Turpin texts, and of the prose phenomenon in general within Old French literature, can be found in Gabrielle Spiegel, *Romancing the Past: The Rise of Vernacular Prose Historiography in Thirteenth-Century France* (Berkeley: University of California Press, 1993, 55–57.

3. *Ronsasvals*: Distorted Discourse and Reliable Reception

1. A particularly sophisticated analysis of the evidence for the text's date can be found in Elisabeth Schulze-Busacker, "La Datation de *Ronsasvals*," *Romania* 110 (1989): 127–66 and 396–425. Schulze-Busacker includes in this article a wide variety of specific sources and relevant trends in Occitan literature of which there are clear traces in *Ronsasvals*. She concludes that the most likely date of original composition would lie between 1180 and 1250 and adds that she believes the text properly belongs to "the context of the Albigensian War" because of its portrait of a society in "irreparable decline" (425). In my view, that remark indicates that the most accurate date would be somewhere in the second quarter of the thirteenth century, either after the end of the war or at an advanced stage where its eventual outcome was becoming clear.

2. The most recent consideration of this issue, however, provides textual evidence to the contrary. Through comparisons of several scenes from *Ronsas-*

vals to their counterparts in multiple rhymed French and Franco-Italian versions, Giovanni Palumbo found that these shared episodes receive a more thorough and logical exposition in *Ronsasvals*, even though the Occitan version is far more compact overall than the rhymed versions. Without drawing overly definitive conclusions, Palumbo suggests that the rhymed versions offer more diluted, and thus perhaps later, adaptations of the general material (and perhaps also some common source texts) they share with *Ronsasvals*. Giovanni Palumbo, "Il *Roland* rimato e il *Ronsasvals*: Problemi di interferenza," in *Les Chansons de geste: Actes du XVIe Congrès International de la Société Rencesvals*, ed. Carlos Alvar and Juan Paredes (Granada: Editorial Universidad de Granada, 2005), 475–97.

3. Specific textual parallels between *Ronsasvals* and Châteauroux are detailed by Schulze-Busacker, "La Datation de *Ronsasvals*," 147 n. 60. She also mentions in this note some laisses that *Ronsasvals* shares with the Paris manuscript. Nevertheless, her overall conclusion in this study is that these resemblances suggest, not that *Ronsasvals* was adapted directly from these rhymed sources, but that it was composed at the same time using some of the same earlier sources, along with, perhaps, other sources unique to an Occitan Roncevaux tradition now lost.

4. Cesare Segre, "Un Procedimento della narrativa medievale: L'Enucleazione," in *Italica et Romanica: Festschrift für Max Pfister*, ed. Günter Holtus, Johannes Kramer, and Wolfgang Schweickard (Tübingen: Max Niemeyer, 1997), 3:361–67.

5. Ibid., 3:362. He also describes enucleated reworkings as characterized by their "saturazione di valenze narrative in modo allusivo" (saturation with narrative valances in an allusive mode), 363.

6. Ibid., 3:367. See also Cesare Segre, "Il Sogno di Alda: Tra *chanson de geste, chanson de femme* e *romance*," *Medioevo Romanzo* 8.1 (1981): 3–9.

7. "Ces personnages font tout autre chose que de passer dans le récit: ils viennent tour à tour, et reviennent parfois jouer une scène dont ils sont le centre, où leur caractère se dégage avec une valeur dramatique et humaine. Pour certains on a l'impression que l'auteur s'est attaché à étoffer un peu leur rôle." Mario Roques, "*Ronsasvals*, poème épique provençal," *Romania* 66 (1940): 477–78.

8. "[U]n poème dramatique beaucoup plus qu'une chanson de geste ou qu'une histoire." Ibid., 480.

9. See especially the discussion of this point by Guy R. Mermier, "Roncevaux-*Ronsasvals*: More about the Originality of the Old Provençal Poem within the Tradition of the *Song of Roland*," in *Studia Occitanica in Memoriam Paul Remy*, ed. Hans-Erich Keller (Kalamazoo: Medieval Institute Publications, Western Michigan University, 1986), 164–65.

10. For a detailed examination of the appropriateness of the term *crusade* to this military conflict, see William Paden, "Perspectives on the Albigensian Crusade," and Eliza Miruna Ghil, "*Crozada*: Avatars of a Religious Term in

Thirteenth-Century Occitan Poetry," in *Tenso* 10 (1995): 90–98 and 99–109 respectively.

11. *Le* Roland *occitan: Roland à Saragosse; Ronsasvals,* ed. Gérard Gouiran and Robert Lafont (Paris: Christian Bourgois, 1991). All citations from *Ronsasvals* are taken from this edition, and all English translations are my own.

12. For background on Occitan regional feuds at this time, see Jonathan Sumption, *The Albigensian Crusade* (Boston: Faber and Faber, 1978), 21–24.

13. "Occitania" is the topic of the first chapter of Joseph Strayer's study of the Albigensian Crusade, in which he considers to what extent the medieval inhabitants of that region may or may not have viewed themselves as a cohesive cultural group. Joseph Strayer, *The Albigensian Crusades* (New York: Dial, 1971), 1–14, esp. 11.

14. Mermier, "Roncevaux-*Ronsasvals*," 163.

15. Amelia van Vleck, *Memory and Re-Creation in Troubadour Lyric* (Berkeley: University of California Press, 1991), 19–20. It is interesting to note that this set of meanings has been attached to the word *jouissance* in modern criticism as well.

16. "Si donc Turpin peut attribuer aux chrétiens la supériorité morale, c'est parce que leur être a été affiné par une civilisation de l'amour." Robert Lafont, *La Geste de Roland* (Paris: l'Harmattan, 1991), 2:195–96.

17. "Vel manus artificis multas ita conflet in unam, / Mentis ut intuitu multae videantur in una" (vv. 700–701). Quoted in Linda Paterson, *Troubadours and Eloquence* (Oxford: Clarendon Press, 1975), 99. Her translation.

18. Van Vleck, *Memory and Re-Creation,* 21.

19. Although the narrators in the songs of female Occitan poets, the *trobairitz,* also speak of unfulfilled desires, it is interesting to note that they seldom use the rhetoric of denial when doing so; their resentment toward the unresponsive object of their desire is usually stated quite clearly. I have made this observation as a reader of the *trobairitz,* but it has also been confirmed by the conclusions to a more systematic study of their rhetoric by Joan Ferrante, "Notes toward the Study of a Female Rhetoric in the Trobairitz," in *The Voice of the Trobairitz,* ed. William Paden (Philadelphia: University of Pennsylvania Press, 1989), 71.

20. Peire Rogier, "Entr' ir' e joy m'an si devis," cited and adapted by Sarah Kay, *Subjectivity in Troubadour Poetry* (Cambridge: Cambridge University Press, 1990), 60.

21. Although this view is not universal, some critics have commented that the Lady who is the supposed addressee of a troubadour poem actually represents another side of the poet's own self: "The woman the poet loves is a mirror in which he sees his ideal self, what he might be." Joan Ferrante, *Woman as Image in Medieval Literature* (New York: Columbia University Press, 1975), 67–68. See also Paolo Cherchi, *Andreas and the Ambiguity of Courtly Love* (Toronto: University of Toronto Press, 1994), 70–71.

22. See Stephen G. Nichols Jr., "Roland's Echoing Horn," *Romance Notes* 5 (1963): 78–84.

23. Dominique Boutet has observed this use of tears to show the dawning of a new awareness for Charlemagne in other *chansons de geste*. Such tears are positive in that they show regret for past policies and a willingness to choose a better direction for the future. Dominique Boutet, *Charlemagne et Arthur ou Le Roi imaginaire* (Paris: Champion, 1992), 406.

24. A biblical reference also noted by Hans-Erich Keller, *Autour de Roland: Recherches sur la chanson de geste* (Geneva: Champion-Slatkine, 1989), 328.

25. Cherchi, *Andreas*, 52–53.

26. Charlemagne, too, is linked with Ganelon and Roland as a potentially guilty party: his absence from the prebattle scene is emphasized by a list of the swords carried by the twelve peers of France, a list ending with Charlemagne's absent sword Joyeuse: "si hi fos Joyosa, payans foran dolans" [If Joyeuse had been there, the pagans would have suffered] (v. 96).

27. In one of the more serious discrepancies between the 1991 edition of *Ronsasvals* and its first modern edition by Mario Roques ("*Ronsasvals*," *Romania* 58 [1932]: 9–28, 161–89), the last two lines fall outside Olivier's speech in the more recent edition, while Roques attributed them to Olivier. Because of the rarity of first-person narrative commentary in *Ronsasvals* as a whole, I agree with Roques on this issue and my citation of this particular passage includes his punctuation.

28. Riffaterre, "Mind's Eye," esp. 31–34.

29. For an explanation of the circumstances of Galian's conception, see ch. 4 below, "About the Text."

30. Keller, *Autour de Roland*, 149–53.

31. Thanks to Joseph Duggan for noting this parallel in his review of this book for the press.

32. In a comparative study on Roland's death scene in several Roncevaux narratives, André Moisan emphasized the unusually humble and personal nature of Roland's confession in *Ronsasvals*: "L'aveu des fautes à la Vierge se fait avec les précisions d'une confession intérieure et personnelle. Le repentir est sincère, comme l'appel à la miséricorde divine. . . . Il mourra comme le plus humble des hommes." André Moisan, "La Mort de Roland selon les différentes versions de l'épopée," *Cahiers de Civilisation Médiévale* 28 (1985): 117.

33. *An Anonymous Old French Translation of the* Pseudo-Turpin Chronicle, ed. Ronald Walpole (Cambridge, MA: Mediaeval Academy of America, 1979), 75.

34. As André Pezard has noted, this frequent comparison between characters is one of the defining elements of *Ronsasvals* within the Roland tradition. See André Pezard, "La Mort de Roland dans *Ronsasvals*," *Romania* 97 (1976): 155–56.

35. "Le roi donne souvent les apparences de la déraison et semble méconnaître l'état de délabrement dans lequel se trouvent ses hommes: la guerre

qu'il veut entreprendre s'annonce comme une sorte d'auto-extermination de l'armée franque. Cependant, la volonté du roi correspond bien à sa mission, tandis que l'apparente sagesse des barons dissimule un refus de leur vocation. Pour Charles, comme pour Dieu, rien n'est excessif, rien n'est démésuré contre les Sarrasins. Une sorte de dialectique de l'être et du paraître oppose deux couples: d'un côté Dieu et le roi, de l'autre le roi et ses vassaux. . . . Le roi, qui a tort au regard du second . . . , a raison au regard du premier, dont la supériorité se manifeste clairement dans la suite des événements."
Boutet, *Charlemagne et Arthur*, III.

36. "Pour le commun des vassaux, cette relation directe est inexistante. Pour eux, servir Dieu tout en restant dans leur ordre n'est possible qu'en servant leur roi." Ibid., 156.

37. It is worth noting that I have altered the punctuation slightly in my translation from that offered in the modern edition to make completely clear that Charlemagne is attributing this "great sin" to himself and not to his sister.

38. Giorgio Agamben, *Stanzas: Word and Phantasm in Western Culture*, trans. Ronald L. Martinez (Minneapolis: University of Minnesota Press, 1993), 3. On the modern sense of *sloth*, Agamben comments, "Modern psychology has . . . emptied the term *acedia* of its original meaning, making it a sin against the capitalist work ethic" (5). For this reason, I have opted to retain the medieval term *acedia* in my discussion of Charlemagne's behavior in *Ronsasvals* in order to retain, as well, a consistent sense that this is depicted in *Ronsasvals* as a spiritual crisis rather than merely a regrettable reaction to loss.

39. Saint Thomas Aquinas, *Summa theologiae*, ed. Thomas R. Heath, O.P. (New York: McGraw-Hill, 1972), 35:20–21.

40. "Fugiendo quidem, quando continua cogitatio auget peccati incentivum. . . . Resistendo autem, quando cogitatio perseverans tollit incentivum peccati, quod provenit ex aliqua levi apprehensione. Et hoc contingit in acedia: quia quanto magis cogitamus de bonis spiritualibus, tanto magis nobis placentia redduntur, ex quo cessat acedia. . . . Ad primum ergo dicendum quod acedia, aggravando animum, impedit hominem ab illis operibus quae tristitiam causant. Sed tamen inducit animum ad aliqua agenda vel quae sunt tristitiae consona, sicut ad plorandum, vel etiam ad aliqua per quae tristitia evitatur." [Turning tail is the answer when continual thinking about it increases the incentive to sin . . . whereas resistance is called for when steady thought would help to remove the incentive arising from some less pressing persuasion. This is what happens with spiritual apathy, since the more we think about spiritual goods the more delightful they become to us, and spiritual apathy goes away. . . . Spiritual apathy because it weighs down the soul does indeed block those activities which cause sorrow. Even so, it induces a man towards those actions which are consonant with sorrow, weeping, for example, or those through which sorrow is avoided.] Ibid., 24–25; 32–33.

41. Agamben, *Stanzas*, 6.

42. Distinctions can, of course, be made between *acedia* and *melencolia*, but again, the post-Freudian connotations of *melancholia* in modern culture can muddy the waters. Agamben, in *Stanzas*, speaks of the "reciprocal penetration of sloth and melancholy" in medieval culture (13) but separates both clearly from the notion of "melancholia" as defined by Freud (19ff.).

43. "Nam cum Adam bonum scivit et pomum comedende malum facit, in vicissitudine mutationis illius melancolia in eo surrexit, quae sine suggestione diaboli non est in homine. . . . [D]e qua tristitia et desperatio in eo surrexerunt, quoniam diabolus in casu Adae melancoliam in ipso conflavit, quae hominem aliquando dubium et incredulum parat. Sed quod forma hominis ligata est, ita quod se sursum supra modum elevare non potest, ideo timet deum et tristis est, ac sic multotiens in tristitia illa desperat diffidens, ut deus eum observet." Hildegard of Bingen, *Hildegardis causae et curae*, ed. Paul Kaiser (B. G. Teubneri, 1903), 143–44. English translation mine, adapted from that of Manfred Pawlik, *Holistic Healing* (Collegeville, MN: Liturgical Press, 1994), 127.

44. This aspect of Charlemagne's behavior and discourse also dramatizes the well-known passage in which the apostle Paul describes a similar inner spiritual warfare: "For the good that I wish, I do not do; but I practice the very evil that I do not wish. But if I am doing the very thing I do not wish, I am no longer the one doing it, but sin which dwells in me." Rom. 7: 19–20, NAS.

45. Mario Roques, "*Roland à Saragosse et Ronsasvals*: Examen comparatif," *Romania* 69 (1946–47): 355. Other examples Roques cites of this comic role for Naime include the earlier scene in which Ganelon's treachery was revealed and Naime demanded that Ganelon be held prisoner: according to Roques, Ganelon's clever response gives him the win over Naime in a verbal skirmish between them. Roques also sees Naime as a doddering fool when he initially guesses that it is Ganelon's son bringing the message from Roland after the battle. Roques proclaims with smug terseness, "erreur: c'est Gandelbuon; l'empereur ne s'y est pas trompé."

46. The sexual connotations of the word *joy* are widely accepted in modern readings of troubadour poetry, but one does not even need to look outside the text to appreciate the sexual nuance of Naime's vocabulary. As we have seen, Roland also used the phrase "joy entier" (v. 924) to describe the consommation of his marriage to Aude. Aude, in turn, will use the same phrase later to explain her refusal to marry: she would only be willing to experience "joya entier" with Roland (vv. 1773–74).

47. *Le Roland occitan*, 134.

48. Ibid.

49. In other medieval narratives, Charlemagne is shown confessing his sin of incest to a priest, so such a confession may have been an option well known to the *Ronsasvals* author. The fact that Charlemagne's discussion of his incest in this scene occurs in such a different context only serves to emphasize that it is *not* a formal confession. This practice of inappropriately announcing one's own wrongdoing is typical of a state of Freudian melancholia, or an exaggerated

clinging to grief for selfish reasons. See the discussion in Juliana Schiesari, *The Gendering of Melancholia: Feminism, Psychoanalysis, and the Symbolics of Loss in Renaissance Literature* (Ithaca: Cornell University Press, 1992), 48–51.

50. Gabrielle Oberhänsli-Widmer, *La Complainte funèbre du Haut Moyen Âge français et occitan*, Romanica Helvetica 106 (Berne: Francke, 1989). See also the extensive discussion of possible troubadour sources for the *Ronsasvals* laments in Schulze-Busacker, "La Datation de *Ronsasvals*," 396–423. Lafont mentions these sources, as well, in his introduction to *Le* Roland *occitan*, 29–30.

51. Linda Paterson offers as possible meanings for *razon*: specific lines of argumentation, poetic themes (of which mourning could be considered one), or the meaning of words, as opposed to the words themselves (*Troubadours and Eloquence*, 11–13 and 72).

52. Oberhänsli-Widmer, *La Complainte funèbre*, 18–26.

53. This may or may not be a deliberate reference to the closing portrait of Charlemagne in Châteauroux and Venice 7, but the relevance of this rhymed version is affirmed by Charlemagne's awareness that remembering Roland would cause him some kind of heart failure, just as he had foreseen Aude's heart failure from grief in the Châteauroux version.

54. Jules Horrent's commentary about Aude's death in the "rhymed *Rolands*" provides a good example of both sides of the issue: Horrent clearly states that Aude's death was an important element of the reworkings and not just an effort to introduce elements of the romance genre at any cost, "as people often claim." Yet while he protests that Aude hardly resembles a character of courtly romance in the reworkings, he characterizes her instead as "a heroine from a drama, and even from a melodrama," which maintains the notion that Aude's expanded role is nonepic. (Horrent, *La* Chanson de Roland, 354–55). The melodrama, furthermore, is not a respected genre among most readers or literary critics but rather a term evocative of a trite "tearjerker."

55. Hans-Erich Keller has discussed at length this evocation of the *chanson de toile*, suggesting that the indicators of the Aude scenes' affiliation with that genre make them a self-contained narrative that could be easily (and perhaps beneficially) detached from the rest of the text. See Keller, *Autour de Roland*, 306–8. Although I believe the scenes featuring Aude are vital to the overall structure of *Ronsasvals*, the medieval Spanish ballad *Sueño de Doña Alda* suggests that Keller was not alone in envisioning the possibility of a separate *chanson de toile* depicting this scene.

56. An image of fire entering Aude's mouth confirms the link between Aude and Charlemagne, whose prophetic dream portrayed the Battle of Roncevaux as a fire consuming Paris and burning his beard and face (vv. 946–47). Herman Braet pointed out a connection between both of these scenes and Charlemagne's dream at the beginning of *Roland à Saragosse*, the Occitan text that precedes *Ronsasvals* both in the medieval manuscript and in the modern edition by Lafont and Gouiran (*Le* Roland *occitan*). In this companion text, Charlemagne dreams of a falcon that turns on him, ripping out half of his

beard, after which a flame from the sky burns down all the tents at his camp outside Saragossa (*Roland à Saragosse*, in *Le Roland occitan*, 13–31). Herman Braet, *Le Songe dans la chanson de geste* (Gent: Romanica Gandensia, 1975), 132, 175.

57. For example, Eugene Vance has described Roland as a poet in his death scene in Oxford, in that he constructs his messages out of visual images ("Roland and Charlemagne," 64–66).

58. Scholars have offered complex and varying definitions of *trobar clus*, any of which might be relevant here, but I derive this specific comparison between *trobar clus* and Roland's rhetoric from R. Howard Bloch's discussion of the contrasts between the chronologically coexistent epic and lyric genres in *Etymologies and Genealogies*, 108–16.

59. This reading is discussed most thoroughly by Joseph Duggan in his article "Legitimation and the Hero's Exemplary Function in the *Cantar de Mío Cid* and the *Chanson de Roland*," in *Oral Traditional Literature: A Festschrift for Albert Bates Lord*, ed. John Miles Foley (Columbus, OH: Slavica, 1981), 217–34. Charlemagne's sin is also understood as a central organizing principle of the Oxford *Roland* in a semiotic/Freudian reading by Alina Clej, "Le Miroir du roi: Une Réflexion sur la *Chanson de Roland*," *Romance Philology* 44 (1990): 16–53. Clej states already for the Oxford *Roland* that "on retrouve dans les profondeurs du texte, dans le *géno-texte*, le bien et le mal coexistant dans le corps du roi" (45).

60. "Plutôt que de parler de dégradation de l'image royale, il faudrait donc évoquer un changement dans la perception de la condition du roi, une crise de la *représentation* de la royauté, qui devient comme un symbole de la finitude de l'humanité. . . . la société paraît n'aspirer plus qu'à sa sublimation dans la mort, conçue comme une assomption" (Boutet, *Charlemagne et Arthur*, 609).

61. In fact, this mentality was not limited to literary kingdoms: in his biography of Louis IX, Jacques Le Goff describes the new vision of Louis IX for his kingdom upon returning from a failed crusade: he would "faire régner ici-bas la justice dans la perspective de l'accomplissement des 'derniers temps,' de promotion d'une cité terrestre évangélique; bref, devenir un roi eschatologique." Jacques Le Goff, *Saint Louis* (Paris: Gallimard, 1996), 213.

62. Given this explicit reference to literary beginnings, and indeed specifically to literary "renewals," I consider it unlikely that the text is missing lines at the beginning, or even that the plot of *Ronsasvals* begins *in medias res*, as some critics have argued (see especially Keller, *Autour de Roland*, 299–301). It is true that the French and Saracen armies are already assembled near Roncevaux when the text begins, but in this opening section the warriors on both sides are still arming themselves for the battle to come. Therefore these lines do not appear at the start of the text through an accident of omission but rather serve as the text's introductory self-identification as both lyric and epic.

63. Ibid., 306–8.

64. Elisabeth Schulze-Busacker, "Réminiscences lyriques dans l'épopée occitane de *Ronsasvals*," in *Charlemagne et l'épopée romane: Actes du VIIe Congrès International de la Société Rencesvals* (Paris: Belles Lettres, 1978), 2:715.

65. This strategy of the Oxford *Roland* has been described in many ways, but Yves Bonnefoy has offered a particularly concise statement of it: "Qu'est-ce donc que le mal qui menace cette harmonie? Et de quel espace extérieur peut-il venir? Il n'y a pas d'extérieur à une forme qui s'approprie le réel, pas d'*autre* concevable dans l'architecture du *même*." Yves Bonnefoy, "Les Mots et la parole dans le *Roland*," in *La Chanson de Roland* (Paris: Union Générale des Éditions, 1968), 297.

66. Keller's article on the structure of *Ronsasvals* emphasizes these confusions of genre at moments of introduction or transition, ultimately claiming that these multiple beginnings show this text to be an awkward combination of three previously separate narratives (*Autour de Roland*, 299–308).

67. "Comme tous les autres personnages de la littérature médiévale, mais peut-être à un degré plus aigu, le personnage épique est un *type*, c'est-à-dire la réalisation exemplaire dans une figure déterminée de vertus ou de vices liés au système de représentation de l'auteur et du groupe pour lequel il travaille. Le type est donc à l'opposé de toute démarche individualisante." François Suard, *La Chanson de geste* (Paris: Presses Universitaires de France, 1993), 40.

68. All of these interpretations can be found in chs. 1 and 2 of my dissertation: Margaret Jewett, "Remembering Roncevaux: Collective Identity and Literary Commentary in Medieval French and Occitan Adaptations of the Roland Legend" (PhD diss., University of Chicago, 1998).

4. *Galïen restoré*: Rewriting and Reception as Remembrance

1. *Le* Galien *de Cheltenham*, ed. David M. Dougherty and Eugene B. Barnes (Amsterdam: John Benjamins, 1981). All citations from *Galïen restoré* will be taken from this edition and noted by line number in the body of the text. The one adjustment I make to the text of this edition is to use the form "Galïen" rather than "Galien" in the title and in certain citations from the text, in an effort to preserve in writing the name's trisyllabic sound. This issue was discussed by Peter Dembowski, "Whom and What Did Galïen Restore?" *Olifant* 10.3 (1984): 83–98, 89. It is also worth noting from the outset that this edition was harshly criticized by a number of reviewers when it was published. See reviews by Peter Dembowski, *Romance Philology* 38 (1985): 537–42; William Kibler, *Speculum* 58 (1983): 1033–35; and Claude Régnier, *Cahiers de Civilisation Médiévale* 27 (1984): 374–77.

2. Jules Horrent, the scholar who has studied the entire Galien tradition more thoroughly than anyone else, summarized this difficulty with the remark, "Localiser le *Galien* de Cheltenham est une entreprise qui n'a jamais tenté personne" (*La* Chanson de Roland, 70).

3. Introduction to Dougherty and Barnes, *Le* Galien *de Cheltenham*, x.

4. A thorough summary of this version is provided in the introduction to *Le* Galien *de Cheltenham,* under the subtitle "Analyse" (xvi–xxi). More information on the plots and interrelationships of the other texts in the Galien tradition can be found in Jules Horrent, *La* Chanson de Roland, ch. 2, "Les Aventures de Galien," and ch. 7, "Galien le Restoré."

5. These events can be found in *Le Voyage de Charlemagne à Jérusalem et à Constantinople,* ed. Paul Aebischer (Geneva: Droz, 1965), vv. 484–92, 691–729, 849–56.

6. Robert Morrissey also noted this contribution of the Galien texts in his book on the significance of Charlemagne for French culture of all periods, *L'Empereur à la barbe fleurie* (Paris: Gallimard, 1997), 98–101.

7. Nine manuscripts from the late fifteenth century are noted in the inventory by Ronald Walpole, *The Old French Johannes Translation of the* Pseudo-Turpin Chronicle: *A Critical Edition, Supplement* (Berkeley: University of California Press, 1976).

8. William Kibler, "Relectures de l'épopée," in *Au carrefour des routes d'Europe: La Chanson de geste,* ed. François Suard (Aix-en-Provence: Publications du Centre Universitaire d'Etudes et de Recherches Médiévales d'Aix, Université de Provence, 1987), 1:103–40.

9. Kibler, "Relectures de l'épopée," 113–15.

10. According to Horrent, the anonymous author of the original Galien text "a inventé un héros et ramène tout à lui: Galien est la clef de voûte de tout son édifice. Galien fait tout, achève tout, sauve tout, remporte toutes les victoires." (*La* Chanson de Roland, 401).

11. Although this scene does not appear in *Galïen restoré,* it plays an important part in other *Galien* texts. See, for example, *La* Geste de Garin de Monglane *en prose (Manuscrit Paris, Bibliothèque de l'Arsenal, 3351),* ed. Hans-Erich Keller (Aix-en-Provence: Centre Universitaire d'Etudes et de Recherches Médiévales d'Aix, Université de Provence, 1994), 180–93.

12. "Ce récit très particulier, où Roncevaux n'est plus qu'un événement parmi d'autres . . ." (Horrent, *La* Chanson de Roland, 377). "Mais Roncevaux n'est qu'un épisode dans *Galien,* et les deux grandes pages de cette vie chevaleresque portent ces deux noms: Montfusain et Constantinople." Léon Gautier, *Les Epopées françaises* (Paris, 1880), 3:341.

13. Consider, for example, this comment on the episodes wholly devoted to Galien: "Ces épisodes, qui sont romanesques dans le sens le plus actuel de ce mot, forment le centre de cette très médiocre chanson qui débute et qui se termine par une imitation fort affaiblie du *Pèlerinage à Jérusalem* et de la *Chanson de Roland.* Ces deux beaux poèmes sont le cadre et le reste est le tableau; mais, comme il arrive trop souvent dans nos Salons contemporains, le tableau ne vaut pas le cadre." Gautier, *Les Épopées françaises,* 2:414.

14. "Un poème tel que le concevait le créateur de *Galien* réclamait de sa part une puissance inventive indéniable. Certes, il ne manque pas de variété

imaginative. . . . Mais souvent son trait reste empâté, son dessein incertain, ses trouvailles peu heureuses. Défauts partiels d'une mise en forme artistique qui n'est pas toujours à la hauteur de la conception. Mais tel que nous pouvons l'imaginer, le *Galien* primitif est loin d'être une oeuvre médiocre" (Horrent, *La Chanson de Roland*, 403; my English translation). Previous commentators had also offered confident hypotheses along the same lines: "[L]e *Galien* primitif, celui du commencement du XIIIe siècle, aurait été une oeuvre trés-supérieure à celle du XVe et véritablement héroïque" (Gautier, *Les Épopées françaises*, 3:318).

15. Horrent, *La Chanson de Roland*, 378–91.

16. Ibid., 406.

17. "Le prosateur est plus appliqué quand il se met à raconter la bataille de Roncevaux: voilà son vrai sujet. Alors les détails ne lui font pas peur. Il en est même prodigue" (Ibid., 407–8).

18. "Curieuse oeuvre que ce ms. 3351 qui traîne où l'on presserait le pas, et prend sa course où l'on voudrait muser!" (Ibid., 409).

19. Of course, determining the "first" laisse was up to the judgment of the modern editors, since the Cheltenham manuscript shows no structural division between the two narratives that modern medievalists discuss as "Girart de Vienne" and "Galien restoré." It is interesting to compare this editorial decision to that of Hans-Erich Keller in his edition of the prose version of *La Geste de Garin de Monglane* from Arsenal manuscript 3351. Keller handles this part of the larger *Geste de Monglane* by dividing it into several sections: "L'Histoire de Girart de Vienne," "Transition," "Le Pèlerinage de Charlemagne à Jérusalem et à Constantinople," "Transition," and "L'Histoire de Galien le Restoré" (163–91). This format brings some clarity to the multiple textual traditions being combined in this portion of the *Garin* compilation, although, by the same token, it represents an act of interpretation on the part of the editor.

20. This historical context, and Charles VIII's evident desire to emulate Charlemagne, are discussed by Morrissey, *L'Empereur*, 143–52.

21. Horrent's comments about the adaptor's procedure in this section: "S'il renonce à écouter les suggestions pressantes de la fin de 'Girart,' s'il retarde avec invraisemblance le combat de Roncevaux, c'est qu'il se trouvait en face d'un récit déjà composé où le voyage d'Orient précédait 'Roncevaux.' C'est qu'une rédaction de *Galien* existait déjà indépendamment de lui" (*La Chanson de Roland*, 394).

22. Although it is extremely unlikely that the author of the Cheltenham manuscript would have had access to the surviving Oxford manuscript, there is a certain parallel between line 4910 and the Oxford *Roland*'s famously ambiguous last line, "Ci falt la geste que Turoldus declinet." What may have survived between the writing of one manuscript and the other is the notion that the lasting significance of Roncevaux should cause authors to state at the close of each retelling the material end of this present version while also stressing the legend's independent and continuing elaboration.

23. "Le sujet de *Galien*, quoique moderne, était fort beau. . . . Par malheur, ni le versificateur du XIIIe siècle, ni, à plus forte raison, les prosateurs du XVe, n'étaient de taille à traiter un tel sujet. Cette oeuvre offre en réalité tous les caractères de la décadence. . . . Le roman de *Galien* est complètement fabuleux; il n'est même pas fondé sur une tradition légendaire. Tout y est de convention; tout y est faux. C'est un vrai 'roman' dans le sens le plus moderne et le plus mauvais de ce mot." Gautier, *Les Epopées françaises*, 3:318–19.

24. For more on the way in which the phenomenon of the medieval specialist affected late medieval epics in general, see Cook, "'Méchants romans,'" 64–74.

25. I assume this rising enthusiasm because of the large number of sixteenth-century printed editions of *Galien*, some of which carried strongly worded printing permissions *(privileges)* indicating that competition among printers was fierce when it came to selling this popular text.

26. Jacques Le Goff, *Les Intellectuels au Moyen Âge* (Paris: Seuil, 1957), 167–72.

27. Domenico Pietropaolo, "Eco on Medievalism," *Studies in Medievalism* 5 (1993): 137.

28. Heather Arden, "Editorial II," *Studies in Medievalism* 2 (1983): 5–6.

29. In his description of this tension, Peter Dembowski paired the French term *continuité* with *rupture,* a formulation that captures well the jarring effect of those elements of the text that represent a break with the earlier medieval literary tradition but that appear within an overall context of reverence toward that tradition. See Peter F. Dembowski, "Continuation ou restauration? La Littérature française du Bas Moyen Age: Le Cas de *Galïen*," in *Actes du XVIIIe Congrès International de Linguistique et de Philologie Romanes* (Tübingen: Max Niemeyer, 1988), 6:439.

30. Georges Doutrepont, *Les Mises en prose des épopées et des romans chevaleresques du XIVe au XVI siècle* (Brussels: Palais des académies, 1939), 393.

31. *Aimeri de Narbonne*, ed. Joseph Couraye du Parc (Paris: Firmin Didot, 1884), vv. 3055–57. Joseph Duggan brought this example to my attention and provided the English translation.

32. Peter Dembowski stressed that the choice of verse was an effort to associate this epic narrative with those that were written centuries before: "Rien n'est plus manifestement archaïsant, c'est-à-dire 'restaurateur,' que cette forme" ("Continuation ou restoration," 440).

33. For these arguments, as well as a summary of previous commentaries on the name(s) Galien(s) (li) Restoré(s), see Dembowski, "Whom and What Did Galïen Restore?"

34. Although Galien did not grow up in France, the fact that he was knighted by Charlemagne and that his father was a prominent French warrior should have qualified him to be the answer to Roland's prayer.

35. Moisan, "La Mort de Roland," 116.

36. Especially because at least one more recent text had already been written in which Olivier's son did inherit Durendal. In a fourteenth-century Italian

Roncevaux narrative, *Li Fatti de Spagna*, ed. Ruggero Ruggieri (Modena, 1951), Olivier's son Galleant inherits Durendal with the clear endorsement of the dead Roland: Charlemagne knights Galleant with Roland's hand around the hilt, "e fu fato chevalere Galleant per mane de K. e de Rolando, bene che Rolando fusse morto" [And Galien was knighted by the hand of Charlemagne and of Roland, even though Roland was dead] (137). Galleant goes on to use the sword in the battle against Baligant but is then killed and returns Durendal immediately to Charlemagne (142). If the author of *Galïen restoré* had been aware of this text, which is unlikely in light of geographical and linguistic barriers, it would only provide more proof that Galien's winning the sword was indeed a possibility, but one that did not fit *Galïen restoré*'s perception of what was unchangeable about the Roncevaux material.

37. Peter Haidu, "Fragments in Search of Totalization: *Roland* and the Historical Text," in *Modernité au Moyen Âge*, ed. Brigitte Cazelles and Charles Méla (Geneva: Droz, 1990), 73–99, 81–82.

38. Ibid., 87–88.

39. This epic is generally called *Lohier et Maillart* by French critics who believe that it originated as a fourteenth-century French text that has now been lost. It has survived only in German versions from the fifteenth century and later. One of these, printed in Leipzig in 1613, refers directly to the Galien-Mallart link in its title: *Ein schoene warhafftige Geschicht von Keyser Loher eines Koenigs sohn aus Franckreich und Maller sohn aus Gallien*. Léon Gautier, *Bibliographie des chansons de geste* (Paris: Welter, 1897), 140.

40. For example, Roland's description of the physical suffering that vassals should be prepared to endure in service to their lords, vv. 1117–19.

41. Horrent, *La Chanson de Roland*, 389.

42. "Pourquoi ainsi rapetisser un héros que l'on veut magnifier? Les remanieurs ont leurs raisons que l'art ne connaît pas. Je ne serais pas étonné que notre homme se soit refusé à faire de Galien le concurrent de Charlemagne" (406).

43. For example, see laisses 407–13 of the Châteauroux manuscript.

44. Dembowski, review of *Le Galien de Cheltenham*, 539.

45. Giuseppe Di Stefano, "Flexion et versification," in *Essais sur le Moyen Français* (Padua: Liviana Editrice, 1977), 99–131. Di Stefano used the portion of the manuscript that contains the pre-Galien sections of the *Geste de Monglane* because that was the only portion of the manuscript that had been published in a modern edition at the time of his study. Having compared the Galien section to the rest of the manuscript, I can confirm that Di Stefano's findings hold true for the manuscript as a whole.

46. "La médiocrité même des textes permet en outre d'analyser certains phénomènes d'un point de vue purement linguistique plutôt que stylistique" (Ibid., 99).

47. "Au niveau de la transmission et de la compréhension du message, la non-ambiguïté de la communication écrite est une condition qui doit être ré-

solue implicitement à l'intérieur d'un système linguistique pluridimensionnel jusqu'au point d'englober des élements qu'on pourrait tenir pour contradictoires" (Ibid., 100).

48. *La Geste de Monglane*, ed. David M. Dougherty and Eugene B. Barnes (Eugene: University of Oregon Books, 1966), line 114. All subsequent citations from this edition will be indicated by line number in the body of the text.

49. Dembowski, review of *Le Galien de Cheltenham*, 538.

50. François Villon, *Le Testament*, ed. Jean Rychner and Albert Henry (Genève: Droz, 1974), lines 393–400.

51. "[O]ù les formes de CS [cas sujet], parfois barbares, sont rarement utilisées à bon escient, n'est qu'une preuve de plus, si cela était nécessaire, que le système de la déclinaison n'a plus aucune pertinence (au moins dans le domaine grammatical) pour les écrivains, copistes et lecteurs du XVe siècle." Christiane Marchello-Nizia, *Histoire de la langue française aux XIVe et XVe siècles* (Paris: Bordas, 1979), 98.

52. M. K. Pope, *From Latin to Modern French*, 5th ed. (Manchester: University of Manchester Press, 1966), 316.

53. In his review of *Le Galien de Cheltenham*, Dembowski suggested that because of the form *ve le ci* in line 822, *veci* should have been written *ve ci* throughout the text (540). My examination of the manuscript showed that Dougherty and Barnes were true to its representation of this phrase as written in the manuscript, with the exception of line 965, where the manuscript writes *ve cy* and the edition *vecy*. The manuscript's spacing in line 822 was indeed exceptional, further supporting my suspicion that Aude's utterance was meant to look, as well as sound, old-fashioned.

54. Marchello-Nizia, *Histoire de la langue française*, 250.

55. The following are occurrences of this word, with dates, as cited by Frédéric Godefroy, *Dictionnaire de l'ancienne langue française* (Paris, 1883; reprint, 1961), 2:417. *damaseal* (1290), *damaseas* (1295), *damasealx* (1299), *damexeux, dommexeuz, dommexou* (all from one text, 1479). While Godefroy probably did not search every possible text for examples, the long gap between these thirteenth- and fifteenth-century occurrences, as well as the lack of final *l* in any of the fifteenth-century variations he found, would appear to support my assertion that *damoisel* was an antiquated form for the late fifteenth century.

56. Pope, *From Latin to Modern French*, 316. See also Claude Régnier's review of *Le Galien de Cheltenham*, 376.

57. That is, it appears to have been an outdated adjective for describing people: fourteenth- and fifteenth-century occurrences cited by Godefroy, *Dictionnaire*, 4:614, apply *isnel* to horses, rivers, and other nonhuman entities. By 1561, Joachim Du Bellay explicitly stated that he used the word when he wished to achieve an old-fashioned sound; other sixteenth-century poets seem to have used it for pragmatic reasons, since it is nearly always a rhyme for *aile*.

58. Marchello-Nizia, in *Histoire de la langue française*, describes in some detail the gradual disappearance of *cil*. She found no fifteenth-century occurrences

of *cil* as a demonstrative adjective (120), while its appearances as a demonstrative pronoun showed that it was used as often in the accusative case as in its proper Old French nominative case. When used as a subject it was usually reinforced by *qui*, forming a set phrase, *cil qui* (124–25).

59. Although *rien* is, of course, a word that has survived into modern French, in fifteenth-century French it was no longer used to refer to people (Marchello-Nizia, *Histoire de la langue française*, 145); perhaps it is for this reason that the author felt the need to include the whole explanatory phrase "rien qui soit vivans."

60. Although past and present tense alternate rather freely in many medieval narratives, it is interesting to note that *voir* is in the past when it is Galien who is seeing and in the present when it is Charlemagne, as if Galien were arriving from a past more remote than that inhabited by Charlemagne.

61. Gérard Moignet, *Grammaire de l'ancien français* (Paris: Klincksieck, 1973), 24.

62. Marchello-Nizia, *Histoire de la langue française*, 140.

63. Ibid., 232.

64. Ibid., 296.

65. Ibid., 248–49.

66. Moignet, *Grammaire*, 192.

67. Marchello-Nizia, *Histoire de la langue française*, 365.

68. Dembowski, review of *Le Galien de Cheltenham*, 539.

69. Régnier, review of *Le Galien de Cheltenham*, 376.

70. Other examples in the Baligant section appear in lines 4281, 4282, 4285, 4327, 4332, 4334, 4339, 4363, 4371, 4387, 4430, 4441, 4547, 4566, 4569, and 4573.

71. As Morrissey commented with regard to a contemporary prophecy that Charles VIII would eventually become king of France, Rome, and Greece, "En somme Charles est décrit comme une sorte de nouveau Galien" (*L'Empereur*, 153).

Conclusion

1. Vance, "Roland and Charlemagne," 83.

2. As medievalists have long recognized, and as college instructors have a responsibility to convey to their students, this representation of the supposedly Muslim Saracens as polytheistic idol worshipers features immense and fundamental distortions of Islam.

Bibliography

I.   Medieval Sources

Aebischer, Paul, ed. *Le Voyage de Charlemagne à Jérusalem et à Constantinople*. Geneva: Droz, 1965.
Aquinas, Thomas. *Summa theologiae*. Ed. Thomas R. Heath, O.P. New York: McGraw-Hill, 1972.
Beretta, Carlo, ed. *Il Testo assonanzato franco-italiano della* Chanson de Roland: *Cod. Marciano fr. IV (=225)*. Pavia: Università degli Studi, 1995.
Brault, Gérard J., ed. *The Song of Roland: An Analytical Edition*. Vol. 1: Introduction and Commentary. Vol. 2: Oxford Text and Translation. University Park: Pennsylvania State University Press, 1978.
Couraye du Parc, Joseph, ed. *Aimeri de Narbonne*. Paris: Firmin Didot, 1884.
Dougherty, David M., and Eugene B. Barnes, eds. *Le Galien de Cheltenham*. Purdue University Monographs in Romance Languages 7. Amsterdam: John Benjamins, 1981.
———, eds. *La Geste de Monglane*. Eugene: University of Oregon Books, 1966. (Version recorded in the Cheltenham manuscript)
Duggan, Joseph J., gen. ed. *La Chanson de Roland, The Song of Roland: The French Corpus*. Turnhout: Brepols, 2005. Vol. 1: Introduction, Joseph Duggan; Concordance of Laisses, Karen Akiyama; Part 1, The Oxford Version, ed. Ian Short; Part 2, The Venice 4 Version, ed. Robert F. Cook. Vol. 2: Part 3, The Châteauroux-Venice 7 Version, ed. Joseph J. Duggan. Vol. 3: Part 4, The Paris Version, ed. Annalee C. Rejhon; Part 5, The Cambridge Version, ed. Wolfgang van Emden; Part 6, The Lyon Version, ed. William Kibler.
French Corpus. See Duggan, Joseph J., ed. *La Chanson de Roland, The Song of Roland: The French Corpus*.

Gouiran, Gérard, and Robert Lafont. *Le* Roland *occitan; Roland à Saragosse; Ron-sasvals*. Paris: Christian Bourgois, 1991.

Hildegard of Bingen. *Hildegardis causae et curae*. Ed. Paul Kaiser. Liepzig: B. G. Teubneri, 1903.

———. *Holistic Healing*. Trans. Manfred Pawlik. Collegeville, MN: Liturgical Press, 1994.

Keller, Hans-Erich, ed. *La* Geste de Garin de Monglane *en prose (Manuscrit Paris, Bibliothèque de l'Arsenal, 3351)*. Aix-en-Provence: Centre Universitaire d'Études et de Recherches Médiévales d'Aix, Université de Provence, 1994.

Mortier, Raoul, ed. *Les Textes de la* Chanson de Roland. Paris: Éditions de la Geste Francor, 1940–44. Vol. 1: La Version d'Oxford. Vol. 2: La Version de Venise IV. Vol. 3: La Chronique de Turpin; Carmen de Prodicione Guenonis; Ronsasvals. Vol. 4: Le Manuscrit de Châteauroux. Vol. 5: Le Manuscrit de Venise VII. Vol. 6: Le Texte de Paris. Vol. 7: Le Texte de Cambridge. Vol. 8: Le Texte de Lyon. Vol. 9: Les Fragments Lorrains. Vol. 10: Le Texte de Conrad.

Roques, Mario, ed. *Ronsasvals*. Romania 58 (1932): 9–28, 161–89.

Ruggieri, Ruggero, ed. *Li Fatti de Spagna*. Modena: Società Tipografica Modenese, 1951.

Samaran, Charles, ed. *La Chanson de Roland: Reproduction phototypique du manuscrit Digby 23 de la Bodleian Library d'Oxford*. Paris: Société des Anciens Textes Français, 1933.

Segre, Cesare, ed. *La Chanson de Roland: Édition critique*. 2nd ed. Geneva: Droz, 2003.

Short, Ian, ed. *La Chanson de Roland*. Paris: Librairie Générale Française, 1990.

Walpole, Ronald, ed. *An Anonymous Old French Translation of the* Pseudo-Turpin Chronicle. Cambridge, MA: Mediaeval Academy of America, 1979.

II.   Critical Works

Aebischer, Paul. *Préhistoire et protohistoire du* Roland *d'Oxford*. Bibliotheca Romanica 12. Bern: Francke, 1972.

Agamben, Giorgio. *Stanzas: Word and Phantasm in Western Culture*. Trans. Ronald L. Martinez. Minneapolis: University of Minnesota Press, 1993.

Akehurst, F. R. P. "Murder by Stealth: *Traïsun* in Old French Literature." In *Studies in Honor of Hans-Erich Keller: Medieval French and Occitan Literature and Romance Linguistics*, ed. Rupert Pickens, 459–73. Kalamazoo, MI: Medieval Institute Publications, 1993.

Anderson, Benedict. *Imagined Communities: Reflections on the Origin and Spread of Nationalism*. London: Verso, 1983.

Arden, Heather. "Editorial II." *Studies in Medievalism* 2 (1983): 5–6.

Auerbach, Erich. "Roland against Ganelon." In *Mimesis: The Representation of Reality in Western Literature,* trans. Willard Trask, 96–122. Princeton: Princeton University Press, 1953.

Bender, Karl-Heinz. *König und Vasall.* Heidelberg: C. Winter, 1967.

Bloch, R. Howard. *Etymologies and Genealogies: A Literary Anthropology of the French Middle Ages.* Chicago: University of Chicago Press, 1983.

Bonnefoy, Yves. "Les Mots et la parole dans le *Roland.*" In *La Chanson de Roland,* 295–307. Paris: Union Générale des Éditions, 1968.

Boutet, Dominique. *La Chanson de geste.* Paris: Presses Universitaires de France, 1993.

——. "Les Chansons de geste et l'affermissement du pouvoir royal (1100–1250)." *Annales* 37 (1982): 3–14.

——. *Charlemagne et Arthur ou Le Roi imaginaire.* Paris: Champion, 1992.

Braet, Herman. *Le Songe dans la chanson de geste.* Gent: Romanica Gandensia, 1975.

Brault, Gerard J. "*Sapientia* dans *La Chanson de Roland.*" *French Forum* 1 (1976): 99–118.

Brook, Leslie C. "Expressions of Faith in the Rhymed Versions of the *Chanson de Roland.*" In *Charlemagne in the North,* ed. Philip Bennett, Anne Cobby, and Graham Runnalls, 145–56. Edinburgh: Société Rencesvals British Branch, 1993.

Cazelles, Brigitte, and Charles Méla, eds. *Modernité au Moyen Âge: Le Défi du passé.* Geneva: Droz, 1990.

Cerquiglini, Bernard. *Éloge de la variante: Histoire critique de la philologie.* Paris: Seuil, 1989.

——. "Roland à Roncevaux, ou La Trahison des clercs." *Littérature* 42 (1981): 40–56.

Cherchi, Paolo. *Andreas and the Ambiguity of Courtly Love.* Toronto: University of Toronto Press, 1994.

Clej, Alina. "Le Miroir du roi: Une Réflexion sur la *Chanson de Roland.*" *Romance Philology* 44 (1990): 16–53.

Cook, Robert Francis. "'Méchants romans' et épopée française: Pour une philologie profonde." *Esprit Créateur* 23.1 (1983): 64–74.

——. "Roncevaux symbole de la nécessité." *Olifant* 8.4 (1981): 352–66.

——. *The Sense of the Song of Roland.* Ithaca: Cornell University Press, 1987.

Crist, Larry. "À propos de la *desmesure* dans la *Chanson de Roland*: Quelques propos (démesurés?)." *Olifant* 1 (April 1974): 10–20.

Dembowski, Peter F. "Continuation ou restauration? La Littérature française du Bas Moyen Âge: Le Cas de *Galïen.*" In *Actes du XVIIIe Congrès International de Linguistique et de Philologie Romanes,* 6:437–45. Tübingen: Max Niemeyer, 1988.

——. Review of *Le Galïen de Cheltenham*, ed. David M. Dougherty and Eugene B. Barnes. *Romance Philology* 38 (1985): 537–42.

——. "Whom and What Did Galïen Restore?" *Olifant* 10.3 (1983–84): 83–98.

Di Stefano, Giuseppe. *Essais sur le Moyen Français*. Padua: Liviana Editrice, 1977.

Douglas, David. "The *Song of Roland* and the Norman Conquest of England." *French Studies* 14 (1960): 99–116.

Doutrepont, Georges. *Les Mises en prose des épopées et des romans chevaleresques du XIVe au XVIe siècle*. Brussels: Palais des académies, 1939.

Duggan, Joseph J. "Ambiguity in Twelfth-Century French and Provençal Literature: A Problem or a Value?" In *Jean Misrahi Memorial Volume: Studies in Medieval Literature*, ed. Hans R. Runte, Henri Niedzielski, and William L. Hendrickson, 136–49. Columbia, SC: French Literary Publications, 1977.

——. "The *Chanson de Roland* and the *chansons de geste*." In *European Writers: The Middle Ages and the Renaissance*, vol. 1, *Prudentius to Medieval Drama*, ed. W. T. H. Jackson, 89–111. New York: Scribner's, 1983.

——. *A Concordance of the* Chanson de Roland. Columbus: Ohio State University Press, 1969.

——. "L'Épisode d'Aude dans la tradition en rime de la *Chanson de Roland*." In *Charlemagne in the North*, ed. Philip Bennett, Anne Cobby, and Graham Runnalls, 273–79. Edinburgh: Société Rencesvals British Branch, 1993.

——. "Franco-German Conflict and the History of French Scholarship on the *Song of Roland*." In *Hermeneutics and Medieval Culture*, ed. Patrick J. Gallacher and Helen Damico, 97–106. Albany: SUNY Press, 1989.

——. "Legitimation and the Hero's Exemplary Function in the *Cantar de Mío Cid* and the *Chanson de Roland*." In *Oral Traditional Literature: A Festschrift for Albert Bates Lord*, ed. John Miles Foley, 217–234. Columbus, OH: Slavica, 1981.

——. *The* Song of Roland: *Formulaic Style and Poetic Craft*. Berkeley: University of California Press, 1973.

Eisner, Robert. "In Search of the Real Theme of the *Song of Roland*." *Romance Notes* 14 (1972–73): 179–83.

Emden, Wolfgang van. *La Chanson de Roland*. Critical Guides to French Texts. London: Grant and Cutler, 1995.

Ferrante, Joan. "Notes toward the Study of a Female Rhetoric in the Trobairitz." In *The Voice of the Trobairitz*, ed. William Paden. Philadelphia: University of Pennsylvania Press, 1989.

——. *Woman as Image in Medieval Literature*. New York: Columbia University Press, 1975.

Fleischman, Suzanne. *The Future in Thought and Language: Diachronic Evidence from Romance*. Cambridge: Cambridge University Press, 1982.

——. *Tense and Narrativity: From Medieval Performance to Modern Fiction*. Austin: University of Texas Press, 1990.

Foulet, Alfred. "Is Roland Guilty of *Desmesure*?" *Romance Philology* 10 (1956–57): 145–48.

Gaunt, Simon. *Gender and Genre in Medieval French Literature*. New York: Cambridge University Press, 1995.

Gautier, Léon. *Bibliographie des chansons de geste*. Paris: Welter, 1897.

———. *Les Épopées françaises*. 5 vols. Paris, 1880.

Gérard, Albert. "L'Axe Roland-Ganelon, valeurs en conflit dans la *Chanson de Roland*." *Moyen Âge* 75 (1969): 445–66.

Ghil, Eliza Miruna. "*Crozada*: Avatars of a Religious Term in Thirteenth-Century Occitan Poetry." *Tenso* 10 (1995): 99–109.

Godefroy, Frédéric. *Dictionnaire de l'ancienne langue française*. Paris, 1883; reprint, New York: Kraus, 1961.

Gumbrecht, Hans. "'Un souffle d'Allemagne ayant passé': Friedrich Dietz, Gaston Paris and the Genesis of National Philologies." *Romance Philology* 40 (1986): 1–37.

Haidu, Peter. "Fragments in Search of Totalization: *Roland* and the Historical Text." In *Modernité au Moyen Âge*, ed. Brigitte Cazelles and Charles Méla, 73–99. Geneva: Droz, 1990.

———. *The Subject Medieval/Modern: Text and Governance in the Middle Ages*. Stanford: Stanford University Press, 2004.

———. *The Subject of Violence: The* Song of Roland *and the Birth of the State*. Bloomington: Indiana University Press, 1993.

Heinemann, Edward. *L'Art métrique de la chanson de geste: Essai sur la musicalité du récit*. Geneva: Droz, 1993.

Horrent, Jules. *La Chanson de Roland dans les littératures française et espagnole au Moyen Âge*. Paris: Belles Lettres, 1951.

Hunt, Tony. "Roland's 'Vermeille Pume.'" *Olifant* 7 (1979–80): 203–11.

Jewett, Margaret. "Remembering Roncevaux: Collective Identity and Literary Commentary in Medieval French and Occitan Adaptations of the Roland Legend." PhD diss., University of Chicago, 1998.

Kay, Sarah. *The Chansons de Geste in the Age of Romance: Political Fictions*. Oxford: Oxford University Press, 1995.

———. *Subjectivity in Troubadour Poetry*. Cambridge: Cambridge University Press, 1990.

Keller, Hans-Erich. *Autour de Roland: Recherches sur la chanson de geste*. Geneva: Champion-Slatkine, 1989.

———. "The *Song of Roland*: A Mid-Twelfth Century Song of Propaganda for the Capetian Kingdom." *Olifant* 3.4 (1976): 242–58.

Kelly, Douglas. *The Art of Medieval French Romance*. Madison: University of Wisconsin Press, 1992.

———. "*Matiere* and *Genera Dicendi* in Medieval Romance." *Yale French Studies* 51 (1974): 147–59.

Kibler, William. "Relectures de l'épopée." In *Au carrefour des routes d'Europe: La Chanson de geste*, ed. François Suard, 1:103–40. Aix-en-Provence: Publications du Centre Universitaire d'Études et de Recherches Médiévales d'Aix, Université de Provence, 1987.

———. Review of *Le Galien de Cheltenham*, ed. David M. Dougherty and Eugene B. Barnes. *Speculum* 58 (1983): 1033–35.

———. "Roland's Pride." *Symposium* 26 (1972): 147–60.

Kinoshita, Sharon. "'Pagans Are Wrong and Christians Are Right': Alterity, Gender, and Nation in the *Chanson de Roland.*" *Journal of Medieval and Early Modern Studies* 31 (2001): 79–111.

Lafont, Robert. *La Geste de Roland.* 2 vols. Paris: l'Harmattan, 1991.

Le Gentil, Pierre. "À propos de la démesure de Roland." *Cahiers de Civilisation Médiévale* 11 (1968): 203–9.

Le Goff, Jacques. *Les Intellectuels au Moyen Âge.* Paris: Seuil, 1957.

———. *Saint Louis.* Paris: Gallimard, 1996.

Lejeune, Rita, and Jacques Stiennon. *La Légende de Roland dans l'art du Moyen Âge.* 2 vols. Brussels: Arcade, 1960.

Leupin, Alexandre. *La Passion des idoles: Foi et pouvoir dans la Bible et la* Chanson de Roland. Paris: L'Harmattan, 2000.

Long, Joseph. "'Cest mot mei est estrange . . .': La Belle Aude and the Irreducible Difference of Words." *Nottingham French Studies* 38 (1999): 114–19.

Lord, Albert Bates. *The Singer of Tales.* Cambridge, MA: Harvard University Press, 1960.

Marchello-Nizia, Christiane. *Histoire de la langue française aux XIVe et XVe siècles.* Paris: Bordas, 1979.

Matlock, Jann. "The 'Clear Visions' of 'la Bele Aude': Dream Form and Function in *La Chanson de Roland.*" *Pacific Coast Philology* 15 (1980): 35–44.

McCash, June Hall. "'Scientia' and 'Sapientia' in the *Chanson de Roland.*" *Mediaevalia et Humanistica* 11 (1982): 131–47.

Medeiros, Marie-Thérèse de. "Temps de l'histoire, temps du récit dans la *Chanson de Roland.*" *Le Moyen Âge* 88 (1982): 5–28.

Menéndez Pidal, Ramón. *La Chanson de Roland et la tradition épique des Francs.* Trans. I. Cluzel. Paris: Picard, 1960.

Mermier, Guy R. "Roncevaux-*Ronsasvals*: More about the Originality of the Old Provençal Poem within the Tradition of the *Song of Roland.*" In *Studia Occitanica in Memoriam Paul Remy,* ed. Hans-Erich Keller, 153–68. Kalamazoo: Medieval Institute Publications, Western Michigan University, 1986.

Moisan, André. "La Mort de Roland selon les différentes versions de l'épopée." *Cahiers de Civilisation Médiévale* 28 (1985): 101–32.

Morrissey, Robert. *L'Empereur à la barbe fleurie.* Paris: Gallimard, 1997.

Nichols, Stephen G., Jr. "Remodeling Models: Modernism and the Middle Ages." In *Modernité au Moyen Âge: Le Défi du passé,* ed. Brigitte Cazelles and Charles Méla, 52. Geneva: Droz, 1990.

———. "Roland's Echoing Horn." *Romance Notes* 5 (1963): 78–84.

———. "Roncevaux and the Poetics of Place/Person in the Song of Roland." In *Romanesque Signs: Early Medieval Narrative and Iconography,* 148–203. New Haven: Yale University Press, 1983.

Oberhänsli-Widmer, Gabrielle. *La Complainte funèbre du Haut Moyen Âge français et occitan.* Romanica Helvetica 106. Berne: Francke, 1989.

Ong, Walter. *Orality and Literacy.* New York: Routledge, 1982.

Paden, William D. "Perspectives on the Albigensian Crusade." *Tenso* 10 (1995): 90–98.

———. "Tenebrism in the *Song of Roland.*" *Modern Philology* 86.4 (1989): 339–56.

Palumbo, Giovanni. "Il *Roland* rimato e il *Ronsasvals*: Problemi di interferenza." In *Les Chansons de geste: Actes du XVIe Congrès International de la Société Rencesvals,* ed. Carlos Alvar and Juan Paredes, 475–97. Granada: Editorial Universidad de Granada, 2005.

Paterson, Linda. *Troubadours and Eloquence.* Oxford: Clarendon Press, 1975.

Payen, Jean-Charles. *Le Motif du repentir dans la littérature française médiévale.* Geneva: Droz, 1968.

Pezard, André. "La Mort de Roland dans *Ronsasvals.*" *Romania* 97 (1976): 145–94.

Pickens, Rupert T. "Roland's Apple: Truthful and Untruthful Discourse in *la Chanson de Roland.*" In *Studies in Honor of Hans-Erich Keller: Medieval French and Occitan Literature and Romance Linguistics,* ed. Rupert Pickens, 73–80. Kalamazoo: Medieval Institute Publications, Western Michigan University, 1993.

Pietropaolo, Domenico. "Eco on Medievalism." *Studies in Medievalism* 5 (1993): 127–38.

Pope, M. K. *From Latin to Modern French.* 5th ed. Manchester: University of Manchester Press, 1966.

Régnier, Claude. Review of *Le Galien de Cheltenham,* ed. David M. Dougherty and Eugene B. Barnes. *Cahiers de Civilisation Médiévale* 27 (1984): 374–77.

Riffaterre, Michael. "The Mind's Eye: Memory and Textuality." In *The New Medievalism,* ed. Marina Brownlee, Kevin Brownlee, and Stephen Nichols, 30–44. Baltimore: Johns Hopkins University Press, 1991.

Roques, Mario. "*Roland à Saragosse* et *Ronsasvals*: Examen comparatif." *Romania* 69 (1946–47): 317–61.

———. "*Ronsasvals*, poème épique provençal." *Romania* 66 (1940): 433–80.

Sarbin, Theodore R., ed. "The Narrative as a Root Metaphor for Psychology." In *Narrative Psychology: The Storied Nature of Human Conduct,* ed. Theodore R. Sarbin, 3–21. New York: Praeger, 1986.

Schiesari, Juliana. *The Gendering of Melancholia: Feminism, Psychoanalysis, and the Symbolics of Loss in Renaissance Literature.* Ithaca: Cornell University Press, 1992.

Schulze-Busacker, Elisabeth. "La Datation de *Ronsasvals.*" *Romania* 110 (1989): 127–66, 396–25.

———. "Reminiscences lyriques dans l'épopée occitane de *Ronsasvals.*" In *Charlemagne et l'épopée romane: Actes du VIIe Congrès International de la Société Rencesvals,* 707–18. Paris: Belles Lettres, 1978.

Segre, Cesare. "Un Procedimento della narrativa medievale: L'Enucleazione."
In *Italica et Romanica: Festschrift für Max Pfister*, ed. Günter Holtus, Johannes
Kramer, and Wolfgang Schweickard, 3:361–67. Tübingen: Niemeyer,
1997.

———. "Il Sogno di Alda tra *chanson de geste, chanson de femme e romance.*" *Medioevo
Romanzo* 8.1 (1981): 3–9.

Siegle, Robert. *The Politics of Reflexivity: Narrative and the Constitutive Poetics of Culture*. Baltimore: Johns Hopkins University Press, 1986.

Spiegel, Gabrielle M. *Romancing the Past: The Rise of Vernacular Prose Historiography in
Thirteenth-Century France*. Berkeley: University of California Press, 1993.

Strayer, Joseph. *The Albigensian Crusades*. New York: Dial, 1971.

Suard, François. *La Chanson de geste*. Series "Que sais-je?" Paris: Presses Universitaires de France, 1993.

Sumption, Jonathan. *The Albigensian Crusade*. Boston: Faber and Faber, 1978.

Taylor, Andrew. "Bodleian MS Digby 23." In *Textual Situations: Three Medieval
Manuscripts and Their Readers*, 26–70. Philadelphia: University of Pennsylvania
Press, 2002.

Uitti, Karl D. "'Ço dit la Geste': Reflections on the Poetic Restoration of History in the *Song of Roland*." In *Studies in Honor of Hans-Erich Keller: Medieval
French and Occitan Literature and Romance Linguistics*, ed. Rupert Pickens, 1–27.
Kalamazoo: Medieval Institute Publications, Western Michigan University,
1993.

Vance, Eugene. *Reading the Song of Roland*. Englewood Cliffs, NJ: Prentice-Hall,
1970.

———. "Roland and Charlemagne: The Remembering Voices and the Crypt."
In *Mervelous Signals: Poetics and Sign Theory in the Middle Ages*, 51–85. Lincoln:
University of Nebraska Press, 1986.

———. "Roland et la poétique de la mémoire." *Cahiers d'Études Médiévales* 1 (1974):
103–15. Reprinted in Eugene Vance, *Epopées, legendes et miracles*, 103–15.
Montreal: Bellarmin, 1974.

Vleck, Amelia van. *Memory and Re-Creation in Troubadour Lyric*. Berkeley: University of California Press, 1991.

Walpole, Ronald. *The Old French Johannes Translation of the* Pseudo-Turpin *Chronicle: A Critical Edition, Supplement*. Berkeley: University of California Press,
1976.

Warren, Michelle. "The Noise of Roland." *Exemplaria* 16.2 (2004): 277–304.

Zumthor, Paul. *Essai de poétique médiévale*. Paris: Seuil, 1972.

Index

author(s), 22, 70, 78, 125. *See also*
Cheltenham poet; Oxford poet;
Turoldus

Baligant
battle against, 7, 77, 109–10
—Battle of Roncevaux, comparison
to, 246–47
—omission of, 130
—post-, 110–14
Charlemagne and, 25, 27, 202
episode, treatment of, 245–46,
269–70
la geste, interpretation of, by, 27
See also battle scenes
Basan. *See* Basin
Basile, 50, 201, 212
Basin, 50, 201, 212
Battle of Roncevaux. *See* Roncevaux,
Battle of
battle scenes, 93–108, 143, 152–53,
156–59. *See also* Baligant, battle
against; Roncevaux, Battle of
biblical narrative, 28, 36, 83–84,
119–20, 131, 154, 183. *See also*
Christian(s); Christ image; God/
God's will; religion
Bibliothèque Muncipale de
Châteauroux, 76
bird (as symbol), 142, 157, 188
Blancandrin, 36
Bodleian Library, 20
Boutet, Dominique, 163–64, 190

Caliph, 38
Cambridge manuscript, 77, 79
case markers, 254–57
censorship, 197
Chalcidius (translator of Plato's
Timaeus), 21
Champion des dames (Le Franc), 224
la chanson de geste, 1, 11–12, 194–96
La Chanson de Roland, use as modern
title, 2–3

la chanson de toile genre, 180, 193–94
*The Chansons de Geste in the Age of
Romance* (Kay), 11–12
character(s)
alienation of, 134
audience, relationship to, 9–10,
13–14, 105–6, 117, 134–35, 161
credibility of, 37, 52
discourse (*see* discourse, character)
epic, 195
inner struggles of, 135–39, 190,
196
interpretation and narration by,
4, 7–8, 45–46, 192, 195
language depicting role of,
258–60
minor, 131, 151
plot hidden from, 8–9, 35–36,
144–46
reception, 142–43
reflection of society in, 4
Charlemagne
alienation of, 164–67, 182
audience perception of, 13–14
battle, relationship to, 9, 66–67,
72, 95, 142–43, 150–51
dreams of, 153
failings of, 83, 135, 153, 159,
162–64, 167, 174–75, 183,
186
false narrative by, 113–14, 119,
181–83
God's will, relationship to,
110–12, 152, 163–67, 173–74,
210–11
grief of, 54–6, 110–13, 123–24,
129, 170–72, 176, 189
history of, 5, 26, 156–57
lament by, 174–76
leadership of (*see* leadership, of
Charlemagne)
nostalgic language, portrayal with,
258–63, 266–69
on peace agreement, 46–47